NARRATING SOCIAL WORK
THROUGH AUTOETHNOGRAPHY

Narrating Social Work Through Autoethnography

Edited by Stanley L Witkin

 COLUMBIA UNIVERSITY PRESS   NEW YORK

COLUMBIA UNIVERSITY PRESS
Publishers Since 1893
New York   Chichester, West Sussex

cup.columbia.edu
Copyright © 2014 Columbia University Press

"Leslie Is Different," words and music by Fred Small © 1983 Pine Barrens Music (BMI), from the Rounder album *No Limit* (www.rounder.com).

Library of Congress Cataloging-in-Publication Data

Narrating social work through autoethnography / edited by Stanley L Witkin.
    pages cm
    Includes bibliographical references and index.
    ISBN 978-0-231-15880-0 (cloth : alk. paper) — ISBN 978-0-231-15881-7 (pbk. : alk. paper) — ISBN 978-0-231-53762-9 (e-book)
    1. Social service—Research. 2. Social service—Practice. 3. Social workers. 4. Ethnosociology. 5. Autobiography. 6. Narrative inquiry (Research method) I. Witkin, Stanley L, 1947–

    HV11.2.N37 2014
    361.301—dc23

2013040523

Columbia University Press books are printed on permanent and durable acid-free paper.
This book is printed on paper with recycled content.
Printed in the United States of America

c 10 9 8 7 6 5 4 3 2 1
p 10 9 8 7 6 5 4 3 2 1

Cover design: Lisa Hamm
Cover image: © plainpicture/B. Jaubert

CONTENTS

I MET STANLEY WITKIN IN 1988 at a meeting of the Group for the Advancement of Doctoral Education in Social Work. Stan was there as a Ph.D. program director and I as a member of the Task Force on Social Work Research, sponsored by the National Institute of Mental Health. The meeting would serve as the official launch of the task force. As we walked and talked, I realized that Stan and I shared the aim of making social work research and its recognized knowledge more consistent with the field's historical values of deep respect for people and their self-determination. This was a time of heady progress for those academics working to make social work a research-based profession. Achieving that status would mean sharing resources, status, and hierarchical organization with the biomedical professions supported by the big federal institutes. My own outlook on social work knowledge and research, which I attribute largely to the strong dialectical quality of my undergraduate education in Chapel Hill, was consciously critical, always trying to find the flaws and possibilities for whatever was presented as knowledge. Stan was clarifying his position as a social constructionist. He was already showing evidence of the proverbial innovator—he was ahead of the pack, with arrows in his back.

In the end, my work on the task force to advance the aims I shared with Stan proved to be something of a fool's errand. The mainstream version of science prevailed on the highest tiers of the social work scaffolds. But there was also a lot more going on. There was a strong but less visible alliance of talented, mindful social workers whose energy and ideas led to the book you are reading now. Few knew what to call these pioneers—constructionists,

new-paradigm advocates, postmodernists, or humanists; they were a growing chorus of increasingly compelling social work voices advocating recognition of broader ways of understanding people and their experience of life,
as mediated by culture. The core of their argument was that the field must
recognize the views and enhance the influence of the purported beneficiaries of social work, as well as clarifying and strengthening the voices of practicing social workers.

Throughout their history, social workers have inhabited a contentious
profession, debating, for example, whether to emphasize social causes versus
social functions, the value of Freudian versus Rankian practice, or whether
the field was deprofessionalizing itself or advancing itself with the bachelor
of social work degree. The positivist versus social constructionist debate of
recent years is also a part of that history. Out of the vigorous disagreements,
limited accommodation has occurred. Means of expression and communication have broadened, and now there is a much wider recognition of the
legitimacy of knowledge found and portrayed in a social constructionist
frame. Even many of the federal funders now advocate including qualitative
and quantitative perspectives in some research projects, a small but significant step in the peace process. History is not just what happened; it is also
where we are now. The publication of this book is proof.

A popular aphorism states that "Social workers have a front-row seat at
the drama of human existence." And indeed social workers do get to learn
firsthand about some of the most extraordinary aspects of the human condition. At the same time, social workers live in the midst of a social movement to make the records of these experiences as concrete as possible. Our
professional culture rests on the idea, whether carefully enacted or fudged
in practice, that we must know the "hard facts" or measurable dimensions
and diagnoses of almost every situation, whether we are conducting a child-
protection investigation, charting eligibility for assisted living accommodations, or figuring out what might occur in a community. The overarching
model assumes that we must count how often something undesirable
occurs or something desirable does not occur before we get too involved,
in order to count again later, once we have been involved, to see how much
things have changed. Managers and auditors may assign financial terms to
each element of the equation, and the result often dictates the all-important
bottom line. For the practitioner, this metamodel almost always involves
assuming a role (putting on a performance) dictated by some authority,

regardless of whether they believe in the value of the model. But the social worker's prized seat at the human drama is wasted unless the social worker goes beyond this surface layer of observations. It is essential to carry observations into realms of memory, context, imagination, and the shared experience of relationship. This book offers accounts that serve as exemplars for ways to seek deeper understanding of both the self and the other. Autoethnographies such as these, and the ones that social workers help clients and communities develop daily, not only describe what was and is, they pull us into what happened and what is happening, here and now, and they make us authors of the future, whatever it confronts us with.

Most of the authors of the superb autoethnographies in this book are friends of mine. I know some of them quite well. I recognized some of their characteristic ways of relating to the world or presenting themselves. But in reading their accounts, sometimes I marveled at how much better I understood them by learning something new about how they see their own relationships with other individuals and with the culture in which they live. In some cases, the authors related experiences that were familiar to me, but that I never appreciated so deeply. Ambiguity, irony, disappointment, anger, sadness, and joy are all revealed, either where I did not know that they existed or in forms that I never would have imagined. The power of the autoethnography lies in its ability to deepen the author's understanding and respect for the self in context while doing the same for the other. Particularly when the text is very emotive or surprising, one's capacity for understanding the writer is enhanced, as is one's ability to seek fuller understanding of other people.

How does it work? Reading each of these accounts is much like reading any compelling story. The author tells us about an important motive force in his or her life, as experienced as a professional and a participant in an ongoing culture. In each case the individual encounters an obstacle, something that disrupts or jolts the movement. And in each case the author realizes that he or she has to try to change or adapt to the obstacle, resulting in more, largely unplanned movement, usually in the form of vectors that make the author's world wobble. But in each case the autoethnographer–social worker is not simply tossed around by outside forces. Rather than dramas to be attended and watched from the front row, the dramas are compelling because they are participatory affairs. The narratives are not only descriptions of the experience of the effects of strong forces beyond anyone's control. In each case they are also accounts in which the author has a key role in the action.

Stan still has some arrow scars. His own shining autoethnography is a classic study of the individual wrestling with his profession while developing it. He helps us to understand his arduous process of innovating while healing, maintaining a long-term perspective on life. Similarly, each of the other accounts in this book is a shining facet of the whole gem. While each has a conclusion or coda, there are no endings. Considering these narratives encourages us (i.e., gives us courage) to appreciate other people's unending life stories more fully. And by doing this we hope to be able to support others in shaping their own lives, the raison d'être of social work.

W. David Harrison

THE EMERGENCE OF THE POSTMODERN movement in the social sciences can be traced back at least to the period following the Second World War. The devastation of that war and the disclosure of its unimaginable atrocities weakened the sacrosanct authority of science and its metanarrative of inevitable progress. Over the following decades, critiques of the scientific canon from different perspectives as well as a changing social environment created conditions conducive to the development of alternative understandings of knowledge and innovative approaches to inquiry. Two are apposite. First was the social constructionist movement, which highlighted the social, interactive production of our realities (e.g., Berger and Luckmann 1967), integrated the major critiques, and articulated how knowledge is embedded in historical, cultural, and social contexts (Gergen 1985). Second, what became known as the qualitative research movement (e.g., Denzin and Lincoln 2000) rejected positivist-oriented standards and spawned new approaches to inquiry that did not assume the "scientific method" as described in textbooks about science and insisted on a more holistic portrayal of researchers and researched. Autoethnography is one expression of these movements. Located somewhere between the binaries of what is taken to be science and the arts, objectivity and subjectivity, truth and fiction, the individual and the social, and the past and the present, autoethnography can be viewed as a site where these liminal spaces are explored.

I have always been attracted to such spaces. The ambiguity and uncertainty that characterize postmodern thought, although troubling at times, have usually seemed more representative of my phenomenal world than have the seemingly more precise and predictable portraits of conventional thought.

This may explain, in part, my affinity for metatheories like social construction, my primary intellectual framework (see, for example, Witkin 2011).

Three interrelated characteristics of social construction support autoethnography. First, social construction makes no claims to truth in any transcendental sense. Truth claims gain legitimacy through social processes. Thus social construction invites the questioning of truths that claim universal or timeless status or origins. Second, given the plurality of truths, social construction favors multiplicity over singularity. If we cannot know ultimate Truth, then it might be useful to broaden the space in which multiple truths and ways of representing such truths can be generated. Third, rather than focusing on what is "really" true or not true in the sense described above, social construction encourages exploring how such claims get constituted, and particularly how they function. For instance, whose realities are privileged and whose are silenced? Together these characteristics of social construction enable new forms of inquiry, understanding, and relating. In a world that seems in dire need of such innovative alternatives, exploring the potential of autoethnography seems like a worthwhile endeavor. This book is an illustration of this endeavor, in particular as applied to issues germane to social work.

Autoethnography seems especially poignant for the social work profession. Although social work identifies with socially progressive causes and ideals, I find it to be an intellectually conservative profession. This state of affairs seems particularly characteristic of the United States, my home country, where the dominance of conventional scientific thinking— philosophically realist, method based, truth seeking, technocratic, and narrowly reflective—has kept social work a handmaiden of the dominant discourses of society. Thus the present effort has the added task of trying to loosen this grip and argue for greater legitimacy for approaches that, in my view, seem more consistent with the day-to-day realities and issues confronting social work practitioners and the profession at large. It attempts to make its case not by providing a set of instructions about how to do autoethnography "properly," thereby replicating the method-based approach of conventional research, but by providing examples of autoethnographies conducted by social workers on experiences that were highly relevant to them. Done well, such examples should be substantive, analytical, and relevant. That is, they should provide potentially useful, accessible information, grounded in the historical, cultural, and social realities that render experiences and their interpretations intelligible. I hope that you will find this book consistent with these aims.

The possibility for this book would not have been seriously considered without having contributors with the interests, skill, and courage to undertake this task. Fortunately I was able to identify such a group who graciously agreed to explore this relatively unfamiliar territory, not only in the sense of autoethnography's novelty but in its unpredictability. That is, to varying degrees the very process of conducting an autoethnography generates its findings. Emergence was the guide as authors wrote and rewrote their way into their inquiry. The result, I hope you will agree, confirms the wisdom of their decision. I extend my deepest gratitude to each of them. This is their book as well as mine.

Of course, as with any endeavor of this sort, there are many voices, named and not, who inhabit these pages. Some are people I have been fortunate to know over the years; others I have encountered only in print or through some other medium. Our dialogue, overt or silent, has enriched my thinking, informed analyses, sparked ideas, and provided encouragement. Although it is not feasible to individually acknowledge everyone, a small number particularly stand out in relation to this book. First, my wife, Fran Joseph, has been an indispensable part of this work from its inception. Her critical but constructive feedback on half-formed ideas and drafts, insights, encouragement, and tolerance for my long working hours and the ups and downs that accompany a project such as this one have been invaluable. Thank you, Frannie, for your love and support. Board members of the Global Partnership for Transformative Social Work (www.gptsw.net) and participants at our annual gatherings have been and continue to be a source of inspiration and enthusiasm for exploring unconventional ideas and inquiry. Almost all the contributors to this book have at some time participated in these gatherings. Brenda Solomon, Susan Roche, JB Barna, and Suzie Comerford, colleagues in the Department of Social Work at the University of Vermont, have been professionally and personally supportive and comrades in the struggle to maintain an academic environment that supports projects such as this one. Ken Gergen's writings initially drew me to social construction, and he continues to be a source of inspiration and support, both in print and in person. My courses at UVM, particularly Advanced Social Work Research, have provided a place for me to explore autoethnography and its utility for students who most likely will constitute the primary readership of this book. Their questions and reactions have been extremely useful. Although this book would not have been possible without these sources of inspiration and support, they are, of course, not responsible for the final product.

Finally, I hope that those of you reading this book, whether as required reading for a course, as part of your own process of inquiry, or simply out of interest or curiosity, will find your effort enjoyable and rewarding. Feel free to share your reactions with me.

Stanley L Witkin

REFERENCES

Berger, P. L., and T. Luckmann. 1967. *The Social Construction of Reality: A Treatise in the Sociology of Knowledge*. New York: Anchor Books.
Denzin, N. K., and Y. S. Lincoln, eds. 2000. *Handbook of Qualitative Research*. 2nd ed. Thousand Oaks, Calif.: Sage.
Gergen, K. 1985. "The Social Constructionist Movement in Modern Psychology." *American Psychologist* 40 (3): 266–75.
Witkin, S. L. 2011. *Social Construction and Social Work Practice: Interpretations and Innovations*. New York: Columbia University Press.

NARRATING SOCIAL WORK
THROUGH AUTOETHNOGRAPHY

CHAPTER 1

Autoethnography

THE OPENING ACT

▸ *STANLEY L WITKIN*

IT'S A COLD, BRIGHT DECEMBER DAY in my home town of Burlington, Vermont. I am out walking my dog when I meet my neighbor, Bob, out with his dog, Woody.

"Hi Stan," he says. "I hear you are going to Florida." (A noteworthy topic in Vermont in December.)

"Yes," I reply. "I'm on sabbatical."

"Is that like a vacation or do you have work that you need to do?"

"No, it's not a vacation," I explain, "but it's not like my usual university routine either. I am free from teaching and other university responsibilities. I did, however, have to write a proposal describing what I would do during my sabbatical and how it would benefit my career and the university."

"Oh, so what are you doing?" Bob asks.

"Well," I reply, "my primary goals are to complete an edited book I've been working on and to begin another one. So most of my time will be spent writing. That's why I can go to Florida—as long as I have my laptop, I can travel."

"What's the book about?" he asks further. "The one you hope to finish?"

"Um, something called autoethnography." (I am a bit hesitant since I know that most people will not understand the term.)

Predictably Bob asks, "What's that?"

I begin searching for a way to explain autoethnography to someone who, as far as I know, has little background related to this topic. "It's not that easy to explain," I begin (wondering if I sound somewhat defensive or even a bit superior). "You may have heard the term ethnography, which is a study of people from the perspective of their own culture. It's an approach to research often associated with anthropology." I'm feeling like I sound too much like an academic—it's become so second nature to me. "So," I continue, "an *auto*ethnography is an ethnography of one's self—usually focusing on a particular experience or life event—from a social and cultural perspective." (This is not going well, I think.)

"Hmm," Bob murmurs, "I'm not sure what you mean."

"Yeah, that was kind of vague," I reply. "Let me try an example. Suppose that I wanted to conduct an autoethnography about the death of my father.[1] My focus might be on my experience of his dying and eventual death. However, my analysis would not be limited to describing my personal reactions but would include an exploration of how death and dying are understood in our society and its influence on my experience. For instance, how did my experience of the process of my father's dying, his being in hospice care, relate to my beliefs about death, and how did these beliefs reflect the ways in which our culture constructs death as, for example, a hidden experience?"

"Uh huh," Bob says unconvincingly. "So you're describing the experience."

"Yes, but more than that," I say. "What I am trying to do is to reflect in the present on how I experienced this event in the past. How can I understand my feelings, thoughts, and reactions at that time from my current vantage point? Can I learn something that will help me and others to understand better the experience of those close to a dying person and its connection to our death and dying practices?" I realize, too late, that I have delivered a mini lecture and exceeded the norms of neighborly conversation.

Sure enough, Bob says, "Yeah, that's interesting. Well, if I don't see you, have a good time in Florida."

•   •   •

Autoethnography is a topic of increasing interest in the social sciences. A Google Scholar title search (July 1, 2010) on the word "autoethnography" yielded 363 hits. About 42 percent of these (152) date from 2007 to the present. What was a relatively rare topic or methodology only a short time ago now frequently appears in journals such as *Qualitative Social Work*, *International Journal of Qualitative Methods*, and *Qualitative Inquiry*.

Nevertheless, as the vignette above illustrates, autoethnography can be somewhat slippery to grasp. If you approach it using the framework of conventional (i.e., positivist-oriented) research, you will likely find yourself trying to wedge it into categories like method and objectivity that do not quite fit. That's because autoethnography is not a variant of conventional research; rather, it resides in the interstices between research and literature. So rather than trying to move it somewhere that will provide the comfort of clear boundaries and definitions, I ask that you tolerate a degree of ambiguity and see where it goes.

Of course, this does not mean that there is nothing we can say about autoethnography. My opening vignette, for example, illustrates several common aspects.

First, it is a little story, a narrative. Autoethnographies are typically written as narratives, often using well-known narrative elements such as plot and character development. Autoethnographers use this form to explore the historically and culturally embedded social processes that help explain particular understandings and actions of the author/subject in relation to some significant experience, event, or understanding.

Second, it is written as a dialogue. Autoethnography uses a variety of literary conventions to explore its subject matter and to communicate in ways that will give readers a sense of the author's experience. Dialogue, poetry, prose, imagery, and so on are all possible tools that an autoethnographer may employ. Descriptions tend to be multilayered and the writing evocative. Pragmatism is the guide: how to communicate the lived experience of the author/subject in ways that will help readers gain a sense of that experience.

Third, the focus is on the author/subject. I am both the main character in the story and its narrator. It is my experience that is center stage. At the same time, that experience is not isolated; it occurs within a social and cultural context. Others are inevitably involved. As I explore my own reactions, I also explore the contexts that make those reactions sensible. Even in my mundane interaction with my neighbor, we learn a bit about social practices and norms associated with walking dogs, talking with neighbors, and differences between academic and nonacademic cultures. More generally, autoethnographies may explore dominant and alternative belief systems as they relate to the topic, institutional practices, and interpersonal interactions in relation to how they express and reflect societal beliefs and practices.

Fourth, there is an active relationship among authors, readers, and text. Unlike a typical research study in which readers are positioned to be relatively passive in relation to an expert author and authoritative text, autoethnography invites readers into an engaged, interactive relationship. Authors interact with readers through the text, evoking varied reactions in which interpretation is encouraged and multiple meanings are welcome. As Ellis and Bochner (2000) put it, the reader is "a coparticipant in dialogue rather than passive recipient of knowledge" (744).

Fifth, autoethnographies show as well as tell. Authors talk not only *about* their experience but *from* it. In my dog-walking vignette, I not only tell you about what happened but bring you into the interaction. This process aspect of autoethnography is related to its product—the kind of knowledge generated.

Sixth, autoethnography is not about discovering truth in any absolute sense but about enriching understanding. I see autoethnography as a kind of "deep talk," a term I learned from the writer Maya Angelou (1969). She writes,

> There's a phrase in West Africa called "deep talk." When a person is informed about a situation, an older person will often use a parable, an axiom, and then add to the end of the axiom, "take that as deep talk" meaning that you will never find the answer. You can continue to go down deeper and deeper.

Similar to deep talk, autoethnography can help us to explore the "multiple interpretive possibilities" and "discourses existing beneath or alongside the primary narrative" (King 1998:1). You can always go down deeper.

•   •   •

Variants of autoethnographic inquiry were being conducted before it became named as a particular inquiry approach (Ellis and Bochner 2000). Just as autoethnographers write about their culture when writing about themselves, ethnographers were writing about themselves when they were writing about culture. What they found interesting, puzzling, difficult, or exciting; the relationships they formed; how they described the culture and the people that were part of it all reflected, to some degree, themselves as social/cultural beings.

I wrote my first autoethnography without knowing it. The year was 1974, and I was a first-year master's of social work student at the University of Wisconsin-Madison in a course on human sexuality taught by Mona Wasow. Mona was a terrific teacher and presented this titillating subject in an engaging way that enabled us to learn the "facts" of sex (Masters and Johnson 1966, 1970) but also sex as a cultural and human experience.

For my semester project, Mona encouraged me to write a paper modeled after a novel we had read for the course, *Memoir of an Ex-Prom Queen* by Alix Kates Shulman. *Memoir* was a feminist coming-of-age story that dealt with a number of gender-related issues that unfortunately are still relevant to women today: harassment, conflicting expectations, abortion, and discrimination. My task was to write a male version of my transition from childhood to adolescence, highlighting the peer pressure, particularly about sex, that I experienced. I called my paper "Memoirs of an Ex-Jock." Besides describing my sexual awakening and the prepubescent initiation rites of male, urban youth, I reflected on the culture of manhood that was an integral part of life for boys in my community. In the context of the time—the late 1950s to early 1960s (the *Mad Men* era)—and my age, my understanding of the female gender and intimate relationships was, by today's standards, primitive. Moreover, the pressure to prove my manhood through meeting phallocentric sex standards and winning peer approval was so great as to drown out whatever sensitivities I might have had.

In my paper I wrote about the game-like, hierarchical nature of sex in which climbing each step on our "stairway to heaven" (i.e., sexual intercourse) was rewarded with accolades from my friends. Conversely, this also meant that a lack of progress was met with derision. Since I was stuck on the bottom step longer than most, I suffered humiliation and feelings of inadequacy. I wrote about how I yearned to be "normal" but was confused as to what that meant, as it seemed that standards were ambiguous and ever-changing. Athletic prowess, the previous "gold standard" in which I had modest success, no longer held sway. As with Sasha, the protagonist in Shulman's novel, "looking good made everything easier." In one passage I wrote about the pressure I felt to "look right."

My appearance had to meet certain strict standards. I would stand for eons in front of the bathroom mirror gobbing Vaseline on my hair, slicking it back except for the front which I would deftly flick forward with two fingers of my right hand. Then would begin the minute, systematic search for pimples and blackheads, the arch enemy. If one was spotted, a crucial decision needed to be made: camouflage or squeeze, and, if the latter, to do so with enough skill to make it look like a shaving nick (although I didn't have a hair on my face).

I described in what now feels like surprising detail (especially since I read the paper in front of the class) my first and surreal experience at the age of thirteen of touching a girl's breast—"step two"—while sitting in a dark movie theater, and how its impersonality and objectifying nature were insignificant compared to the achievement. I wrote:

> Marsha's breasts filled my visual field and I feverishly contemplated the ways I might approach them. Unaware of my intricate machinations, she sat as still as a statue, totally engrossed in the movie while my hand dangled silently over her shoulder like a spider about to pounce upon its victim. Slowly . . . with one finger and then another, I delicately entered unchartered territory. Still no movement. Now was the moment of truth; with my heart pounding like a bass drum and my breath coming in short gasps, I made my big move. I've done it! I've done it! I shouted over and over in my mind, although I couldn't feel anything except a stiff bra cup. Still Marsha did not respond and since I was too scared to move, we sat that way for the rest of the movie, two statues linked together by hand and breast. But it really didn't matter. Doing "it" was all that mattered and I had done it.

Although the term autoethnography had not yet been coined, my social work orientation toward understanding behavior in the social environment made this form of inquiry (albeit in an elementary form) a natural offshoot of my studies. Somewhat in the sociological tradition of ethnographic biographies, my paper illustrated, and social workers understood, that self and cultural/social narratives are inseparable. As Gubrium and Holstein (2008:244) note in their discussion of Clifford Shaw's *The Jackroller* (1930), his classic study of Stanley, a delinquent youth from Chicago, in which he presented Stanley's story in his own words: "What Stanley says is a story about a social world, not just about Stanley." Autoethnographers have taken this same principle and applied it to self-narratives.

INTERLUDE

THE EDITOR WHO LIVES IN MY HEAD: OK, you've provided a sense of what auto-ethnography might look like and some of its features. Now you need to get a bit more academic—provide more substantive information as a backdrop to reading the autoethnographies in the book. You're not assuming that readers have a background in autoethnography, so you need to provide a framework that will help them interpret and assess what they are reading.

THE AUTHOR WHO ALSO LIVES IN MY HEAD: You mean mix writing styles *within* this chapter—some dialogue, personal essay, and more academic writing?

THE EDITOR: Yeah, kind of a show and tell.

THE AUTHOR: Ok, I'll give it a try.

A BRIEF ELABORATION OF SOME PREVIOUSLY
IDENTIFIED THEMES

Autoethnography is one of the innovative inquiry approaches to emerge from the qualitative research movement (see Denzin and Lincoln 2002). Born from dissatisfaction with the perceived rigidity and limitations of orthodox research, autoethnography "troubles" the assumptions, methodology, methods, and foci of conventional inquiry. In doing so it complicates many of the taken-for-granted distinctions within research (e.g., researcher and subject) and between research and nonresearch (e.g., research and literature).

Autoethnography does not follow the protocols of mainstream research, nor is it based on assumptions of positivist philosophy; for example, the belief in an independent existing reality. Rather, it encompasses a range of inquiry practices that highlight the cultural and social contexts of knowledge as they were and are understood and experienced by the researcher/subject. This approach enables autoethnographers to investigate lived experiences from a perspective and level of detail not ordinarily accessible in conventional studies.

Autoethnography is written as "a form of self-narrative that places the self within a social context" (Reed-Danahay 1997:9). While focusing on the personal experience of the author/subject, it elucidates the social and cultural contexts that lend meaning to that experience. Thus autoethnography can be considered a special kind of narrative, one that "transcends mere narration of self to engage in cultural analysis and interpretation" (Chang 2008:43).

Two basic subtypes of autoethnography have been recognized: analytic and evocative. In analytic autoethnography, the emphasis is on "improving theoretical understandings of broader social phenomena" (Anderson 2006:375), whereas in evocative autoethnography, understanding is sought through one's personal story and the emotionality it invokes in readers. This is not a rigid duality, as many autoethnographies express both subtypes.

Whichever way an autoethnography leans, however, there is a reaching for a sense of verisimilitude and understanding; that is, a feeling of believability and a sense of what it was like to be in the author's shoes. Authors seek "empathic resonance" with readers (Ellis and Bochner 2000:744), drawing on "the imaginative style of literature with the rigor of social science ethnography" (Ellingson and Ellis 2008:449). Autoethnographers use the tools of literature, such as perspective, scene setting, dialogue, and plot, and a variety of literary devices, such as tropes, dialogue, and poetry, to develop a compelling narrative. At the same time they are mindful of ethnographic imperatives, such as the constitutive properties of cultural and social contexts and language.

As researchers and subjects, authors write from multiple perspectives: from the phenomenological perspective of the experiencing person, from a reflective social and cultural perspective, from the reflexive perspective of a visible author, and from a comparative perspective with the extant literature. In other words, they write about how they made sense of their experience at the time and how they are making sense now of how they made sense then.

Autoethnographic writing has "grab" (Gilguin 2005); it holds readers' interest. Although the writing can be highly engaging and evocative, it does not eschew erudition or careful analysis. Social issues are described from the inside out. In contrast to the canons of positivist-oriented research, autoethnography's accessibility and its complex, "messy" rendering of lived experiences are viewed as strengths, connecting with readers in meaningful ways.

Similarly, unlike conventional research writing, which is viewed as a kind of reporting that is neutral in tone, autoethnographic writing "evokes thought and imagination" (Nicol 2008:316). For autoethnographers, neutrality is not a statement of fact but a claim to a "positionless" position. All writing is interpretive and expressive of value positions. Rather than a neutral conveyer of facts, writing is a selective representation of interpreted experiences or observations. With varying degrees of consciousness, authors select from among numerous words and sentence structures. Each choice inevitably favors certain understandings, bringing certain aspects of experience (e.g., emotion, analysis) to the foreground and others to the background. Rather than deny or attempt to control these features of writing, autoethnographers embrace them. For example, authors not only are present in their texts but are reflexively present. They strive to be self-aware of how their assumptions, beliefs, understandings, values, and commitments influence their descriptions, analyses, and representations. They may also discuss how the process of autoethnographic inquiry has affected or changed them.

There is an element of courage in many autoethnographies. To write autoethnography is to go public with aspects or events in one's own life; to reveal thoughts, feelings, and actions that may not be flattering to the author nor known to others. It is to transgress the conventional boundaries of the personal and professional in the interest of generating insight and understanding. This novel positioning gives autoethnographic writing a therapeutic or generative quality for many authors and readers. As Ellis (2008:17) writes, autoethnography "provides companionship and coping strategies for dealing with personal disappointments, traumas, and losses; and helps us understand, reframe, and live through collective natural and human-made disasters that increasingly seem to be part of our lives." It was common, for example, for contributors to this book to comment on how their inquiry helped them gain a deeper understanding of their experience.

TRUTH, METHOD, AND AUTOETHNOGRAPHY

The notion of truth plays a central role in conventional scientific research in three interrelated ways that are relevant to autoethnography.[2] First is the assumption, often associated with the modernist project, that science, as the highest expression of rational thought (based on the ideal of objectivity), brings us ever closer to truth. This truth is ahistorical and acultural—it applies to all people at all times.[3]

Second is the notion of truth as accuracy. That is, when research findings are true, they are assumed to be accurate reflections of reality. This brings up the epistemological issue of how researchers can know this to be the case and not, for instance, what they hoped to find. Scientific research attempts to address this potential problem by employing specialized methods and analysis procedures to weed out false beliefs (e.g., bias, confounds) from true ones (i.e., facts). Also, since these true beliefs need to be represented in some way, scientists use a specialized language (words and numbers) that is assumed to accurately reflect reality.[4]

Third is the notion of truthfulness. Scientists do not make things up. They report what they observe (or what their measures "observe"). To distort or fabricate results (sometimes known as "fudging the data") is a cardinal sin punished by a secular version of excommunication from the scientific community. Collectively, the assumption of a transcendent truth, the use of special methods and language to ensure accuracy, and the commitment to truthfulness distinguishes science from other endeavors such as literature.

Autoethnography, as more representative of a postmodern orientation, tends toward a different view of these assumptions and beliefs. Consequently, it employs a different approach to gathering, representing, and interpreting data. As Zygmunt Bauman (1993) explains the contrast, "for the modernist, knowledge production is contingent on the circumstances of its generation; that is, it must meet certain criteria to be taken as knowledge. For the postmodernist, knowledge production itself is a narrative, one of many possible narratives" (16). In this regard, autoethnography's embrace of the idea of narrative truth (see Ellis and Bochner 2000:745–47) is consistent with the postmodern position. That is, there is no transcendental standard against which truth can be measured, nor is it presumed that language mirrors reality. Rather, it is the narrative in which truth claims are made—"the science story"—that gives those claims their authority. Within this story, claims that adhere to certain criteria are judged as true. However, this is not the only story possible. For autoethnographers, not only is the story itself generative of "truths," but truth in the modernist sense is not the aim of inquiry. Rather, autoethnographic inquiry seeks to enrich our understandings, expand our awareness, increase our sensitivities, and provide insights that can lead to practical action.

When writing about an experience, an autoethnographer does not seek accuracy in the sense of producing an exact representation of what occurred. For the autoethnographer, this is neither possible nor desirable. There is no truth to remember. We cannot communicate a noninterpreted experience (even to ourselves). What is experienced and how it is communicated are socially and culturally contexted interpretations. No matter how comprehensive our recall, the notes at our disposal (e.g., diaries), or the artifacts we consult, we can never reproduce or know if we reproduced the exact words that were said, thoughts that we had, every contextual detail, and so forth. There are innumerable ways to select and combine what might be considered the facts of experience.

Autoethnography presents an interpretation of an interpreted experience. It is an inquiry into the meaning of that experience based on when and where it was experienced from the standpoint of a later time and context. In this sense it is both an insider and an outsider perspective: the researcher/participant/author is separated from her or his own experience and uses that separation to generate a richer, more nuanced understanding.

My story about meeting my neighbor is not strictly true in the sense that I describe exactly and comprehensively what occurred. Rather, it is a recollection of this particular encounter blended with similar encounters I have had with different people. This type of "mindful slippage" (Medford 2006) is inevitable and underscores the difference between truth and truthfulness. That is, autoethnographers try to capture the essence of an event, "a resonance of truth rather than accuracy" (Davis and Ellis 2008:104), knowing that exact reproduction is not possible. This is done not in a cavalier or capricious fashion but by "mindfully" examining what is being knowingly omitted or how an experience is being represented (e.g., the author's choice of words). As Carolyn Ellis writes in the same paper, "I would argue that the stories we write as ethnographers do not have to be factual to be true; actually, they are not 'factual' in the 'accurate representational' sense of the word" (107).

Similarly, writing from our memories is not a reproduction of past happenings but, as Art Bochner notes, "is, in part, a response to what inspires my recollections" (2007:198). In other words, the conditions of recall (e.g., context, intended audience) will influence what is remembered. As a social construction, memory is viewed as a social act, something that is influenced by others and whose legitimation as a memory is contingent on meeting certain social criteria (e.g., sensibleness).[5]

Autoethnographers are aware that their version of events is one among many possible interpretations. Rather than strive for a truth that silences other claims, they attempt to provide interpretative analyses rich enough in detail, context, and aesthetic quality to enable insightful and meaningful understandings of social phenomena.

AUTOETHNOGRAPHY'S RELEVANCE

The embodied, sociocultural understandings of autoethnographies can provide useful information and perspectives on various issues. Emphasizing the phenomenological aspect of experience gives autoethnographic narratives a depth and authenticity rich with possibilities for discovery and action.

For social workers, autoethnography provides a form of inquiry congruent with the values and commitments of the profession. There is no pretense of neutrality but an exploration of how we construct and represent realities in particular contexts while at the same time knowing that any telling will be partial and subject to revision. Thus these constructions and representations are not expressed as isolated, acontextual acts but are connected to the material conditions and social categories that inscribe our lives. Applying this kind of telling to people whose representation or silencing has been controlled by others can be an important source of new information. Ellis and Bochner (2000), although not social workers, eloquently express this notion: "So it's important to get exposed to local stories that bring us into worlds of experience that are unknown to us, show us the concrete daily details of people whose lives have been underrepresented or not represented at all, help us reduce their marginalization, show us how partial and situated our understanding of the world is." They further state that "the goal is to encourage compassion and generate dialogue" (748). This is reminiscent of the philosopher Richard Rorty's (1993) advocacy for "sentimental stories" that enable others to identify with those viewed as "not like us."

Social workers often speak of "giving voice" to marginalized others. Autoethnography is a way to do so without translating the text into inaccessible academic jargon or to have these others represented by a professional in the role of de facto spokesperson. Similarly, autoethnography renders "subjugated knowledge" visible—things that we avoid talking about or that make us uncomfortable. It foregrounds the details of experience often lost in questionnaires and structured interviews. For example, Laura Ellingson's (2005) description of being a cancer patient receiving chemotherapy provides a level of bodily detail that is rarely visible in social science texts and that many would prefer not to read about. Yet such details are central to understanding her experience and probably that of others. She writes:

> A sharp pain in my lower abdomen startled me into wakefulness and I groaned in recognition. I searched the bed for my nurse-call button and pushed it. Glancing over at the rapidly dripping IV line, I cursed the need for continuous hydration to save my kidneys from the onslaught of toxic chemicals that was injected in that morning. The bone cancer had left my right leg a mess of grafts, stitches, and staples; there was no way I could get out of the bed, find my crutches, and hobble to the bathroom without losing control of my bladder. I was beyond exhaustion, and by the time I woke up, my bladder was so full it hurt. I'd have to wait for my nurse, Chris, to bring a bed pan. . . . The hot yellow liquid streamed from my urethra without my consent and the searing flames of shame swept over my face. Defeated, I let the tears flow with the urine. My pelvic muscles relaxed gratefully even as my buttocks cringed in retreat from the growing wetness that surrounded them. (87)

How did you feel reading this passage? Your reactions may tell you something about the social contexts that generate and reflect your own and Ellingson's feelings. Reflecting on these reactions may also create the potential for new understandings and ways of relating to others in such situations.

Autoethnography provides an opportunity for people to contest their stigmatizing labels. This is illustrated in an autoethnography by Heidi Pfau (2007), one of my former students, who wrote about her experience of coming to grips with her loss of sight. Central to Heidi's inquiry is how the cultural and social context of blindness as expressed, for example, through medical practice and interpersonal interactions attempted to equate her identity with her disability and its accompanying negative connotations. She writes about the well-meaning but misguided attempts of others to focus on her accomplishments despite her vision loss and its alienating consequences: "My story is a story about becoming 'other' in the eyes of friends and family members who suddenly didn't know how to relate to me. It is a story about not knowing how to relate to myself and feeling truly alone in the world" (402). Throughout the text she "talks back" to this stigmatization by repeating the line—to readers and herself—"I am more than my vision" and by challenging readers that "to really know me, you must be able to look beyond the distorted reflections of yourself that you project onto me. You must be able to first see my humanity" (404–5). Reflecting on her original version of this autoethnography that she wrote in my course seven years earlier—what Carolyn Ellis calls a meta-autoethnography—Heidi shares the insight that the situation is not either/or but both/and; that is, she needs others (and herself) to consider both her blindness and her shared humanity.

Lastly, as the above examples illustrate, autoethnography generates empathy: what it might be like to be in that person's shoes. This is a kind of understanding that is critical to accepting and respecting differences; what some (e.g., Bauman and Tester 2001) consider the basis of human rights.

EVALUATING AUTOETHNOGRAPHY

All inquiry approaches can be judged according to various criteria as having been done well or poorly. With controversial approaches like autoethnography, there is a tendency to confound the quality of particular autoethnographies with general judgments about the approach. Evaluating a particular autoethnography is different from evaluating autoethnography as a form of inquiry.

It is also important to consider the criteria underlying an assessment. Autoethnographies cannot be judged fairly by the criteria of conventional research. As stressed throughout this chapter, autoethnography is not a form of conventional research. Rather, it expresses alternatives to many of the tenets of research, such as objectivity, method, and protocol. Within the autoethnographic context, these ideas may not be relevant or sensible. Take, for example, validity as a reflection of reality.

For autoethnographers, what is taken as real is contingent and socially constructed. Multiple constructions (i.e., renderings of reality) are always possible depending on the author, audience, and contexts. Therefore alternative concepts such as authenticity and verisimilitude are more relevant.

Narratives exist not in isolation but in relation to other narratives, metanarratives, and discourses (Gubrium and Holstein 2008). Thus a particular autoethnography can be analyzed in relation to these other knowledge contexts; for example, the metanarrative of the inevitable progress of science or medical discourse. Possible questions might include: To what extent does the autoethnographic narrative assume these other knowledge contexts? How do they influence the content and the telling? Would drawing on different knowledge contexts have generated a different story? We might also consider the narrative environment, that is, the circumstances in which the narrative is assembled and expressed. This might include its purpose (why this topic?), the intended audience, or other contextual factors.

In their recent book on a relational constructionist approach to inquiry, Sheila McNamee and Dian Hosking (2012) propose an orientation toward evaluation that resonates with autoethnography. They propose that knowledge is a communal production and that different communities will value different knowledge. This position leads away from a results- or outcomes-oriented approach that seeks to reduce possibilities to ones concerned with preserving diversity and increasing possibilities. It refocuses them to emphasize process and its impact on findings. In the case of autoethnography, this might include, for example, how theory, methods, and even writing formats position the researcher and reader and influence which realities are invited and which are discouraged.

Autoethnographies can be poorly written or executed. They may not generate verisimilitude. They may seem self-indulgent, hardly reflective or reflexive, or only thinly connected to culture (Ellis 2004). Further, their aesthetic qualities (for example, the author's ability to hold readers' interest or evoke emotion) or substantive contribution (do readers learn anything new?) may seem weak (Richardson 2003). Of course, such judgments will vary; however, such variation is not necessarily problematic as multiple assessments can contribute to a rich dialogue around the topic of inquiry.

ABOUT THE BOOK

I hope the previous discussion has provided a sense of what autoethnography is like, what it tries to do, and some of the issues involved in its use as an inquiry approach. Unlike a "how to" book that emphasizes techniques or breaks down autoethnography into discrete categories, I have chosen to focus instead on general principles and illustrative examples. Instructional texts can provide potentially useful ideas; the downside is that they necessarily present a partial view of autoethnography and portray it as more mechanistic and method oriented than it is in practice. Still, these different approaches to learning are not in opposition but are complementary (see, e.g., Chang 2008 and Muncey 2010 for more instructional texts).

This book has three primary aims: to illustrate autoethnography as an inquiry approach, to demonstrate the value of such inquiry for social work practice and related fields, and to provide important, substantive information about topics germane to social workers. No attempt is made to define what an autoethnography should look like or to replicate a particular model of autoethnography. How authors/researchers take up autoethnography will be influenced by many factors: their research orientation, their understanding of the concepts central to autoethnography, its interaction with their topic, their level of comfort with disclosure, their writing skill and styles, and so on. There is no strict protocol that must be followed. "Methods" are varied and emergent rather than prescribed. Thus the book illustrates a diversity of literary formats and tools, investigative techniques, and analytical styles. Some of the autoethnographies are evocative; others are more analytical. All, I hope, will leave you feeling like you learned something potentially useful.

Despite the variability in how authors conducted and wrote their autoethnographies, there was a general agreed-upon structure. This included the following:

- Choosing topics that have been addressed by mainstream research in order to compare its portrayal with the lived experience of the author
- Focusing on the personal experience of the author while elucidating the social and cultural contexts that lend meaning to that experience
- Providing background and contextual information that enables readers to gain a sense of the dominant perspectives and their connection to the authors' and others' interpretations and actions

- Striving for verisimilitude such that readers vicariously experience the topic being addressed
- Making visible the authors' attempts to make sense of the situation or topic they are writing about, including the ambiguities, struggles, doubts, contradictions, insights, tensions, epiphanies, disappointments, and successes that accompanied their experience
- Considering implications for (social) working with people who have had similar experiences

A BRIEF PREVIEW OF THE CHAPTERS

The remainder of the book consists of eleven chapters illustrating autoethnographic inquiry on different topics. Although they can be read in any order, I have tried to group them according to what I interpreted as common or overlapping themes.

In chapter 2, Katherine Tyson McCrea tells the story of her passage to parenthood through the international adoption process. As we journey with Katherine, other stories, both heartbreaking and uplifting, appear: about Guatemala and the Mayan people, about the dark and angelic sides of humans, about parenting a child with disabilities, and about the love between two infant boys. Despite being a professor of social work, Katherine was unprepared for the volatility of the situation she entered and the unevenness of professional competence and values. As she wrote, "Only in Oz are the good and bad people so clearly distinguishable: in an enterprise such as international adoption, one unfortunately often could not know which side a professional was on until one was a recipient of their misbehavior." Ultimately her story provides us with a rare, insider's view of this field as well as the remarkable ability of people to persevere through seemingly overwhelming circumstances.

Chapter 3 is an autoethnographic exploration of Satu Ranta-Tyrkkö's experience in India, first with a Gandhian rural development organization, and then with a theater group, Natya Chetana (Theatre for Awareness). It also is the story of cultural encounters and the struggle for understanding. Satu's experiences challenged her preconceived ideas about social work in ways that required her to seek interpretive frameworks beyond conventional texts to such areas as postcolonial theory, and to extend her vocabulary to encompass culturally foreign concepts central to Natya Chetana's "practice."

In doing so, she was able to reconstruct her understanding of social work practice in a way that was more sensitive to and respectful of the historical and cultural contexts in which such practices emerge. Her study has important implications for reenvisioning social work and related fields from a global perspective.

In the United States, labels such as "minority" and "immigrant" strongly influence social relations and, consequently, personal identity. People who have an ambiguous status regarding these categorizations (that is, people of mixed race) may face challenges navigating this social terrain. Noriko Ishibashi Martinez, the author of chapter 4, was born in Japan to a white American mother and a Japanese father. She immigrated to the United States at age ten. Noriko quickly learned that she inhabited two worlds but was a full member of neither. As she puts it, "I am half majority race, half 'model minority' . . . a U.S. citizen moving to the U.S. for the first time; . . . a Japanese citizen leaving my country of birth." Her autoethnography explores this relationship—which she learns has more in common with others than might be surmised—while examining the contradictory rhetoric that urges people to transcend race while maintaining its importance to personal identity. She also considers the implications of her inquiry for the notion of cultural competence, a concept currently in vogue within the social work profession.

Critical reflection is an approach to practice whose major tenets—self-examination within social and cultural contexts, reflexivity—overlap with features of autoethnography. In chapter 5, Jan Fook, a leading voice in the development of critically reflective practice, blends aspects of both approaches in exploring the development of her personal and professional selves. Like Noriko, Jan too occupied a marginal status in her native Australia, a Chinese woman raised in a relatively rigid fundamentalist family. Using the tools of critical reflection and autoethnography, she explores her experiences as a professional educator and how these experiences led to increased awareness and a "coming together" of how her biography and social position generate her unique professional contributions.

In autoethnographic inquiry, authors/researchers reconstruct events and themselves based on memories supplemented by or checked against others' recollections, artifacts, and records. Social workers also construct narratives of others—narratives that live on beyond the person's lifetime. These narratives are necessarily highly selective, generating a portrait that may tell as much about the narrator as about his or her subject. In her unique autoethnography, which makes up chapter 6, Karen Staller explores the similarities between the reconstruction of others' lives through social work records and our personal records of deceased family members. The connection between her archival research on social work case records of a past generation and the process of sorting through her parents' artifacts following the death of her father sheds light on the relational nature of these records and the construction of historical memory.

Although autoethnographies center on the author/researcher, they are inevitably about relationships—the cultural and social milieus that we inhabit in our day-to-day lives. Sometimes life events move us into unfamiliar or uncomfortable environs in which we search for a connection to help us navigate the terrain. Brenda Solomon explores these types of events in chapter 7, from the seemingly insignificant, an encounter with an airport security guard around her daughter's sippy cup, to the profound, the death of her sister. Her inquiry leads to insights about the dehumanizing consequences of institutional discourses that decontextualize relationships and privilege protocols and rules. It also highlights the primacy of human connection as the basis of our common humanity and sustenance.

The diagnosis of a potentially fatal illness is a life-changing event. When Johanna Hefel's dear friend and colleague received such a diagnosis, she committed to supporting him throughout the remainder of his life. Little did she know that one year later she too would receive a similar diagnosis, making her both a care giver and someone in need of care. In chapter 8, Johanna uses this unusual positioning to explore the meanings and cultural constructions of death and dying. Drawing on her past experiences with death and in particular on the care of her friend (who eventually died), she provides an evocative narrative of coping and affirmation despite a work context in which productivity is the primary value.

The flexibility of autoethnography is illustrated in chapter 9 by Orlagh Farrell Delaney and Patricia Kennedy, who use dialogue to recount and reflect on their experiences of marital separation and eventual divorce. Although there are many differences in their lives—Orlagh has no children and lives in a rural setting, whereas Patricia has four children and lives in Dublin—their home country of Ireland provides a powerful common context that shapes their experiences. Despite many hardships and challenges, both find ways to endure and thrive. Their dialogue-based inquiry illuminates processes of resilience and strength, highlighting the importance of friendship and other supportive relationships.

We all have secret lives that in some cases belie our outward appearance.[6] Often a price is paid for these clandestine selves. Still, overcoming the real or imagined consequences of disclosure can be daunting. Chapter 10, Allan Irving's autoethnography on cross-dressing, an aspect of his life that he has not publicly disclosed before now, exemplifies the courageous aspect of undertaking autoethnography. It is not only informative but performative in that its telling is also an "outing" of a secret life. His inquiry and analysis go beyond the act itself to the relationship between clothing and gender identity, challenging the binary of two genders. More than being simply transgressive, there is an embodied, sensual, and liberating dimension to Allan's cross-dressing that contains important lessons for social workers to ponder.

The notion of change is a central feature of social work and other helping professions. While most change is shallow in the sense of leaving underlying assumptions and beliefs intact, my focus in chapter 11 is on deep or transformative change, which entails a foundational shift in understanding. In contrast to the more common focus on cataclysmic change that comes about through a traumatic event or conversion experience, my narrative explores such change—in my case from a diehard behaviorist to a social constructionist—as a complex, cumulative, and lengthy process characterized by nudgings, fortuitous events, and small epiphanies. Because transformative change often generates a world that is incommensurate with the former one, it can have a disruptive effect on relationships. I examine these relationships and their impact on my change efforts as well as how cultural and social contexts may thwart or facilitate change.

How we name relationships, such as mentor-protégé, parent-child, husband-wife, and employer-employee, provides general expectations regarding roles, statuses, rights, duties, behavior, and emotional involvement. Still, the specific expressions of these culturally informed frames are often negotiated in interaction, emerging as the relationship develops. In chapter 12, Zvi Eisikovits and Chaya Koren draw on their own experience and relevant literature to explore the development of their mentor-mentee relationship within an academic setting in social work. Employing dialogue and critical reflections, they illuminate both the idiosyncratic and common dimensions of their relationship development and how it was influenced by institutional and social/cultural contexts. Their negotiation of the nebulous boundary between the personal and professional, how the meanings of their relationship were constructed and reconstructed through dialogue, and how it affected their social, personal, and public identities can be extended to other relationships of relevance to social workers.

CONCLUDING THOUGHTS

It is now spring. Once again I am out walking my dog, but now the temperature is comfortable and the air is fragrant with the perfume of lilac and azalea bushes.[7] Not surprisingly, I encounter my neighbor Bob with his dog, Woody. Following greetings and an exchange of pleasantries, Bob asks if I finished my book project, "on, what did you call it . . . autoethnography?"

"Not quite," I reply, "but I hope to submit the manuscript to the publisher in about a week. These projects often take longer than expected, and this one has been particularly challenging."

"How come?" he asks.

"Writing these chapters has proven to be quite difficult for many of the contributors," I reply. "Part of the difficulty is that they have been so well schooled in using academic formats—an impersonal, third-person writing style—that it hasn't been easy to put that aside for the more personal, literary style of autoethnography. For example, much of my work with the contributors has been trying to get them to *show* readers how they experienced different situations rather than only telling them about it. Also, going public about personal experiences or life events takes courage, and authors struggle with what to include or omit." (Uh, oh, I think, I'm doing the long-winded, academic thing again.)

"Sounds interesting," Bob responds (although again I am not convinced). "What are you hoping to accomplish?"

"I hope that readers will come away having an understanding of autoethnography as an approach to inquiry, as a process of knowledge production, as a practice, and as a useful tool for professional development that can increase self-awareness and sensitize practitioners to the constitutive aspects of social and cultural contexts. I'd like them to see parallels between autoethnography and social work practice; for instance, how autoethnography expresses the kind of contextual understanding representative of a social work orientation. Finally, I hope that they will learn something valuable about the topics addressed in the chapters.

"I realize that some readers—and many who choose not to read the book—will not accept these aims. For some, autoethnography will be, as Carolyn Ellis, a well-known autoethnographer, put it in 2009, too 'unruly, dangerous, passionate, vulnerable, rebellious, and creative . . . the researcher [too] . . . impassioned and embodied, vulnerable and intimate, and the stories [too] . . . evocative, dramatic, engaging, with concrete and layered details, and when the topic calls for it, even heart-breaking' to be considered legitimate scholarship. I am comfortable with that. My goal is not to try and convince readers that autoethnography is 'really' research or that the knowledge it generates is authoritative. Rather, I tried to invite them to read the chapters with an open mind, putting aside their conventional, research-informed, critical lens, and allow themselves to engage with the text—to see how it calls to them, what it conjures up in their minds, how their sensitivity and understanding of the topic is altered. Does it explicate tacit knowledge about the topic? Did they learn anything about themselves? To quote Ellis once again, 'I want the reader to care, to feel, to empathize, to try to figure out how to live from the story, and then to do something. That to me is what autoethnography is about.' There are no checklists, no specific protocol, just a willingness to step outside the manicured path and into the forest."

I emerge from my passionate soliloquy and look around. Bob and Woody are gone.

NOTES

1   Note that I said "conduct an autoethnography." This is because an autoethnography is a form of inquiry or research—a point I did not feel was important to make explicit in my conversation with Bob.

2   The notion of truth is a complex one that cannot be comprehensively addressed here. Still, I offer some thoughts for readers, especially skeptical readers, to consider.

3   Although researchers often represent their findings as fallible, the assumption is that such truth is the best approximation to the "real" at that time.

4   This is known as the correspondence theory of truth.

5   This discussion notwithstanding, autoethnographers rely on various methods and artifacts to help them reconstruct their memory of events (see, e.g., Chang 2008).

6 This is poetically and musically expressed in Leonard Cohen's song, "In My Secret Life" (2001).

7 Although it is spring as I write this, the encounter is fictional in the sense that I did not have this actual conversation with Bob. Rather, the dialogue could be viewed as one I am having with you, my imaginary reader. I repeat this format as a way of tying the chapter together and to provide an interesting way of communicating some final thoughts.

REFERENCES

Anderson, L. 2006. "Analytic Autoethnography." *Journal of Contemporary Ethnography* 35 (4): 373–95.

Angelou, M. 1969. *I Know Why the Caged Bird Sings*. New York: Random House.

Bauman, Z. 1993. "Postmodernity, or Living with Ambivalence." In *A Postmodern Reader*, edited by J. P. Natoli and L. Hutcheon, 9–24. Albany: State University of New York Press.

Bauman, Z., and K. Tester 2001. *Conversations with Zygmunt Bauman*. Cambridge: Polity Press.

Bochner, A. P. 2007. "Notes Toward an Ethics of Memory in Autoethnographic Inquiry." In *Ethical Futures in Qualitative Research: Decolonizing the Politics of Knowledge*, edited by N. K. Denzin and M. D. Giardina, 197–208. Walnut Creek, Calif.: Left Coast Press.

Chang, H. V. 2008. *Autoethnography as Method (Developing Qualitative Inquiry)*. Walnut Creek, Calif.: Left Coast Press.

Cohen, L. 2001. *Ten New Songs*. New York: Columbia Records.

Davis, C. S., and C. Ellis. 2008. "Autoethnographic Introspection in Ethnographic Fiction: A Method of Inquiry." In *Knowing Differently: Arts-Based and Collaborative Research*, edited by P. Liamputtong and J. Rumbold, 99–117. Tampa, Fla.: Nova Science Publishers.

Denzin, N. K., and Y. S. Lincoln, eds. 2002. *The Qualitative Inquiry Reader*. Thousand Oaks, Calif.: Sage.

Ellingson, L. L. 2005. *Communicating in the Clinic: Negotiating Frontstage and Backstage Teamwork*. Cresskill, N.J.: Hampton Press.

Ellingson, L. L., and C. Ellis. 2008. "Autoethnography as Constructionist Project." In *Handbook of Constructionist Research*, edited by J. A. Holstein and J. A. Gubrium, 445–65. New York: Guilford Press.

Ellis, C. 2004. *The Ethnographic I: A Methodological Novel About Autoethnography.* Walnut Creek, Calif.: Altamira Press.

———. 2008. *Revision: Autoethnographic Reflections on Life and Work.* Walnut Creek, Calif.: Left Coast Press.

———. 2009. "Review of Chang, Heewon, *Autoethnography as Method.*" *Biography* 32 (2).

Ellis, C., and A. Bochner. 2000. "Autoethnography, Personal Narrative, Reflexivity." In *The Handbook of Qualitative Research*, edited by N. Denzin and Y. Lincoln, 733–68. 2d ed. Thousand Oaks, Calif.: Sage.

Gilguin, J. F. 2005. "'Grab' and Good Science: Writing Up the Results of Qualitative Research." *Qualitative Health Research* 15 (2): 256–62.

Gubrium, J. F., and J. A. Holstein. 2008. "Narrative Ethnography." In *Handbook of Emergent Methods*, edited by S. N. Hesse-Biber and P. Leavy. New York: Guilford Press.

King, D. W. 1998. *Deep Talk: Reading African-American Literary Names.* Charlottesville: University of Virginia Press.

Masters, W. H., and V. E. Johnson. 1966. *Human Sexual Response.* Toronto: Bantam Books.

———. 1970. *Human Sexual Inadequacy.* Toronto: Bantam Books.

McIlveen, P. 2008. "Autoethnography as a Method for Reflexive Research and Practice in Vocational Psychology." *Australian Journal of Career Development* 17 (2): 13–20.

McNamee, S., and D. M. Hosking. 2012. *Research and Social Change: A Relational Constructionist Approach.* New York: Routledge.

Medford, K. 2006. "Caught with a Fake ID: Ethical Questions About Slippage in Autoethnography." *Qualitative Inquiry* 12:853–64.

Muncey, T. 2010. *Creating Autoethnographies.* Thousand Oaks, Calif.: Sage.

Nicol, J. J. 2008. "Creating Vocative Texts." *Qualitative Report* 13 (3): 316–33.

Pfau, H. 2007. "To Know Me Now." *Qualitative Social Work* 6:397–410.

Reed-Danahay, D. 1997. *Autoethnography: Rewriting the Self and the Social.* Oxford: Berg.

Richardson, L. 2003. "New Writing Practices in Qualitative Research." *Sociology of Sport Journal* 17:5–20.

Rorty, R. 1993. "Human Rights, Rationality, and Sentimentality." In *On Human Rights*, edited by S. Shute and S. Hurley. New York: Basic Books.

Shaw, C. R. 1930. *The Jackroller.* Chicago: University of Chicago Press.

Shulman, A. K. 1972. *Memoir of an Ex-Prom Queen.* New York: Knopf.

CHAPTER 2

Where's Beebee?

THE ORPHAN CRISIS IN GLOBAL CHILD WELFARE

▸ KATHERINE TYSON McCREA

THIS IS THE STORY of my personal journey to parenthood, which, due to accidents of timing and a fateful coincidence of local and global influences on Guatemalan adoption, quickly swept me into some of the most enshadowed and sinister corners of the orphan crisis in global child welfare. It also led to a story of love between two infant boys that is remarkable and inspiring. The story told here has many ways of telling: one for my little sons on their third birthday, another when they are twelve; one for their doctors and helpers, others for friends; one we sought to tell to an international human rights tribunal for redress. The telling for you here, striving to follow principles of autoethnography, is crafted to best make known what cannot be known if one is limited to scientific traditions and even the most flexible of multimethod social science studies.

This story cannot be otherwise known because the people who are the basis of the facts one could gather using other methods disappear. The infants disappear: kidnapped, sold to Fagins who will turn them into thieves and criminals, or dying slowly of malnutrition, illness, lack of love, grief. Or they are disabled by criminal acts or deprivation of medical care readily available in industrialized nations and live lives of unimaginable pain in countries that have no resources to care for those who cannot fend for themselves in the most basic ways (Lykes 1994). The infants cannot speak, and even if they could, who can gather those statistics and stories into a neatly bound research package? An Institutional Review Board would shudder at the thought of what would be needed to cross national boundaries and take on such questions. Even more harrowing is that Guatemala is among the countries where researchers face profound opposition by those aspects of government seeking to hide their genocidal allegiances (Melville and Lykes 1992). Human rights activists supporting indigenous peoples are frequently murdered in Guatemala (see Human Rights Watch 2009). The story you will read happened, and in that sense it bears witness in a way that cannot be known through customary research methods.

So enough prelude—except for one set of thoughts about the inner place where the story begins. Parenthood starts with some dream, like a seed, born of ancient memories and personal experiences of caring and being cared for, and in this dream every parent is looking, somehow and in however focused or fragmented a way, for a child. In my parent dream, I wondered who that child would be, imagined loving that child, discovering the wonderful person the child could become and hoping to be up to the job of helping the child become that wonderful person. Then, as the dream comes to earth, one gradually knows that this dream will not just live in one's heart but become one's very heartbeat; it is a dream of life, but of life so deeply important it means more than one's own bones and breath: it means the ability to love, to live what life is meant to be, to join the core of the universe with one's tiny, humble breath. Some paths to parenthood become more entangled, and it feels as deeply threatening as tumbling into quicksand or an avalanche crashing; whether entangled or straight, parent-hood can be lofty with fruitful meaning and permanent, like residing in the most beautiful place in the world, doing the most fulfilling work possible with the best partners.

When into these dreams of parent love, with their possible incarna-tions, appear some of the world's over 100 million orphans, the entan-gled or straight road to parenthood suddenly has other dimensions only glimpsed through a glass darkly even by those claiming to be experts. As a professor of social work going for help to adopt a child, I had read about difficulties and controversies in international (Knoll and Murphy 1994) and transracial adoption (Bartholet 1991, 1993), but I could not foresee what a wild country the field of adoption can be from an adoptive parent's point of view.[1]

If you decide to read this story, I hope our encounters with the dark and noble sides of human nature will underscore the importance of cor-rective understandings and actions. I hope you will experience the courage of infant twins who dared to hold on to their love for each other despite disruptions by life-threatening illness, neglect, cruelty, and corruption. I hope you will know a bit more about what actually happens when mothers made desperate by poverty want to spare their newborns the threat of kidnapping, slow death from starvation, or mortal illness and disability, and find the courage to give them over to strangers in the hope the children will find a better life.

BEGINNING

So it was with the birth mother who gave my husband, Bob, and me our boys. During our cold, snow-laden winter in Chicago, she traveled several times from her tropical Mayan city by the sea in Guatemala to the country's capital to register her healthy twin sons' birth and reveal her story to social workers and others seeking to verify the authenticity of her intentions and actions, even making a videotape for the lawyer to satisfy inquisitorial opponents of international adoption in Guatemala. For she had borne and given birth to healthy twin sons, and it was worth all those steps and all that humiliation to try to give them, as she put it, a better life than what she could manage, abandoned as she was by the babies' father and her own family. We never could meet her but knew her through her documents: the phrases she gave the interviewers, her pictures. Her face looked terribly sad but also etched with determination, for she had to give up those babies right away to a foster mother and yet see them several times again, attesting each time that she had not been coerced, bribed, or forced in any way to have the children or give them up for adoption. And she had to give up her blood so it could be matched with her baby twins' blood, to ensure the boys had not been kidnapped. Her mourning process held hostage by the levels of bureaucratic suspicion and drudgery, she nonetheless maintained in her expression a combination of hope and fierce dignity. And we are forever grateful to her for her choice and her courage in carrying it out.

Tragedies usually initiate any adoption story. Legitimate birth parents relinquish their children only because they are overwhelmed by tragic events such as poverty, shame if the child is conceived out-of-wedlock, horrible circumstances such as rape leading to the conception, or being so young as to be unable to care for a child. There are usually tragic reasons why adoptive parents do not conceive, and given corruption in both domestic and international adoption, adoptive parents are prey to being misled and virtually robbed by birth mothers and adoption agencies.

Bob and I had an active domestic application pending but had already experienced one profound disappointment when the birth mother changed her mind. Like many parents aching from a lost domestic placement and wanting to make their dream come true, we looked at international adoption because, while there were hurdles unique to international adoption, in 2006 it was also believed to be more straightforward: when you were given your child's dossier by an international adoption agency, the adoption moved forward. We looked hard for reputable agencies, which also clearly exist, run by people who actually fight to be able to save the lives of orphans by arranging adoptions, ironically despite considerable opposition and negative public opinion. We chose both China and Guatemala, each of which were annually sending to the United States for adoption about four thousand babies who could not be cared for in their countries—China because of discrimination against women (Evans 2000; Johnson 2004); Guatemala because of genocidal discrimination against the Maya. There were some very desirable features of adoption from Guatemala compared with China: the children were in foster care rather than orphanages and were usually adopted in the first six months rather than at twelve months or older. So we filled out what seemed like an endless number of papers documenting that we are who we say we are, with all documents stamped by city, state, and federal authorities and, in the case of Guatemala, by the Guatemalan consulate. We had our fingerprints taken several times. We took classes on international and transracial adoption, read books, signed papers, sent money to guarantee our adoptees would be well cared for in every way, and were in line then for babies from the United States, China, and Guatemala.

HISTORY

When Bob and I started our journey to adopt in Guatemala, we knew some basic facts, and we quickly learned more. Guatemala is a country trying courageously to implement a parliamentary democracy in the wake of centuries of colonialism by the Spanish, a long history with the slave trade, and decades of genocide against the Mayan people who are the majority of the population. The Mayan people in Guatemala suffered some of the worst recent state-sponsored genocide in the world (Sanford 2003). Two researchers who interviewed sixty-eight Mayan child refugees whose family members were murdered, "disappeared," or kidnapped summarized the situation as follows:

> The trauma experienced by the Mayan children in Guatemala resulted from hostile Guatemalan Army incursions into their villages, that involved the indiscriminate torture and physical elimination of individuals, families, and even of entire communities, and the forced relocation of many, especially during the years 1981–1983. The children also experienced random, forced disappearances of family members without respect to age or gender and the concomitant uncertainty of their fate, as well as witnessing horrible mutilations evident in the bodies purposefully left by the army to terrorize the population. (Melville and Lykes 1992:533)

According to the Guatemalan Supreme Court of Justice, over 200,000 children lost one or both parents in the carnage; several hundred thousand families sought refuge in Mexico, Belize, or the United States (Melville and Lykes 1992:535). It is likely the birth and foster mothers of our children, who would have been children at the time, were exposed to the violence. Even in 1992, although the large-scale civil warfare had abated, continued terrorist acts against Mayan villagers by the Guatemalan Army continued.

The reason for the many Mayan infants available for adoption became apparent as we continued our research. In 2007 one of the presidential candidates included a Mayan activist and Nobel Peace Prize laureate, Rigoberta Menchu (Menchu 1984), running against candidates who had been affiliated with the military who carried out the genocide against the Maya. While there was controversy about the veracity of her accounts of her family's role in the counterinsurgency against the government (Arias 2001), Menchu's reporting of Mayan cultural values and practices was not contested. The Mayan people do not believe in abortion: from the moment of conception, life is thought to be sacred, and the people in a pregnant woman's community see themselves as obligated to treasure, protect, and support her, and they stop to greet and pray for her when they meet her in the village. Another important and credible diary by a Mayan, that of Ignacio (edited by James Sexton), confirms the Mayan cultural opposition to abortion, which is deepened by the fidelity of many Maya to the Catholic Church (Ignacio 1992). Customarily a Mayan woman would be married in her early teens and bear many children during her lifetime, many of whom would die from malnutrition or disease.

The recent history of genocide against the Mayan people continues to be a source of intense conflict and tension in Guatemala (Sanford 2003). The United Nations was involved in the peace accords between the government and the Mayan insurgency but terminated its involvement in 2004, citing continued profound problems with racism, corruption, and internal violence. The previous president and vice-president (Portillo and Reyes, respectively) were charged with embezzlement, fraud, and corruption, and Portillo fled to Mexico and was still to be extradited in 2007. A World Bank report in 2005 identified Guatemala as the most unequal country in Latin America. The country's disorder and violence were aggravated by efforts of drug cartels from Colombia to seek a stronghold in Guatemala, but the violence was still promulgated by government security forces, as noted in a respected U.S. security agency report: "Criminal gangs will target wealthy local business personnel and occasionally foreign nationals, especially in the capital Guatemala City. Robbery, burglary and kidnapping predominantly affect Guatemala City, but are widespread nationwide. The involvement of current and former security forces members in serious crime such as drug-trafficking is a growing problem" (Control Risks Group 2007).

Currently, in terms of children's quality of life, Guatemala ranks nineteenth in the world in the frequency of infant mortality, and its children have one of the worst nutritional statuses in the region: UNICEF (2009) estimates 76 percent of Mayan children live in profound poverty, and half of Guatemalan children suffered from chronic malnutrition in 2006.

TWINS

We received a call from our adoption agency in February 2007 that twin boys had been born in the Mayan city of Mazatenango and relinquished for adoption, and that we could adopt them. We were overjoyed. Shortly thereafter we received their photographs and fell in love with them immediately. We learned more about the birth mother from her photographs and statements to the social worker who interviewed her. She worked making tortillas and earned forty dollars a month. With two older sons for whom she was providing, but whom she could not afford to have live with her, and without a husband, the father of the twins, or other family members to help her, she wanted her sons to have a better life in the United States. It was not surprising to us that a single woman with no family support, living in such grinding poverty, at the brink of her resources in caring for two sons already, and likely with a family history of brutalization during the genocide, would find the prospect of caring for twin babies insurmountable. And there was also the concern about the boys having been born out of wedlock, and the shame that might well have attended their residing in the community (Ignacio 1992; Menchu 1984). A mother residing in the United States and faced with such stressors might also certainly have opted for adoption.

Their birth mother's choice of names expressed her expectation that they would be traveling and her hope they would distinguish themselves. As is customary in Guatemala, both boys had the same first name, Alejandro. Jose looked from his birth portrait to be reflectively examining his world and already thinking about it. Fernando (the name means "one who travels") seemed to be born smiling. We wanted to keep their birth mother's names for them, out of respect for her and their heritage, and yet we also wanted to give them names from our families to make it clear that we offered them a family completely. Accordingly, we named them David Jose and Donald Fernando. We were told we would likely be able to bring them home in late spring or early summer.

When we considered going to Guatemala to visit them, we learned that the U.S. State Department was strongly advising against travel to Guatemala: it was impossible to prevent violence against tourists because police were involved in the worst forms, which included surrounding busloads of tourists and demanding money; puncturing tires in rental cars and then ambushing tourists on the road when they tried to fix the tires; and kidnapping infants awaiting adoption to collect ransom money from the desperate adoptive parents. Police would go to the hotels where adoptive parents were caring for their children, demand the children, and tell the parents they had to provide thousands of dollars to get them back. While adoptive parents and their potential children were prime targets, the violence permeated all aspects of society: in the parliamentary elections that were going on in the summer and fall of 2007, forty candidates were murdered. The remaining candidates had to talk behind bullet-proof shields.

TRICK OR TREAT FOR UNICEF?

Ironically, the degrading and often violent racism (by Ladinos, the ruling Spanish-speaking people, against the Maya) still endemic in Guatemala was illustrated in an incident of international adoption. During the time the adoption of our sons was in process, Guatemalan president Oscar Berger and his wife Wendy decided to adopt a child, but instead of adopting a Mayan child, they adopted a Caucasian child from Russia. Their decision was considered unremarkable in Guatemala. Also that fall, UNICEF representatives in Guatemala allegedly gave President Berger (via a donation to his wife's organization) twenty-eight million dollars with the proviso that he would support an end to international adoption and instead build orphanages (Luarca 2006). Berger left office in early 2008 without there being any accountability about the money and without any significant investment and improvement in conditions for orphans in Guatemala.

We expected that our adoption would follow the traditional timeframe. The birth mother and the babies had to have their DNA tests confirmed by a U.S. source to ensure she was their parent; the boys had to be made available for adoption in Guatemala; if no one rose to adopt them, the case had to be passed through the Guatemalan Family Court; and finally the adoption had to be validated by the Guatemalan governmental agency, PGN. We anticipated that the adoption would occur in summer 2007. In late summer our adoption agency told us that there had been an abduction of twin boys. Although the abducted boys were not our sons, nonetheless our boys' case was being delayed in PGN because extra evaluations were needed given the abduction. Then we learned from our adoption agency in August that the boys had been harbored in three foster homes, two of whom were replaced because the agency had been unsatisfied with their care. I was devastated to learn about the shifting foster mothers since, as a child therapist who has treated young children suffering the effects of multiple foster placements (which can range from profound disorganized hyperactivity to elective mutism), I had some sense of what it means for a baby to repeatedly lose his or her parents. Just when the baby's emotional life and identity is being formed and looking ardently for a secure foundation and stable arms to embrace, to suddenly be torn away three times in succession is traumatic at a level so profoundly disorganizing it can hardly be put into words. Pictures we received in August confirmed our fears, as the boys looked scared and were not smiling. We passionately expressed our concerns to our agency and started trying to advance the adoption process. But events in Guatemalan adoption were becoming increasingly chaotic, as UNICEF and other groups stepped up their pressure on the government to abolish international adoptions, despite the efforts of advocates of international adoption, including the director of our agency, who testified in Guatemalan court about procedures to ensure legitimate international adoption.

In September I began weekly calls to the Guatemalan government agency responsible for verifying and finalizing the adoption, PGN, to try to understand the nature of the holdup. In late September I learned from PGN that the twins' case was held up in the Minors Section (a special section for problematic cases, especially when the birth mother is a minor). I immediately contacted an official at the adoption agency, who spoke with the lawyer assigned to our case. He informed us that it was held up in the Minors Section because a police report was needed to prove the children were not the abducted twins.

The Minors Section of PGN was headed at the time by Josefina Arellano, a known critic of international adoption reputed to have said that "it would be better if the children were dead than that they were adopted." This officially hostile bureaucracy subsequently sent the case to the police for further investigation. Aware that, with the timeframe for adoptions coming to an end, the boys might be consigned to indefinite orphanage placements, we decided to hire another set of Guatemalan lawyers, highly recommended by other parents, to advocate for advancing the adoption through PGN.

Meanwhile we learned that tensions in the adoption community in Guatemala were so profound that one adoption lawyer, a human rights advocate who supported facilitation of Guatemalan adoptions, had been held hostage in PGN and threatened for several hours (Luarca 2007). Despite our fears at the time, we could not even comprehend how bad things could have become: as of this writing two years later, seven to nine hundred children who were supposed to be adopted as infants still languish in orphanages in Guatemala, and their adoptive parents have no recourse as the bureaucratic delays put up one obstacle after another (Aizenman 2009; http://guatemala900.org/wp/).

At the last moment our adoption lawyer obtained the police report on October 24 and the boys' case was released from the Minors Section.

It was finally released from PGN in early December. Thus Donald Fernando and David Jose were legally our sons in Guatemala as of December 5, 2007, when their birth mother came to court again, this time to sign her final relinquishment.

They legally became our sons in Guatemala just days before a law was passed by the Guatemalan Congress and signed by the president that created a new adoption-processing bureaucracy, prohibited any financial benefit to anyone involved in an adoption, and mandated that all adoptions be national before they became international. While stating its intent was to comply with the Hague Convention, Decreto 77-2007 has posed insurmountable obstacles for completing adoptions in process and prevented new international adoptions.

OF DISEASES, PHYSICIANS, AND A HOSPITAL: MEETING OUR SONS

Awaiting the children's appointment to be screened by the U.S. State Department in Guatemala City for their visas, which was the last step, we learned that one of the babies was sick with a cold and in the hospital. Knowing the vulnerability of orphans to dying even from measles, we decided to go immediately to Guatemala. We arrived thirty-six hours later, afraid in the airport and while taking a cab to the hotel, but safely.

The next morning, in the lobby of the hotel, we had the joy of meeting David Jose for the first time. Within a minute of starting to get to know him, we received the terrible shock of being told by the foster mother that Donald Fernando was in intensive care, on a respirator, having suffered acute convulsions due to meningitis ten days previously. We frantically called our adoption agency, which had no idea what had happened. The agency made calls and confirmed what the foster mother said: Donald was in the public hospital in Guatemala City. Because he was not yet legally our child according to U.S. law, we could not move him to any other hospital in Guatemala or take formal responsibility for his medical care. We would have to do the best with what was available where he was. In any case, he was too ill to be moved at that point.

Bob immediately went with our translators, Alfredo and Claudia (to whom we are eternally grateful), to Roosevelt Hospital, akin to Cook County Hospital in Chicago or any large, urban hospital serving indigent people, but correspondingly underresourced in Guatemala. When Bob returned he told me that Donald was in a coma, hooked up to a respirator, on a feeding tube, and tied down. "Are you sure you want to go?" he asked when I set off to see the baby. "It's really hard—he looks like Jesus Christ on the cross."

Donald had been stricken with streptococcus pneumoniae, which, as it often does, infected the coverings of his brain, a syndrome termed bacterial meningitis. The worst side effect of the disease is that the blood vessels that supply oxygen to the brain constrict uncontrollably. In the absence of blood supply, cells in many regions of the brain begin to die, which in turn causes swelling in the brain that squeezes the blood supply even more. This profoundly painful process causes extensive, lasting brain damage and is fatal if steps are not quickly taken to halt it. Current estimates are that 14.5 million children are stricken with serious pneumoccocal disease worldwide, resulting in over 820,000 deaths (the majority in non-HIV-positive children); about 11 percent of all deaths of young children are caused by pneumoccocal infection (O'Brien et al. 2009).

We headed for the hospital, through the winding streets of Guatemala City, up and down hills, and then through a marketplace and streets packed full of Mayan people—women in long, striped dresses with lace tops, their children in slings on their backs or holding their hands, the men, some wearing ponchos, in darker colors. The people were selling primarily foodstuffs, pottery, and greens—plants with huge green leaves that I didn't recognize. Some people were waiting by the side of the streets; others in long lines, perhaps for a bus. Then we went through a public park—unkempt compared to the hotel district, with huge, overhanging tropical trees and wild, brilliant flowers sweeping overhead. The driveway turned into a semicircle and there was the hospital—dirty white, many windows panes nonexistent and covered with newspaper, huge and dilapidated.

Bob pointed me to the main door. Only one of us could go at a time, and the identification process was complex. Donald Fernando could not be admitted as an orphan awaiting adoption because of the concern that he would be discriminated against and not receive care. So we were not listed as his parents, even though under Guatemalan law we were. I went to the social worker's office with the patient ID card with Donald's name on it and waited for her to get back. The waiting room steadily filled with

Mayan people. That would be how it would go for all our visits over the next month: only Mayan people at that hospital. Alfredo and Claudia told me that anyone with money went to a different hospital. When the social worker came back, she looked like one of the Spanish-speaking elite (or Ladino). I spoke to her in my elementary Spanish, and she was openly hostile: "Only his mother can come." I showed her that, according to Guatemalan law, I was Donald Fernando's mother. She looked at me with undisguised hostility and waved me toward the guard, also Ladino, who looked at the card and then told me to go upstairs. I walked through winding, institutional blue hallways, past many Mayan families visiting their children; the hallways wound and turned without signs, and I was unsure if I was going the right way until some doctors pointed me toward the pediatric neurology intensive care unit. The door to the unit was closed, and there was a waiting room with parents, many of whom were crying. There was Donald's foster mother, who came up to me with tears in her eyes and embraced me. I went into a large room with children all around the perimeter, all hooked up to various machines so they seemed buried in tubes, all beeping in various ways, with notably few nurses.

I asked for Donald Fernando and was pointed to his bed. There he was, a tiny, tiny baby who looked like David but with hair even darker against the yellowish white sheet, his skin paler, his eyes closed. And he was stretched out as if on a cross, restrained (they later told me it was because as soon as he woke up he would try to tear out the tubes), the IVs in his left arm, a feeding tube and respirator controlling his breathing, keeping him alive. I remembered the comatose patients from my time as chaplain-in-training and medical social worker and hoped that perhaps he knew I was there. All I could do was reach for his tiny hand and pray, and the tears started coming down my face. I stayed that way, and finally someone who looked like a resident came over and I asked in my elementary Spanish how Donald was doing—"the same." "His condition is grave; they are unsure what will happen. Right now he can't breathe or eat for himself, and if they reduce the high dose of antiseizure medicine, he has terrible seizures." I felt numb and in shock. Looking around, I realized how many other children were there in dreadful condition, some of whom looked like they had terrible tumors. I couldn't look any more. I focused on Donald, and then the brief visiting hours were over. I went out into blinding Guatemalan sunshine and could hardly talk as we returned to the hotel.

FIGHTING FOR THEIR LIVES

Every day we went back to the hospital. I would take care of David in the morning while Bob went, and then I would go for the afternoon. The guard came to know me but obviously did not want to have any kind of relatedness and asked for my card very officially every day. I got used to being six feet tall and blonde, waiting in a long line with Mayan families who were terribly malnourished and impoverished. But no one was cruel or even stared; if we made eye contact, they just returned my nod and smile.

Bob, conferring with doctors with the help of our translators, learned that they had not given Donald steroids during the critical first hours of his illnesses. Those might have prevented some of the swelling of his brain. The steroids were more than they could pay for in a public hospital. One day I was stroking Donald's hands and feet and noticed that while his right hand and foot responded, his left did not. I asked the resident and he said "Yes, it is likely his left side is paralyzed." How long will it last? They don't know. Does he feel anything? "Yes, he can feel pain." I thought that was terrible—he couldn't move but he didn't have the blessing of numbness.

Bob, being a brain scientist, could read MRIs and knew Donald's syndrome, having taught physicians how to read MRIs and done thousands of dissections of brains of humans and animals. Bob learned that Donald's doctors did not do an MRI scan on Donald because they did not have the funds—it would cost $30. He also found out that Donald needed a medication that would cost $9. We paid for the MRI and the medication. Donald had lost 20 percent of his body weight. Adults can die when that happens, let alone babies. Our literature search late at night after David was asleep (when the unreliable Internet was working) indicated that infants with his presenting symptoms (severe seizures, comatose) have a 33 percent mortality rate from this disease, and if they recover many are severely disabled with epilepsy, cerebral palsy, paralysis, and retardation. In developing countries bacterial meningitis and encephalitis are not uncommon, especially in the winter months, often resulting from streptococcus pneumoniae bacteria, against which vaccines are used in industrialized countries (e.g., Lovera and Arbo 2005; Natalino and Moura-Ribeiro 1999; Selim et al. 2007; Siddiqui et al. 2006). Our translators told us that their children were vaccinated against the pneumoccocus disease because it can run rampant in Guatemala. Since we had paid our adoption agency to ensure the boys received their vaccines, and the agency had promised to carry out the vaccinations, we had assumed they had been administered. But not so.

We frantically tried to figure out what to do. My family was calling every day, and my sister called her husband's brother, who is a pediatrician; he had done his residency at Roosevelt Hospital and speaks fluent Spanish. He agreed to help us by having a conference call with Donald's attending physician and Bob. So we arranged that for shortly after Christmas and prayed that our cell phone connection would be working.

On Christmas Eve Bob came back from the hospital, furious. He had learned from the residents that Donald (and, we assumed, David) had not been vaccinated against pneumoccocus and many other childhood diseases. Apparently the lawyer and doctor responsible for their care were trying to save money (the vaccine costs $25 in Guatemala). The translators confirmed that their friends called the pediatrician "Dr. Cheap" because he was known to skimp so badly on care. Donald's condition still appeared dreadful; he was still in a coma. We called the adoption agency, and, to their credit, the assistant director was horrified by the news and stayed in touch with us by cell phone for the remainder of our stay.

Then, on Christmas day when Bob was there, Donald woke up. But he would not suck. Bob came back and said, "If he doesn't suck it's all over—they'll have to put the feeding tube back in and the risk of another infection is very high." I frantically thought about what I had learned about babies in medical emergencies—how they can lose their will to live because the physical pain is such a shock it disrupts any sense that they can feel good; like a suicidal adult, they just stop eating or drinking. What could we do? "Let's find lollipops," I said, thinking that the burst of pleasure on Donald's tongue might help him the way it helped my depressed child psychotherapy clients. So we looked around the city to find a store open on Christmas Day that would sell lollipops, and Bob took them to Donald. When he came back, he said that after a few hesitating moments Donald started to suck. But it was clearly hard for him to move his lips, and when the nurse then tried a bottle, he started to choke. Bob suggested that Donald might not be able to swallow—his swallowing muscles might be paralyzed too.

Meanwhile we were caring for David, who had responded to the trauma he had experienced with the curiosity and activity of a baby determined to learn about what was going on around him and to make the best of it. David was incredibly active, curious, and social, standing up in his crib every morning to greet the day and us with a smile and a characteristic "kkkkk" sound that he used to initiate any social interaction. He crawled everywhere and was thrilled when I held his hands to help him learn how to walk. He clung to Bob and me as though he knew from the beginning that we would love him forever and he had just been waiting for us all that time.

But the day after Christmas, David suddenly vomited and got explosive diarrhea and fever. In a panic I contacted our adoption agency, which said I needed to work with its pediatrician, even though we had lost all trust in him, as he was the only pediatrician they knew and could recommend. The pediatrician came to visit us in the hotel and told us there was a rotavirus outbreak among Guatemalan children and this was no doubt it. "It does not have to be serious—we have to feed him Pedialyte, and if he vomits again we will admit him to a hospital." Sitting on the couch with me, the doctor said, "You know your other son, he can grow up to be normal, I've seen many children grow up to be normal who went through that." I started to cry with relief. I translated for Bob, who was horrified and said to him, "How can you lie to us like that?" And from the pediatrician's expression, I realized he was lying.

Then we were worried about David—how could we trust this pediatrician with his care? But we didn't know anyone else, and during the holiday our translators' pediatricians were not available either. Bob recalled that while I was visiting Donald, he and David had been playing in the park and a little girl had wanted to share her ice cream cone with David. No doubt it was there that he contracted the highly contagious disease. The doctor said to be careful of ourselves, since we could catch it too if we had not received a rotavirus vaccine as children. We didn't remember ever being vaccinated for rotavirus. I looked it up on the Internet and learned that it is a protracted diarrhea syndrome with grave risk that a baby can become dehydrated, especially with vomiting. Rotavirus was another vaccine that the boys should have had but were never given. The vaccine is effective in preventing this disease, which rampages through developing countries primarily during the months of November to February. More than half a million children die every year from the virus, most in developing countries (Tanaka et al. 2007; Parashar et al. 2009). As of 2008, the World Health Organization reported that neither pneumoccocus nor rotavirus is part of the normal, publicly funded vaccine schedule for children in Guatemala, although U.S. children routinely receive those vaccines.

During the conference between Donald's attending physician and my brother-in-law's brother, the latter reassured us that the treatment Donald Fernando was getting was, at this point, on a reasonable course. He thought rotavirus was a likely cause of David's condition and emphasized that we should seek immediate hospitalization for David if he vomited, he refused to drink Pedialyte, or his diarrhea did not abate within a week.

I teach classes on global social work in which we talk about structural violence based on James Farmer's excellent work: the physical suffering of poor people caused by the deprivation of basic medical care, contributed to frequently by the exploitation of poor countries by wealthier ones, and by the global imbalance in resources (Farmer 2003). I realized my sons were victims of structural violence, as are so many other children. Meanwhile David's fever went up and he had constant diarrhea; I kept him near the bathtub because it was so painful if the extremely acidic diarrhea had any contact with his skin. David cried because he was so uncomfortable, and I found myself unbearably fearful of losing David too. I started to cry at the same time that I was frantically praying that David would be spared. I realized how much I already loved him more than myself—as someone said about her love for her child, "It's like your heart is walking around outside your body." As I was hugging him and crying, David looked up at me in a puzzled way and expressed the most that he could at that time, stroking my hair with his hands.

By the next day he had not vomited again. David drank down the Pedialyte as avidly as if it were the best milkshake around, and again I was struck by his resilience. He cried when the diarrhea bothered him and was weak but otherwise hung on to me with great determination and retained his insatiable curiosity. He was more uncomfortable at night, and I put him near me in the very large hotel bed so I could tell immediately if he became too sick. Then of course I started to feel sick myself, but it was fortunately a weaker version of the illness afflicting him.

After several days it became clear that the worst of the fever was over; the diarrhea continued and, as we were told, would for a week, and for another week he could not drink milk-based products because of the trauma to his digestive system. So we bought a brand of non-milk-based formula, and fortunately David took to that too. What happens to children whose parents cannot afford Pedialyte and special formulas?

Donald got out of intensive care on New Year's Day. We went to see him on the pediatric neurology floor, in his hospital bed, which looked like beds from movies in the 1930s: dingy metal, tiny, rickety, the sheets worn and yellowed. The children on his unit had terrible conditions—most were in beds or wheelchairs, paralyzed, trembling, some with heads bandaged. Now that I could hold him, I discovered Donald had raw bedsores across the back of his head and a terribly painful diaper rash all over his bottom. Neither of these would have happened in a hospital for more privileged children, and they were excruciating for him. The hospital allowed children only two bottles of milk a day because that was all it had money for, and it would not allow us to bring Donald more. There was also a shortage of water, and we could not compensate for that either.

Donald had two roommates who were older than him. Their parents spoke only Mayan, which was nothing like Spanish so I couldn't understand them, but they were very friendly and showed me where all the necessities were for parents (where to put dirty diapers, etc.). There was a room where the parents kept their things: there were so few nurses that the parents spent the nights with their children and slept on the floor. We could not stay the night as we were not officially Donald's parents, but we could support his foster mother in her desire to do so. When Donald started crying, I picked him up and comforted him and sang to him, and I saw the Mayan mothers point to me and nod approvingly to each other. Over the next several days we parents found ways to communicate, and when Donald's seven-year-old roommate had a birthday, we brought small gifts from the hotel and he and his parents were thrilled. I noticed the Mayan parents were permissive and greatly affectionate with their children. When siblings visited they jumped around and played and seemed to not have any fear of their parents.

While Mayan people we encountered were uniformly supportive of our adoption, there was a significant contrast in our experiences with non-Mayan people in Guatemala (with the exception of our translators). Alfredo and Claudia warned us that we should not leave the few blocks around our hotel for fear that we might be harmed or David kidnapped and held for ransom. One time Alfredo and Claudia took us to the Guatemala City Zoo with another set of parents and their adopted baby. Seeing me with David, a strange Ladino man came up and made some derogatory remarks in Spanish, evidently assuming I would not understand. When I responded in Spanish that my son was a marvelous boy, he looked surprised momentarily but then mockingly said, "He looks like you." We turned and walked away.

EXIT

Shortly after New Year's, the Ladino lawyer who processed the adoption (and hired the pediatrician who did not give the boys their vaccines) came to the hospital to have pictures taken for Donald's passport. Bob and I could not figure out how they thought Donald could look healthy in the pictures, but we saw how he was posed, and indeed he did not look anywhere near as ill as he did in person. The lawyer's only interaction with Bob was to acknowledge his presence with a nod, and we realized how thoroughly unscrupulous he was, and how uncaring he was of his tiny client who had clung so determinedly to life.

Able to take in a bottle, Donald was discharged from the hospital on his birthday. We celebrated with a SpongeBob piñata and dinner with Alfredo and Claudia and the foster mothers. Donald was in a baby carrier, asleep most of the time, sweating profusely, trembling with myclonal seizures, and crying when he woke up. He drank from his bottle, but just barely.

A few days later we took Donald outside in a baby stroller for his first walk in months and ran into Zuleima, a Mayan woman who sold her handicrafts outside of our hotel room, with whom we had become acquainted. When she saw us with Donald, she was most supportive. She had not been easy to get to know: clearly an astute businesswoman, she spoke English, Spanish, and Mayan and sold her work as well as that of others without any bargaining allowed. When I had realized that I would need a baby sling for David, as within a day he had not wanted to be separated from me by more than a few feet, I had talked with Zuleima but finally purchased from another woman one of the large blankets Mayan women use as baby slings. The blanket cost half what Zuleima charged. The next day Zuleima saw me with the blanket she had not sold to me and offered to help me tie it as Mayan women do. While she was doing that she commented, "Oh, it's damp—you had to wash it, it wasn't new?" I nodded and she said, "Mine are new." "Yes," I said, "but this cost a lot less. I don't know how long we'll be here; he has a twin brother in the hospital who is very sick and is needing medications and care." Zuleima's expression of concern had deepened, and she expressed her hope that Donald would recover. Now, seeing Donald with us but obviously still so ill, she escorted us on a walk around the block, full of support, saying, "It is so wonderful you can take him to the U.S. and keep them together—they will know how to help him there." Such support of our adoption was common among the Mayan people we encountered and was also documented in interviews with Guatemalans (Wilson and Gibbons 2005).

That night Alfredo and Claudia said they felt bad for us that the pediatrician had been so dishonest and that they could help us bring Donald to a pediatric neurologist they believed to be one of the best in Guatemala City. Deeply grateful, a few days later we went to Dr. N.'s tiny storefront office with Donald and David. We waited with other parents with children suffering from terrible neurological conditions—some clearly retarded, some with crippling cerebral palsy. Dr. N. examined Donald and then said to us, "I have to tell you, I saw him in Roosevelt Hospital also. He should have had the vaccine for pneumoccocus; it would have prevented this, and it is commonly given now for children here. It's amazing he is alive. I saw his brain scans. You understand the syndrome." Bob nodded but Dr. N. explained it to me: "The infection caused his blood vessels in the brain to spasm. They cut off oxygen to the brain cells, and then the brain reacts by flushing out with fluid. The brain swells and there is more damage. There are now giant holes of water where there should be brain cells. He has lost so many brain cells, most likely he will never be able to swallow, to talk, to feed himself. He'll never be able to walk or even use his arms. He will be deeply retarded and probably never be able to recognize who you are." Finding it hard to believe the doctor, I said, "It seems he knows us in a way now—he looks at us deeply for a long time like a younger baby." Dr. N. responded, "Yes, but he has to do that because he can't make sense of anything he sees. He might recover something, but it would take a miracle. I have seen miracles, believe me, but they do not happen often." Dr. N. refused to take any payment from us and also agreed to be available in the future for help if we should need it. We were both impressed by his obvious honesty, skill, and commitment, shocked as we were by what he told us.

At first Dr. N.'s prognosis didn't sink in. It couldn't be that bad. But then we realized that if Donald did not get significantly better, it would be as bad as Dr. N. said. He was functionally paralyzed, he could not even hold up his own head, and his limbs trembled with seizures when he was awake. He cried continually and could barely stop to take a few swallows of food. He often spit up half of what he swallowed. Bob and I got up to feed Donald at night, and it seemed we were up every two hours. But one night we each thought that it looked like more of his bottle was gone than when we got up the last time. When morning came, we realized that Donald was actually waking up every hour, and we were unknowingly spelling each other and had the illusion he was waking up every two hours. When David crawled over to Donald and patted him, Donald did not respond. It seemed David did not know him—he related with Donald more like Donald was a doll than another person, which was understandable since Donald didn't really respond in any way. We noticed, however, that Donald felt physical pain and expressed more distress if he was in his crib and the rest of us were together at the table. He was happier being near us and didn't like to be alone.

That day and the next we were frantically thinking: we had been assigned by the consulate visa office to adopt both boys at the same time and had perhaps the last embassy interviews we could arrange to get them out before the adoptions were terminated by the government. We assumed the lawyer must be thinking he could bribe the U.S. consulate prescreening doctor to sign that Donald was healthy. But the consulate office staff would also interview us with our adoptees, and we wouldn't lie. We could not imagine how Donald would pass. What would happen to him and to our adoption of David in that case? In part to prepare for the consulate's questions about whether Donald would drain public funds in the United States, we tried to find out what kind of care Donald could get in the United States in his condition. My insurance did not cover long-term care for children, which was what Donald probably needed. I checked institutions in Chicago and found that tube feedings and other treatment that Donald might require would cost hundreds of thousands of dollars a year, which we did not have. Phone calls to our adoption social worker and accountant confirmed that we would be falling into a hole in the United States where there was no financial support. I found myself realizing that if I lived in a country like Finland, where there is better support for families caring for children with special needs, there would probably be some way to bring Donald home.

But I don't, and in the embattled context of Guatemalan adoptions, it was clear that all other international options would be blockaded for Guatemalan orphans indefinitely. Zuleima's supportive, hopeful comments took on a tragically ironic ring.

I don't know how to describe what the next days were like except to say that although there was an earthquake in Guatemala City—the hotel shook, the lights flickered on and off—it seemed like only a very minor event and not the least bit frightening because I was feeling so stricken. We had been in Guatemala a month, but it seemed like years. All I could think about was what would become of Donald, whom I had grown to love, and if we couldn't bring him home somehow, how would David feel about losing his twin?

And then we didn't really have a choice. The consulate's doctor put off Donald's appointment. Bob walked to the consulate visa office early each morning, telling them that we needed an appointment for our adoption of David. Finally, via e-mail, they gave us a date, three weeks away. We couldn't wait that long, not the way the government was terminating adoptions. Planes out of Guatemala were full, and we had reservations to depart in a few days, which would be impossible to change. I insisted on talking to the consul myself and pleaded with her to resolve our concerns. "Everyone else is in your situation, and some have waited longer," she said. "Not all of them have patients at home or a son who has been in a coma here," I replied. She finally relented and gave us an appointment for David's consulate visa review the day before our plane was scheduled to depart.

We went to the consulate visa office with David just after dawn. The office was full of babies, most of whom were younger and quiet or sleeping. David characteristically was wide awake and wanted to see everything and crawl everywhere. I entertained him by singing songs: "We're off to see the Wizard, the wonderful Wizard of Oz." Certainly we were not in Kansas anymore. David decided to be a one-baby greeting committee, sitting by the door, watching how it opened and closed, and smiling at each person who came in. Finally, after five hours of waiting, we had our interview and obtained permission to bring David to the United States, with the assumption that Donald would have an interview when he was well enough to travel. We couldn't share with the consul Dr. N.'s opinion.

That afternoon, numb with exhaustion but unable to rest, we went to the main square in Guatemala City. Alfredo and Claudia urged us, "You should see it, you haven't seen anything of Guatemala while you've been here, and all the other parents do." So we went, carrying our babies. David, soon to be an immigrant, was moving constantly and looking everywhere, and Donald, whom we would have to leave in Guatemala, looked tiny and exhausted by comparison and did not move in my arms. We saw a wall where the names of people murdered in the genocide were inscribed, like the Vietnam Memorial in Washington, D.C. Even more names are being added all the time as graves are dug up. I thought that perhaps the boys' birth mother's family members are listed on that wall. How many orphans are not on that wall, casualties of infanticidal neglect that is no doubt even more common among orphans not on the track for adoption? We went into the church, and at last it was dark. All I could do was cry because I could not fathom leaving Donald. We had only three more hours to be with him. We went back to the hotel, and I couldn't stop the tears from running down my face.

The pediatrician showed up unexpectedly, and it was clear to Bob and me that he was there to try to convince us to stay and take Donald back with us in a few days. Bob angrily asked, "How can you say the consulate would pass him through?" The pediatrician had nothing to say to this and left shortly thereafter. I felt like I was sleepwalking as I showed the foster mother Donald's medicine, how to get it down his tiny throat despite his protests, which food he liked the best, how to treat the bedsores on his head and diaper rash on his bottom. And then they had to take him.

The next day we went to the airport, where other adoptive parents were going through the lines. An ecstatic family had a thirteen-year-old Guatemalan girl who looked like she was Cinderella at the ball, all big eyes and smiles. We were all afraid, until we got through U.S. Customs at the other end of our flight, that something would go wrong again and we would lose our children.

The flight took off, and I had a sense of freedom for David and a terrible sense of doom about Donald. When we landed on American soil, I felt a returning sense of determination and realized how important it was that David would not have to grow up in a country where his people were so hated by their own government that were murdered by the hundreds of thousands and are still being murdered, primarily through terrible deprivation and neglect.

LIMBO

In the United States that winter and spring, I felt my heart divided. There was the joy of caring for David: his first snow, his first steps, his first time in the park in the spring. David was fascinated with a TV show called *Eebee Baby*, where the babies play with other babies doing baby things like peek-a-boo and rolling balls down ramps. We got him the life-size eebee baby doll, and he called it and the show "Beebee." He carried it everywhere.

There was blizzard after blizzard that winter, and it seemed that my soul was getting blanketed with preoccupation with Donald. We obtained our license to be adoptive parents of a child with special needs. We contacted our lawyer and put pressure of all kinds on the adoption agency to monitor care for Donald in Guatemala. We kept in touch with Alfredo and Claudia, who let us know, via the foster mother, that Donald had had to be rehospitalized and put on a feeding tube because he could not eat. Our agency had not told us, so we remonstrated them, "How could you not tell us—we are his parents!" We learned from the translators that Donald had still had no physical therapy, despite the pediatrician's promises to arrange it. But then the lawyer changed foster mothers, so we could not get reports any more through our translators. So we ramped up the pressure on the agency by writing to the U.S. Consulate in Guatemala about our concerns, including Donald's need for physical therapy and our need for reliable medical evaluations and reports that would be sent directly to us. Our agency then assured us that this would be done. An MRI was done of Donald's brain, and we received the report in early March: there were many spaces where he had only air and water where there should have been cortical brain cells. The neurologist concluded that, based on the test, Donald would be significantly retarded and have many other problems as well.

I tried to find social services to care for Donald in Guatemala if we could not adopt him but came up with nothing of the intensity to match his needs. I was thinking about trying to locate a convent or monastery somehow. I realized that in Donald's condition, given the state of services there, he might either die or else live a life in some dreadful institution in terrible pain. I could not fathom how to talk with David about his brother when he reached an age when he would need to know about him.

I finally said to Bob, "I have to go back there—I can't just leave him there." "Have them send us a video," he said, and he wrote down the eight things he wanted the agency to have Donald do for the video: feed himself, sit up, etc. We waited, and the first video came on a memory stick that would not work in any of our computers. We waited some more and finally received pictures of Donald sitting. Bob was angry: "These must be faked." I said, "I have to go back."

Then in mid-April a video came that we could run on our computers. And there was Donald. He was a lively baby, looking like David's twin, feeding himself, smiling, in a baby walker, and communicating his distress because he wanted to go outside and was frustrated. There were pictures of him standing. And we said, "We have to bring him home." We called the agency, which said that he had passed his interview with his consulate doctor, and within a week there was an appointment for us at the consulate to get Donald's visa. We didn't know exactly how this was accomplished but later saw that the lawyer's documents said we were adopting a "completely healthy infant boy." Bob said he would tell the consul the truth, but by that time it appeared that Donald could do enough that there was a good chance he could pass the consul's exam as a special needs child who was still adoptable. Bob went to Guatemala to retrieve Donald while I stayed to take care of David because we did not dare take David back.

Would Donald remember us? From Guatemala, Bob called home and told me that when Donald came in with his foster mother and her family, they handed Donald to him and Donald grabbed him tightly, hugged Bob completely, and would not let go throughout their meeting. When the time came to say goodbye to his foster mother and she wanted to hug him, he would not let go of Bob, hanging on fiercely as his former caretakers said good-bye. Bob said, "Donald is totally winsome and charming, he smiles at everyone. He's paralyzed and can't move but he's eating like a horse even though he drools and his food spills all over, and everyone loves him." He also said that the hotel he stayed in, which was probably the hotel most often used by adoptive parents, was in disarray: facilities and rooms that had been set up for families were being dismantled, staff were losing their jobs, and everyone was wondering what they would do to make a living now.

REUNION

What would it be like when Donald came home? I talked with David for the three days Bob was gone as we bought an extra crib, baby clothes, and things Donald would need for encouraging his ambulation. David could not talk yet, and I had no way of knowing if he remembered his brother or understood what I was saying. On the last day, when I was shopping and putting things in my shopping cart, David became excited, pointing. I set him down and he immediately picked out his own toy red wagon and, having gotten the idea of what happens in shopping, went around the toy department picking out toys he wanted and putting them in the wagon. Did he understand his brother was coming? I didn't know. We went home, the hours and minutes ticked by, and then Bob called to tell us "I'm outside, we're home."

Bob got off the elevator with Donald in his arms, and all questions about whether the boys would remember each other were instantly gone. David yelled "Beebee" the instant he saw him. Donald yelled "AAAAAAHHHHH" and reached out, from Bob's arms, for his brother. We put them on the couch together, and for hours they were ecstatic, putting their fingers in each other's mouth, David often putting both hands over his heart as though it would burst with pleasure. They hugged each other, laughed at jokes only they could know. They peered into each other's face, serious and then laughing. They touched hands and feet and patted each other's head. Donald's left arm was paralyzed and he couldn't move from his seated position on the couch facing David, but he nodded his head enthusiastically and reached constantly with his right hand to stroke David. I had tears running down my face and kept taking pictures—the moments were so precious for them to have forever. Too young to ask each other, "What happened to you?" they had their own vocabulary of reconnecting. Their reunion went on for more than three hours but seemed like lightning, and then Donald became exhausted.

That night David immediately jettisoned the eebee doll to a corner, and David and Donald became inseparable. Since Donald couldn't crawl or walk, David pushed and pulled him places in the red wagon. He helped him drink his bottle, helped him eat, babbled to him, and they laughed together constantly. Donald took to his baby walker and could jet up and down our hall, speeding after his brother so they both ended up at my side, laughing, wherever I was. Donald was ticklish and chortled with glee when we tickled his tummy.

TOWARD RECOVERY

As the days went by, we saw the challenges Donald was facing: he seemed greatly affected by his powerful antiseizure medications and sometimes looked quite disoriented. If he was put down out of his walker, he could only sit and was immobilized. It was clear that somehow, once again, the lawyer had rigged the April pictures of Donald standing. Donald got a high fever the first weekend back and we took him to the emergency room, terrified he would have a seizure. To strengthen his muscles, we practiced sitting and sit-ups and standing, and we arranged for the early intervention team to come, thanks to our neighbor who turned out to be a world expert on cerebral palsy. He gave us the first words of hope since Zuleima's: "Don't go by the MRIs, go by his functioning. Neuroplasticity at this age is such that, with his curiosity, sociability, and determination, he can become a CEO!"

We found a wonderful part-time Colombian nanny who spoke Spanish, hoping the boys would not lose the Spanish that was their first language. But both boys initially had a great fear and aversion to Hispanic-looking women. Donald would cry upon seeing a dark-haired woman, and David became panic-stricken and screamed bloody murder. Being a child therapist, I understood from their reactions that they had been traumatized by some form of abuse, probably in the second foster home. I noticed the first time we took them to the park that if our nanny took Donald to a different part of the park away from David (who could do so many things Donald could not), David became almost paralyzed with fear, staring and pointing at Donald. I reassured him, "Donald will stay with us forever, she's helping," but he never took his eyes off his brother. It would be months before David could feel reassured that he would not lose his "beebee" again. Our nanny was exceedingly gentle, and after a short time Donald relaxed with her, and after months David also relaxed with her. Their traumatic reactions gradually faded as well.

The early intervention team and other therapists and doctors worked with us seven times a week. They agreed Donald was experiencing hemiplegia (a form of cerebral palsy, which means his left side was abnormally weak, with some muscles on the left side overly tight and causing contractures) and oral apraxia (failure of the mouth muscles to form speech, even though he knew what he wanted to say). They also all said they had never seen such a determined baby.

In addition to times of progress, there were times of great trepidation. Waiting for an orthopedist to examine Donald for leg braces, I saw a tiny mother trying to carry her fourteen-year-old son with cerebral palsy who was immobilized by casts on his legs. We learned from reading about cerebral palsy that surgeries to break and reform bones to correct joint malformation are annual experiences when the cerebral palsy is severe. At the park I saw another mother struggling to lift her six-year-old son with cerebral palsy out of the only swing he could use, which was made for infants. Another mother told us about her son whose cerebral palsy was so severe he could not swallow; his public school did not provide adequate supervision, and at school one day he aspirated his food and died. We could not help but feel that this could be our experience with Donald.

And then there was Donald, who struggled with great determination to do the next thing: first commando crawling, then crawling, then pulling up to cruise, then, at last a year later, walking. Every accomplishment was hard won, and each one initially seemed out of reach. Yet, in the end, it seems Zuleima was right.

A FUTURE FOR INTERNATIONAL ADOPTION?

What about international adoption and the orphans remaining in Guatemala (see "Room for Debate" 2009 for a recent debate)? In 2009, seven to nine hundred Guatemalan orphans who were assigned to families in the United States were still languishing in orphanages while federal governmental agencies delayed adoption processing with often meaningless red tape under the rationale of investigating corruption (Aizenman 2009; http:// guatemala900.org/wp/). Consider the possibility that Donald and David had not had the option of adoption. They would have lived in orphanages, and access to medical care and nutrition would likely have been worse than what they received in Guatemalan foster care. Donald's meningitis might well have led to his death; David's rotavirus could have as well. If they had survived, Donald would have lived in a society lacking early intervention services and would have faced a future of being severely crippled and in pain. Assuming David had survived rotavirus, how would his twin brother's plight have affected him? There is considerable documentation that Guatemalan orphans who survive live like the homeless five-year-old we saw in Guatemala City selling CDs on the street, obviously the virtual slave of an abusive adult.

We now know that normal brain development depends on family care in the years from birth to three. Is it not a violation of human rights to deprive children of the opportunity of family life by consigning them to orphanages where, if they survive, they can be permanently handicapped? It is remarkable that some opponents of international adoption who discuss corruption in Guatemalan adoptions (e.g., Graff 2008) never include in their discussion the impact of state-sponsored genocide against Mayan families and children, and the often-fatal impact of profound poverty and inadequate orphanages and foster care on Mayan children. As Elizabeth Bartholet (2007) notes, those who oppose international adoption globally do so by documenting abuses that have occurred, but they lack evidence based on larger analysis of international adoption outcomes and also do not discuss the evils that occur on the other side: child abuse and neglect, malnutrition, disease, grossly inadequate orphanage care, and so forth.

Currently international adoption of infants as one solution for infants and children in crisis has been significantly hampered because, in the name of human rights, some policy makers (including UNICEF) press for governmentally enforced legal restrictions on international adoptions (Bartholet 2010; Roby and Shaw 2006). The practical impact of those restrictions is ignoring orphans in need, leaving them homeless or dying on the streets, or consigning them indefinitely to institutional care as the adoptive process grinds on (Child Advocacy Program 2008). For example, consider the recently publicized situation of children whose orphanages were destroyed by the 2010 earthquake in Haiti. It was taking a minimum of three years for the government to process their adoptions (McKinley and Hamill 2010), by which time the most crucial period in an infant's brain development has elapsed and a child can be irrevocably injured (Perry 2002).

While corruption in international adoption is a serious problem, corruption exists in many governments in the world. Rather than abolishing the institutions, customarily efforts are made to reduce and abolish corrupt practices. While that may be easier said than done, it is not impossible, as some might claim. There are many ways to promote transparency in adoption, especially given DNA tests, photographs of birth parents and infants to verify identities, licensing standards and associations, and Internet blogs where parents review the capabilities of lawyers and adoption agencies. The danger in relying only on public governments to carry out adoptions is exactly what has been learned by child welfare specialists in the United States (Bartholet, 2007): public bureaucracy and inadequate accountability can be such that human services are generally carried out more effectively by private agencies whose work is reviewed and contracted by local, state, and federal government bodies.

Opponents of international adoption cling to a narrow concept of adoption as justifiable only when both parents are dead and all possible relative placements have been tried and exhausted, which can take years (see quotes from Save the Children staff in Pidd 2009, and UNICEF personnel in McKinley and Hammill 2010). By contrast, in the developed countries of the world, some parents relinquish their children for adoption if they believe they cannot adequately care for them. In Illinois, for example, birth parents have to wait three days after their baby is born before signing a relinquishment. Thus a double standard exists where adoption is a viable alternative for parents and children in crisis in developed countries, but not in the severely impoverished countries of the world, which actually lack the social service infrastructure to support poor families or provide adequate foster care and adoption services locally.

While the importance of children growing up in their own culture is often cited as a reason to oppose international adoption, aren't the opinions of birth parents worthy of respect? We were struck by the fact that in our domestic adoption, our daughter Naomi's birth parents could choose who would adopt her. They said they wanted a family who would love and cherish her and give her siblings to play with and a fine education with opportunities to travel. They clearly felt those qualities were more important than whether the adoptive parents were of the same African American race. Our twins' birth mother expressed similar beliefs. But Mayan parents who might want a child they cannot care for to grow up in a country where there is no recent history of genocide and terrorism against Mayan people, and where services for children and families are greatly improved over what exists now in Guatemala, cannot make that choice now.

Finally, while opponents of international and transracial adoption state that it is better for children to grow up in their country and community of origin, other child advocates argue that such a restriction is based on "extreme romanticism" rather than systematic study of international adoption outcomes and common sense (Bartholet 2010; Child Advocacy Program 2008; see also Aronson's comments in "Room for Debate" 2009). Moreover, in some countries a commitment to adopting children runs against custom or religious values, and while change certainly happens, it is not in time to save the lives of many orphans: in a prominent Sudanese orphanage that admits hundreds of orphans every year, conditions are so bad that a child dies every other day despite the best efforts of child welfare workers and UNICEF over several years to improve conditions (Polgreen 2008). If orphans reside in countries where their lives are threatened because of religious values, racism, gender bias, or extreme poverty, shouldn't they be able to reside in environments where they are safe and valued (Roby and Shaw 2006)? While research has failed to document that transracial or international adoption endangers children's mental or physical health, it has demonstrated the dangers of the alternatives of homelessness, institutionalization, or inadequate foster care (Bartholet 2010; Child Advocacy Program 2008).

PRESENT: REFLECTING ON AUTOETHNOGRAPHY

Writing this autoethnography has been cathartic and also an opportunity to reflect on the causes of and potential solutions to the suffering inflicted on David and Donald and other orphans in crisis. While autoethnography's primary method is to delve into the very personal, I felt as a social worker it was important to give readers the benefit of additional literature about the central topics. Of course this particular autoethnography is also a work of advocacy, and it felt personally as well as scientifically important to document that there are other scholars whose arms are linked with mine in seeking to remove obstacles to international adoption and to improve care for homeless and orphaned children.

It seemed important also, given my research training, to consider whether in autoethnography one has to abandon all efforts to manage the challenges associated with intersubjectivity. Perhaps not. Since Bob was so involved with the process, I asked him to review what I had written and make any changes he felt were needed to improve accuracy. There were only a few, but they are all included here, so this rendition has had an additional validation of its accuracy. Readers may also consider that the central facts have many witnesses: the twins' third foster mother, our translators, Dr. N., Zuleima, my brother-in-law's brother, and so forth.

I have been struck in writing this autoethnography that, just like in any research project, what one chooses to focus on and to leave out is of utmost importance (akin to Wimsatt's wonderful conceptualization of the environment-system boundary in scientific research, 1986). In the spirit of reflectiveness, it is important to talk about my choices of what to include and what to leave out. As probably always occurs, I had to leave out much more than I could include: I talked little about my ongoing relationship with Bob, which would occur in a chronicle about a marriage, or about the hotel, Guatemalan Christmas traditions, the earthquake, or what we ate and saw in Guatemala, which would occur in a tourist article. I spared the reader details of our advocacy for adopting the twins both before and after our visit to Guatemala, and also how we coped with the anger and sadness we felt at what was done to Donald and David. A chronicle focused on David alone would have recounted much joyful relating and many funny times, such as my changing his poopy diaper for the first time while listening to the Bach cantata version of "A mighty fortress is our God." He became so excited he started rolling around the bed (with predictable results including laughing by all). We enjoyed his spunky antics and chuckled about our neophyte parenting ineptitude, but for space reasons I could not include those moments in this account.

The straight track of the story I did tell here concerns the relationship between David and Donald, what happened to them as orphans, their near brush with being orphans indefinitely, their courage in coping with the diseases and loss they faced, and finally their dedication to each other. What I left out was omitted because it might detour from following the straight track of their story.

Finally, autoethnography embraces and builds on the subjectivity of the researcher's perspective, which has for years been scorned by positivistic social scientists as tainting the research process. In examining the connection between subjectivity and the knowledge-building process, autoethnography makes an invaluable contribution to social science research. After all, subjectivity cannot be eliminated, and it is important to understand how it works and also to set a standard that helps researchers reflect on how their own subjectivity invariably influences their research. The experiences one has and the meaning one makes of them no doubt influence many aspects of one's work as a scientist, as was noted most famously by Thomas Kuhn (1962). For me the trauma and inspiration of the events chronicled here will no doubt influence my choice of research questions to pursue in the future, how I interpret the relatively sparse data that is available on the conditions of international orphans and outcomes of international adoption, and how I respond to scientific controversies that exist in the fields of global child welfare and care for children with special needs. For instance, the *New York Times* article that chronicled global child welfare agencies' efforts to reduce the massive death rate of children in a Sudanese orphanage was quite laudatory of the results the agencies received (they cut the death rate in half). However, it was striking to me that an orphan still dies every other day in that orphanage. When I pictured our orphans as among those who die, the data reported reflected an ongoing and fundamentally preventable tragedy.

Consider also that the experiences a scientist has *not* had can color the research process. It was striking to me how many people comment on international adoption (policy makers as well as researchers) without ever acknowledging potential sources of their own personal bias (for a notable exception, see Bartholet 2010). It might affect one's research conclusions if one has never experienced a family united by motivation rather than by sharing genes. Similarly, if one never had to give up a child for adoption or confer deeply with birth parents, it might be hard to adequately comprehend and respect birth parents and their wishes. Those who have not personally experienced the terrible suffering of orphans sickened, starving, and dying may find it easier to take an exclusively muckraking focus on corruption in international adoption and to ignore the urgent needs of orphans and the many happy and productive families created through such adoptions.

A researcher's passionate interests can be powerful incentives to think and investigate deeply and thoroughly, so perhaps subjectivity compromises the quality of scientific research only when its impact is ignored and researchers, assuming they can be purely objective, ignore important realities.

Before I end this autoethnography, readers may want to know more about how the parent dream is coming to earth in the present.

THE PARENT DREAM, AS IT IS HAPPENING NOW

When David and Donald were two and a half, we had the joy of being able to adopt a beautiful baby daughter, Naomi, through a domestic adoption. David and Donald are excited about her, help feed her her bottle, offer her their trains to play with, and pat her lovingly. Space does not allow a focus on the gift of parenting Naomi, but readers may understand the wonder of being able to help a brand new person experience so much of life for the first time: first bird songs, first summer sunlight streaming through trees, first waves on the lake and ocean, and, most of all, getting to know the wonderful person she is. Caring for Naomi in her first months of life, I realized the terrible vulnerability of our sons, how frightening it was to be with foster mothers who did not give them the care they needed, and to feel their surroundings were so unpredictable. The tragedy of infants who don't even have foster mothers but instead are neglected in orphanages has an even more profound meaning now. When we took Naomi to get her vaccines, I saw her receive not just once but several times vaccines for rotavirus and pneumoccocus. Each time I thought about our sons and what other poverty-stricken children do not get; how simple the vaccines are to give, and how grave the illnesses are when the babies do not receive them.

And here, now, at this writing in the winter of 2009, it is almost exactly two years since we first met our wonderful sons in Guatemala—David in the hotel, and Donald in the hospital. Outside a blizzard is howling, as it did when we got the news that one of our sons was ill, and while we were packing to go to Guatemala. That time is most alive inside me and may always be as the snows of winter blanket Chicago and represent to me what seemed to be a numbing blanket of corruption and brutal inhumanity in seemingly snow-free Guatemala. Orphans and poor children in Guatemala are starving for food, medical care, and love. The adoptive parents to whom Guatemalan children were assigned are in anguish while the current bureaucracy goes around in circular investigations of investigations of adoptions "in process," with no hope of recourse (see Aizenman 2009).

In our home, we are recipients of what Dr. N. said could only be a miracle. Now three, our boys are rambunctious and ready to go at life with all their gusto and infant integrity. Donald hasn't had a seizure since his illness and no longer takes the medication that made him so spacey. With new hinges on his leg braces, Donald can run. He can reach out and hug with his left arm, and although he can't speak words yet, he communicates in all kinds of ways that his understanding of English and Spanish is nuanced and at a three-year-old's level of sophistication. He is incredibly social and active, dancing in his own way along with David, hugging everyone he meets. His eyes are full of sparkle and laughter as he makes jokes for himself, David, and Naomi that are best understood only by babies. He chortles with glee when tickled and sharing jokes with us. He feeds himself steadily and with great concentration, and there is no food he refuses. He reads books avidly and adores his trains and trucks, and he is completely fearless about going on rides at amusement parks and zoos.

There are other kinds of miracles, too. David and Donald hear each other in ways we cannot fathom. Donald fell a few months ago, and when he was still limping the next day I told the boys I was taking him to the doctor because maybe he hurt his ankle. David said, "His toe." I said "Oh, which toe?" David pointed. We took Donald to the doctor, and sure enough, the little toe David identified had been slightly fractured in the fall, and everything else was fine. Donald can't talk, so how did David know? Last night Donald sat down and David said, "Donald want braces off." I said to Donald, "Do you want your braces off?' Donald said, "Yeah!" and David said, "Let me." He carefully took off Donald's shoes, then the several latches on his braces, then his braces, then his socks, and inspected Donald's feet. "That red," he said, and I said, "Yes, the braces are new. They can hurt while he's getting used to them, so it's great you let us know they started to hurt and helped take them off."

While we were going through our journey to parenthood, there was so much to do I could not think much about what I was experiencing. Now I think about my parent dream, where I started, and I realize how, as that dream came to earth, it was so much richer and also so much more fearsome than I could have imagined. For all of us, every time we love anew we can be faced with terrible loss and have to overcome our fear of loss in order to love. Sometimes the loss of the person we love stares us in the face as it did with Donald; sometimes it is more lurking and flares up, as in David's bout with rotavirus; sometimes we know it is inevitable, like old married partners who talk about who will die first and who will be left with the grief. It is so terribly difficult to let ourselves love in the face of the chasms of loss and attendant pain that open up in each relationship. And yet an essential part of our humanness is denied if we run away from the loss and try to stop love. No other fulfillment of our human nature can possibly equal what happens when we embrace our love of another and let ourselves fall into it completely as it should be.

The future for David and Donald is full of challenges. They will learn of the injustices done to them and also will know about the many people who helped them with the impact of those injustices. Donald will need multiple therapies for years and special schools, and, just as important, help knowing his strength and value, given how he was horribly injured. He will need Botox treatments to have even a hope of being able to use his left hand, and he is struggling to make his mouth muscles form even the smallest words. "Yes!" he says with great gusto, raising his right hand in the victory sign. And "No!" he can say with great determination. But other words come out only as vowels, like "oooo" for juice. He gets terribly frustrated, with so much to say but muscles that won't work to say it. The part of his brain that was the most damaged was Broca's area, and his brain will need to make new connections to enable his speech. He tries enormously hard, and we try to do him justice.

This morning when I came into their bedroom, I saw David saying to Donald, "Want help getting down?" Donald said, "Yeah," and scooted toward the end of the bed, where David then took him by his night braces and his feet and pulled while Donald pushed. Donald started sliding down, and David put his arms around his waist to stabilize him, saying, "Okay, Donaldy?"

Tonight David and Donald, getting ready for bed, are playing at their train table. In the delicate language of a three-year-old trying out his words for the first time, David makes up a story of how Thomas the Train runs into a pig on the track. What will he do? They talk to the pig, and the pig decides to get off the track so they can go further. But then Thomas and the trains he is pulling hit another obstacle and need the hero, Harold the Helicopter, to save them. In their world, Harold comes and can save them. Problems solved; pig and trains and heroes intact. We put on Donald's night braces. Going to bed, the boys invariably sleep snuggled close. "Ever and ever," says David as he goes to sleep, his refrain that means we will love them both, and be a family together, forever and ever. Donald pops up to check on David, and, reassured, makes a snoring sign to indicate that David is sleeping and he will too, and lies back down. Donald's right arm reaches out to hold my hand, and his left arm that was paralyzed reaches out to hug and hold onto David as he falls asleep. With these gestures he speaks volumes.

EPILOGUE

As this book goes to press, there is an opportunity to look at some elements of our story from a present vantage point. First, Donald can now speak several syllables at a time. He runs, he shouts, he sings, and he is still laughing. He is in a great special education preschool and has therapies four times a week, made affordable thanks to President Obama's healthcare legislation. He plays continually and avidly with David and Naomi. While many aspects of Donald's future abilities remain highly uncertain and can be a cause for great worry, at the same time he makes steady headway, so we have grounds for much hope. While I was writing this, Donald ran in from going on an errand with Bob, said, "Your lap," and climbed on my lap. While eating a chocolate cupcake and doing a train game with me on the computer, he periodically reached up and pulled my face down to kiss with a chocolate kiss and a big smile.

Information is now available about what would likely have happened if we had not been able to adopt David and Donald in early 2008. As was noted previously, the Guatemalan law that was passed in December 2007 that mandated establishing new oversight processes, as well as new government structures for international adoption, brought international adoption to a screeching halt. As of 2012 there were still 900 Guatemalan children who had families ready to adopt them internationally, but whose cases were stalemated in the bureaucracy. The children are growing up in transitional situations, including institutions (*Guatemala 900*).

Many commentators remark the new law resulted in no substantive improvements for orphans in Guatemala. In fact, one orphanage director, who says her orphanage is privately funded because the public funding red tape is convoluted and corrupt, comments that the government made a terrible mistake ending international adoption. Now, she says, the government has to pay for all the orphans and does not allocate the resources. Previously the fees paid by adoptive parents funded a considerable child welfare infrastructure of foster parents, medical care, social services, and legal oversight for child welfare processes (Reason 2011). Meanwhile, the numbers of Guatemalan street children and orphans in dreadful conditions are growing exponentially—one of the babies growing up in the director's orphanage was found abandoned in a garbage can, with dogs starting to eat her (Reason 2011). Guatemalan children are victimized through forced labor (such as forced begging and working in garbage dumps), trafficking in Guatemala and via kidnapping to other countries, and child sex tourism (U.S. State Department 2012). One of the leading humanitarian organizations protecting Central American street children estimates over 15,000 Guatemalan girls are victims of brutal sex trafficking (Casa Alianza 2012). In 2010 a student in my global social work class volunteered on several occasions helping street children in Guatemala. She described and showed pictures about how police in Guatemala City routinely doused sleeping street children with gasoline and set them on fire. The existence of such conditions makes it impossible to reasonably claim that international adoption should be halted in order to preserve "cultural values." Indeed, policies that preserve values of child homicide and genocide appear to be, as James Garbarino (2008) writes, the "dark side of human experience."

Elizabeth Bartholet (2010) comments that international adoption was "a remarkably effective social program," in that it provided immediate and enduring life-saving help to thousands of orphans every year, using private rather than public funds. Some hope that with enough public awareness, the tide may turn again in favor of supporting international adoption (*Both Ends Burning*).

It seems to me that perhaps a major motive behind autoethnography is the hope that by telling one's story and listening to each other, we can make a better world based on the truths we learn. So thank you, the reader, for reading and listening.

NOTE

1   Figures on the number of orphans are controversial because some define "orphan" as those without parents or family, such as estimates that there are 25 million orphans due to HIV-AIDS alone (TvT Associates/The Synergy Project 2002; Roby and Shaw 2006). Others include those children whose birth families relinquish them, often because of poverty.

We were both very aware of the opinion that international adoption is highly problematic because of imbalances in resources and power available to poorer countries (usually sending countries in international adoptions) and wealthier countries (usually receiving countries). For us, the view that national boundaries take precedence as the major considerations in deciding the fates of children is a relic of the view that infants and children are not persons with their own autonomy and boundaries to be respected but are instead first and foremost property (in this case, of their nations). In other words, from a perspective prioritizing the human rights of the individual child, the impact of the claim that infants and children are first and foremost property of their countries in effect subjects large numbers of infants and children to infanticidal sexism; genocidal racism; brutal neglect or maltreatment because of cultural values that relinquished children of unmarried persons or orphaned children have "bad blood"; institutionalization that damages their brains (Nelson et al. 2009); or lives of perpetual abuse on the brink of starvation as street children. In short, the country-prioritizing perspective is adultcentric and oppressive of infants, children, and youth (Petr 1992). By contrast, the opportunity to be adopted internationally offers infants, children, and youth the human right to live the best lives possible and develop their own freedom of choice about their familial, cultural, and national allegiances, and it offers many countries resources to develop a child welfare infrastructure that otherwise would not be available (we side completely with the articulate analysis in Bartholet [2007, 2010]).

REFERENCES

Aizenman, N. C. 2009. "Guatemalan Children in Limbo of Orphanages: Parents Push U.S. Officials to Help." *Washington Post.*

Arias, A. 2001. *The Rigoberta Menchu Controversy.* Minneapolis: University of Minnesota Press.

Bartholet, E. 1991. "Where Do Black Children Belong? The Politics of Race Matching in Adoption." *University of Pennsylvania Law Review* 139 (5): 1163–1256.

———. 1993. *Family Bonds: Adoption and the Politics of Parenting.* New York: Houghton Mifflin.

———. 2007. "International Adoption: Thoughts on the Human Rights Issues." *Buffalo Human Rights Law Review* 13:151–203.

———. 2010. "International Adoption: The Human Rights Position." *Global Policy* 1 (1). http://ssrn.com/abstract=1446811.

Both Ends Burning. http://bothendsburning.org/.

Casa Alianza. 2012. http://www.casa-alianza.org.uk/northsouth/CasaWeb.nsf/Casa_News/664F53A2DF5FFB6F80257A7D003B41D2?OpenDocument.

Child Advocacy Program, Harvard Law School. 2008. *International Adoption Policy Statement and Supporting Report.* Cambridge: Harvard Law School.

Control Risks Group. 2007. *Guatemala Country Report.* Bloomberg.

Evans, K. 2000. *Lost Daughters of China: Abandoned Girls, Their Journey to America, and Their Search for a Missing Past.* New York: Penguin/Putnam.

Farmer, P. 2003. *Pathologies of Power: Health, Human Rights, and the New War on the Poor.* Berkeley: University of California Press.

Garbarino, J. 2008. *Children and the Dark Side of Human Experience: Confronting Global Realities and Rethinking Child Development.* New York: Springer.

Graff, E. J. 2008. "The Lie We Love." http://www.foreignpolicy.com/story/cms. php?story_id=4508.

Guatemala 900. http://guatemala900.org/wp/.

Human Rights Watch. 2009. *World Report 2009, Guatemala.* http://www.hrw. org/en/node/79213.

Ignacio. 1992. *Ignacio: The Diary of a Maya Indian of Guatemala,* translated by J. S. Philadelphia: University of Pennsylvania Press.

Johnson, K. A. 2004. *Wanting a Daughter, Needing a Son: Abandonment, Adoption and Orphanage Care in China.* St. Paul: Yeong & Yeong.

Knoll, J., and M.-K. Murphy. 1994. *International Adoption: Sensitive Advice for Prospective Parents.* Chicago: Chicago Review Press.

Kuhn, T. 1962. *The Structure of Scientific Revolutions.* Chicago: University of Chicago Press.

Lovera, D., and A. Arbo. 2005. "Risk Factors for Mortality in Paraguayan Children with Pneumococcal Bacterial Meningitis." *Tropical Medicine and International Health* 10 (12): 1235–41.

Luarca, S. 2006. "President Berger and the Hague Convention." September 28. http://www.guatadopt.com/archives/000498.html.

———. 2007. "Susan's Statement on PGN Events." http://www.guatadopt.com/ archives/000733.html.

Lykes, M. B. 1994. *Terror, Silencing, and Children: International Multidisciplinary Collaboration with Guatemalan Maya Communities.* Center for Human Rights and International Justice, Center Affiliated Faculty Publications, Boston College.

McKinley, J., and S. Hamill. 2010. "53 Haitian Orphans Are Airlifted to U.S." *New York Times.*

Melville, M. B., and M. B. Lykes. 1992. "Guatemalan Indian Children and the Sociocultural Effects of Government-Sponsored Terrorism." *Social Science and Medicine* 34: 533–48.

Menchu, R. 1984. *I, Rigoberta Menchu,* edited by E. Burgos-Debray. New York: Verso.

Natalino, W., and M. V. Moura-Ribeiro. 1999. "Acute Bacterial Meningoencephalitis in Children. Complications and Neurologic Sequelae." *Arq Neuropsiquiatr* 57 (2B): 465–70.

Nelson, C. A., E. A. Furtado, N. A. Fox, and C. H. Zeanah. 2009. "The Deprived Human Brain." *American Scientist* 97:222–29.

O'Brien, K. L., et al. 2009. "Burden of Disease Caused by Streptococcus Pneumoniae in Children Younger than 5 Years: Global Estimates." *Lancet* 374 (9693): 893–902.

Parashar, U. D., et al. 2009. "Global Mortality Associated with Rotavirus Disease Among Children in 2004." *Journal of Infectious Disease* 200, Suppl 1: S9–S15.

Perry, B. D. 2002. "Childhood Experience and the Expression of Genetic Potential: What Childhood Neglect Tells Us About Nature and Nurture." *Brain & Mind* 3 (1): 79–100.

Petr, C. 1992. "Adultcentrism in Practice with Children." *Families in Society* 73: 408–16.

Pidd, H. 2009. "Malawian Court Defers Madonna Adoption Decision." *Guardian*.

Polgreen, L. 2008. "Overcoming Customs and Stigma, Sudan Gives Orphans a Lifeline." *New York Times*.

Reason, D. 2011. "Reason TV: Abandoned in Guatemala: "The Failure of International Adoption Policies. *Washington Times*, October 17. http://communities. washingtontimes.com/neighborhood/red-thread-adoptive-family-forum/2011/oct/17/drew-careys-reason-tvs-video-unicefs-impact-adopti/.

Roby, J., and S. Shaw. 2006. "The African Orphan Crisis and International Adoption." *Social Work* 51:199–210.

"Room for Debate: Celebrity Adoptions and the Real World." 2009. *New York Times*, May 10. http://roomfordebate.blogs.nytimes.com/2009/05/10/celebrity-adoptions-and-the-real-world/#more-6787.

Sanford, V. 2003. *Buried Secrets: Truth and Human Rights in Guatemala.* New York: Macmillan/Palgrave.

Selim, H. S., et al. 2007. "Microbial Study of Meningitis and Encephalitis Cases." *J Egypt Public Health Assoc* 82 (1–2): 1–19.

Siddiqui, T. S., et al. 2006. "Etiology of Strokes and Hemiplegia in Children Presenting at Ayub Teaching Hospital, Abbottabad." *J Ayub Med Coll Abbottabad* 18 (2): 60–63.

Tanaka, G., et al. 2007. "Deaths from Rotavirus Disease in Bangladeshi Children: Estimates from Hospital-Based Surveillance." *Pediatr Infect Dis J* 26 (11): 1014–18.

TvT Associates/The Synergy Project. 2002. *Children on the Brink: A Joint Report on Orphan Estimates and Program Strategies*. Washington, D.C.:U.S. Agency for International Development, Contract No. HRN-C-00–99–00005–00; UNAIDS and UNICEF.

UNICEF. 2009. *Information by Country: Guatemala*.

United States State Department, Office to Monitor and Combat Trafficking in Persons. 2012. *Trafficking in Persons Report 2012*. http://www.state.gov/j/tip/rls/tiprpt/2012/192367.htm.

Wilson, S., and J. Gibbons. 2005. "Guatemalan Perceptions of Adoption." *International Social Work* 48:742–52.

Wimsatt, W. C. 1986. "Heuristics and the Study of Human Behavior." In *Metatheory in Social Science: Pluralisms and Subjectivities*, edited by D. W. Fiske and R. A. Schweder, 293–314. Chicago: University of Chicago Press.

A Finn in India

FROM CULTURAL ENCOUNTERS TO GLOBAL IMAGINING

▸ SATU RANTA-TYRKKÖ

MANALI, HIMACHAL PRADESH, northern India, 1993. I am at a local police station, wanting to report that my bag was stolen in a local bus a few hours earlier. The police officer is seemingly reluctant to register my case, not least for the reason that it would not look good on the station's statistical records. Instead he is randomly asking me about my traveling and what I do in my own country, Finland. When he learns that I am a social work student, he assumes the case is completed: "Then you don't want to report the crime."

Mumbai, India, December 2007. I am on a social work teacher exchange trip at a local university, having an opportunity to make field visits. I have spent my day accompanying Shubha Benurwar, who is a social worker responsible for the welfare of slum dwellers in two regions of the city. She has two assistants and an abandoned classroom, half of which functions as the storage and the rest as a meeting place, where she holds constant meetings, thirty to forty women at a time, each of them representing a local women's group. Earlier the same day, in one of her slums, we visited one such group and the local kindergarten, which she has also organized. After the day, we count the number of the people she is responsible for—at least 1.2 million.

GRAMIN VIKAS VIGYAN SAMITI AND NATYA CHETANA AS VANTAGE POINTS ON VOLUNTARY SOCIAL WORK IN INDIA

I went to India for the first time as a student in 1993. My trip turned out to be the beginning of a long process of learning that still continues. In the following, I recall certain encounters, reactions, and reflections that have been significant for my learning, many of which deal with the challenges to come to terms with otherness and myself. As my journey proceeded, it included various attempts to identify meaningful disciplinary, discursive, and practical frameworks to discuss and better understand social work in both India and Finland.

My learning while in India was to a great extent bound to two local organizations, Gramin Vikas Vigyan Samiti (GVVS), which in English means Center for Human Science and Rural Development, located in the state of Rajasthan in northwestern India, and Natya Chetana, Theatre for Awareness, in the state of Odisha in eastern India. As will unfold in detail later on, I lived several months with GVVS during the visits I made to India during 1990s, whereas Natya Chetana has been my main stop in India since then.

GVVS is a Gandhian rural development organization founded in 1983. The qualifier "Gandhian" implies that the organization relates its value base and modes of work to the thoughts and practices of Mohandas "Mahatma" Gandhi (1869–1948), who for over two decades was the leading figure of the Indian nationalist movement and already in his lifetime the acknowledged father of the Indian nation. Because of his method of nonviolent resistance and his ability to mobilize Indian masses into politics, Gandhi is still widely known in the world. As Gandhi himself disliked all "isms," he refused to found any movement in his name. Nonetheless, a whole milieu of activists has claimed inspiration from him (e.g., Markovits 2004:62). In retrospect, for example, Nandy and Jahanbegloo (2006) have identified four different Gandhis that survived after Gandhi's assassination in 1948: "Gandhi of the Indian state," "Gandhi of the Gandhians," "Gandhi of the eccentrics," and "Gandhi who is basically not read but only heard" (35–36). Of these, GVVS belongs to the Gandhians: the organization is part of a broader movement consisting of individuals, organizations, and communities who share similar views and seek ways to adapt what they see as the essence of Gandhi's life's work to present conditions.

From modest beginnings, GVVS has grown into a substantial nongovernmental organization (NGO) in western Rajasthan. In 2012 it had about 580 workers, 400 of them part-time. This growth is largely based on the organization's strategy and ability to collaborate with both the state ("we cooperate when we can and resist when we must") and international donors. The organization's motto is "working with desert communities for the empowerment of the poor." The actual work in the arid, subtropical Thar Desert, also known as the Great Indian Desert, focuses on re-creation of village institutions, such as village committees, which are representative of all sections of the community, women and marginalized castes included. In collaboration with them, other key areas of work are sustainable development of local natural resources, conservation and development of village commons, public health, income generation, promotion of savings, and education, with particular emphasis on girls.

On the other side of the country, one thousand miles to the east in the state of Odisha, Natya Chetana is a local theater group. Initially founded by drama students in the state capital Bhubaneswar in 1986, its early orientation was primarily artistic, career-boosting, and income-providing theater. However, as a result of several concurrent processes, such as personal disillusionments with the commercial entertainment industry, opportunities available in social and community development work, and the strong societal calling felt by many in the group, the decision was to change Natya Chetana's course. While the group did not give up its artistic ambitions, it identified itself as a people's theater group with a specific "propeople" agenda and commitments. In this, to embed its social commitments into its theater work, the group utilized learning and insights from various sources. These included the example set by Badal Sircar, a renowned Bengali theater maker who from the early 1970s pioneered in drawing from traditional Indian forms in performing artistic theater for large, diverse audiences with little money while addressing current social issues to catalyze social change (see, e.g., Sircar 1978; Yarrow 2001:154). Furthermore, Natya Chetana utilized available training in participatory methods, as well as ideas about participatory theater. These elements also connect Natya Chetana's work with various forms of socially committed theater globally. In other contexts, largely similar theater is made, for example, under the labels of community, political, and popular theater (e.g., Byam 1999; Kerr 1995; Kershaw 1992; Mlama 1991; Nellhaus and Haedicke 2001; Schechter 2003; Van Erven 1988).

Over the course of years, grounded on the idea of doing Indian theater with contemporary content but building on locally existing modes of theatrical expression, Natya Chetana has developed two practical and conceptual formulations of its own theater: cyco theater, for rural, largely poor audiences; and intimate theater, for urban, mainly middle-class audiences.

The idea behind both performance forms is to take the theater to the people. Accordingly, Natya Chetana's theater is made to be portable: cyco theater by bicycles, and intimate theater by a bus or a truck.

Typically, cyco theater plays are around thirty minutes, performed to a village audience that is gathered around the performing troupe after having been called to the spot by drumming and singing; there is no other advance advertising. As everything has to move by bicycles, only a few essential props are used, and the plays, performed mostly in daylight, depend neither on lighting nor on sound reproduction. The audiences are not charged any fees, but after the performance those who want have an opportunity to assist the group, for example, by giving money or foodstuffs such as rice, which can then be used to feed the group during the tour.

Intimate theater plays last one and a half to two and a half hours. They are usually performed to a one-sided audience, either in an auditorium or outside on a constructed stage with a back cloth, and rely on more complicated staging solutions, simple lighting techniques (mainly a dimmer at the beginning and the end of the play), and sound reproduction. While the shows are usually ticketed, outdoor performances can also be followed for free from outside of the ticketed area.

In both forms, the plays are grounded on local issues and background research and built up through a participatory process. Most of the plays have a climbing action and end in the middle of crisis in the storyline. Thematically, through the destinies of their characters, they depict and address structural violence, unmet basic needs, and lack of social justice, but they refrain from offering solutions to the issues staged. In addition to the major theme—as, for example, the issue of farmers' suicides, which was the topic of the cyco theater play *Dhola Suna* (White Gold), performed in 2007 and further developed in 2008 into the intimate theater play *Maati* (Mother Earth), the storylines incorporate one or several subthemes. Common themes for Natya Chetana's plays are the importance of unity and solidarity (often addressed through the lack of them), cultural alienation, gender inequality, corruption, as well as issues related to environment, health, food, work, or education. As theater provides scope for multilayered, nonblaming ways of presentation, despite the grimness of the situations depicted, the plays are not necessarily black and white.

Throughout the years, the size of the most actively involved team of Natya Chetana has varied from three to four individuals to more than a dozen, reflecting the financial situation of the group as well as the tasks at hand. However, in response to occasional greater need, such as to take part in a special production, assist on a tour, or volunteer at a theater festival, the group can recruit many more volunteers from its wide social network. Financially, the group has sustained itself mainly with intermittent, project-based development cooperation funding, usually receiving funding for a set number of plays and related performance tours, but has from time to time suffered from severe scarcity of money.

GVVS and Natya Chetana are very different from one other in several aspects, as are the states in which they are located. Much of Rajasthan is sandy and dry desert, whereas Odisha has both mountainous highlands with rapidly reducing forest cover, and fertile plains and river valleys suitable for intensive rice cultivation. Despite the differences, there are certain similarities between the approaches of the two organizations. Importantly, both identify their work as social work, as do the local people who know them and their work. However, worth noting is that their conception of social work is not bound by professional training and related qualifications, which are neither demanded nor a topic of much interest in either of the organizations. Instead, social work marks most of all an ideology and a specific social commitment built on the notion of voluntary social service. Accordingly, the salary level of GVVS workers is on average significantly lower than salaries from equally demanding jobs in government or the private sector, whereas Natya Chetana does not pay any salary for its volunteers. Instead, if the financial situation of the group so allows, its full-time volunteers get a monthly "scholarship" with which they can cover their basic food and other minor expenses so that full-time participation is possible. Beyond this, Natya Chetana has no professional staff, whereas GVVS recruits professionals, like physicians or engineers with higher salaries, when needed for special tasks.

All in all, the idea of voluntary social service is strongly emphasized in both organizations; it covers the entire lifestyle of the people involved and expects from them deep personal commitment and embodiment of the values the work stands for. In the actual work, both organizations deal with social justice issues, which are inescapably political in nature. This is because in both Rajasthan and Odisha, as throughout India, governmental neglect of the rural poor, who make up a major part of the population (Census of India 2011) and are an important reference group both for the GVVS and Natya Chetana in their own regions, is commonplace. In Rajasthan, GVVS's response to the situation is largely service delivery and village-level work to strengthen the civil society. In Odisha, Natya Chetana delivers no material aid but attempts to "disturb the minds" of its audiences, thereby generating the kind of questioning and discussion needed for critical citizenship and stronger civil society to take root.

How then should we conceive of GVVS's or Natya Chetana's kind of social work in relation to other social work approaches? My experience is that despite recent calls for better acknowledgement of "popular" in contrast to "official" (e.g., Lavalette and Ioakimidis 2011) or "amateur" versus "professional" (Ranta-Tyrkkö 2010:305–8) social work in mainstream Finnish and more broadly Western, or North Atlantic, surroundings, the kind of work that the GVVS and Natya Chetana are doing does not necessarily translate as social work. In my case, while I worked on my doctoral thesis on Natya Chetana in Finland, my colleagues often asked me what my study had to do with social work. Curiously enough, even though in my mind it had a great deal of relevance, I had difficulties coming up with answers. While feeling expected to prove the validity of my case—the social work relevance of the kind of work that I had witnessed India—I lacked a path and the vocabulary needed for intelligible bridging of the Indian voluntary and the Finnish professional social work approaches. In part the situation also reflects the culturally specific nature of social work understandings, as well as the centrality of waged work and professionalism in Western societies. In Nordic countries, the Nordic welfare state model, even if historically relatively young and at present increasingly threatened politically and economically, may further limit the capability to recognize and imagine other kind of foundations for social work. At any rate, GVVS and Natya Chetana may seem too different to be thought of as social work organizations despite endeavors to create understanding and unity among social workers around the globe, or the globally applicable definition of social work (IFSW 2000), which in principle could be signed by both the GVVS and Natya Chetana.

Utilizing my experiences in Finland and India, one of my interests has been to understand why practices that are self-evidently social work in one place are not recognized as such someplace else. In so doing, I am fully aware that both India and social work are entities far beyond the scope of one individual. My learning about both these realms started from personal encounters, moments of curiosity, fears, fervor, occasional disillusionment, and difficulty, added to and fed throughout the years by learning from books and new encounters and discussions in and outside the academy, and in the midst of the rest of my life. With the typical ethnographic dilemma of how to tell my story in a way that attains meaning beyond my personal experience, I have tried to use the opportunity that ethnography allows to use my own personhood and experiences as a condition for knowledge claims (see Cerwonka and Malkki 2007). The knowledge claims I am targeting deal with ideas of what constitutes social work as understood in different regions, and how to negotiate and possibly reexamine those ideas in a cross-cultural dialogue. In short, what does it take to try to conceive of social work on a truly global scale? As a matter of fact, noting the disparities of wealth, political power, and cultural influence between different countries and regions of the world, I see this as a crucial issue for a field that claims to be concerned about the poor and vulnerable. In a globally interconnected world, social work cannot exclude the realities of places where, for example, public welfare structures are lacking, or where there are no trained social work professionals. Rather, to understand and intervene in processes that keep people poor and vulnerable, social work as a field and discipline has to expand its understanding and build on various local sources of thinking and action (see also Connell 2007).

In what follows I start with a summary of my personal journey to wonder at social work in India and, because of the kind of questions that arose, consequently back home in Finland. As is typical of cross-cultural and interdisciplinary ethnographic work, my challenges have been quite different in these two environments. In India they have mostly been about doing highly interactive and relationship-based work in another cultural context, whereas in Finland the task has been to figure out what and how to think about the learning and experiences gained. One of my dilemmas has been how to explain my experience in a manner that is understandable to a variety of audiences, in Finland and in India, without overly distancing my narrative from what I have witnessed and lived. Rather than trying to explain away the many differences between social work and its practitioners in Finland and India, I have tried to take these differences seriously and to think about their implications.

MY ENTRIES TO SOCIAL WORK IN FINLAND AND INDIA

My history with both India and social work originates in Finland in the early 1990s. I was a social science graduate student with international relations as my major. To earn a living, I got a job as an assistant in social rehabilitation camps for people with cerebral palsy. Liking the work, I looked around for studies that could support me in my work and found first rehabilitation studies and then social work. Before that I had also found my way to the student union. In a solid, rustic, downtown house, the union offered some facilities and a rather free hand for students willing to work on specific issues such as gender equality, international exchanges and solidarity, racism, and of course student views on educational and social policies. In addition to holding meetings, students often approached these issues through little demonstrations or rallies, organizing events, and taking part in broader political campaigns. As my interests fit well with what was going on in the union's international and women's branches, I engaged myself with them, attending and organizing meetings, campaigns, and cultural events. What's more, I had fun, which is not an insignificant aspect of volunteer work.

In the student union many of the campaigns I was involved with had equality, social justice, and sustainable development as their ultimate goals, both locally and globally. We sought these goals through small, practical steps, for example, by acquiring funds for reforestation work for certain NGOs in Africa and Asia. At the same time, such activities provided us a way to personally participate in cooperative development projects. Through them we learned how development and social justice issues, to which there are always multiple parties, are actually complicated matters to grasp. In retrospect, this increased understanding of the complexity and ambiguities of development cooperation was one of the reasons I started to question what I really knew about the lives and preferences of the people in distant lands for whom I was campaigning. I felt the need to be better grounded. Together with others with similar concerns, we decided to approach one of organizations for which we had raised funds, the aforementioned GVVS, and to ask whether it would allow us to visit. They agreed, and I began saving money for the trip. I also established a study group with my friends in which we tried to orient ourselves to forthcoming cultural and social issues and learn a bit of Hindi. Finally, in August 1993, along with seven other young women, I left for India.

At the Delhi airport we recognized from photographs a few people from the GVVS, who then packed us promptly into two rickshaws. Squeezed tightly together, we stared at the muddy monsoon road scenes of Delhi, crowded not only by all kinds of vehicles and pushcarts, but also by cows, dogs, buffalos, and large numbers of people, some in their daily tasks on a patch of street, others hurrying somewhere: we had indeed arrived in India. Our accommodation turned out to be in the basement of another organization called Gandhi in Action, run by GVVS's friends. That served as our base during a packed, three-day program in Delhi, which introduced us to monuments and temples but, in line with GVVS's ideology, also a biogas production unit and other small-scale village industries at the surroundings of the city. Then we headed by night train to GVVS's home state of Rajasthan, the land of rajas (kings), camels, mighty turbans, and bright colors. That first train trip further introduced us to the kind of diversity at its best typical for India, yet somewhat exotic and alien for welfare-state kids born in the rather closed corner of strongly Lutheran Christian northeastern Europe. One Sikh man, for example, gently advised us to make room for the prayer of a Muslim cotraveler in the packed train compartment, introduced the symbols of his own faith, and gave us good practical advice about the train and its facilities, including how to use the Indian-style squat toilet, which many of us saw for the first time.

The train took us to the city of Jodhpur, Rajasthan's second biggest city, where GVVS had its office in a neighborhood that specialized in cow keeping, and therefore hundreds of cows were always around. Having spent plenty of time in the countryside in Finland, I found the presence of cows cozy. As most GVVS work takes place in the surrounding countryside, the organization runs several rural centers, from which it works in nearby villages. The centers vary in size from just a room or two for the workers to live in, to having a couple of hectares of land and several buildings. Some of the centers also serve the villagers by running an informal school and day care for small children, providing basic health care facilities, offering a space to conduct meetings, or building a well from which the villagers can fetch water. With the GVVS, we spent much of our time in two such centers.

As was agreed upon beforehand, we set ourselves to planting trees, an essential part of GVVS's forestation program, as well as learning about the organization, the area, and its people. GVVS was working together with local communities and their subgroups on a wide variety of issues, such as water scarcity, nutrition, child marriages, and opium addiction, and problems like bonded labor and silicosis, a lung disease with no cure, prevalent at local sandstone mines. Strangely to me, whatever the actual content of the work, it was talked about either as social or as Gandhian work. Accordingly, the staff of the organization, from village workers to car drivers, identified themselves as social workers. In their view, rather than formal qualifications, which only a few of them had, the essence of social work was "simple living and high thinking." As became clear in frequent discussions, the idea was that the test of a true social worker was a commitment to and capability for voluntary poverty. Following Gandhi's stand that the Earth can sustain everyone's need but not anyone's greed, social workers in particular should be able to be content and satisfied with a simple lifestyle fulfilling basic needs. In so doing, they can set the standard for others, as well as be more approachable for those who are truly needy and poor. Furthermore, education, while useful, does not guarantee becoming a good social worker. What matters is a personal awakening and commitment, including truthfulness and nonviolence, and how one embodies these in his or her everyday life. In actual work, then, the main tasks were seen as working with villagers toward the self-sufficiency of the villages, awareness and team building, and education (Ranta-Tyrkkö 1997). Some GVVS people were also aware of social work as a profession but saw it as a dubious government job. When government jobs in India are commonly associated with lack of commitment and chances for corruption, the GVVS workers emphasized the true meaning of social work as voluntary social service.

As simple as it might appear, it took me time to grasp that, for the GVVS workers, being Gandhian equaled being a social worker. Coming to terms with that took time not only because of my limited knowledge of Gandhi, but because it did not fit into my presuppositions of social workers as professionals with specific tasks and training. In retrospect, however, the visit to GVVS gave me a lesson about the diversity of social work understandings, for it made me acknowledge that social work can be conceived as something far more pervasive than I had considered before—that it is not only a profession and a discipline, but also a movement with various streams, one of them being the Gandhian approach.

Although this was my first time outside of Europe, I don't remember feeling much of a cultural shock. Rather, I was keenly spotting what I had learned from books and movies. Even so, those first days and weeks in India were a constant and wholesome stream of experiences, trying to grasp the other culture and to make sense of the new surroundings, issues, people, and differences. And vice versa: we also were objects of curiosity. As an important part of our exchange with GVVS was to discuss the possibilities for future collaboration, we were expected to explain our own behavior, interests, and culture. Many local people were, for example, puzzled by the fact that we were a group of young women traveling "alone," without guardians, and GVVS people wanted to know who the leader of our team was. We did not always have carefully thought out, clear-cut answers to provide but had to often start by elaborating what our stand was, and thereafter how to explain it in an understandable manner against the cultural expectation of our new surroundings. For example, we tried to explain that not being accompanied by our family members does not mean that they would not care about us.

After returning home from that first, ten-week trip, I continued my studies and finally graduated as a master of social work, which in Finland equals the competence requirement for a qualified social worker. Meanwhile, I remained in contact with GVVS and did one of my social work practice internships with the organization in 1996. During that time I also collected material for my master's thesis, an ethnography that dealt with the GVVS and its Gandhian social work discourse. In my thesis I struggled to understand what was for me the often vague, but for GVVS workers clear, mode of talking about their social work. I ended up claiming that, in a way, in English, Hindi, or Marwari, the local language, the workers of the organization actually talked "Gandhi." Further, although I was not yet able to articulate it very clearly, one of my findings was that being without scientific professional education in social work does not necessarily mean lacking a solid practice and theoretical base; a strong and well-defined philosophical and political orientation, such as the Gandhian approach, can also serve as one.

RESEARCHING THEATER AS SOCIAL WORK IN INDIA

I graduated during the time when Finland was slowly recovering from a severe economic recession that had hit the country hard in the beginning of 1990s. Banks were saved with state money, but people got less. Social security was cut, and vacant posts were rare even for social workers, who usually have good employment prospects. When seeking a job, I found that neither my eclectic study history nor my social work internships outside mainstream Finnish social services were seen as strengths. Even if I got positive feedback at a job interview, I did not get the job. I felt discouraged and began thinking that there might not be space for persons like me at social welfare offices. Thus, after vain efforts to secure a social work position, I returned to the university as a coordinator of an interdisciplinary research and teaching project on welfare services. Despite my initial longing for practical social work, in the enthusiastic research environment of my new job I started to consider further studies. Considering possible topics, I realized that instead of topics of more domestic nature, I was more excited to expand my understanding on what I had come across in India.

I had no illusions that obtaining a Ph.D. degree would make securing a social work post in Finland any easier, as those with a Ph.D. are easily seen as overly educated for practical work. On the other hand, I had nothing to lose. Reasoning that with an arduous task like a doctoral dissertation the best guarantee for long-lasting motivation and endurance is a true interest in one's topic, I spent some time identifying mine. In so doing, I realized that in India I had run across performing and performances since my first moments. In 1993, when we moved around in the GVVS working area in the Thar Desert as a team of students, people sang and danced for us—and expected similar favors in return. We responded with a set of Finnish folk songs, which, when translated ad hoc from Finnish to English to Marwari, turned out to connect quite well with local sentiments. Our set of songs contained, for example, a bride's weeping song in advance of marriage, when she has to say good-bye to everything until then dear and familiar to her. In short, with the GVVS, performance was crucial for our daily interaction with local people.

After a month with the GVVS in 1993, we traveled further, to central India, to visit another NGO, Narmada Bachao Andolan (NBA; Save the Narmada Movement), whose main task was to fight against a megascale project consisting of several dams meant to tame the mighty Narmada River. While the supporters of dams claimed the project would bring improved welfare, that is, electricity, irrigation, and drinking water, the critics of the project were appalled by the human and environmental costs of the approach and questioned its sensibility on the whole. For the latter camp, the project and its implementation—in the name of development— was symptomatic of big development policies and their inherent violence and disinterest toward local people, many of whom were subjected to loss of their homes, land, and livelihoods. During our visit the NBA volunteers were building a papier-mâché replica of the river, its goddess, a crocodile, and all other parties involved in the dispute. These were made to be part of a forthcoming display, through which the opponents of the project wanted to articulate their protest. Unable to stay until the actual spectacle, we were told that in the final scene the World Bank, a huge round face with a gaping mouth, would eat everything and everybody. It was obvious that for the local NBA activists, the performance was a way to bring their struggle alive, and that from their perspective there were important issues and parties that the World Bank or other financiers had not until then recognized.

Three years later, in 1996, during my social work practice internship at GVVS, I had several opportunities to witness how the GVVS communication team, as the organization's performance team was called, made miracles. In certain rural villages in the Thar Desert, which at that time were notorious for their tense intercaste relations, the performances managed to gather whole village communities together, men at one side, women and children at the other side of the stage (basically a space on the ground) at various little village squares, to enjoy a relaxed and humorous atmosphere. Noting the often delicate social and cultural atmosphere of the villages, which included a conceivable threat of outbursts of communal violence, rather strict ideas of honor and shame, and highly gendered codes of behavior, I thought that already this was an achievement in and of itself. What's more, the performances raised a number of hard topics on the stage, discussing them bravely, skillfully, and above all with humor. Songs and a number of short dramas brought the oppressed position of local women, corruption, treatment of malaria, and the consequences of opium addiction all to the stage. Being known by the villagers, the performers utilized the collision between their civil and stage roles in the making of drama. When a high-caste woman appeared at the stage as a lowly sweeper, the audience was just silent.

To me the apparent success of the performances and the fact that the local communities so obviously accepted this kind of an intervention from the GVVS were both a relief and a source of enthusiasm, as beforehand there had been some doubts about how the villagers would respond to the show. Though I was not really able to conceptualize what was going on,

I felt that the performances crated a space of being together that was different from the ordinary. More important, such events seemed to enable communication and interaction so that despite the prevailing disputes and the
oppressive nature of many of the prevalent social norms and hierarchies,
coming and being together was both possible and bearable for the villagers. What's more, this came about through a performance that to some
extent dealt with the very disputes and power positions that were dividing
the spectators. The alienating effect of the drama worked—the comicality
of the performance made it possible for everyone to keep his or her face,
and not to take the performance too personally. In subtle ways and on various levels, the performance events advanced and actually epitomized many
important social work goals of the GVVS.

When I was considering doctoral studies, the above-described events
returned to my mind. Recalling my enthusiasm and the social atmosphere
at the time of the performances, my hunch was that learning more about
such type of performances and their social dynamics could be highly relevant for social workers beyond the immediate cultural context of the actual
performances. Thanks to a successful scholarship application, I was back
in India by the end of 2000. Wanting to expand my horizons beyond the
GVVS, I sought out other NGOs as well as theater groups making socially
committed theater in order to find a team with which I could engage for
study purposes.

As there are numerous socially committed theater groups as well as
NGO-bound performers in India, I started my search and visits with the
contacts I had, aided by new ones gained along the way. I got Natya Chetana's address from a Finnish community theater teacher who had met the
group's leader at a festival in Kenya. Visiting the group took me to Odisha,
a state of India where I had never been before. Once with Natya Chetana,
I found that, unlike many other performances I had seen, its plays were not
forcefully propagandistic or marketing a particular ideology—if refraining
from propaganda is not counted as an ideology. Nonetheless, they were
strongly political in the choice of topics, showing, for example, what being
a migrant laborer or a poor agricultural worker in a cyclone-prone coastal
area possibly means in the present local-global economy. While the plays
refrained from offering any action plan, they were thought provoking and
touching in the way they examined the difficulties of their protagonists. It is
one thing to tell the audience what to do and quite another thing to pose a

question and ask the audience what they think they should do. In comparison to many NGO performances with a more educative or edifying focus, I found Natya Chetana's approach refreshing. Moreover, the plays of Natya Chetana suited my yet fairly unarticulated ideas about theater as a tool for cultural or political sensibility or awakening, which could be essential also for social work, at least social work seeking to be political. I felt this was my chance to witness work that is serious about facilitating social change but does not predetermine its steps and direction—taking the complexity of people's life conditions as well as democratic processes seriously.

After having been with Natya Chetana and seeing two of the group's plays, I felt I had found my research subject. Happily, the Natya Chetana team agreed to allow me to study them. The condition for my coming was that I should live with the group and not on my own in some rented apartment nearby where I would just visit the group, even if on a daily basis. That sounded fair enough and was the beginning of a collaboration, one outcome of which has been my Ph.D. dissertation (Ranta-Tyrkkö 2010).

LEARNING ABOUT LOCAL STANDPOINTS AND MYSELF

Living together with the people of GVVS and Natya Chetana has been significant for my learning and relationships in India. Among other things, it has meant that local people introduced me to local social norms, dress codes, and proper behavior of everyday life. Furthermore, they offered me a huge amount of information about how the society functions, starting from mundane matters such as how to go where I want to go, how to get the things I need, what and where to safely eat, and where to go when I am ill. I was casually introduced to activists, government servants, and family members, and most of all, given time and attention, even a bit of protective warding. This process of learning Indian social norms and codes forced me to reconsider my own identity, background, behavior, and even outlook from new angles. In particular, a number of such crucial cultural encounters had something to do either with money or with gender.

My gender has often been unclear to local people in India. I assume this has been mostly because of my different size (taller) and skin color (lighter) when compared to local women. Moreover, especially on my first trips to India, I often wore clothes that are culturally coded as men's, such as kurtas (long shirts) and pyjamas (pants). Because of this, I have had my moments to grasp how uncomfortable it can be to be seen as "the Other." For example, in 1996 when I traveled alone by local buses in the Thar Desert, often dozens and sometimes hundreds of local men, at least so I felt, gathered around me just to stare at me silently until my bus finally came. I had been pretty thoroughly informed by GVVS about the subordinate position of local women, as the organization was working with various issues related with women's long-lasting oppression in the region. Thus when I was surrounded by the staring crowd, the minutes and sometimes hours waiting for a bus felt truly long and uncomfortable. Initially I found such staring both frightening and irritating, although the men always remained at least a few meters away from me. Yet when I was more used to such occasions, I felt that the staring silence around me was mostly merely attentive rather than purposefully offensive. Against the fact that the local women present were all fully veiled, squatting somewhere aside, I was clearly paying the price of my strangeness: probably a woman, but dressed in men's clothes, white and odd, and with no veil for anyone to see.

Albeit uncomfortable, these experiences were in a sense healthy for me. They gave me a glimpse of how it might feel being constantly othered and marked as "not one of us" in everyday encounters—as many of the people with whom social workers work are. Among other things, these incidents made me think about whether the first dark-skinned people in Finland experienced something similar because of their different skin color, as Finland remained for a long time rather closed and is still predominantly white. I later learned that the first Africans in Finland indeed had to live with the burden of being sure crowd pullers, a fact that, for example, Lutheran parishes utilized when they organized church gatherings to acquire funds for missionary work and wanted to draw in lots of church members (e.g., Jonkka 2010).

Turning to money, my life with GVVS and Natya Chetana involved various kinds of transactions on a symbolic level, as well as cash and in-kind exchanges. To GVVS I initially represented the funder in Finland, for, although on a small scale, the student union was financing some GVVS work. To Natya Chetana I donated money to duly compensate the costs of my accommodation, food, and travel with the group. More critical, perhaps, has been the financial imbalance between the volunteers of these organizations and me. However meager my own study grants or research scholarships on a Finnish scale, compared to the situation of many of my

Indian friends I surely appeared wealthy. Most of the time I was able to afford basically anything I considered useful, needed, or just wanted to buy—a position that is totally beyond the financial range of an average social work volunteer in India.

One occasion in which my different orientation to owning and wearing things became clear was when Natya Chetana's leader, Subodh, was involved in a serious traffic accident, which nearly took his life. In the accident Subodh incurred a head injury that resulted in unconsciousness for several days. As I often traveled on the backseat of motorbike or moped driven by someone on the Natya Chetana team, I thought that I should learn a lesson from Subodh's accident and buy myself a helmet. I even considered that, as a helmet was a rare scene on the road, my purchase would publicize its use. To my surprise, when finally home from hospital, Subodh strongly opposed my intention to buy a helmet. In his opinion, no helmet was needed in the Indian traffic culture, which is based on continuous negotiation and generally low speeds. Furthermore, he was convinced that my whiteness made other road users drive more carefully. I had numerous counterarguments, and physical counterevidence with still visible scars from a recent minor scooter accident. What's more, against the fragile, bolster-supported, and painful condition of Subodh, whose own survival had been anything but granted, I felt the whole discussion nonsensical, and I felt greatly irritated by Subodh's persistence in the matter. It took me time to figure out, with difficulty, that, for Subodh, safety really was not the number one issue in the use of helmet. The main reason he opposed my intention to buy the best available helmet was that he was convinced that in the eyes of the local people, such a helmet was merely a symbol of the wealth and privileged position of its user. As he explained, if two people are on a motorbike, the helmet should be on the one who drives. If both have helmets, the driver should have the better one. If I, a tall, white Finn, just sat on the back with an expensive helmet, people would wonder why I traveled on the back of a motorbike when I could obviously afford a taxi. In short, Subodh was concerned about my relationship with local people. In the end, the compromise between us was that I bought a cheap copy of a better brand of helmet, hoping it would nonetheless prove useful in an accident. On the other hand, I also started to move more regularly by taxi.

Although in Finland I don't consider myself as particularly materialistic, living with GVVS and Natya Chetana forced me to acknowledge, to my own surprise, how habituated I am to a consumer identity. In an environment in which chances for consumption are limited because of tight personal budgets, the ideology of the organization, like boycotting certain multinational companies, as well as the bare fact that in small rural and semiurban shops there is not a great selection available, I have been surprised how truly delighted I have been when I have had a chance to choose, pay for, and get what I want, even if it is a kilo of guavas. Having the chance to decide over such simple matters made me feel like a doer, as if the capacity to make such small consumer choices attested that I was, after all, an independent and free being, that I had agency. Yet, as I later learned, the freedom of consuming can be also questioned. In consumer societies, consuming is discursively attached to ideas about self-realization, autonomy, and willpower to change, and therefore many of us try to approach the kind of ideals we entertain about ourselves through consumer choices (e.g., Cronin 2000). At the same time, the indisputable fact is that the mass consumption–based economic system produces an abundance of unnecessary products, debris, and pollution that harm the ecosystems on which we depend. More than ever, our consumption and convenience are economically, ecologically and socially untenable, disadvantaging the nature and the lives of future generations.

While the episodes of finances and consumption related above tell their own story about fundamental material and cultural aspects regarding my position within GVVS and Natya Chetana, it is equally worth noting that in the eyes of the more well-to-do members of the local cultural elite, there was nothing to envy about my wealth or lifestyle. Often when I was politely asked about my parents' professions on various family and official visits, my answers caused a recognizable silence. This is because after some decades as a welder in various factories, my father was for a long time unemployed until his retirement, while my mother worked as a factory worker and a cleaner. From an Indian perspective, the sons and daughters of an unemployed father and a cleaning lady simply do not roam around other continents writing doctoral dissertations; in their case, foreign travel and university education are highly improbable and even unimaginable. From my own perspective, there is no reason to hide my working-class background; thus I did not take the aforementioned silences personally. Rather, I sometimes tried, although not very successfully, to tease the discussion on the matter a little further. At any rate, such silences do tell their own story about class- and education-bound expectations. While my case clearly attests that the Nordic welfare state model has been successful in reducing class- and income-based disparities, such fluidity of educational and class positions can be difficult to imagine and come to terms with in India, where more often than not one's social status, education, class, and caste background go tightly together. In fact, despite being enabled through free education and a study grant system, crossing class barriers is not the most common reality in Finland either. In India, then, against the obvious fact that I could afford to fly there, one of the questions often posed in casual discussions was how many cars do I have at home—my bewildering answer being that I have none and get along well with bicycle and public transportation. Likewise, many middle-class Indians found it strange that I had done various forms of wage work, from assisting handicapped people to working in a cafeteria, to sustain myself during my undergraduate and graduate studies, whereas in Finland combining work-ing and studying is common and a necessity for many.

In my mind, the irritations and moments of fear and uneasiness that I described above, as well difficulties in fitting the frameworks of others, and vice versa, epitomize something of the kind of resistance, discomfort, and difficulty typical of cross-cultural encounters. Writing from a perspective of a not yet thoroughly multicultural society (Finland), it seems to me that elaborating on such difficulties is actually important for social workers, who in general try to make way for greater tolerance and understanding, and who avoid posing different marginalized groups against each other. Addressing difficulty is not contrary to seeing cross-cultural and cross-border efforts and dialogue important and necessary. Rather, the point is to acknowledge, as travel writer Philip Briggs (2009:112) does, that other cultures are not always easily accessible and assimilated—a fact that may be forgotten, for example, in cosmopolitan cities where it is possible to cel-ebrate diversity with a variety of cuisines and cultural centers.

Reflecting back, my first journeys to India were well informed in the sense that I had researched relevant background information about the country and its culture. My initial trap was that while things were largely as I expected, I assumed that something more secret and real would reveal itself during a longer stay. In retrospect, my own standpoint during my first trips was nonetheless quite narrow. While I thought I was seeking the real and hidden, I largely stuck to the kinds of issues and aspects of the other culture that were familiar to me from home. This is highly evident, for example, from what I documented and photographed. Having been active in NGOs in Finland, I viewed India from the standpoint of an NGO activist, and my photographs were filled with local NGO activists, mostly posing on newly built rainwater-harvesting tanks. While there is nothing wrong with that, many other issues, perhaps equally worth documenting, did not get my attention.

What further flavored my first trips to India was a certain duty to witness and in a way renew what I thought to be authentic images of India, especially when it came to local social problems. In part, my idea of "real" India and what I should witness there was actually colored by the problem-centered way of depicting India, and in general much of the developing world, in Finnish media. Furthermore, what kind of social science student would travel in India not paying attention to social problems, especially when folks at home expected the journey be nothing but beggars, tropical diseases, and poverty? I, for sure, was careful to recognize malnourished children, child wives and widows, women practicing purdah, drying up wells, and children working in appalling conditions in sandstone mines. I visited an arranged marriage wedding party but saw little good in the form of marriage itself. And so forth. What I was not yet very attentive to was the amount and speed of positive changes, despite obvious problems, taking place in the lives of girls and women of the region, or that mostly the people around me were happy with their arranged marriages, many of which actually end up being full of love and affection.

There were also images and responses that did not quite fit my presuppositions. In Rajasthan, knowing the strongly patriarchal culture and the prevalence of absolute poverty among many low-caste and class groups, what was I to think of the impressive presence of some local women, even if they did nothing but watch me silently? What's more, when I was concerned with how to come to terms with the kind of poverty I saw, I realized I was being pitied for needing to travel on my own, for my pale, skinny, and dowdy outlook, and because in my country marriages reportedly break up easily, alcoholism is common, and many older people are not properly cared for by their children. In the Thar Desert, even in the poorest of houses where there were not enough dishes for every family member to eat and drink at the same time, efforts were made to offer me and my friends at least something. From earth to sky the desert provided us plentifully with its beauty. To me, one of the unforeseen luxuries of the journey was the chance, night after night, to count the falling stars before falling asleep under a warm quilt on the rooftops that served as my bedroom in the desert.

Gradually, various cultural encounters led me to reexamine my own perspective. Furthermore, although my understanding of the kinds of social problems that exist in the Indian and Finnish societies grew, I also realized that it is equally important to ask what do I lose, or what remains unseen to me, if I only focus on the most dreadful or the most wonderful aspects of the other culture. While, for example, hierarchy, fear, and violence are part of Indian and, in different forms, also Finnish societies, they are not necessarily simple and straightforward issues to recognize and deal with, especially for a person coming for a short visit from outside. Moreover, as I hope some of the episodes I write about illustrate, one's personal location, history, and background forge one's orientation and standpoint, and thus how and what one experiences and understands. In other words, our locations and backgrounds are inscribed to us, even when we travel—for example, in the ways we measure things or approach other people, and, vice versa, in the ways we are interpreted against our assumed background.

Whether I have liked it or not, as a Westerner in India I have often been taken as the representative of Europe or America, money and power, good and bad. On the other hand, notwithstanding the warnings given for female tourists in India, I have been able to do things that for my local female friends are not considered safe. As a white foreigner already seasoned with Indian culture, I can, for example, by and large stay without special cautions in cheap hotels, pick up random taxis, and dine alone as a woman. While I might, in doing so, come across occasional discomfort or harassment, I can generally expect a friendly response and help from local people. It seems that my behavior is acceptable because of my background, whereas similar behavior by local women would mark them as persons inviting trouble. What's more, should something happen to me, the police and the embassy would surely be involved. For many Indians, such safety guarantees do not exist. On the contrary, they can be questioned and challenged, and even taken to a police station, as happened to a musician friend of mine at a railway station in Delhi. Because of his beard and long shirt, he was considered by the local police officer to be a Muslim, and in a country where every seventh or eighth person is Muslim, the officer decided that he had to be questioned at the police station. My friend was released, with no excuses, only after he was able to prove that he had been invited to perform at the local music academy. Sadly for a country proclaiming unity in diversity, merely looking like a Muslim was enough to be interrogated and discriminated against. One can only assume what actual Muslims experience on a daily basis. My friend was a highly educated, self-confident man from a high-caste community, aware of his rights. For those who are not, the basic rule is not to stand out, and not to end up in situations in which one is vulnerable and in trouble. Unfortunately, my friend's case demonstrates how anyone can be targeted for discrimination, even by those whose supposed duty is to protect the rights of every citizen.

While I have not been free from the kind of images, attitudes, and postures that I have imbibed in throughout my life in Finland, social work education included, a central part my learning of new cultural contexts and logic has been relearning what I thought I already knew, and tracing attitudes I was not aware of having. Gradually I learned to see India increasingly in light and shade. As noted, this required plenty of self-reflection, and willingness to try to see things from the standpoint of the Other. In my case, my process of learning in and about Indian culture has been necessary also for my work. At any rate, the lesson is that in research, traveling, and social work alike, it is useful to be critically aware of one's own standpoint and location before judging others. Although commonplace, this is also the greater relevance of my story.

LEARNING, RELEARNING, AND IMAGINING SOCIAL WORK IN THE GLOBAL CONTEXT

Having been born and raised in a country and at a time in which many of the benefits of the Nordic welfare state model seemed certainties, learning of the contrasting realities of India has been illuminating, and it has influenced my thinking on social work. First, it has made me more sensitive toward the multiplicity of realities and has helped me to better realize my own location and standpoints and the culturally specific, location-bound nature of all social work. Second, it has generated a personal interest in social work histories—how and why social work got formed in different places, and how local constructions of social work have been influenced by broader social, cultural, and economic processes. Third, my travels in India made me realize not only differences but certain odd similarities between Finland and India. For example, in the nationally peripheral regions of northern Finland or eastern India, some of the topics at stake sound surprisingly similar: fights over land rights, mining sites, whether logging equals environmental destruction or sensible forestry, and whether there is a future for indigenous cultures and lifestyles.

This process has generated many questions with a personal, professional, and political edge, to which I have no easy answers. What, for example, should one think of the vastly different global realities, and the differences between social work approaches? While moving between cultures develops one's sense of proportion, how should one deal with disparities of conceptual worlds and worldviews when they do not neatly translate from one language and worldview to another? My attempts to bridge the worlds of social work in Finland and in India have benefited from finding working theoretical and discursive connections, such as postcolonial theory and the discussion on international or global social work. In my view postcolonial theory, which I understand as theoretical sense making of colonial pasts and their consequences (e.g., Gandhi 1998; McLeod 2000), provides intriguing opportunities to think about pasts and presents of social work. This applies not only to formerly colonized countries like India, but also to Finland, a country that never had any colony, but which has nonetheless been a party to various kinds of colonial relations and which is home to the indigenous Sami people (Ranta-Tyrkkö 2011). On a global scale, postcolonial theory helps recognizing the "Northernness" (Connell 2007) of much of globally distributed social work theory and practice models, as well as the fact that from certain southern, popular, or nonprofessionally oriented standpoints, they may embody a position of privilege. Further, as postcolonial theory suggests, legacies of colonialism are still around, influencing people and regions beyond the actual colonizing or colonized nations. In social work, examining these legacies is useful for attempts to understand social work histories, and to distinguish inherited but not always well-recognized biases prevalent in present practices. In Finland and other Nordic countries, for example, these include racism (despite our fondness for the idea that, as we rarely met people from other races, we were never racist), strong heteronormativity of services, and an inability to see what is exclusive in Nordic welfare policies and practices (Mulinari et al. 2009).

As I hope my story attests, when taken as a call to learn more both about oneself and the others, difficulties in coming to terms with the Other can sometimes provide a fertile ground for cross-cultural dialogue and learning to develop, and new questions and understanding to emerge. I learned, among other things, to place the parochial concerns of my own cultural background, and sometimes also those of others, in perspective. Further, learning about the Indian realities taught me to value, far more than initially, the persistent, long-term work to combat poverty structurally, in India and Finland alike. In particular, it clarified for me the need for political, structural social work, and strategic collaboration and solidarity between various kinds of social workers locally and globally, be they trained professionals or volunteers or activists with various political and spiritual backgrounds. It also awakened me to the centrality and acuteness of environmental issues for the quality and continuity of human life. While the poor in countries like India are often at the front line experiencing the present environmental crisis, with little chance for protection and adaptation, the challenge is global and requires, in my view, social work as a profession, discipline, and movement to confront it head on.

Last but not least, being in India highlighted for me the value of theater and other arts for imagining new ways of living and fostering solidarity. Being moved and touched by other people's destinies facilitates negotiating and collaborating, as well as bearing with conflicts, contradictions, and imperfection. Isn't that what much of social work is about? At the same time, however, it is also important to question one's own comfort zones, which is not always an easy task. Of late, the academic world has increasingly become my own comfort zone, so how can I remain connected outside of it? And what about the ecologically and socially just but truly challenging idea of voluntary poverty? How should that oblige social workers, or researchers like me, in rich countries and with massive ecological footprints? At the time of writing, part of my personal response to these questions is to try to remain attentive to popular movements addressing issues of social and environmental justice. Regarding efforts to consume less and thus cause less harm, one of my daily attempts is to try to be content with the things I already have.

REFERENCES

Byam, D. L. 1999. *Community in Motion: Theatre for Development in Africa*. Critical Studies in Education and Culture Series, edited by H. A. Groux. London: Bergin & Garvey.

Briggs, P. 2009. *Ethiopia. The Bradt Travel Guide*. Chalfont St Peter: Bradt Travel Guides.

Census of India. 2011. Statistical information provided by the Office of the Registrar General and Census Commissioner, Ministry of Home Affairs, Government of India. http://www.censusindia.net.

Cerwonka, A., and L. Malkki. 2007. "Fieldwork Correspondence." In *Improvising Theory: Process and Temporality in Ethnographic Fieldwork*, edited by A. Cerwonka and L. Malkki, 44–161. Chicago: University of Chicago Press.

Connell, R. 2007. *Southern Theory: The Global Dynamics of Knowledge in Social Science*. Cambridge: Polity Press.

Cronin, A. M. 2000. "Consumerism and 'Compulsory Individuality': Women, Will and Potential." In *Transformations: Thinking Through Feminism*, edited by S. Ahmed, J. Kilby, C. Lury, M. McNeil, and B. Skeggs. London: Routledge.

Gandhi, L. 1998. *Postcolonial Theory: A Critical Introduction*. New Delhi: Oxford University Press.

IFSW. 2000. Definition of Social Work. Adopted by the IFSW General Meeting in Montreal, Canada, July 2000. http://www.ifsw.org/.

Jonkka, M. 2010. *Afro-Suomen Historia* (History of Africans in Finland). Documentary. Broadcasting Company of Finland.

Kerr, D. 1995. *African Popular Theatre from Pre-Colonial Times to Present Day*. London: James Currey.

Kershaw, B. 1992. *The Politics of Performance. Radical Theatre as Cultural Intervention*. London: Routledge.

Lavalette, M., and V. Ioakimidis. 2011. "International Social Work or Social Work Internationalism? Radical Social Work in Global Perspective." In *Radical Social Work Today: Social Work at the Crossroads*, edited by M. Lavalette, 135–51. Bristol: Policy Press.

Markovits, C. 2004. *The Un-Gandhian Gandhi. The Life and Afterlife of the Mahatma*. New Delhi: Permanent Black.

McLeod, J. 2000. *Beginning Postcolonialism*. Manchester: Manchester University Press.

Mlama, P. M. 1991. *Culture and Development: The Popular Theatre Approach in Africa*. Uppsala: Nordiska Afrikainstitutet.

Mulinari, D., S. Keskinen, S. Irni, and S. Tuori. 2009. "Introduction: Postcolonialism and the Nordic Models of Welfare and Gender." In *Complying with Colonialism: Gender, Race and Ethnicity in the Nordic Region*, edited by S. Keskinen, S. Tuori, S. Irni, and D. Mulinari, 1–16. Farnham: Ashgate.

Nandy, A., and R. Jahanbegloo. 2006. *Talking India in Conversation with Ramin Jahanbegloo (2006)*. New Delhi: Oxford University Press.

Nellhaus, T., and S. C. Haedicke. 2001. "Introduction." In *Performing Democracy: International Perspectives on Urban Community-Based Performance*, edited by S. C. Haedicke and T. Nellhaus, 1–27. Ann Arbor: University of Michigan Press.

Ranta-Tyrkkö, S. 1997. "Gandhilaista sosiaalityötä autiomaassa. Kertomus intialaisesta Gramin Vikas Vigyan Samiti—järjestöstä" (Gandhian Social Work in Desert: An Account of the Social Work of the Indian NGO Gramin Vikas Vigyan Samiti). Master's thesis, University of Tampere.

———. 2010. *At the Intersection of Theatre and Social Work in India: Natya Chetana and Its Theatre*. Ph.D. dissertation, Acta Universitatis Tamperensis 1503. Tampere: Tampere University Press. http://acta.uta.fi.

———. 2011. "High Time for Postcolonial Analysis in Social Work." *Nordic Social Work Research* 1 (1): 25–41.

Sainath, P. 2009. "Neo-Liberal Terrorism in India: The Largest Wave of Suicides in History." *Counterpunch*, December 12. http://www.counterpunch.org/sainath.

Schechter, J. 2003. "Back to the Popular Source. Introduction to Part 1." In *Popular Theatre: A Sourcebook*, edited by J. Schechter. London: Routledge.

Sircar, B. 1978. *The Third Theatre*. Calcutta: Sri Aurobindo Press.

Van Erven, E. 1988. *Radical People's Theatre*. Bloomington: Indiana University Press.

Yarrow, R. 2001. *Indian Theatre: Theatre of Origin, Theatre of Freedom*. Richmond, Surrey: Curzon.

CHAPTER 4

Being of Two Minds

CREATING MY RACIALIZED SELVES

▸ NORIKO ISHIBASHI MARTINEZ

A YOUNG GIRL, probably six or seven years old, is sitting on her patio, looking over the railing at the river and the walkway below. The house is on the side of a mountain in Kobe, Japan. She sees another girl, about her age, walking by. She looks to be walking home from school, as she is wearing a red backpack. She looks up and notices the girl on the patio looking at her.

"*Gaijin*!" she hollers. The word, which just means "foreigner," is meant to be insulting. The girl on the patio is surprised at this, because of the meanness, but her mother is American, so she's not that surprised, because she is kind of *gaijin*.

"*Ninjin*!" hollers the girl on the patio. The word, which means "carrot," rhymes nicely with *gaijin* and feels like a good retort.

"*Gaijin*!"

"*Ninjin*!"

Eventually they realize they are at an impasse, and the girl on the walkway walks on, as the girl on the patio moves away from the railing.

•   •   •

When I lived in Japan, I categorized people largely in terms of nationality. Because I had family who lived in two different countries, I recognized that I was not entirely Japanese in nationality. It did not mean anything about who I was, but perhaps something about where my allegiances were supposed to lie. When I moved to the United States, I had to be enculturated in the American version of categorization, which is based more heavily on race. As the vignette above illustrates, I would not want to pretend that Japan is some paradise where everyone loves everyone else, regardless of provenance; rather, the point is that we culturally construct our ways of recognizing difference and sameness, so that different people don't understand their difference in the same way.

As a newcomer to the United States, I had to learn how I was supposed to recognize difference by learning what racial and ethnic stereotypes were, and then pretend that I did not know them. This was confusing, but it seems to be the same confusion that lies at the heart of race relations in the United States: no one seems clear, from an individual level to a policy level, whether we are supposed to notice people's races, and whether we are supposed to treat people differently based on race. As I struggled to learn the racial stereotypes, and then the steps in the dance of race relations, it took some time before I turned that lens on myself and began to wonder about my own race and racism.

My mother is essentially a white woman from the Midwest, though with frequent relocations to various naval bases based on her father's assignments, she tends to be flexible and tolerant in response to individual and cultural difference. That's probably what made it possible for her to marry my father, who was born and raised in Tokyo. His parents were both from Fukushima Prefecture, a place very few people in the United States had heard of until the Fukushima Daiichi nuclear disaster in 2011. They met when my father was completing his master's degree in business in the United States, and in spite of the fact that their fathers had fought on opposing forces during World War II, and that my Japanese grandfather disowned my father and his family as a result of my father's choice, the two got married and eventually moved to Japan.

I used to think of myself as half Japanese and half American, but when I moved to the United States I had to start thinking in American terms. I was born in Japan but moved to the United States when I was ten years old. Am I a minority? Yes and no. I am considered half "model minority," half majority race. I imagine I don't experience much discrimination, aside from the odd "What are you, anyway?" to "Oh, you must know karate" or "We kicked your ass in World War II." (In fairness, given my grandfathers' being on both sides of the conflict, I actually kicked my own ass.) My minority status doesn't seem to carry much burden. When I moved to the United States, I was a U.S. citizen moving to the United States for the first time;

I was also a Japanese citizen leaving my country of birth for a new, foreign country. So was I an immigrant? No and yes.

In the decades since then, I have married a Mexican American man whose father's family has lived in the Colorado area since before it became a state. His grandfather was among the first Hispanic train engineers and suffered violent discrimination in order to achieve that; he literally fought his way to the top. My husband, on the other hand, who is six feet tall with blue eyes, has a hard time convincing people that he is actually of Mexican descent. His brother, with red hair and freckles, has an equally difficult time. For both of us, the extreme gap between our grandparents' generation and ours leaves us with complicated stories of race, ethnicity, and culture; moving down to the next generation, it seems our children's stories will be impossible to untangle.

At first I thought perhaps I was simply an extremely unusual case, but what I find is that, in fact, most of the people I talk to have a complicated and conflicted relationship with their race. How much they identify with the stereotypes (both positive and negative) of a particular race, how much it informs their self-narrative, and how much they have even examined race are all unique to each person. In the clinical context, we have to add in the consideration of whether the other person shares the same idea about what cultural competence is and whether it is valued. I have worked with clients who specifically chose a clinician of a different cultural background so that they would not have to follow their own cultural norms: would that be greater or lesser cultural competence on the part of the clinician? When we talk about cultural competence, we have to make space for all that, and that starts with noticing how much of the world fits along the blurry margins of any racial or cultural label rather than in the center.

My story is one that does not fit neatly into the accepted dialogue about race and culture, and I suspect that it is not all that unusual in that regard. I imagine that many people's stories look something like mine, where we all somewhat identify or are identified with various defined categories and accept none of them completely. We need to move beyond race and ethnicity as reified and defining concepts, and yet it is unclear how can we do that in the present U.S. context where they form such an important part of people's identity and experience.

Strangely, as I was writing this chapter, a woman wrote to the Social Q's column of the *New York Times* with the following question:

> I am an Asian-American woman living in a mostly white town. Every day, I am asked bluntly: "What are you?" I get it from colleagues at work and people who have known me for less than five minutes. I find it so intrusive that sometimes I respond rudely. But even then, people will say, "You sure don't look it." First, how should I respond to this question? And can you tell me why it upsets me so much? (Galanes 2011)

Ten years ago, when I was waiting tables to pay for school, I could have written the same question, although the town was fairly diverse. Some nights I would tally how many people asked that same exact question: "What are you?" And I, likewise, would get snarky and answer such things as, "A human being, what are you?" In my experience that wouldn't end things, though, as the conversation went something like this: "No, I mean, where are you from?" Me: "I'm from Chicago." Them: "No, you know, where are your *people* from?" or "What are your *roots*?" Other nights I would feel magnanimously open and educational, and I would take the time to explain my ethnic and racial heritage. I laugh with my students when I tell them about those experiences: "Isn't it funny that people have a hard time knowing how to interact with you when they can't place you into their preformed categories of ethnicity and race?" This gets at the heart of the problem: we base too much of our peripheral interactions on generalizations rather than knowledge of an individual.

Galanes's (2011) answer to the original question above, in part, was:

> For a nation that claims "race blindness" as the road to equality, that's disturbing—and makes our route a little hard to believe in when race and ethnicity are the first things people want to know about us.
>
> Worse, the question itself ("What are you?") has a demeaning edge, as if you were a rare breed of dog or a rock formation. But that may be my tenderfooted inexperience showing. The worst I get is "What kind of name is that?" (Greek, thank you very much.)

Galanes goes on to add that she has no duty to respond, though it might be beneficial, giving her instead something to say to remind the asker of people's common humanity: "What am I? Mostly water and carbon—just like you." I do wish it were that simple. Within the question, "What are you," is information that the person needs in order to resolve his or her own discomfort and uncertainty. It includes, I think, questions like "How should I interact with you?" and "Are there things I should avoid talking about in order to avoid being awkward or rude?" When someone is more easily identified, racially speaking, then determining that person's ethnic or racial background happens on first glance without thought, notice, or conversation. In a way I am fortunate that this aspect of interaction, which would generally pass unnoticed, is forced out into the light, allowing the construction of race as an aspect of our interaction to proceed with awareness.

RACE AS A SOCIAL CONSTRUCT

The young girl, now ten years old, starts at a new school in the middle of the school year. Not surprisingly, the other kids are curious about her. Some are friendly, asking about what Japan is like. Others are less kind, teasing her for her hairstyle, her clothing, the way she carries her backpack. Some are classic bullies. They ask about Japan, too: "Is that how they do it where you're from?" but they don't seem to expect an answer, and they walk away giggling.

•   •   •

When I left Japan, I had been a foreigner because I was not fully Japanese and attended an international school. I came to the United States with assumptions about what it meant to be American (as a nationality), but without any clear sense of *race*. I did not think of myself as any particular race. When I experienced the cruelty of children who were unfamiliar with encountering difference, I understood it as something like culture associated with nationality, rather than an issue of race. My ten-year-old mind constructed a story that was about how people did things differently in America, and I was doing it wrong by American standards. I certainly did not think that the other kids were *racist*. As I examine my experiences, I wonder: when did I become aware of race, and how did that affect my understanding of culture? Again, I am in the fortunate position of having something that would normally pass unnoticed (the development of my understanding of race) happen with more awareness (since I was older than when racial identity formation normally happens).

The complexity of race as a concept is clear when considering how to operationalize it for the purposes of quantitative research. The most common approach, in my experience, is to simply ask a question like "What is your race?" and then provide a limited set of possible answers, including the catch-all response, "other." The problem with this is that if the point of the research is to determine the effects of race on some other variables, then which is more important: self-identification or other-identification? I had a professor in my undergraduate degree program who, as I found out later, was biracial: African American and white. This came out when he was sharing an anecdote where he expressed surprise at having to tell someone that he identifies as black. The implication of the story was that, in his own eyes, he was quite obviously a black man, although by his appearance I would not have been able to identify him as such. Perhaps I am less race-conscious than others, but I suspect I was not the only person whose response was "You are?" This is probably similar to the reaction in others when I identify my racial and ethnic background as well, and it highlights the distinction between race and ethnicity as an aspect of identity versus race and ethnicity as a basis for social interaction. He had a racial identity that he seemed to be holding as a key component of his identity, but also one that would be the basis for the ways others would interact with him. But was he experiencing race-based discrimination as heavily as another man whom most observers would identify as African American? In that case, if we are trying to understand his experiences of discrimination, is it methodologically sound to categorize these two men together: one, who is clearly identified as African American, and the other, who some categorize as African American but some others think of as Latin, or Mediterranean, or Middle Eastern, or simply Unknown?

It seems to me, as someone who avidly participates in research as a subject in order to generate good karma for my own research endeavors, and as someone who takes note of the operationalization of race, that it has become increasingly common to allow respondents to mark more than one category, or to include a category of "biracial or multiracial." This change is exemplified in the change between the 1990 and the 2000 U.S. Census: whereas the former instructed respondents to "Fill ONE circle for the race that the person considers himself/herself to be," the latter instructed respondents to "Mark [X] one or more races to indicate what this person considers himself/herself to be" (U.S. Census Bureau n.d.).

I suspect that most people can understand what a step forward this was. As a person who is biracial, I often hesitate when answering the question if I can only mark one category: if I mark white, then I am denying my Asian heritage; if I mark Asian, I'm overplaying my minority status; if I mark other, then I am glossing over both of these since I'm more white or Asian than neither of those. Often I prefer not to answer, since I don't want my answers to be assumed to be race-based anyway, but if I don't allow my answers to be connected with my racial/ethnic category, then I am limiting the ability for me and others like me to be represented. In conversations with my students during research methods classes, I often bring up the issue of how to measure race. I find that many students are equally hesitant to respond to the traditional questionnaire format. One white student reported that she will not answer the question if it uses the term "Caucasian" since, as she puts it, "I'm not from Caucasia." Again, while I imagine that my experience of the complexity of raceness is due to unusual circumstances, it is perhaps rather more common. This is complicated further by the fact that the self I step into when I am participating in research is the self who is also a researcher, attempting to be a good research subject while also critiquing the methodology, and further trying to make sure that the me that gets represented by the measurement feels like an accurate portrayal of the me I see myself as. That self has ideas about race and thinks about race in particularly academic ways; it does not express racial identity or orient toward race in the same way that all my other selves do.

THE HISTORY OF RACIAL CATEGORIES

But returning to this jump forward of allowing for bi- or multiracial identities: is it, in fact, a jump forward? The acceptance of multiraciality as even a possibility has had a varied history in the United States. There was a time when the term "yellow" referred to people who were of African and European descent.[1] Hickman (1997) argues that people of mixed African and European descent have been treated as essentially black since the earliest legal records in America, in 1656. However, the existence of words for mixed-race people implies a distinct category, meaning that the current return in the United States to the concept of multiracialness does not represent a new idea.

Miscegenation (whose Latin roots mean the mixing of genuses) refers primarily to interracial marriage and procreation; it seems to have a negative connotation, perhaps in part because of association with the prefix mis- in such words as misanthrope and misogyny (where it means hatred) or misfortune and mistrial (where it means erroneous or bad). People who were of mixed race were neither one nor the other and were considered a weakening of both races. Because of that, some would argue that getting rid of a multiracial category was better for all involved (for a full discussion, see Davis 1991, esp. chap. 6). For example, when races were defined by the one-drop rule, such that "one drop" of African blood made a person black, a unified African American identity and culture became possible.

The first state law on the books outlawing marriage to a specific Asian group was in 1861 (Nevada's law prohibiting white-Chinese intermarriage); Montana was the first to include Japanese people specifically in its antimiscegenation laws, in 1909 (Sohoni 2007:597). However, one consequence of the antimiscegenation laws regarding Asians was the creation of the category "Asian." Just as the one-drop rule allowed for the reification of an African American identity, antimiscegenation (and citizenship) laws reified Asian as a racial category (Sohoni 2007). It wasn't until the 1967 U.S. Supreme Court decision of *Loving v. Virginia* that antimiscegenation laws were declared unconstitutional; my parents were married two years later.

There continue to be people who are strongly against miscegenation, perhaps in part because of what Davis (1991) describes as the five foundational beliefs of racist ideologies: (1) races can be ranked according to physical superiority and inferiority; (2) races can be ranked according to intellectual superiority and inferiority (a task undertaken by the infamous book *The Bell Curve* [1994], and ably refuted by Stephen Jay Gould in the revised and expanded version of *The Mismeasure of Man* [1996]); (3) ethnicity or culture is genetically transmitted along with race; (4) individual temperament or personality is genetically transmitted along with race; and (5) miscegenation biologically weakens the human race. These five beliefs are the foundation of such movements as the eugenics movement and the fitter families ideal, both of which strive to breed out qualities perceived as inferior in the human race, preferably by sterilizing people who possess those undesirable qualities (e.g., the "feeble-minded" or the criminally inclined). Ultimately, though, they support the notion that pure races are better than mixed races.

Of course, this is where the heuristic of race breaks down; race as a concept seems deeply rooted in its distinct boundaries. Mixed races might not weaken the gene pool, but they certainly weaken the utility of racial categories. Culture, on the other hand, seems to be more fluid, as it already has within it hierarchical organization (subcultures and sub-subcultures) and an expectation of some sharing, if only at the geographical boundaries. It certainly feels easier for me to have a complex relationship with my identification with Japanese culture than with my identification with the Asian race, in part because it feels like a vague, falsely reified construct whose rigidity does not allow for my sense of self. And these days it seems like biculturality in general is more appreciated in this country; for example, in nearby Evanston, Illinois, the elementary and middle school district has a program known as Two-Way Immersion, or TWI (pronounced "twee"). This program teaches bilingually in English and Spanish, working to develop bilingual proficiency in both native English and native Spanish speakers; native Spanish speakers are automatically included, and native English speakers apply to be included. My children attend a Spanish immersion preschool in Evanston; not surprisingly, many families who speak Spanish at home drive some distance in order for their children to be able to attend. More surprising, perhaps, are the Caucasian, American mothers who have enrolled their children in the preschool to give them a better chance of being accepted into TWI. These white, English-speaking mothers I spoke to had applied to the program and waited in agony to hear whether their children would be accepted into TWI. If language is a stand-in for culture, then being bicultural is not only acceptable but desirable. The mothers gossiped about who among their neighbors had children accepted into TWI, and what everyone's chances were based on neighborhood of residence and level of experience or fluency in Spanish. Perhaps the growing recognition of bi- and multiculturality is a reflection of growing pride and admiration for people who can move into and out of different cultural universes, in our increasingly globally connected society. Of course, that admiration of TWI is from the parents' perspective; when I spoke to a child in the program, he reported that the general education grade-school kids think the TWI kids are bad at sports and probably need to be bilingual to get a good job because they come from poor families and wouldn't be able to otherwise. Perhaps the underlying bias against mixed culture and mixed race is not so far gone after all.

As a parent, then, the value of the bicultural piece is growing, but the best course for my children is still not clear. How much raceness and ethnicness should I claim for my children as I fill out their school paperwork? As I described above, my husband is of entirely Mexican descent, but he does not speak Spanish. He "passes," much to his chagrin, as this entails having to stop people from making racist comments around him. Is it really fair to claim that my children are Hispanic? Does cooking tamales and homemade tortillas really suffice? My children would not fit in if they were suddenly dropped in Mexico, and yet I did not fit in when living in Japan, even having been born there. But surely cooking *daikon-nabe* and *yuudofu* doesn't really suffice, either. The tension is around all the assumptions built into asking me (the parent) what race my children are. The researcher in me comes out once again: Why are you asking about race in this way? What will it actually tell you? As an adult, a clinical social worker by profession, having a multicultural-sounding name like Noriko Ishibashi Martinez allows me to lay claim to diversity in a way that is probably beneficial (I don't have to prove that I am not racist in the way that a white American might have to), but often I am less ethnic (whatever that means) than people expected prior to meeting me. I end up in some ambiguous space where I'm ethnic but not ethnic enough. That was, in fact, a comment I received from a white woman when I was asking about minority fellowships: "Are you ethnic enough to apply for those?"

This is the complexity of the interplay between race and culture, because factually (to the extent that we take race to be purely a result of blood relations) I am descended from two races. My children are also descended from two races, plus one "ethnicity" (since Latino is usually categorized as an ethnicity rather than a race). But how many cultures do I contain, how many cultures do my children contain, and how does that map onto our racial and ethnic heritage? As a parent, do I want my children to capitalize on their diversity, or does that somehow diminish what it means to be a minority? As a social worker, do I want to claim automatic cultural competence based on my own mixed background, or does that diminish the complexity of what people are striving for when they talk about cultural competence?

The change in stance toward mixed races is overdue, given that it has been over forty years since *Loving v. Virginia*. Families handle the one-drop rule in their own ways. Roth (2005), drawing on the work of Rockquemore and Brunsma (2002), lists five possible identities for biracial black/white people (note that the human propensity for creating categories never ends): *black singular identity*, which is the one that would be assumed under the one-drop rule; *white singular identity*, which is also sometimes referred to as "passing"; *border identity*, where the person identifies as a unique blend of both races; *protean identity*, where the person shifts racial identities according to the situation; and *transcendent identity*, where the person does not identify with any race. It's tempting to place myself cleanly in one of those categories (substituting Japanese or Asian for black), but I partake of each, when it suits my mood and the occasion: there are still times when I don't really think in terms of race, and then I suppose I am enacting a transcendent identity. I would often argue, though, that since I don't fit squarely in either race, I am some other, border category. This might be a reflection of resistance to being categorized or simplified, or resistance to accepting all the assumptions that go along with singular identities. The border identity is the one that allows me to bond with other biracial people, regardless of whether it is the same two races that we share, as when a friend of mine had a biracial/multiracial party, just for "people like us." It's interesting how defining an exclusive group in that way can be so comforting: we may be excluded from either race, but all those one-race people are excluded from our group! The protean identity doesn't quite capture the movement across transcendent and border identities. Of course, Roth explains that people do not always fit neatly into one category.

Roth (2005) goes on to examine how parents identify their biracial children. Interestingly, of the families who are mixed white and Asian, in the 2000 U.S. Census (as mentioned previously, the first year that people could mark more than one racial category), 54.7 percent of the households identified the children as an exact combination of the parents' races, which she argues is a reflection of the border identity, assuming that the transcendent or protean identities would be reflected by marking "other" (which 4.4 percent of those households did). Since starting this inquiry, I asked my mother what she would have done. She said she would have marked me as "other." As a white American woman who moved to Japan, and had her own difficult-to-categorize cultural background as a result of moving around the world to different naval bases as a child (evidence of formative years in the Philippines certainly remains), I think she embodied the optimism of the civil rights era: soon (she thought), we will be living in a postracial society. Interestingly, that same optimism surged when the United States finally elected its first nonwhite president: now that Barack Obama has been elected to the highest office, the United States will move into an era where race is no longer relevant. As a parent, I relate to the position my mother held: Are my children really a different race from what I am? Is it possible that we are fundamentally different in some deterministic way? Yet, from discussions with my brother, two years older, he dealt with significantly more hostile, overt racism when we moved to this country than I did. Perhaps my children would suffer the consequences of my idealism if I socialized them to think that race and ethnicity are no longer relevant, given that social constructions and interactions around race and ethnicity might not change as quickly as I would like. I know my mother wonders whether she could have better prepared my brother for that by talking explicitly about race and racism.

DIMENSIONS OF RACENESS AND CULTURE

I like to imagine that there is growing awareness of the value of racial *and* cultural diversity. After all, the very idea of cultural competence, so prominent in social work, evokes a kind of learned multicultural/multiracial status. Having a biracial president helps, too. So perhaps the United States is moving toward a point where people categorized as biracial would want to identify themselves—and be allowed to identify themselves—as biracial. The problem is that this continues to represent race as a static, categorical understanding of people's experience. There are more options for which box to check, but you still have to check a box; this is often the case for identifying a client's culture in order to be culturally competent as well. In this conceptualization of race, it is still considered a static trait. Perhaps it would be better viewed as an aspect of identity that is enacted to varying degrees depending on internal and external factors. When I am with Japanese friends, my Japaneseness comes out much more. I suspect that I would make different kinds of decisions in those moments from those I would make when I am with my white American friends, who bring out a very different part of my identity. I notice it most in terms of how I orient toward people outside of the group I am with, and it manifests itself in relatively stereotypical ways: I am more considerate and circumspect toward strangers when I am being more "Japanese," and I am more gregarious or simply ignore others when I am being more "American." The key is that the extent to which I experience my Japaneseness in those different moments varies significantly, and I simply cannot agree that I am being truer to myself in one situation than in the other. In both situations, who I am is emergent out of the context and the relationship. This insight leads me to wonder about the influence of cultural competence as a relational orientation. It seems that sometimes it is harmful, evoking stereotypical behavior, rather than beneficial, and the trick, perhaps, is to identify when that will happen.

Claude Steele's work on stereotype threat was telling to me in regard to race enactment. What Steele and his colleagues, Joshua Aronson and Steven Spencer, were trying to understand, was the experience of worrying that others will see oneself through one's race, or worrying that one will act in ways that support the stereotype. Steele (2003) described some of this work, in which they had white and black Stanford University students take a thirty-minute section of the Graduate Records Examination in English literature. It was meant to be challenging for the students. In one condition, researchers mentioned to participants that "the test was a measure of verbal ability" (114). In this condition, the black students performed one full standard deviation lower than the white students. In the other condition, researchers described the test as part of research to "study how certain problems are generally solved"; they emphasized that it was *not* a measure of intellectual ability. In this condition, the black students and white students performed the same. Steele interprets this drop in performance among the black students as being due to their fear of fulfilling a stereotype about African Americans being less intelligent than Caucasian Americans. Steele and his colleagues repeated the same test with white and Asian students using math tests (the white students did worse in the stereotype threat condition); with women and men using math tests (women did worse in the threat condition, though not when they were told there was no gender difference); and with white and black students with golf (when it was described as "natural athletic ability," the white students did worse; when it was described as "sport strategic intelligence," the black students did worse).

Based on these findings, Steele suggests that performance in these situations is not a matter of internalized stigma, but rather a response to conditions where a person feels threatened in relation to a stereotype. Stereotype threat is the same process that a white social worker might go through when she does not want to appear racist (which would fulfill a stereotype about white people). And perhaps my experience of stereotype threat is one area where I can plumb the distinction between my own racial identity and my race as a basis for social interactions. If I believe that others see me as white, then I might feel more tension around trying to prove that I am not racist. When I first began to think in terms of race and racism, since I had not thought of myself in terms of race, I assumed that others would assume I was racist. This is one aspect of stereotype threat that white people supposedly struggle with: they do not want to fulfill a stereotype about white people by appearing to be racist. For me, this experience of stereotype threat was not predicated on my identity as white, but rather my identity as racially anonymous. However, this is the default racial identity that white people may have ("I'm not any race"); essentially, this is an aspect of white privilege, to be able to be unaware of or discount race. My background, which likewise held the privilege of not being aware of race, aligned my experience more closely with whiteness than nonwhiteness. In this way, at least, I was more white than biracial or Asian in what I expected out of social interaction, regardless of what I identified as.

When I was eighteen, I went to Tokyo to visit my father. While walking through a bustling train station, filled with a sea of relatively homogenous faces, suddenly I spotted a black man. We made eye contact. In my recollection, his facial expression was one of pleasant surprise; at the time, I thought he was relieved to see another face that was not so Asian. I was taken aback by my own confusion, though. When I lived in Japan, I didn't notice that there were not really any black people. When I moved to the United States, I didn't notice that there were (it should be noted that I lived in a predominantly white suburb, so it wasn't exactly the most diverse area either). Yet, once again in Japan, my contextually specific expectations of "what people look like" had quickly been enacted, so that I was personally surprised to see someone who was so clearly *not* Japanese! That moment stands out in my memory as one in which I started some self-examination: am I, in fact, racist? I wondered if I should not have been so surprised to see a black man, because I probably would not have been surprised to see a man in a wheelchair, even though that would also have been uncommon. I also wondered whether I made a face that was one of not-so-pleasant surprise, revealing some unconsciously held racism. I plumbed the depths of my initial response to determine whether there were other associated feelings, stereotyping thoughts that were lurking below my full awareness. That was the beginning of my dance with stereotype threat, in which I wanted to assure myself that I did not come across as racist to others. Here cultural competence can be a security blanket: "Because I value cultural competence and strive toward it, I am not like the stereotype." And certainly one stereotype of social workers is that of a well-meaning, middle-class white woman who is nonetheless paternalistic and supports the status quo.

There are two other components of Steele's (2003) discussion of the research that are particularly intriguing. First, when given eighty word fragments, of which twelve could be filled out to be words related to stereotypes about African American intellectual ability, African American students in the threat condition completed more of the words to be stereotype-related than when they were in the nonthreat condition (and more than Caucasian students in either case). This suggest that race and racism, as heuristics, were more available or salient in their minds. In other words, the extent to which a person interprets a situation in terms of race or racism is just as context-dependent as anything else. As with all the schemas we use to organize our experiences, it makes sense that the availability of the race/racism heuristic will be especially important in interpreting ambiguous situations. Yet it was only in the utterly unambiguous racial situation of seeing the unexpected black man in the Japanese subway that the heuristic was created for me at all; it was the emotional salience of confronting myself about my own racism that made the heuristic stick.

The second intriguing component that Steele describes pertains to asking students to state preferences regarding some things associated with African American culture and some not (examples Steele gives of the former are basketball, jazz, and hip-hop; of the latter, tennis, swimming, and classical music). In the threat condition, African American students reported less interest in the things associated with African American culture; in the nonthreat condition, they reported a strong preference for those same things. This finding is a little bit trickier: is this an attempt to seem less of a racial stereotype, in a direct bid to counteract the stereotype threat? Or is this a reflection of some level of disownership of a racial identity? This distinction might seem minor, but it gets at the heart of the nature of racial identity. As someone who has gradually learned about utilizing race as a way to understand myself and my behavior, there are times when I have to consider the extent to which it has infiltrated my ways of being. When I am not acting out of my Asianness, for example, I could be attempting to avoid seeming Asian, I could be disowning my Asianness, or perhaps I am simply returning to that space in my mind where race is not a factor. And perhaps my continuing interest in race, ethnicity, and culture is based on that unresolved, and unresolvable, question. When I struggle with cultural competence, though, it seems important to know whether I am disregarding the importance of race because I am being insensitive to it, or whether I am moving beyond it to recognize the richness of experience that is not solely determined by race. In the context of the United States, where there is such a long-standing history of racism and discrimination, this gets back to the question of whether we should notice and respond to race. I suspect that it is likewise an unresolvable question, and the answer will always be maintaining some kind of dialectical balance between the two.

So when I am expressing my own race as Asian or biracial, it might be in part due to stereotype threat, because enacting my minority status is a way to distance myself from the stereotype of white people as racist. That seems to reflect intention on my part; on the other hand, it could also be that the context creates me, without my active intention. I find myself enacting and interpreting race differentially by context. I don't really know how to bow unless I am with a bunch of Japanese people, and then I find myself bowing without thinking about it. It doesn't feel like an intentional enactment of a particular self. This is more of a cultural artifact than a racial one, but here once again race and culture intertwine. On the other hand, it does not have to be solely racial or cultural identity that can come to the fore. Gender identity, religious identity, generational identity, national identity; all aspects of identity might be fluid and dimensional, so that any action or experience can be understood to reflect any aspect to varying degrees. More important, the person may *feel* a particular identity more or less strongly in any situation. In social work the goal of cultural competence requires one to then ask: can a person learn to act in the way that is appropriate according to the impression one wants to make? If you know how to act in a way that makes a client aware that you are trying to make him or her comfortable, that may be enough; that is different, though, from acting in a way that actually *makes* the client comfortable. Learning to bow appropriately would be a reflection of cultural competence, perhaps, but would not make anyone think that a white person is actually Japanese.

Based on those distinctions, I would argue that there are three distinct purposes of cultural competence: the first is about the signal that you make by putting in the effort: "I want to know you on your terms as best I can; I respect you and your perspective and I will demonstrate it with actual effort." This version of cultural competence requires continuous work but seems to have the potential to be able to transcend static interpretations of others and their identifications. It is a communication based on process and thus is continually developed.

The second is to actually make others more comfortable, or to blend in, by becoming thoroughly fluent in another culture. This requires deep knowledge of the culture, deep experience, and seems to be the aim of cultural competence as it is often discussed; it also seems like it can veer toward rigidity or complacence, as in "I'm Japanese so I know how to act around Japanese people." Or, as a student was telling me about recently, that you might be able to get a certificate indicating achievement of cultural competence. It can also be unnecessarily limiting because it makes it so that you can never "truly" connect with someone who is of a different culture. This version of cultural competence is based on content, which is what leads to the possibility for rigidity.

The third purpose is the one that people also seem to strive for, possibly in place of the second; it is the desire to appear culturally competent because it is valued per se, not as a tool for the work it is meant to support. This is a more self-serving purpose and seems to be only peripherally about the client. It is the self-congratulatory version of cultural competence, and I think anyone is susceptible to it. If I am meeting with a client and I am satisfied that I am culturally competent, then I have to check myself: am I satisfying my own feelings of wanting to be culturally competent, or have I actually reached across to demonstrate as best I can that I am trying to know this client on his or her own terms? I was talking with a clinical supervisor, a white woman, and tangentially mentioned my race; her eagerness to delve into the meaning of my race, her race, and our race relations felt like a diversion, unrelated to the main issue I had been trying to discuss. It felt more like she was trying to prove her cultural competence than to actually *be* culturally competent.

If we look across cultures, the concept of self is widely variable; in comparing the Western conceptualization of self with Buddhist and Confucian conceptualizations, Giordano (2011) gives examples of selfhood that are entirely contextually dependent or an illusion, emergent out of context. The notion that we are each independent, rational beings with a stable core that is continuous and separate from other people is a culturally constrained idea that makes it more difficult to understand that race itself is truly a *social construct*, meaning that it is constructed anew in every single social interaction, and thereby can be different in every single social interaction. When I was learning the racial categories as practiced in the United States, first I had to learn the categories; over time, each emergent self had to acquire a raceness that was appropriate for the cultural context. To put it another way, for each emergent self, the American context required that race be defined as a characteristic of self. I struggled with how much I identified with any of my racial identity options and how much I expressed any of those identities.

Looking back, I can reinterpret earlier experiences in the light of race and suddenly see them quite differently. In my senior year of high school, I was in a class that involved working with a partner for the entire school year. I ended up partnered with the Korean American girl, although I don't remember how that happened; I'm fairly certain that we somehow chose each other, rather than being assigned together. We were acquaintances previously, but how did we end up together, the only two Asian girls in the class? Did she think we were the same race? Did the other, mostly white, students think we were? To me she was clearly American, not an immigrant like I thought of myself (to the extent that I was an immigrant). She had been born and raised in the United States and just seemed very American to me. Also, I would never have lumped Korean and Japanese together as being the same in any regard, because in terms of nationality (still my preferred method of categorization at the time), we couldn't be more different. Did she make bids for racial connectedness, based on a different sense of what race meant? How strongly did she feel her race when she was with me? Looking back, if I had already developed the race aspect of the self that emerged in that interaction, I might have understood her behaviors differently. As it is, behaviors that could be interpreted as race-based simply were not encoded in my memory.

When acquaintances were pressuring me to date the one African American boy in the school, was it because we were both minorities? It never occurred to me at the time. And they never said anything about race, simply insisting that "he likes you!" Perhaps he did, but their enthusiasm for this particular pairing seemed out of proportion. In my last year of high school, I had many people ask me if I had a younger sister in the freshman class. I did not, but she was biracial, and this is perhaps a microcosm of the problem with racial categorization: we conflate levels of generalization. I didn't think we looked anything alike, but the other people thought we did. From what I could tell, she had some with Asian heritage, which others perceived as a family resemblance. The salience of race as a way to perceive other people overwhelmed any differences between her and me.

RACIAL AND ETHNIC SOCIALIZATION

Roth (2005) explains that the most significant contributor to the racial identity development of children of black interracial couples is the way that parents socialize their children into their race. When they see their children as black and their job as parents to help the children develop black identities, the children grow up to have black singular identities. When they don't see their children as any race, and they try to help their children develop universal human values, then the children grow up to have transcendent identities. Based on a review of the literature, Hughes and her colleagues (2006) describe multiple possible methods for what they term ethnic-racial socialization: cultural socialization, or the promotion of cultural knowledge and pride; preparation for bias; promotion of mistrust, specifically in regards to interracial interactions; egalitarianism, or valuing individual qualities over group memberships; and silence about race, which they describe as less frequently studied, and yet clearly as powerful a communication about race as the other, more explicit strategies. Hughes and her colleagues lay out these components of ethnic-racial socialization as a way to promote more accurate and consistent research into its role in human development. The idea is that parents can, depending on the context, utilize any one of those strategies to varying degrees. Based on my experience, I would conjecture that a person's experienced racial identity will reflect the ethnic-racial socialization strategy that her or his parents tended to utilize in similar contexts. When I am in contexts that evoke prior experience of Japaneseness by virtue of my father's socialization, I experience that corresponding identity. In places clearly demarcated as Japanese (restaurants, the Japanese Buddhist temple in Chicago), I feel my Japaneseness more clearly. In what appears to be fairly standard for Asian cultures, my father never had much to say by way of parental wisdom about race or racism, so I perhaps in those Japanese-ish places I feel inclined not to feel my race; however, I certainly invoke the culture, for example, in my heightened awareness of not wanting to be a nuisance to anyone else. In Japan I attended international schools, where most of the children were migratory in some sense, and there was little attention paid to race or ethnic origin; that would explain why I tend not to feel my racial identity with any particular strength when I am in an educational setting. As a student or a lecturer, I feel less of any particular race and am more likely to assume some transcendent posture and see others in the same way. In one confusing instance, I was working in a small group in a linguistics class with a man who was from Hawaii and spoke Japanese: when he first called me by name, he pronounced it exactly as my father would have. Internally I was completely destabilized, as I muddled through how I should act toward that classmate who insisted on invoking my Japaneseness. I think I probably avoided him the rest of the term. So I am not any less susceptible to uncertainty around how to act than the customers at the restaurant who asked me, their waiter, my race. But again, I could reinterpret some of my experiences by applying the racial lens, if I wanted to. When I rethink my experiences from a racial perspective, is it a more accurate reflection of reality? Not really: the racially tinged and nonracially tinged perspective are equally valid interpretations, both of which can enrich my understanding of a situation. If the goal of cultural competence is to apply a particular lens in the interpretation of experience, then it is necessarily limiting in its scope because it is rigid; if the goal is to open up space for consideration of the individually determined importance of race and assess the role that race and racial identity play for an individual client, then there is more space for a flexible and nuanced understanding.

THE PROBLEM OF CULTURAL COMPETENCE

The woman, now in college, decides to study anthropology and language. Race, culture, ethnicity: the pieces still feel strange and interesting to her, even with over eight years of learning the American way, in part because so many things seem to be taken for granted or assumed when others talk about them. To her it seems obvious that you cannot simply translate a Japanese phrase into English, or vice versa, without losing meaning or else having to explain the full contextualized sense of what each word means.

And yet her linguistics class spends whole sessions talking about signifiers and concatenation, and how each word contains implied within it all the words it can connect to and is associated with, so that words are not always equivalent across languages.

"So you can't really ever translate the meaning of a word from one language to another?" she asks a professor.

"I suppose you could argue that, but that doesn't get you anywhere," he replies.

•   •   •

As a clinical social worker who works in practice and education, I can see the importance of and the value placed on cultural competence, but it is difficult to define exactly what cultural competence is, or whether it is attainable. It seems impossible that we could translate human experience across cultural divides, given that every word and every construct is culturally distinct; yet we cannot give up the endeavor as hopeless and stop trying to connect with others. Still, the depth of the possibility of difference cannot be dismissed either, as my professor did so many years ago. Some definitions of cultural competence are about functionality, as in having certain culture-related skills and knowledge (see Dana, Behn, and Gonwa 1992; Schultz 2004); some are about intentionality, as in avoiding prejudice and increasing awareness (see NASW 2008). As I mentioned above, it can be about knowing, doing, or simply appearing to know and do to meet requirements.

In my own coursework for a master's degree in social work, cultural competence boiled down to reading a textbook that described how to work with African Americans, Muslim Americans, Asian Americans, and so forth; I found that somewhat disheartening, and I had a difficult time reading the text. When I was designing a course on cross-cultural clinical work, it was difficult to find any textbooks that took a different approach. This chapter-by-chapter background information about various racial and cultural groupings may be the basic cognitive knowledge necessary for clinical practice. It is a way to help practitioners decenter from their own cultural practices and recognize the broad range of normal human behavior, and then again at an advanced level, when practitioners are aware of the complexities around the ways in which any individual within a group can partake of or identify with the norms of that group. By itself, though, it can be dangerously simplistic. It promotes the idea that we can, in fact, understand another person's experience solely through the lens of race or culture; in other words, it can be misused in the service of racism. This is the level of knowledge that can be distancing, as when my Japanese step-mother asked me, "So all Americans eat turkey on Thanksgiving, huh?" It sounds like a harmless question, but in the moment it made her seem very Japanese and made me feel very American. In other words, it heightened rather than reduced our ability to bridge a cultural divide, and that level of "cultural competence" can achieve the same results in clinical social work. Likewise, when I read about Asians or Japanese Americans in those text-books, it's more likely for me to think, "Oh, is that what I'm supposed to be like?" than "Yes, that's me!"

This is not news. This is the underlying conundrum in any attempt to address racism: how can we teach about race and remediate racial dispari-ties without noticing race, and yet when we underscore the importance of race, are we not further reifying it and ultimately contributing to racism? Asian could be referring to a geographic area or to a race, what used to be known as "Mongoloid." I have had arguments with other "Asians" about whether Asian should include Russians, which geographically, of course, it does, but many seem to imagine Russians to be more European than Asian; we have also argued about whether perhaps Oriental is a better term to refer to East Asians, though the stores that sell "orientals" (rugs) make that a bit problematic; and of course most Asians prefer to be called by their specific nation rather than a general term that covers all of them. When I was analyzing a particular set of data and looking through the race/ethnicity question, I noticed that some people marked "other" and wrote in "Indian." I am fairly certain these were people who did not feel that "Asian" included South Asia and preferred to have a more specific label. I am also fairly certain that there were more people who were from India than the few who marked "other," and I assume they marked "Asian." What mean-ing does Asian have as a racial category when it is mixed up so thoroughly with culture, nationality, and geography? Personally I often have difficulty marking Asian, since I'm not really fully Asian, neither racially nor cultur-ally, but I certainly don't want to deny my heritage. Marking white never seems right either. When I can check more than one, I check both, but I prefer to leave those questions blank. Which, in essence, drops me from statistical analysis, and so the people who orient toward race in the way that I do are simply never counted.

And yet people do have commonalities of experience based on various shared identities. Dean (2001) eloquently described a more fluid concept of cultural competence:

> If we believe that culture is a moveable feast and ever evolving, then understanding and self-understanding are, in Gadamer's terms, "always on the way" (1989:102). In that sense, our knowledge is always partial and we are always operating from a position of incompletion or lack of competence. Our goal is not so much to achieve competence but to participate in the ongoing processes of seeking understanding and building relationships. This understanding needs to be directed toward ourselves and not just our clients. (628)

Dean is talking about culture more generally, but to the extent that racial identity is constantly in flux and enacted in similar ways to culture, then Dean's statement can apply to race as well. Even within myself, I can feel that my racial identity is not fixed, and frankly my own knowledge of Japan and Asianness is incomplete; even my own knowledge of where I fall in relation to that racial aspect of myself (in any particular situation) is also incomplete. I am still developing the racial aspects of my selves. The problem is not the categorization, but the assumptions that follow the categorization: (1) that a person has a static experience of self in relation to that categorization; (2) that generalizations about the category can say anything about any individual within that category (what's known as the ecological fallacy); (3) that the category is *real*, rather than a heuristic that necessarily simplifies the rich complexity of human experience. My experience as I've described it does not fit with those assumptions, and I maintain that I am not a fringe or unique case in that regard.

When I am working with children in my private practice, there seems to be so much that is simply about two people being together, even with the cultural baggage of parenting traditions lurking in the background. I try to imagine, as a parent, whether I would prefer someone who took pride in "cultural competence." I have certainly had the experience of talking with white people who seemed overeager to discuss race and culture and seemed to care much more about it than I did, again demonstrating that stereotype threat behavior and the desire to prove nonracism. And yet when choosing our first family physician, as we whittled down our list, the final deciding factor was "someone who is not a white man."

Yes, we reverse-discriminated, because we wanted our children to see, from birth, people of color and women in positions of authority, so that it would be something taken for granted and not at all noteworthy. As a social worker, I feel some sympathy for the culturally competent, white, male doctor who never had a chance with us. There are aspects of who we are as clinicians that will always be what they are, and there are some clients who will not be able to connect with us, regardless of how culturally competent we are.

As a person whose race is not immediately clear to most, I often find clients struggling with how to identify with my race; that struggle itself becomes a space for us to consider and discuss issues of race and identity in the context of our relationship. For a while I worked in a program with many African American kids, and their responses to me would range from, "Well, you're white, so, you wouldn't know," to, in response to something I had said, "Aha! I knew you had a little black in you." They were enacting their race in different ways through their perception of what their race meant in relation to mine. In one happy instance, a young African American man simply said to me, "Are you racist?" Excellent, I thought to myself. Let's roll up our proverbial sleeves and get right in there.

CONCLUSION

Now, older and wiser, I think back to my frustrations with being asked, "What are you?" To me, racial identification is contextual, in that it emerges out of a specific place and moment; it is dynamic and multidimensional, in that it is constantly shifting across infinite gradations; it is both personal and social, in that it carries the weight and investment of being an aspect of self identity and yet contains within it a sense of shared, social identity; and it is larger than an individual in its scope and yet less than an individual in its ability to define a person. And part of the frustration of that question was not really about race but had more to do with the context: as people being waited on, my customers often seemed to have a paternalistic manner toward me, giving them the right to pry into personal matters and dispense advice and guidance to me. Other common topics of conversation included where I was in school and what I was studying; what was my plan for the future; and with a personality like mine, I should be a [insert profession here]. Even the convention that the customer should know the waiter's name without any indication that the waiter should know the customer's name felt, at the time, like an expression of imbalance and power in the relationship. The customer can pry and know anything he or she wants about me, but I must respect the customer's privacy. The parallel in social work is fairly obvious: the clinical relationship can have a similar imbalance and can likewise tilt toward a paternalistic interaction where the social worker gets to know everything about the client and pry into every aspect of the client's life, while supposedly maintaining professional boundaries by limiting self-disclosure. We can hide behind our status, our clinical aloofness, and perhaps even our cultural competence. Maybe the goal of cultural competence is simply to avoid creating the feeling in the client that I felt from my customers when I was a waiter: that of being a specimen with no status as a human being deserving of respect.

There seem to be some who would argue that we should eliminate racial categorization altogether. I disagree, for several reasons: first, to eliminate the use of racial categories would simply propagate the status quo. Unless we notice that people are, in fact, being treated differently according to their race, we will never be able to do anything about it. Intervention research, for example, often seems to be conducted with primarily Caucasian participants; when the research does not report the racial makeup of its sample, then we can pretend that research generalizes to all people, when in fact it may not. Furthermore, for some people, race has been defining of their experience in fundamental ways. To deny them their right to claim and own a significant portion of their identity is problematic.

Second, it is impractical. As human beings, we will always find ways to group other people. The very nature of language requires that we categorize objects together, so that we can see a tree we have never seen before and still be able to call it a tree. Of course, the problem is that then we assume that tree will be like all the other trees we have ever known, but that danger inheres in language itself. We need labels, which is just another word for "words," but they can limit our understanding and necessarily fall short of the rich detail of reality (which is particularly relevant in clinical work; see Ishibashi 2005).

Third, eliminating racial categories would eliminate the rich strengths and connections that come out of having a sense of shared identity. I enjoy connecting with my Japanese heritage, and having a special shared connection with another person around the joy of eating *yakiimo*, literally juggling a hot potato. While the ugly side of that is the exclusion of people who do not share that identity, the beautiful side has inspired all manner of creative and joyful expression.

We benefit from racial categories, so the trick is to alter our stance toward them so that we can partake of their benefits without getting stuck in the mire of racism (assuming people can be understood by their race alone). Race is simply one aspect of how we in the United States constitute people, and it means something different to each person. We have to do the arduous work of maintaining flexibility in our understanding of how a race is being enacted in any social situation. When we are working toward cultural competence, all the while aware that we can never be fully competent in anyone's culture (Dean 2001), we are constantly challenging our own automatic categorical thinking and allowing our clients to be fluid in their definition of who they are (and who we are).

Ultimately racial identity is only one aspect of our multiple selfhood, and it varies from self to self in the same way that many of our characteristics vary from self to self. Right now, when I interact with another person, am I acting based on my identity as Japanese, white, or biracial? As an immigrant or an American? As a mother, a woman, a clinical social worker, a child psychotherapist? As a teacher, a writer, a researcher? I carry all these identities with me, and to imagine that one of them determines my actions in any one moment belies the fact that I have a whole range of cards in my hands that I could play. What am I? Now, I know the answer depends: Where am I? Who are you? What are we doing together, and why? Out of all my identities emerges the me that I am with you right now. It may pull from my race; it may not. And that is why relationships are so powerful: they allow us to define ourselves.

NOTE

1   In the Spanish colonies there was a much more explicit set of terms for multiracial people: there were sixteen possible mixed-race labels, ranked in status from mestizo (Spaniard father and Indian mother) down to ahi te estás (Coyote mestizo father and mulatto mother). For a fascinating look at the one-drop rule and definitions of race, see Davis (1991).

REFERENCES

Arredondo, P., and R. Toporek. 2004. "Multicultural Counseling Competencies = Ethical Practice." *Journal of Mental Health Counseling* 26 (1): 44–55.

Bridge, T. J., E. G. Massie, and C. S. Mills. 2008. "Prioritizing Cultural Competence in the Implementation of an Evidence-Based Practice Model." *Children and Youth Services Review* 30:1111–18.

Dana, R. H., J. D. Behn, and T. Gonwa. 1992. "A Checklist for the Examination of Cultural Competence in Social Service Agencies." *Research on Social Work Practice* 2 (2): 220–33.

Davis, F. J. 1991. *Who Is Black? One Nation's Definition.* University Park: Pennsylvania State University Press.

Dean, R. G. 2001. "The Myth of Cross-cultural Competence." *Families in Society: The Journal of Contemporary Human Services* 82 (6): 623–30.

Galanes, P. 2011. "Social Q's: What's Race Got to Do with It?" May 26. http://www.nytimes.com/2011/05/29/fashion/questions-about-social-situations.html?scp=5&sq=social%20q's&st=cse.

Giordano, P. J. 2011. "Culture and Theories of Personality: Western, Confucian, and Buddhist Perspectives." In *Cross-cultural Psychology: Contemporary Themes and Perspectives*, edited by K. D. Keith, 423–44. West Sussex: Wiley-Blackwell.

Gould, S. J. 1996. *The Mismeasure of Man.* Revised and expanded. New York: Norton.

Hernstein, R., and C. Murray. 1994. *The Bell Curve: Intelligence and Class Structure in American Life.* New York: Free Press.

Hickman, C. B. 1997. "The Devil and the One Drop Rule: Racial Categories, African Americans, and the U.S. Census." *Michigan Law Review* 95 (5): 1161–1265.

Hollinger, D. A. 2005. "The One Drop Rule & the One Hate Rule." *Daedalus* 134 (1): 18–28. http://www.jstor.org/stable/20027957.

Hughes, D., J. Rodriguez, E. P. Smith, D. J. Johnson, H. C. Stevenson, and P. Spicer. 2006. "Parents' Ethnic-Racial Socialization Practices: A Review and Directions for Future Study." *Developmental Psychology* 42 (5): 747–70. DOI: 10.1037/0012-1649.42.5.747.

Ishibashi, N. 2005. "Barrier or Bridge? The Language of Diagnosis in Clinical Social Work." *Smith College Studies in Social Work* 75 (1): 65–80.

Mesquita, B., and R. Walker. 2003. "Cultural Differences in Emotions: A Context for Interpreting Emotional Experiences." *Behavior Research and Therapy* 41:777–93.

NASW. 2008. *Code of Ethics of the National Association of Social Workers*. http://www.socialworkers.org/pubs/code/code.asp.

Rockquemore, K. A., and D. L. Brunsma. 2002. *Beyond Black: Biracial Identity in America*. Thousand Oaks, Calif.: Sage.

Roth, W. D. 2005. "The End of the One-Drop Rule? Labeling of Multiracial Children in Black Intermarriages." *Sociological Forum* 20 (10): 35–33. DOI: 10.1007/s11206-005-1897-0.

Schultz, D. 2004. "Cultural Competence in Psychosocial and Psychiatric Care: A Critical Perspective with Reference to Research and Clinical Experiences in California, US, and in Germany." *Social Work in Health Care* 39 (3/4): 231–47.

Sohoni, D. 2007. "Unsuitable Suitors: Anti-Miscegenation Laws, Naturalization Laws, and the Construction of Asian Identities." *Law & Society Review* 41 (3): 587–618.

Steele, C. 2003. "Stereotype Threat and African American Achievement." In *Young, Gifted, and Black: Promoting High Achievement Among African American Students*, edited by T. Perry, C. Steele, and A. G. Hilliard III, 109–30. Boston: Beacon Press.

U.S. Census Bureau. n.d. *Major Differences in Subject-Matter Content Between the 1990 and 2000 Census Questionnaires*. http://www.census.gov/population/www/cen2000/90vs00/index.html.

CHAPTER 5

Learning From and Researching (My Own) Experience

A CRITICAL REFLECTION ON THE EXPERIENCE OF SOCIAL DIFFERENCE

▸ *JAN FOOK*

WHEN I FIRST SAT DOWN to write this chapter, I struggled with the difference between writing an autoethnography and writing a critical reflection on my experience. I finally reasoned that focusing on the connections between personal experience and social context, which is an integral part of autoethnography (Chang 2008), is also integral to my own approach to critical reflection. This is explicitly based on a critical analysis of the person in social, cultural, and political contexts (Fook and Gardner 2007). I am aware that not all understandings of critical reflection take this view (Fook, White, and Gardner 2006), but it is the one I explicitly adopt for our purposes here. Neither, of course, does such an approach necessarily produce a work that looks like a conventional autoethnography, which might typically include a good deal of personal experience and emotive content. However, conducting an autoethnography using a critical reflection framework is an important choice for me. First, it allows me to illustrate more directly the research element of a type of autoethnography. Second, and perhaps more important, such an approach feels congruent with my own biography, and how I see myself both personally and professionally. I have therefore deliberately chosen to adopt a critical reflection framework as a vehicle for my autoethnography.

What is it about my biography that leads me to this choice? I am a later-generation, Australian-born Chinese woman, raised in a "white" Australia in the mid-twentieth century, from a lower-middle-class background.

Academic skills came relatively naturally to me, both personally and cultur-ally, but carving out an academic career in the 1970s for someone of my back-ground, even in a female profession like social work, did not. In some ways my career has involved a constant struggle with dominant cultures: white male–dominated academia; positivist-dominated social work research; and theory-dominated teaching cultures. Even as an Australian, I felt marginal on the international scene. Luckily analysis and intellect were valued in my home culture, and they also proved useful strategies for being accepted into mainstream academic society. My social marginality also taught me the importance of understanding and using the whole person and their experi-ence in professional work, rather than seeking to make everyone conform to an unstated mainstream ideal. Critical reflection, with its incorporation of solid analysis of all aspects of experience, provides a meaningful framework for me to combine the learning from the experiences of my own background with the analytical skills I cherish. I firmly believe that the approach I have developed works as a method for unearthing, celebrating, and rework-ing aspects of experience and personhood that have been easily devalued, denied, or dismissed in dominant professional cultures.

This account may therefore appear too intellectual, with minimal per-sonal descriptive detail. This is intentionally so. The approach is induc-tive, in that it starts with a very small, often banal example of experience and delves into this to find the richness of meaning and connections with other experiences. What is therefore privileged is the reflections on these experiences for what they say about the broader experience of identity and meaning making in social context. The actual stories or descriptions of experiences fade into the background—they act simply as peepholes into a bigger world. What I hope comes to the foreground is a reflective analysis of how I have made meaning of my own life from both the posi-tion and experience of social difference—in fact, from a marginal social background. I have written this chapter as I believe befits who I am, both socially and emotionally. I write this paragraph now with the benefit of several stages of feedback from valued colleagues. Their feedback has been informative, as it has clarified for me how the chapter I have constructed is very much an artifact of who I believe I am, as a specific person, culturally, socially, and professionally.

My chapter, then, is a critical reflection on my experience, which also functions as a type of autoethnography, and a broader researching of my own experience using my own approach to critical reflection. (I will say more later about the specific theories involved). I illustrate my approach to critical reflection, how I have used it to research myself and (learn from) my own experience, and in so doing show how more than just the connections between personal experience and social contexts are analyzed and used. In the process I hope to convey how critical reflection has taken on a larger meaning for me. In the same way it provides a vehicle for many professional practitioners to make meaning of their experiences, it has allowed me to make meaning (and good use) of my own personal experiences and identity in professional context. Working with critical reflection has enabled me to find a professional mission that integrates my background, values, and capacities. This in turn provides a direction that endows a deep personal and professional satisfaction and sense of contribution, which I hope will sustain me until the end of my career.

A RECURRING EXPERIENCE

I begin the reflection by recounting a simple experience of mine that recurs fairly frequently in many of the different professional contexts in which I've worked.

One of the things that happen frequently in my professional life is that I find myself in a meeting. In this meeting may be several executive and senior-level managers, as well as people of my own rank. The meeting may be a planned meeting for the purposes of drafting a strategic plan. I usually look forward to such meetings with a sense of positive anticipation that important issues will be discussed, and important decisions will be made. I am hopeful that I will emerge with a renewed sense of vision.

What tends to happen is that some important issues may be mentioned, but not much discussion ensues, and it is not even clear to me when (or even that) decisions are being made. I end up not participating very much, as I cannot follow what is happening. I tend to assume that everyone else knows what is going on; it's just me who doesn't. I usually leave the meeting frustrated that a strategic plan has not been developed, and annoyed at the apparent waste of time and my own lack of voice.

This is a story I often tell when I am modeling critical reflection in workshops I conduct with practicing professionals. The specific times and settings may vary, but I have had similar experiences in the many different positions I have held since the beginning of my career.

The story represents a critical incident for me. I relate it now because when I critically reflect on it, I realize that it encapsulates much that is about me, and who I am personally, socially, and professionally. It will therefore provide perfect raw material for researching myself, for the type of autoethnography included in this book, and for illuminating the connections between myself as an individual and my social context.

I also relate it in my workshops, as it is a pertinent example of a critical incident, that is, something that happens (all too often) to me, and from which I would like to learn. It is therefore relevant material to use for critical reflection, as an example of an experience that can be used to illustrate the process of learning from experience. Additionally, critical incidents have been used in research for some time (Flanagan 1954), and they also accord nicely with Dewey's (1933:9) idea of the perplexing or uncertain situation that triggers reflection.

WHAT I MEAN BY CRITICAL REFLECTION

For our purposes here, I understand critical reflection to be ultimately about learning from (or making meaning of) experience, begun by a process of unearthing and examining fundamental assumptions that are implicit in a person's account of his or her experience (see Fook 2011). The experience may be critically analyzed by showing how these assumptions are connected with social and cultural contexts, and it may also therefore be about power and its creation and maintenance. (This is, in a nutshell, applying a critical theory framework, using a variety of theorists.) However, it is often difficult to identify core implicit assumptions, as they may be deeply hidden, or their actual origins may be shrouded in the mists of time. So, to identify core assumptions, a person may also need, for example, to notice her or his emotions as indicators of significant values or past experiences. (These of course are often intertwined; that is, we derive deep values from past significant experiences.) The process therefore involves integrating all aspects of experience and understanding how they are interconnected. When this is done, the central meaning of an experience usually emerges. (By delving into all aspects of experience, it is easier to pinpoint the crucial meaning, since experience is often complex and multifaceted.)

Critical reflection, then, in this approach, is more than an analysis and interpretation of personal experience using a critical theoretical framework. That is, it is more than an analysis of the connections between personal experience and social or cultural context. It is also a plumbing of all facets of experience (thoughts and values, feelings and actions) in order to remake its meaning in current context. In addition, in this process of making deeper meaning, people generally remake broader guidelines for further action, as a specific follow-on from remaking the meaning of the experience. (This latter emphasis was most famously developed by Dewey [1933] and is taken further by contemporary authors such as Mezirow et al. [1990] and Boud et al. [1984].) Obviously the deeper the meaning involved, the more fundamental and far-reaching are the guidelines for action.

The idea of learning from and making meaning of experience therefore acts as a kind of rubric that integrates the use of different theoretical frameworks. These theoretical frameworks involve different ways of interpreting and understanding the influence of the social realm on personal experience, thoughts, and actions. There are, in this sense, many different theoretical perspectives that might loosely come under the rubric of "critical" in critical reflection.

Elsewhere I have documented in great detail a process of critical reflection and some of these specific theoretical frameworks (such as reflective practice, concepts of reflexivity, postmodern and poststructural thinking, and critical theory) that inform it (Fook and Gardner 2007). In essence, such frameworks allow us to theorize personal experience through concepts related to each of these frameworks. For example, reflective practice acknowledges the role of tacit knowledge (Polanyi 1966). The concept of tacit knowledge draws attention to the fact that we are often barely aware of the knowledge (or theory or assumptions) that are implicit in our experience and actions. Therefore it is almost impossible to articulate them without assistance. This lack of awareness of, and difficulty in articulating, assumptions means that they are all the more powerful as a result.

The concept of reflexivity introduces an understanding of the influence of our own selves, being, experience, and contexts in creating the knowledge we use and believe to be valid. Postmodern and poststructural thinking shows the role of language in helping to construct our knowledge, the categories we construct, and the power that is integral to the discourses we create and maintain. Critical theory sensitizes us to the connections between personal and social worlds and the importance of personal agency in making social changes. I have as yet not documented in detail how such frameworks are integrated under the rubric of learning from experience, but I hope this chapter will illustrate this to some degree.

As part of the process of critical reflection, I devise questions that help elicit an awareness of implicit assumptions using the several different frameworks outlined above. I usually find that when people are asked specific questions based on particular theoretical frameworks, these may help provide several potential interpretations of their experience. People not only are able to reflect on their experience in more ways but are also able to compare different interpretations, giving them more of a sense of choice in how they understand their experience. For example, questions about where fundamental beliefs come from can shed light on the many social and cultural sources of interpretation, as well as the sources of power operating in people's definitions of themselves. Questions about whether binary or polarized constructions are evident in the way people categorize situations can illuminate the powerful discourses underlying how people organize their knowledge about their worlds. Questions coming from a reflexivity perspective can underscore the influence of our own biases in how we value or recognize legitimate perspectives.

Pondering such questions can help to plumb the fundamental meaning of experience and allow people to remake their understanding of their experience (and themselves) in a form that also provides new guidelines for action.

CRITICAL REFLECTION AND AUTOETHNOGRAPHY

For our purposes, the process might be used as a form of autoethnography, to research personal experience in a systematic way. Sue White (2001) points out how a reflexive inquiry into one's own experience can be a form of autoethnography in that the process might help identify the implicit thinking involved in personal experience. I agree with this view but would extend the idea to include more than notions of reflexivity (as per my outline of theoretical perspectives above). In other words, a process of critical reflection, used to examine multifaceted experience and based on a number of theoretical frameworks, can be used to research experience in a more complex way. I believe that, using the approach to critical reflection outlined above, it is possible not only to unearth fundamental assumptions that make a connection with social and cultural contexts, but to use this process to remake understandings of experience and to provide further (critical) guidelines for action. In this way critical reflection can provide a more integrated understanding of experience—both personal and social realms may be better integrated, but also analyses may be better connected with actions. I am currently developing this process as a systematic methodology for better researching experience (Fook 2011). I believe that the structured process for critical reflection that I advocate can actually lead to a better expression of experience in terms the person who is experiencing it can identify and engage with. In this way it is also possible to develop new labels and expressions to better communicate and discuss experiences.

BACK TO MY STORY

Having outlined the process and framework for critical reflection, I will begin to reflect on my meeting story above.

When I look back at it, I am immediately struck by several things. First, there is an underlying discourse about power, or at the very least about hierarchy. I speak about myself in a passive way ("finding myself") in the meeting, as if I took no action, or exercised no agency or choice in being there. I am also quick to mention the relative status of people at the meeting, and to place myself in a less powerful position. It is also clear that I have some strong values about clear communication, the importance of transparent decision making, and achieving a task.

These are assumptions that are reasonably apparent on fairly superficial scrutiny of the story. It appears I have constructed myself (rather embarrassingly in hindsight) as a fairly "eager beaver," ready to participate positively in a jointly shared creative experience, after which "we all live happily ever after" (i.e., I go away with "renewed vision"). I have evidently built the meeting up to be a highly important and significant event in my professional life, something that will be so momentous that it will give me renewed vision. (I really like having a vision, since I mention it so much!) I think there is also something here about assuming that mixing with senior people will allow this vision to be developed. Perhaps this also implies that I believe that at the very least senior people will want to, and be able to, develop vision fairly efficiently. So I seem to be assuming that seniority equates with competence.

However, as soon as I recognize this doesn't seem to be the case, I am readily disillusioned, and I immediately stop participating as a result. It is as if, when my view of things doesn't seem to pan out, I lose my compass. I'm unable to find direction, and therefore I effectively silence myself.

SILENCING MYSELF, FITTING IN, AND BEING VALUED

If we examine this a little further, this silencing of myself seems to come about because of a convoluted set of assumptions. First, I appear to be assuming that I can't (or won't) speak effectively unless I can understand what is going on. I need to understand the situation in order to have direction. Being able to speaking sensibly assumes being able to speak with understanding, in order to be able to contribute meaningfully. Contributing meaningfully for me is equated with getting the meeting going in the right direction. So in order to get the meeting going in the right direction, I need to understand the situation, and I cannot speak until I am sure I can make a meaningful contribution. So I need to understand before I can speak. There is a definite value placed here on intellectual ability, and the power or rationality or intellectual ability. Perhaps I am implying that "thinking precedes action"?

This assumption is mostly related, I think, to not wanting to appear like I don't know what is happening. I want to look like I "get it" and don't want to seem stupid by "not getting" what everyone else seems to. (Note here also an assumption that everyone else does get it, and that I am the only person who doesn't.) On a more sinister note, I think, my assumptions are related to wanting to fit in, to show that I have been able to analyze the situation and can act appropriately. Notice here that my deeper assumptions (and values) are not really about making a contribution, or even about moving the meeting on. These would be consistent with my stated values about wanting a clear outcome from the meeting. However, my assumptions really appear to be about not wanting to appear out of place or out of step. My concern is to be up to speed (with the senior people, I wonder?) and not to be thought inadequate. Notice here also that I equate being "out of place" with being inadequate. So much of my behavior here can be seen to be built on a desire to fit in and to be accepted—especially to be accepted as worthy or good enough.

Now that I have unearthed a relatively fundamental set of assumptions that appear to be connected, it is appropriate to stop here and ask, where do these assumptions come from? What is it about my background and experiences that may have cultivated this way of thinking?

WHO AM I?

I once responded to the question "Who am I?" with the answer "a banana" (Fook 2001). This means, to the initiated, an Australian-born Chinese person (yellow on the outside, white on the inside). Of course it refers more broadly to anyone of Chinese descent raised in a predominantly white country. I am in fact a fourth-generation person of Chinese descent born and raised in a predominantly white Australia. I grew up in the 1950s and 1960s in suburban Sydney, in an era when assimilationism ruled. Post–World War II migration was still a novelty in suburban Australia, and European migrants were called "New Australians." Asian Australians were viewed with considerable suspicion. I recall often being told to "go back where I came from" and taunted with the term "Jap" by fellow schoolchildren. In postwar consciousness, all people of Asian appearance were seen as Japanese and were therefore viewed with hostility. The White Australia policy was particularly significant, as it marked a distinctive form of racism in the Western world. As Fitzgerald notes (2007:2), other Western countries such as Canada and the United States also had harsh policies of discrimination against Chinese people. However, Australia distinguished itself by trying to build its sense of nationhood on the principle of keeping Australia white. Fitzgerald builds a strong argument to show how Australian historians have systematically cast the Chinese, and Chinese culture, as somehow deleterious to an emerging Australian culture. In this way he argues that Australian historians themselves have been guilty of racism toward Chinese. He implies that this inbuilt prejudice has been a strong undercurrent in the development of (white) Australian culture.

In my own household, it was an article of faith in my own parents' version of being Chinese in Australia to fit in. This meant not making waves or causing trouble, trying to be as pleasant and accommodating as possible. I understood this at the time as being a well-recognized Chinese way of making a success of migration into foreign cultures or countries. It is of course arguable that even if Chinese people did speak out more forcefully to defend their positive contributions, their voices would have been heeded (Fitzgerald 2007:227). However, in my and my family's case, we did not even put it to the test. I in fact did not have much trouble with this "fitting in" adage and for a long time suffered little conscious tension. I simply saw myself as an Australian—after all, I spoke and understood no Cantonese language except for a few words for my favorite Cantonese foods. In fact, I recall being startled, my identity somewhat jolted, when I was about sixteen years old. I was window shopping and caught a glimpse of my own (Chinese) face staring back at me from the window. There was something about seeing myself in a public setting that brought home my Chinese appearance with some force.

For a young woman of Chinese appearance especially, it seemed there was an even greater expectation of acceptable behavior than for Chinese men. I have found that this expectation in particular seems to have been reinforced in many of the professional circles in which I have worked throughout my life. I imagine that other people view my social persona of visible appearance as a relatively accommodating, passive, articulate, but nonthreatening Chinese woman. This has often felt at rough odds with my own inner life, which comprises a (sometimes biting) social analysis of gendered, power, and race relations, combined with strong values of creativity, intellectualism, and quick efficiency. This dissonance between my social persona and my own perceptions of myself runs as a current throughout my biography. In the study of identity, of course, it is well understood that there are both social and personal elements that combine to produce a person's understanding of themselves (Fook 2001). However, in my case, I think the contrast between the exterior social and interior personal identity is perhaps more than normally pronounced. I in fact felt like a white Australian, and to a large degree I identified as one. It was only the way other people related to me, and the views of other people, that constantly reminded me that I was not seen that way. I have constantly had to remind myself throughout my professional career that my own view of myself does not necessarily accord with the way other people see me.

In looking back at my meeting story again, I see further connections with the view of myself that comes out in the story. I appear to construct myself as relatively passive, "finding myself" in a meeting, and so forth. This denial of my own power seems to be linked with the desire to fit in. Perhaps I do adopt the view I believe other people have of me—that is,

I do adopt what I believe is my social persona. I also acknowledge, from ongoing reflection, that I do have an identity of relative powerlessness, having experienced this social position for a good deal of my life. In my meeting story, it also seems as if having power may suddenly render me visible, as potentially threatening, and therefore as potentially not fitting in. I think these views can also be connected with other assumptions—about what my rightful place is (presumably to fit in), and that my rightful place of fitting in also means not being "better than" other people in the situation. "Fitting in" means it is all right to be equal with other people (or perhaps less than equal), but not being better than other people. Presumably these ideas are based on some kind of belief that people *of my type* should not be better than others.

When I recently presented this scenario for critical reflection at a workshop in London, one person asked an astute question. She was searching for binary constructions in my story. She asked how I constructed the idea of "leading" and the idea of "following." I replied, honestly, that I thought I did not have a concept of following—for me the binary is between leading and fitting in. That is, it does seem that I have only two categories for ways of being professionally—either to lead or to fit in, and that I have constructed these as binary opposite categories—they are both opposite and mutually exclusive, and that I must operate in one or the other category. As I said this, the penny dropped. I suspect that what emerges from my meeting story is that I do not feel comfortable with the idea that someone like me should lead, because I do not feel that leading, or being "better than," is appropriate for someone like me—it is not my rightful place. Fitting in seems both safer but also right, on a social level, although obviously there is great personal frustration involved. Hence the tension between social persona and personal characteristics is upheld.

RACE, GENDER, AND "MAKING IT WORK"

Many of you reading this now, especially those of you who are female and from an Asian background, will recognize these ideas as being an integral part of your own upbringing. You will probably wonder why this issue of race (and gender) difference has lain unexamined for so long in my own story of myself. Is there something here that implies that acknowledging difference will mean having to acknowledge not fitting, which means acknowledging the potential power associated with this, and therefore the potential to be exposed? Does this imply a lack of safety?

I remember vividly a female academic colleague of mine (from a minority background) who once made the astute observation that people like us tend to feel we have to "make it work." By this she meant that we do not have the luxury of being able to simply land other people with problems, but that we have to manage relations and gloss over differences and conflicts in order to make it work. Otherwise, I suppose, being the people with the least standing, we would risk being blamed for causing whatever the problems were at the time. This is an interesting take on "blaming the victim."

I also recall feeling terribly comfortable with this view, because I felt that making it work was an important principle (which just happened to accord with an important social work principle as well). On the other hand, this also implies a discomfort with not making it work—a discomfort with not accepting status quo social relations, and a discomfort with challenging and confronting problem behavior on a micro level. This makes me begin to wonder whether my choice of social work as a profession and the perspectives I take within it are linked to this.

So a major question for me now becomes, how does the wanting to make it work sit with my identity of difference? And how does my identity of difference sit with wanting to fit in and not being "better than"?

Let me start to respond to this by reflecting a little more on my identity of difference, and what that means to me. I begin to wonder whether I have made myself "fit" to some extent by constructing myself as someone different. In other words, perhaps I have tried to carve out an acceptable social place for myself as someone who doesn't conform. However, for me, this nonconformity is not about cultural or ethnic difference but more about social or political difference. Why this choice? Given the fact of my growing up in a predominantly Anglo country, and being raised to fit in, I have, as I said above, roughly identified to some extent as a white Australian. However, having made academia my career choice, I have felt my class and other social differences to be of greater disadvantage in being accepted and successful in such an environment. I do, I think, construct myself as someone who has had to do it the hard way, that is, make a career pathway without a privileged background (my parents and grandparents were involved in small businesses). "Doing it the hard way" has meant getting there through hard work (congruent with a Chinese upbringing), a high value on intellectual ability, and sheer achievement. In a strange way I have felt that I have had to be better than others in order to attain equal status (as many feminists complain). In my case, this was an acceptable form of being "better than." In other words, it was all right to be better than in order to gain similar positions to other people, but not to be better than in order to gain higher positions. I accepted that I had to do more to achieve the same.

These ideas all connect with the importance I place on the ability to get it right, as evident in my initial meeting story. I also suspect they connect with the supreme significance I place on having a vision as a guiding direction for professional work. In other words, I suppose, I have constructed myself as someone who has had to stand out (not conform) through higher than ordinary achievement in order to attain an equal place with others (as I see it). I fit in by trying to be better, to do and give more, and, even more important, by trying to make it work for others.

I wonder how much this is the story for many people of difference. Perhaps for them the choices of direct confrontation or powerful challenge, or of attaining positions of greater power, do not even seem to be an option. The dominant templates for people who hold legitimate power do not even include a definition or category for people of difference.

Again I recall a fascinating conversation I once had with a colleague of indigenous background. We were speaking of her people's tendency toward fatalism, in particular an acceptance of uncertain and severe weather conditions, and therefore the need and ability to adapt as a matter of survival. We wondered whether this way of being also translated to unpredictable or adverse social conditions—the response was not to challenge but to adapt. I recall also at the time a related conversation with another colleague, a person of Anglo descent. She was lamenting the behavior of an indigenous student in her class because he did not openly protest and rage against obvious racism. We wondered together whether his silence was his form of protest, and whether our desire to hear his voice arose more from our own assumptions about the forms protest should take.

Such reflections lead me to rethink where the dominant views about race, racism, intolerance of social difference, and acceptable responses to these, and even the idea of fitting, come from. How much of these views have infused my own thinking about my experiences and the sort of identity I have forged as a result? I wonder, perhaps, if I have assumed that the "proper" ways of speaking out and resisting a lack of acceptance are perhaps Westernized and maybe masculinist ways of being. Have my own views been "colonized"? And as such, have I constructed my own, perhaps less socially confronting ways, as somehow NOT resistance or protest, and therefore less than adequate? After all, following the postmodern idea that there may be many perspectives and ways of knowing and being, then there may be many ways of being active, resisting, or giving voice, indeed, of interpreting a situation.

REVISITING THE ORIGINAL STORY

Recounting the specific incident that sparked my story makes me recall another meeting incident, some years earlier. I remember that this meeting was of some type of curriculum committee, and it was our role to revise a lengthy document. There had been several drafts of this document to date, and the current meeting was to revise the latest draft. All meeting members had copies of the document, and we were proceeding through it page by page, making suggestions and discussing alterations as we went. Early in the proceedings, I found I could not follow the page numbers, nor find the exact points people were discussing and making changes to. I kept looking over my colleagues' shoulders to see if I could find any clues on their papers. My colleagues were unable to assist me. I repeatedly looked frantically around the room, only to see that everyone else was studiously nodding and discussing, and making relevant marks on their own papers. Finally, toward the end of the meeting, I admitted to the chair of the meeting that I was lost and couldn't trace where many of the relevant points were in the document. Imagine my total surprise when one by one, sheepishly, other people acknowledged that they were in the same position. Finally the chair noted that in fact the wrong document had been copied, and that all committee members had been working off a different document from the chair! I guess I wasn't really out of step here, except insofar as voicing my position. Perhaps the meeting culture that I didn't understand was nothing more sinister than the culture of saving face!

This story pulls me back to the stark realization that there may be many (simpler) ways to interpret "not getting it" in a meeting, and it is still interesting that I privilege the idea of my difference as the reason for being out of step.

This realization leads me to revisit my original story: I wonder whether there might be a completely different way of rewriting it. Clearly there may have been a meeting culture and agenda being adhered to that simply did not fit my own interpretation, and which I did not see, given my own set of values and assumptions. Also, my own assumption of my own difference did not allow me to recognize that there may well have been other people in the room who also did not understand and also did not speak up as a result. Instead of assuming I would expose my own lack of ability to fit and get it right, I could just as easily have assumed that other people might feel the same (even if for different reasons). In this case I might have shown some leadership, or exercised some power, by attempting to reshape the agenda by registering my own confusion. This could have functioned as a rallying point for others who were confused or frustrated. Incidentally, it might also have given me an opportunity to identify and perhaps even understand the culture that was operating in that meeting situation. At the very least it may have been useful learning for future meetings.

Or I could also have assumed that acknowledging a lack of clarity might have at least introduced some more clarity in the situation, and perhaps allowed some discussion of the meeting process. Interestingly, the assumptions I made were in a sense all about me (judgments of myself or my own situation in relation to others) as opposed to being open to trying to understand what was happening for other people. My behavior, in that sense, did not actually function to give me more information but only functioned to reinforce my implicit assumptions about myself and my difference.

BACK TO THE PROBLEM OF DIFFERENCE

This reflection has made me fully aware that I have also constructed difference as being a problematic thing, a source of difficulty and tension, a feature that does not necessarily contribute to making things work. In fact, even as I say these words, I am acutely aware that there is no rational reason to suppose that difference might not actually function toward better working. This can be especially the case if it is understood in a way that allows for a range of differences to be recognized and for creative tensions to result. This realization is hardly rocket science, but the fact that it remains relatively silent in my story shows how dominant views actually do dominate.

And of course, when I look back over my academic career, I find it easy to celebrate, on a rational level, that my own social difference has in fact bequeathed a considerable advantage, especially to me as a social scientist. A minority background means that I automatically carry an alternative perspective, one that allows a relatively natural critical stance toward the mainstream and taken-for-granted. It also creates an opening to envision other perspectives and possibilities, enabling great creative potential. On an interpersonal level, it has also proved invaluable for me as a social worker, giving me a ready empathy with those who feel excluded, and them with me. I derive from these experiences a tremendous sense of commitment to relating inclusively and to creating inclusive environments.

Having been able to list the many advantages social difference affords, I wonder then why this perspective clearly does not seem to provide an adequate picture of my own experience, and why my difference continues to sit in my story as a thing of difficulty.

This continuing reflection makes me ponder the complexities of the experience of social difference. While it may be somewhat easy to reel off the positives of a socially different background, it is evident from my own account that the experience does not feel positive. I can give it a positive meaning and spin, but this is not the whole story. There is hurt, some anger, self-doubt, and the fear of social rejection and not being understood behind the desire to fit in. And, in the very act of putting these words down on paper, I am struck by the importance of recognizing these elements in order to make meaningful meaning of the whole experience.

Yet it is also interesting that they have not figured to a large degree in my easily remembered experiences. It is only when I am discussing, with a very good friend, my reflections on writing this autoethnography that I recall vividly some of the many experiences of exclusion I have suffered in my professional life. Some are small (like not being invited to the party everyone else in the department has been invited to) and others larger (like feeling like a social pariah in professional circles in an entire city). It is sometimes hard, in the web of micro interactions, to put a finger on how and where exclusion manifests (you constantly wonder if you are being too paranoid), but it has a way of slowly adding up to point with surety in that direction. The entire experience is obviously painful, but it is also perplexing for those excluded, since they are often highly valued by some groups (usually lower-status groups). In my own case, in all the academic departments I worked for over a period of about fifteen years, I was never popular with my own colleagues but was generally appreciated by students. My friend, also from a minority background who had similar professional experiences to myself, lamented plaintively, "Why don't they [our colleagues] like us? I wish I could sit one of them down and ask them to tell me concretely why."

This sparked a fascinating discussion. I attempted to respond to his question by asking him to think about a particular person from that mainstream, rejecting circle he disliked, and his reasons for disliking her. My friend readily admitted that his reasons for his dislike were cultural, but that at least he could recognize this. He posited, however, that he was sure that this woman disliked him, but that she would say her reasons for disliking him were to do with his personality, so "why can't she recognize that the basis for disliking me is cultural?" We pondered together whether this was one of the differences between being marginal and being mainstream. People in mainstream cultures have the privilege of being able to construct difference as problematic and blame the source of these differences on the "different" individual, not on the cultural assumptions or norms that construct the differences in the first place. They have the luxury of pathologizing difference as originating from personality difficulties. This is a particularly subtle form of "blaming the victim," I think, which for me holds great currency in providing a better understanding of the micro relations in social difference and the operation of exclusion.

It is perverse, though—even as I speak about the tough emotional experience of exclusion, and I construct a damning analysis of exclusionary micro relations—I can, at the same time, almost imperceptibly, start to feel the need to speak about them slipping away. It is as if acknowledging them begins to make them fade back into the texture of the canvas in which they had stood out in stark relief. Suddenly they do not dominate the picture, but they slide into perspective as part of the whole picture. Whether or not it is a beautiful, sad, angry, or even banal picture does not matter. Whatever it is, that whole picture is who I am now, and who I have become, from incorporating all these aspects of my experience. These many disparate aspects hang together with a congruency that seems to give my understanding of myself and my life a type of authenticity. I am able to see a picture of myself that is recognizable in my terms, and to own that I have had, and will continue to have, a substantial role in painting that picture.

MAKING MEANING OF DIFFERENCE

So how does the story of fitting in (or not), social acceptance, power, and an identity of difference come together to provide a coherent understanding of myself and sense of direction?

Somehow it now seems less important whether I fit in, or even whether I am socially accepted. These concerns seem too driven by people, groups, or cultures that are not mine, or of my own making or choosing. What stands out in stark relief for me is the realization that I have power, and that I have the potential to seize or create more power than I have wanted to acknowledge in the past, and that my difference may be a useful tool in this task. Neither power nor difference is something to be feared in and of itself. It is as if I can now see these phenomena in perspective, and I have become empowered to face the risks that having power (and difference) involves. What has become of much more fundamental and prime importance to me is the vision and direction that guides the use of power. And it is this vision that has become far more apparent to me through the critical reflection process.

And what is the specific vision that gives my professional life direction? It is a vision of social inclusion, forged through my own fear of being different. It is a critical stance, developed through small personal traumas combined with big intellectual analyses of countless social situations in which social difference loomed large. It is a dogged optimism in the possibility of social change, of belief in the possibility of alternative, and better, ways. It is a firm commitment to recognizing and valuing all aspects of experience, and bringing the learning from it to bear in human relationships, academic study, and professional practice.

A CRITICAL REFLECTION ON CRITICAL REFLECTION

What have I learned about my own experience from critically reflecting on it? What has the process of researching my experience in this way actually unearthed?

Interestingly, I have identified a lot more about the operation of social difference and how it is constructed in everyday relations. I have become more aware of the potential colonizing of identity, and of the many appropriate ways of expressing resistance. Even more important, I have become more sobered by the reinforced realization that transformation is possible, and that identities and experiences are complex, are changing, and can be changed. And perhaps for identities to change, and for transformation to happen, the complexity of experiences must first be accepted.

I have gained more interpretive frameworks from which to understand my own life. For instance, I can now see how my own background of social difference has fueled my passionate concern with people and views on the margins. Not only does this explain my interest in critical perspectives, but also my lifelong interest in championing minority causes. Thus I am concerned with practice, in an academic culture that privileges theory; concerned with practice research, in an academic environment that values more purist research; and concerned with alternative research methods, in a prevailing positivist climate.

Critical reflection on my own experience brings home to me how I am both a product and a producer of my social world and reality. There are gaps, biases, and blind spots in even my own carefully developed analyses. My own vulnerabilities can leap up at any time and bite me on the back unawares. Perhaps, more surprisingly for an academic, I can concede that the intellect is a necessary but insufficient tool for plumbing the depths of experience. This leads me on a continuing quest to find research tools that will illuminate complex experience, tools that combine a mixture of ways of knowing but which can nevertheless be replicated and can make a recognized contribution in the intellectual world of the academy.

In this way my personal background and professional quests become merged. I can now see how and why my own background and experiences, although painful and problematic, have combined to give me a perspective on social and academic problems that is uniquely mine. This gives me the vision (I hope) to make a unique professional and academic contribution.

These are the very realizations that give impetus to my interest and belief in critical reflection as a significant contribution to professional life and practice. Just as critical reflection on my own experience allows me to integrate the disparate aspects into some meaningful whole, I often see this process happening for the people I critically reflect with.

The process I have witnessed and participated in countless times starts with a person's account of a specific incident, one which is critical because it somehow is significant. It stands out perhaps because it is puzzling, distressing, annoying, or it simply can't be forgotten. In the process of reflection, begun by searching for unspoken and implicit assumptions, the person may unearth many assumptions, some more superficial than others. Usually, however, it is possible to delve more deeply to discover fundamental assumptions that may underlie and therefore connect the sometimes seemingly unrelated, more superficial ideas. In this process the person is usually also mining his or her experience to identify the crux or essence of its meaning. I normally find that in order to do this, the person may need to recognize feelings, actions, and the thinking associated with these. All these aspects are bound together in a way that represents the whole experience for the person. In the course of this process, the person tends to become aware of how specific assumptions he or she hold may have derived from specific situations or events, and may be led to question whether these assumptions are relevant for the current contexts in which he or she lives or works. This then provides them a basis for further questioning and rebuilding of different interpretive frameworks or principles as a guide for further actions.

What this process embodies can be understood as a transformative experience, one in which deeply rooted and influential beliefs can be challenged and changed, to be brought more in line with a person's own conscious, chosen value stance. My experience of this process (both my own and others' reflections) has been both humbling and inspiring. I have learned about, and shared, many people's vulnerabilities, dilemmas, struggles, and triumphs, and come to recognize a lot more of my own. No experience is too trivial or banal to have meaning. I have come to both understand and accept that there is a lot more to human experience than we have the words to express, and a lot more complexity and elusiveness than we can presume to pin down.

My experiences with critical reflection have provided that vehicle for me. I can recognize, from both critically reflecting on my own experience and participating in critical reflection on others' experiences, that the many disparate aspects of myself developed from my own background and experiences have come together in a way that allows me to make a unique contribution. "Social difference" is not necessarily just an experience to be endured or even changed, but simply something to be incorporated, something that becomes part of the total picture that I and all people are.

My own critical reflection on my experiences illuminates how a background of social difference and wanting to fit in can be transformed into an innate critical edge, an openness to difference and inclusion, and a sympathy for marginal experiences. Even more fundamentally they bespeak an acceptance of many points of view, and an enhanced capacity to engage with many forms of social suffering and the fragilities and ambiguities of human existence. These are the transformations that I believe are the essence of the profession of social work, and, incidentally, of the business of living.

REFERENCES

Boud, D., R. Keogh, and D. Walker, eds. 1984. *Reflection: Turning Experience into Learning*. London: Kogan Page.

Brookfield, S. D. 1995. *Becoming a Critically Reflective Teacher*. San Francisco: Jossey-Bass.

Chang, H. 2008. *Autoethnography as Method*. Walnut Creek, Calif.: Left Coast Press.

Dewey, J. 1933. *How We Think*. Boston: D. C. Heath.

Fitzgerald, J. 2007. *Big White Lie: Chinese Australians in White Australia*. Sydney: UNSW Press.

Flanagan, J. 1954. "The Critical Incident Technique!" *Psychology Bulletin* 51:327–58.

Fook, J. 2001. "Emergent Ethnicity as a Framework for Social Work." In *Beyond Racial Divides: Ethnicities in Social Work*, edited by H. Soydan, L. Dominelli, and W. Lorenz, 9–22. Avebury: Aldershot.

———. 2011. "Developing Critical Reflection as a Research Method." In *Creative Spaces for Qualitative Researching*, edited by J. Higgs et al., 55–64. Rotterdam: Sense Publishers.

Fook, J., and F. Gardner. 2007. *Practising Critical Reflection: A Resource Handbook*. Maidenhead: Open University Press.

Fook, J., S. White, and F. Gardner. 2006. "Critical Reflection: A Review of Current Understandings and Literature." In *Critical Reflection in Health and Social Care*, edited by S. White, J. Fook, and F. Gardner, 3–20. Maidenhead: Open University Press.

Mezirow, J., et al. 1990. *Fostering Critical Reflection in Adulthood*. San Francisco: Jossey-Bass.

Polanyi, M. 1966. *The Tacit Dimension*. New York: Doubleday.

White, S. 2001. "Auto-ethnography as Reflexive Inquiry." In *Qualitative Social Work Research*, edited by I. Shaw and N. Gould. London: Sage.

CHAPTER 6

What Remains?

HEROIC STORIES IN TRACE MATERIALS

▶ KAREN STALLER

Let me ask you this question: "What make heroes? Why are some real heroes unsung, while others being overrated?"
—John Chester Munn to Helen Baxter, April 10, 1943

THE FIRST TIME—but far from the last time—John Chester Munn's[1] case file reduced me to tears, I was sitting at an ancient wooden table in the library of the New-York Historical Society (N-YHS), trying to stifle my sobs so as not to disturb the other researchers in the reading room. At the time I was midway through a seven-month sabbatical in New York City doing historical research. John's Children's Aid Society (CAS) case file was enormous. It was so big, in fact, that it filled several folders. His life story spilled out in front of me as a disjointed narrative, rising up from treatment logs, professional assessments, and personal correspondence. Truthfully, I was a bit emotionally raw even before I began reading John's file.

My much beloved father died on July 13, 2009. It was a peaceful death at eighty-two. As deaths go, it couldn't have been better executed. He wanted to be pain free. He was. He wanted to stay in our family house, "the Homestead," he called it, as long as possible. He died there. He drew his last breath surrounded by his wife of fifty-four years and all four of his adult children. His health had been declining for decades. I can still hear him say "aaccch yaahh," a guttural sighing sound he made that was heavily influenced by his native Czech tongue, "it's a terrible thing to grow old." I still miss him so much it hurts. Following his death, I somehow limped through the remainder of fall semester with its full load of regular business. However, I was emotionally depleted and exhausted by the time I arrived at the N-YHS in January 2010 to begin my sabbatical work.

PICKLED FISH

Years ago I was introduced to the opening paragraphs of a book written by John Steinbeck and Edward F. Ricketts and published in 1941. The passage of interest is about a fish called the Mexican sierra. It reads:

> The Mexican sierra has XVII-15-IX spines in the dorsal fin. These can easily be counted. But if the sierra strikes hard on the line so that our hands are burned, if the fish sounds and nearly escapes and finally comes over the rail, his colors pulsing and his tail beating the air, a whole new relational externality has come into being—an entity which is more than the sum of the fish plus the fisherman. The only way to count the spines of the sierra unaffected by this second relational reality is to sit in a laboratory, open an evil-smelling jar, remove a stiff colorless fish from the formalin solution, count the spines, and write the truth "D. XVII-15-IX." There you have recorded a reality which cannot be assailed—probably the least important reality concerning either the fish or yourself.
>
> It is good to know what you are doing. The man with his pickled fish has set down one truth and has recorded in his experience many lies. The fish is not that color, that texture, that dead, nor does he smell that way.

Just over a decade before Steinbeck wrote those paragraphs, Thomas D. Elliot published an article in *Social Forces* about the "objectivity" of social work case records. Elliot (1928) wrote, "The old-fashioned case record has all the juice squeezed out, and is displayed, like a botanical specimen, from which even a soaking cannot revive a semblance of the original in its ecological setting" (541).

In 1942, a year after Steinbeck wrote *Log*, John Chester Munn had penned a letter to his guardian and social worker, Miss Helen Baxter, about his experience in the U.S. Navy during World War II. The letter resides in his social work case file. A partial passage of the wartime correspondence reads: "I've changed a great deal since the beginning of this fracas. Honestly, I developed a wider vision of seeking the true facts in the reality of life. If the people only knew the truth. I've undergone many stirring and harrowing experiences which will remain in my memoirs until the end of my days" (October 8, 1942).

It may be true that social work case records are like a desiccated botanical specimens or pickled Mexican sierra; however, none of this helps explain why I would be moved to tears reading John's social work case record. Nor why I am still haunted by its content. Nor why I feel like John and his social worker, Miss Baxter, have become real characters in my life, although I never met either one. Nor why I have felt a paralyzing need to tell John's life story "truthfully" and "correctly," in spite of the fact that reconstructing a life can never be fully achieved from the trace evidence of its existence.

Social workers routinely preserve selective information in their case records and, with every action or inaction, compose a portrait of a person's life created both by what is present as well as by what is absent. Beyond this "botanical specimen," there was a fully lived, complicated, and historically, culturally, and politically situated life. There was *somebody*. In making their decisions and carrying out their jobs, social workers play an important but largely unrecognized role in producing a sliver of both human and social welfare history. Yet no matter how rich the case file may be, at some point the documentation simply stops leaving behind millions of unanswerable questions about that *somebody*.

SELLING THE HOMESTEAD

By the time I had reached John's file—well into my sabbatical stint—my mother was in the process of selling "the Homestead." She had moved quickly to rid herself of the burden of caring for an aging house. At some point along the way she also said to me, "Your father filled that house." Ever a glass-half-full optimist, my Mom would never complain that the house felt empty without Dad. It was more that his presence was like helium to a balloon; it had given the house its shape and was its life-force. The Homestead was simply unfilled and formless in his absence.

She was correct—as she always is—in her decision to sell the Homestead. She was eager to create a new space for her new life. However, her four adult children were slower to embrace the idea. "What about us?" we whined. It had been our home for four decades. The house had been there for every landmark event, good and bad, not to mention every mundane day in between. Although education and jobs had led me to Bloomington,

Pittsburgh, New York, Tuscaloosa, and Ann Arbor, more often than not when I talked about home, I still meant the Homestead. Through every crisis and every celebration, large and small, it had been a stable, permanent, and dependable fixture. Where would home now be? Would it cease to exist altogether?

It wasn't just the sense of homelessness that was disconcerting. In fact, it turned out this wasn't even the most disconcerting part of selling the Homestead. More unsettling was the fact that when Mom put the house on the market, we began the onerous task of "downsizing." That is what my father had called the abstract concept—never realized during his lifetime—of shedding stuff. With the pending house sale, the theoretical project of downsizing was suddenly a reality. We were thrust into the new emotional territory of disposing of things that had been the embodiment of home for decades.

PICKLING, PRESERVING, AND RECONSTITUTING

This autoethnography is forged from these personal and professional threads: downsizing the family homestead, and holding on to memories of Dad, while reading the turn-of-the-twentieth-century case records of homeless children served by the Children's Aid Society. By intertwining the personal and professional story lines, I hope to point to the ephemeral nature of the things that define our lives while we are living, the places and spaces those things reside, and the stories they may still tell when we are no longer here.

More broadly I struggle with three issues. First, what remains of people's lives when they are gone? What traces of evidence are preserved? What is missing? How does this remaining patchwork relate to our fully lived lives, our legacy, and our place in history? Second, who decides what to preserve? What is cast off from our lives, intentionally and unintentionally? When, how, and why are these things scattered? The third is about whether people can be reconstituted from the bits and pieces of trace evidence left behind. Can we be raised from the dead? Can the Mexican sierra be withdrawn from formaldehyde and made to thrash?

Here, alternating between the two story lines and dancing between memories and interpretations, I attempt to reconstitute and understand John's life from the inert, incomplete specimen I found before me in his

CAS case file while preserving my dad's life even as material elements of it were scattered. In the process, I discovered new sources of evidence and revisited entrenched understandings of old stories. Taken together, I suppose, I am seeking to understand the lives of these treasured characters in my life—some of whom I have never even met—and my role, professional and personal, in preserving and interpreting their lives.

MIGRATING REMAINS, CASE READING, AND RECORDING

My primary sabbatical research focused on early services for poor, mostly immigrant, street youth provided by the CAS. CAS was founded in 1854 and is still an active social service agency today. During the intervening century and a half, documents accumulated in basements and back offices of CAS buildings scattered across the city. More recently the CAS's former executive director had the foresight to donate these old records to the N-YHS. So material was excavated from the moldy basements and dusty backrooms and migrated to its new home, in a climate-controlled environment provided by the N-YHS. In the process, old stuff and junk were transformed into valuable historic artifacts available to scholars, writers, journalists, and other researchers.

Today the archived collection includes 996 boxes of material, 490 bound volumes, and 30,000 case files. Access to the case files, not surprisingly, is restricted. After spending several months delving into the general business records of the agency, I secured permission to examine the case records of individual children and began to explore this treasure trove. I expected to read these records as a detached social scientist. I was not prepared for those children and young adults to take up residence in my heart and head as their lives were laid out before me, plucked from boxes of files and bound volumes of service notes.

In an editorial in *Social Work* on the importance of "reading," Stanley Witkin (2001) notes, "As social workers, our written artifacts inscribe clients' lives. Written texts—whether in the form of a case record or journal article—form an 'official record' about clients and are used to render judgments and inform decisions about them" (5). He makes an argument for care in the *reading* of these artifacts. It is the interactive effect of a written record with the reader that produces meaning, since the report has "no fixed meaning" in isolation (6).

Accordingly it quickly became apparent to me that not only was I being moved by the lives and living conditions of these children on their face, but my interpretative reading of the CAS files was nearly as significant as the act of recording them had been in the first place. For example, the earliest CAS "agents"—social work practitioners of their day—kept daybooks with sequentially dated entries documenting their day-to-day encounters with children and families. An early entry from March 15, 1854, reads:

> Mary C_____. Don't live any where—has no father or mother—lodges at acquaintances house in 25th St (moving today) English Protestant. Can't read or write. Aunt Mary paid passage to N.Y. and died on the way, buried in the water. Lived in Harlem 5 months with Mrs. D___ —14 years would like to go to Sunday school. Will go anywhere and do anything.

Sitting at the reading room table looking at the faded ink entries scrolled into the daybooks, I felt my mind wander in intellectually interpretive and speculative directions. How difficult Mary C's life must have been. By fourteen she had lost her parents as well as Aunt Mary. Did she watch her aunt's ocean burial? If so, what was it like seeing her body slip below the water, knowing that she herself was suddenly heading to a strange new homeland all alone? My heart ached for her.

I couldn't help but think about how, immediately following my father's death while my mother, brother, and one sister had stayed upstairs with the undertaker who would remove his body from the Homestead, my sister Helen and I had fled the upstairs bedroom, scurried down a flight of stairs, through the kitchen, and out the back door to the safety of the Homestead's back porch. The porch overlooked a tranquil wooded garden and koi fish pond (with soothing gurgling fountain) that my parents had cultivated over the decades, bird feeding stations over which my Dad had expressed utter delight whenever he spotted one of "his" female cardinals, and the old Weber grill where he produced all those charcoal-broiled summer dinners. The back porch was also physically located as far from the sights and sounds of the solemn procession that was taking place in the house behind us as possible. Although it was the middle of the day, my sister had wisely grabbed a bottle of wine and goblets as we darted through the kitchen. We sat together—experiencing an indescribable mixture of grief and relief all filtered through a Chardonnay-induced haze—comforted by our mutual confession that although we had witnessed Dad's demise and death, the practical act of removing his inert remains from the house was simply more than either of us could bear to witness.

I can still summon up how painful that moment was, and through the tears, wonder how CAS's little Mary C had handled this disposal of her aunt. Was she there? Was it a memory that stayed with her for life? Was she sad? Scared? What became of her? What was her life like without a family? What had the CAS done for her? Had the agents helped in any meaningful way?

A CASE AND A LIFE, IN THIRTY-SEVEN WORDS

Four days after the Mary C entry, the CAS agent recorded Elizabeth S's story:

> Elizabeth S____ 13-years old Irish Catholic apparently an honest girl, reported by Mrs A . . . much abused by her parents who are unwilling that she should leave. The girl desires to get away. Can read and write a little.

Certainly these facts will sound familiar to any social worker in today's child welfare system. But what are the limits of this familiarity? What was Elizabeth's life destined to be like at a time when there was no foster care system? What did this newly created society and its agents do with her case? How did they make sense of the information? Who was Mrs A anyway? What was her motivation for reporting this case? Did Elizabeth ask Mrs A to speak with the CAS agent? What form did the "abuse" take? Why, exactly, did Elizabeth desire to get away? How "unwilling" were her parents to part with thirteen-year-old Elizabeth? What happened to her? What kind of life did she end up living? Of course, the list of unanswered questions dwarfs the original thirty-seven words that comprise the entire entry on Elizabeth's life, the pickled version of it.

So what should we make of the activity of both *recording and reading* a preserved Mexican sierra? How do you write just thirty-seven words? What if it were to be the sum total of that person's earthly legacy? What story would it tell? What story would be left untold? I tried out the exercise on my dad. Who was he, in thirty-seven words?

> George S. Generous, loyal, funny, and ethical to a fault, gifted teacher and mentor, devoted family man and consummate provider, adored cardinals, fresh flowers, charcoal grilling, saltwater swimming, women's soccer, Beckerovka, sweet vermouth, and bad Czech jokes.

Certainly this portrait leaves out so much more than it includes. But even the clauses included are there without the added support of stories that would breathe life into them. Take the words "saltwater swimming," for example. How would someone know that when I was a child, Dad would wade waist-deep into the water holding me firmly under my arms and begin swinging me side to side through the water, reciting his made-up rhyme, "swishy, swishy," then toss me upward and outward into the water—as I squealed with delight—to the closing stanza, "scare the fishies." Or how would anyone know from those words that, as an adult, I watched my frail and fragile elderly father fearlessly enter a turbulent sea, my stomach seized with fear and breath bated, knowing that neither he nor I could fight the tide and bring him back safely if he were dragged out to sea? Sure enough, I watched in abject horror as a wave washed him under and he vanished from sight. But I can still chuckle at the sight of him bobbing up like a cork from the frothy sea, giggling with glee like a two-year-old and exclaiming, "That was a good one!"

How would these thirty-seven words have differed if they were written not by a loving daughter but by a CAS agent? What portrait would they produce? What would be gained and what lost? What meaningful questions could never be asked because these scraps of information didn't give rise to them?

SOCIAL WORK CASE RECORDS

It is unlikely that today's professional social worker, or social work student, would deny the importance of a client's case record. The current NASW Code of Ethics requires that social workers maintain these records. Section 3.04 specifies that social workers should take "reasonable steps" to ensure accuracy in their records and that they reflect service provided. The documentation must be "sufficient and timely" in order to "facilitate" service delivery and to ensure its "continuity." In addition to protecting privacy, social workers should include only "information that is directly relevant to the delivery of service" and should retain accessible records as required by "state statutes or relevant contracts."

In the early days of professional social work, educators and practitioners spent considerable time opining on the content, purpose, and function of the case record. The debate was relatively expansive and reflects the struggles of an early profession trying to make a place for its work, but also trying to determine the proper scope, content, and even tone of that product. Arguably this conversation has narrowed significantly over time.

For example, in 1938 Margaret Cochran Bristol wrote a book, *Handbook on Social Case Recording*, devoted to the topic. She identified four main categories of functions of case records: to facilitate treatment, to "study and research social problems as a basis for social reform," to train students and for teaching purposes, and finally to "educat[e] the community as to its social needs and the place of social case work in filling some of these needs" (5). Furthermore, she offered practical advice on conducing first interviews, writing narratives and summaries, collecting and preserving letters, conducting case analyses, and the ethical implications of practice.

Given the centrality of case recording to the everyday business of social work, remarkably little current scholarship has paid sustained intellectual attention to the task. An exception is found in the work of Jill D. Kagle (1984; 2002). Broadly speaking, Kagle (2002:28) summarizes the reasons for keeping records as threefold: to promote accountability, to support practice, and to improve practice. She identified the core content of a complete case file as including an opening summary, assessment, service planning, interim notes, emergencies, and a closing summary (29–30). She notes that good case records are "accurate, unbiased, and objective"; include only crucial information; are up-to-date and well organized; document the source of information; provide rationales for action; focus on "the agency's mission and the purpose of service in the case"; document compliance with policy and practice guidelines; document "risks and benefits of services offered" and the client's role in decision making; "consider the special nature of the client situation"; and provide a "coherent picture of service" (30). The principal uses of the case work record were for maintaining the continuity of cases, documenting services, and communicating with other professional organizations (Kagle, 1984:150).

Kagle (1984) has expressed concern about the fact that social work recording has become more of an administrative, rather than clinical, activity. She also noted that the "era when social work agencies could keep detailed narrative records on each client has passed" (48). So there has been an evolution in the function of the case record that has necessarily also affected the kind of information recorded. This evolution in function and content is arguably the result of both economic pressures and privacy concerns. However, the end of any era has implications, both positive and negative.

Barbeau and Lohmann (1992) have contrasted this current truncated version of the case record with the products of social workers from the early twentieth century who "were aware of the historical importance of their efforts" (15). There was a time when social workers recognized that the significance of the information they were collecting and recording extended beyond the simple relationships of client and worker. These records were deemed to have both historical and sociological significance. Social service agencies of yesteryear left "a considerable record of achievement and accomplishment," which has "been preserved for our use. Unfortunately," Barbeau and Lohmann noted, "the same may not be as true of the present generation of social workers and the executives of social agencies where they practice" (15). The pair argue for the historical preservation of today's administrative records in order to document the accomplishments of the profession in general, as well as the work and contribution of individual agencies. Presumably a similar argument could be made for the preservation of clients' individual case records as well.

Case records can provide a lens for telling agency stories and thereby understanding social work. They also offer a way of making sense of people's lives and actions in a historically situated moment. Certainly when the former CAS administration made the decision to turn over agency records to the N-YHS, it had the longer historical view in mind. It remains to be seen if the current CAS administration will see the significance of administrative data and case records and preserve them for a next generation.

BREATHING LIFE INTO CASE RECORDING

In 1928, at a time when the CAS was routinely using the "Treatment Record" as a way to organize a client's file, a debate was unfolding in the scholarly journal *Social Forces* about what a social work record should contain for the purposes of sociological investigation. It was a time when the roots of social work were still deeply intertwined with sociology.

"What should social case records contain to be useful for sociological interpretation?" is the opening sentence in an article by Ernest W. Burgess (1928) addressed specifically to social workers and sociologists. His response to his own question seemed—in his own words—"too easy to be entirely honest" and was that social case records should contain "what will render them valuable for social case work, that and no more" (524).

Burgess identified dissatisfaction on both sides of the disciplinary aisle because "sociologists" were "quick to point out that social case records as they stand are not satisfactory for sociological analysis," and social workers "are dissatisfied with their present methods of record keeping for the purposes of social diagnosis and treatment" (524). It seemed natural to him to raise the question of their "joint interest" in the "content and form of social case records." His concern, ultimately, is framed as a question about the relationship of the "individual" to the "group." I too am concerned about this link, but my interest has a historical twist to it. What can the individual youth and families served by the CAS tell us about the course of history?

Ultimately Burgess directed his critique at the lifelessness of the case record. "Characters in case records do not move, and act, and have their being as persons," he wrote, "they are depersonalized, they become robots, or mere cases undifferentiated except by the recurring problems they present of poverty, unemployment, drunkenness, feeble-mindedness, desertion, bad housing" (526–27). In short, they were like pickled Mexican sierras removed from their watery environment.

Burgess locates the problem with the fact that "characters in case records do not speak for themselves" and that "they obtain a hearing only in the translation provided by the language of the social worker." The solution he argues for is "to enter the interview in the words of the person." In this manner the individual becomes a participant in the "life history . . . in his own plans, in his philosophy of life" (527). In short, Burgess sought a way to bring clients alive by making their voices heard.

Certainly by the late 1920s, the CAS had a well-developed idea of what constituted a case record. Each youth had an individual file folder, which contained a summary placement log with intake and discharge dates, intake assessments, health and education records, internal and external correspondence, and all sorts of miscellaneous notes. Many records contained correspondence with clients that extended well past the official discharge date of the youth from agency supervision. CAS interest in its former chargers continued for life. More important, these personal letters, written by the clients themselves, seem to come closer to Burgess's call for permitting the client to speak for him or herself; for finding a way to capture the client's philosophy of life from his or her own point of view, and thereby making clients come alive. Such was the case with John Chester Munn.

JOHN'S STORY

John Chester Munn was "received" by the Children's Aid Society on September 17, 1936, from the Society for the Relief of Half-Orphan and Destitute Children. He was sixteen years old at the time. Aside from arriving in "good physical condition" and being of "average intelligence" (even if a bit "careless about details"), he was also characterized as being "willing and reliable" as well as "kind and thoughtful toward other children." More significantly, however, the referral letter introduced him as "very anxious to learn farming." At that time the CAS was running a farm training school for boys known as the Bowdoin Farm School. John was immediately placed at the farm school even as CAS social workers set to work—with some evident difficulty—trying to make sense of his family tree.

For all intents and purposes, John was an orphan when he arrived at CAS. His mother, Eleanor Creek, had given birth to him on October 3, 1920, as an unmarried nineteen-year-old. Just two days after John's eighth birthday, his mother died at Metropolitan Hospital after a four-month illness. John's biological father was more of a mystery. It appears Eleanor married a John Munn a month after giving birth to baby John, although actual paternity remained in question. John's fictive stepfather, Vincent Caldron, on the other hand, was more actively involved and a sporadic presence in John's life. John's younger half sister, Faith Caldron—an ambidextrous, shy, athletic girl with sallow skin and wavy hair—was the closest thing John had to family.

In hindsight it appears that John's eagerness to attend farm school was part of a lifelong pattern of seeking out opportunities for advancement. But John was both insightful and painfully aware of the limitations imposed on him by his social class, family background, and lack of formal education. His drive to overcome these obstacles was a recurring theme. By most outward measures he was successful. However, he took notice of the barriers along the way, and they upset him. He was capable of expressing his disappointment and able to focus his consternation on the institutional and structural nature of his roadblocks.

John finished the Bowdoin Farm School training program and was well respected in his six subsequent farm placements. In late October 1937 he began attending Delhi Agricultural School in order to further his education. However, he instinctively seemed to know that all this vocational training was not a good substitute for formal education. A year later, in September 1938, he expressed a desire to attend high school rather than return to Delhi. He broke the news to Miss Baxter in a letter: "I am changing my mind in going back to the agricultural School. I can see more advantages in going back to high school. I want to get a high school diploma so as be ready to a higher education." He explicitly worried about disappointing Miss Baxter, and, perhaps partly in an effort to demonstrate his maturity, he included $75 in his letter paying back money previously borrowed from the CAS.

Miss Baxter responded with encouragement: "I must admit when I heard that you were not going back to School at Delhi I was very disappointed but now that I know the reason why it is quite different." She goes on to say she is "perfectly delighted" because "no matter what a boy does a high school diploma is very valuable to him." In fact, she confides that a graduate "can go ahead and do just about anything he wants to, whereas without that he is handicapped." She applauds his "ambition and desire" and even notes that his year at Delhi will probably make school easier "because of the studying you did there" (September 21, 1938).

EDUCATION: STALLER FAMILY BUSINESS

I can't help wondering where John got this deep-seated belief about the importance of traditional education. How could I make sense of that? I could certainly relate to it. I grew up in a house where education was like air or water; it was a life element. But my family background and circumstances made it so.

My paternal grandfather was an engineer; my maternal grandparents, a doctor and a nurse. My father had completed seven semesters of law school at Charles University in Czechoslovakia before being driven from his homeland. From a displaced persons camp in Vienna, he was "saved" by a scholarship to Hastings College in Hastings, Nebraska.

In his own words, Hastings College was "heaven on earth," and his loyalty to everything about the people and the place stayed with him until the day he died. He flourished at Hastings, attributing his success to the fact that he was older than the average college student, and better trained. Perhaps, but I think his humility often resulted in underestimating his natural intelligence. Besides, he was harder working and more determined than most. Economics was his chosen field of study at Hastings because he wanted to make sure that he acquired skills and knowledge that were readily transportable in case he was ever uprooted from his homeland again. His Czech transfer credits had included science, physical education, and language. Dad was fluent in Czech, Russian, German, and French and knew Latin, but his English was limited. He often recounted—with obvious amusement—that at Hastings he had accidently registered for a course in "home economics," thinking that it must be the English term that distinguished the study of the U.S. economy from international economics. After graduating from Hastings magna cum laude, he was accepted in a doctoral program in economics at Cornell University. There he met and married my mother, a liberal arts student. After a postdoc at Harvard, he landed a job on the faculty of the economics department at Cornell, a position he held for a half century.

In short, I was born into a family where the value of education was bedrock; it was an unquestioned and unquestionable given. I remember once asking my father about the possibility of getting a part-time job in order to earn pocket money, only to be reminded, in no uncertain terms, that *his* job was earning money for the family; *my job* was to study and be a good student. My parents invested in summer dance camps and private ballet lessons, but always accompanied by the story about how my grandfather, a well-educated engineer, had managed to support his family in exile in a displaced persons camp by playing piano for barroom tips. The moral of the story was that a well-rounded education was critical because it was impossible to predict how various knowledge and skills might need to be deployed in an unpredictable world.

Only as an adult did I become aware of the fact that my education-infused upbringing might be unusual. While recounting an inconsequential story to a first-generation college-educated colleague on the faculty at the University of Alabama, I happened to mention my childhood bedroom study. She gasped in disbelief, "You had a desk in your bedroom?" Indeed, I did. Each of the Staller children did. Where else would you do your homework? My study nook consisted of a desk, an office chair, a strong desk lamp, and a bulletin board. One wall of my bedroom housed floor-to-ceiling bookshelves. They were made from plywood boards and rested on movable metal brackets hooked into metal runners. These bookshelves were utilitarian, not decorative. My colleague couldn't believe I had grown up with the luxury of having an office and library in my own bedroom. I had never before stopped to think about a childhood without them. I couldn't have imagined it.

In short, the very privileged path that I followed from high school through college, law school, and finally a doctoral program seemed both predictable and inevitable. Being a student was what I had been trained to do since birth. It was a natural path. But why was John so driven? Where had that passion for education and advancement come from? Who had instilled it? Certainly it did not come from his fictive father.

JOHN'S PLANS FOR ADVANCEMENT

John's high school plan failed, largely because it rested on resources his stepfather was unable—or unwilling—to provide. So John again turned to CAS for help. With Germany's invasion of Poland in September 1939, he saw a new opportunity. John decided he wanted to enlist. Enlisting, however, required the signature of a responsible legal guardian. Miss Baxter stepped up to the plate and was appointed in that capacity by New York surrogate's court on November 18, 1939. A month later, on December 17, 1939, John enlisted in the U.S. Navy.

John began serving before the United States had officially entered World War II, and he made the transition—along with the navy itself—into active combat. Ultimately he saw considerable action in the Pacific theater, serving on the U.S.S. *Enterprise*, the U.S.S. *Dixie*, and the *Bunker Hill*. Throughout, Miss Baxter and John exchanged letters. He struggled with the challenges of growing up quickly, living life, and being at war.

John's earliest letters from the navy bristled with enthusiasm. "Believe it or not, Miss Baxter, I have a million and one things to relate, but I don't know where to begin" (November 3, 1940). He eagerly asserted that the navy "is really becoming part of me" and expressed pride in wearing a uniform (January 16, 1939). He narrated his new experiences to Miss Baxter with evident zeal. These included his travels (like his first trip west of the Mississippi); flying for the first time and looking down, from above the clouds, at a fleet of aircraft carriers and destroyers; as well as his daily routine (including enduring inspections: "Boy, they don't miss a thing at these inspections! . . . The neater and cleaner you are, the harder the inspecting agent looks."). He peppered his letters with a new vocabulary—signing one letter to Miss Baxter from "the saltiest hombre afloat"—while apologizing to his landlubber reader for the jargon. Miss Baxter's responses were encouraging and reflected her interest and support. "You certainly are having one of the finest experiences in the world," she wrote in March 1940.

As I delved ever deeper into the enormous file, each letter drew me further into John's life and his relationship with Miss Baxter. She was tender at times, scolding at others, while she played mother, social worker, legal guardian, and friend. Although Miss Baxter is alleged to have corresponded with some three hundred boys during the war, John was clearly special. The letters became more complicated, as did their relationship. In 1943 John managed to send her red roses from a South Pacific port on Mother's Day, and that Christmas—after a four-year absence in the navy—he visited New York City over the holiday. He sent photographs, and they exchanged small gifts. "Speaking of Christmas gifts," he wrote in 1944, "what could be more sensible and practical than a good pair of men's hosiery? A man's gift, indeed."

CHRISTMASES AT THE HOMESTEAD

I can't imagine a more magical time of year than Christmas. Unlike John, who arrived at the CAS without certainty about his date of birth, I knew mine. I was born on December 22, three days before Christmas. I grew up hearing the family tale about how my mom had insisted on opening her gifts before leaving for the hospital, and how she had received a fur muff from my grandmother that special year. I absolutely loved the notion that I was welcomed into the world (and celebrate my birthday each year) with the good cheer and rituals that surround the Christmas holiday. I don't have to wonder about what was going on at the time of my birth; I can hear the carols that were being sung, see the decorated evergreen trees, and smell the spicy aroma of cookies baking in the oven.

As a child, we celebrated my birthday by inviting all the other girls from my grade school class—at *that* time in my life the boys had cooties—over to the house to make Christmas ornaments for the tree. My mother would put out an assortment of raw materials—colorful construction paper, ribbons and twine, sprinkles and glue sticks—and set the creative juices of a pack of giggling girls to work. Although the point, as I understood it at the time, was to decorate *our* Christmas tree, inevitably the nicest creations left the Homestead with the girls who had created them. Our tree ended up adorned with family ornaments accumulated over the decades, and that particular year's rejected party creations.

But there was a darker side to Christmas as well. My Dad would grow somber on Christmas Eve before he gave himself over to the family festivities. I grew up knowing that this was the day Dad escaped from Czechoslovakia, but he didn't like to talk about it. Somewhere in my childhood I learned or at least sensed it was not a topic area where questions from children were welcome. It had been a dangerous and daring escape that opened up opportunities for my dad and thrust him on a new life course. Although my father was eternally grateful for everything he had in the United States—more grateful than many U.S. citizens, in his view—the Christmas Eve anniversary was always bittersweet. In my own life, his moments of melancholy were experienced as a temporary and transitory cloud in the overall festive flow of the holiday.

THE DARKER SIDE OF MISS BAXTER'S RESPONSIBILITIES

Miss Baxter's guardianship of John Munn also had a darker and more serious side. John began sending her legal documents for safekeeping. These included the confidential fact sheets required by the navy in case of his death or serious injury. The information recorded identified beneficiaries, other persons to be notified in case of his death, and his assets, including insurance policy information and bank accounts. "I hate to be bothering you with such small gear" he wrote, "but in uncertain times as these one doesn't know what'll happen . . . from day to day" (June 14, 1941). Although he continued to apologize for burdening her with such "small tripe" and expressed his gratitude to her for attending to these chores, the forms came regularly and were repeatedly updated and amended. For example, his first instructions for disposing of his remains in the case of his untimely death were "to be buried at Arlington Cemetery, Wash., D.C.," but within three years, an increasingly jaded John responded to the same question with "Suit yourselves" (July 19, 1943). Miss Baxter must certainly have understood the seriousness of John's request, but nonetheless, as if to underscore its importance, John wrote, "You see, I want this piece of document to be fool proof. My original sheet is aboard ship and, as you know, there is a possibility that this may be destroyed in the event in the loss of the ship" (October 8, 1942). Miss Baxter was John's land-based lifeline. He appointed her his executrix, designating his stepsister, Faith, as his primary beneficiary.

John's drive for advancement was evident from the start. Miss Baxter served as constant cheerleader, coach, friend, and parent. From a host of possible specialty ratings in the navy, John was assigned yeoman with clerical responsibilities for his squadron in November 1940. He initially progressed through the navy's enlisted rates quickly, moving from seaman to petty officer by June 1941. He also skipped up the rating scale within the yeoman classification from third class to second then to first by August 1943. He was appointed his ship's chief yeoman in early 1944.

John clearly wanted to capitalize on the broader opportunities offered by the navy. He set his sights on enhancing his professional skills by putting in a request, as part of a quota system, to attend stenography school. It seemed like a good choice. It would further the skills he employed as the squadron's yeoman, and Miss Baxter thought there would be a good market for male secretaries after the war. John quickly realized that his social class and lack of formal education were impediments to his permanent advancement in the navy. He alternated between handling these hurdles with cheerful and insightful philosophical resignation and indignant outrage and depression.

John submitted requests to attend stenography school several times, the first in the fall of 1941. He declared this would make him "the happiest fellow in the world if only this request is granted," a claim he continued to repeat in his letters to Miss Baxter for years. He applied himself with zealous determination, taking up the study of shorthand in his spare time. By February 1942 he was promoted to lead yeoman, but his hopes of stenography school were dashed. "I was informed by my Commanding Officer that my services at present are needed for the best interest of the Service." John chose to dwell on the positive side of this development, expressing disbelief that "most of the boys, who are my subordinates, are senior to me in educational standards" and recognized that his superiors "placed full confidence in my work."

Admitting that he had been "discouraged" but was not inclined to give up, John submitted another application to stenography school and was recommended by his superiors again in April 1943. He understood and commented on the inequities: "why is it that in peace-time when competitive examinations were in their stride I have made rapid advancement; then in wartime these same fellows—whom I have surpassed—are stepping ahead?" By August he had still not been put on the quota list for stenographer school and was increasingly resentful about it. "I've been told by some of these glorified pedants that I have a restricted level for learning," he wrote Miss Baxter.

> After all, who are they to judge when they show their mediocre abilities in such exaggerated ego. After being repressed of personal liberties and restricted to a certain social level, I look forward to a world of unlimited opportunities. They'll be plenty of dark days ahead, so what? A man who has the will power, dogged-determination to face his problems with all of his available resources is bound to win.

In October 1943 he submitted yet another request for stenography school, with the full support of his supervising officer. Among other things, he noted that he had been "serving on a combatant ship from December 7, 1941, until January 28, 1943 which was operating extensively in the South Pacific arena in all the major campaigns," and that he had served nearly four of his six-year enlistment term. By January 1944 he wrote to Miss Baxter that he expected to "leave for steno school "very shortly."

Then came silence.

BACK ON THE HOMEFRONT: DOWNSIZING THE HOMESTEAD

At first, it seemed like the task of downsizing the Homestead would mostly involve material possessions and be a matter of either allocating or shedding. Allocating necessarily included the tussles—some small and some larger—between and among my mother, sisters, and brother over things that held some meaning. Who would get the unusual coffee table sliced from a tree trunk, the marble-topped chest of drawers, or the brass bed?

What would happen to the battered Weber grill on which my dad had produced a lifetime of hamburgers and pork chops? Or the oversized asbestos gloves that served as protection from the dancing flames as he hoisted those three-inch-thick steaks for which he was so famous that students and colleagues fondly recalled them even after his death?

Disposing of material things that none of us wanted was an altogether different task from this allocation exercise, which served a basic preservation function. There were useful and serviceable items like furniture, dinner plates, artwork, garden equipment, and clothes that needed to go somewhere. Some of it was hard to let go and some not.

But there were also the outdated and useless items that held special meaning. Was there any reason to save the 8-millimeter films capturing family events and the antiquated equipment necessary to play them? What about all the family photographs in negative and slide form and the light boxes used to scan through them? There were LP record albums and a phonograph, but who wanted them? I didn't, in spite of the fact that memories exploded like fireworks with each record jacket. Privately I worried that the memories themselves would disappear without the physical triggers that ignited them.

So shedding items—as distinct from allocating them among family members—involved saying good-bye permanently as things went off to the Service League or found new adoptive homes on eBay. It all disappeared, but not without some parting tears and mourning the fact that these familiar things would never surround and comfort me again.

JOHN'S UNTOLD STORY: WHAT WASN'T SAID

Coterminously with the developments in John's naval career, the war was escalating and mail was slow. Receiving a letter within one month, said John, was a "phenomenon"; letters averaged a two- to three-month delay. This time lag caused Miss Baxter worry and she fretted, but John repeatedly tried to reassure her, "Whenever you are uncertain of my well-being, remember the old proverbial expression: 'No news is good news.' As I told you before the mail situation is simply fierce" (April 24, 1943).

If the mail situation was metaphorically "fierce," the fighting John was seeing was literally fierce. Complicating the matter was the fact that mail was heavily censored. The public service campaign of the day touted, "Loose lips might sink ships," and everyone—inside and outside the military—was repeatedly warned not to talk about ship movement or war production. Although some war correspondence was attacked by heavy-handed censors with scissors and arrived stateside looking like Swiss cheese, John was careful to self-censor his content, and most of his letters arrived intact. "The secrecy around us is so dense that one hasn't much to say these days," he wrote on February 19, 1942. Although he was having "many unusual experiences" and had seen "a little excitement," he confided to another CAS worker, "due to strict censorship regulations I am compelled to save these exciting stories until the restrictions are lifted" (February 13, 1942).

While he could not provide Miss Baxter with details, he could allude to the horrors and his life learning curve. He wrote:

> Back again from a successful and eventful cruise. Yes, I was in the thick of things. Oh, Miss Baxter, I only wish we were permitted to relate our many experiences and exploits. . . . At present everything seems to be in dense secrecy, so I guess we'll have to tuck these sea stories away for a later date. (ca. February/March 1942)

> You must believe me when I say that I have experienced the horrors of war. I have seen with my own eyes my fellow shipmates go to their destiny. (June 15, 1942)

> Truthfully speaking, I have seen sights which were indescribable. The most underestimated statement ever uttered by any man in history was the fact that "war is hell!" (a letter to Mr. Lane, another CAS worker, November 3, 1942)

> I have learned many things about human nature. Fighting for self-preservation brings out the hidden character. (April 10, 1943)

However, all this secrecy had a cost. John had to keep what he was seeing to himself. So while he was experiencing more, he was saying less. The pressure built.

There were plenty of indicators that the war was taking its toll on John. On August 23, 1943, John admitted in writing that his "spirits were so depressed that my enthusiasm and interests just couldn't be aroused." Miss Baxter responded that she was "disturbed" but hoped it was only "a passing phase." If John felt the additional burden of needing to curtail expressing his true feelings to Miss Baxter, he didn't put it in writing; instead he apologized for his "depressing account," saying he did not "mean to have you bear with me the 'ups and downs' of my moods." He promised to try "not to write any more dispirited letters" (November 9, 1943).

Instead, what followed was a dearth of letters from John altogether. In fact, nine of Miss Baxter's letters went unanswered. She grew so concerned that she went to the unprecedented measures of scolding him on April 14, 1944: "we just cannot figure out your silence. Tell us frankly, Johnny, what's wrong?"

Miss Baxter finally received a four-page letter dated June 21, 1944. John had had his orders modified, and he was once again denied the opportunity to attend stenographer school. In spite of admitting he was "bitterly disappointed in not obtaining the Steno School quota, for it was my highest hopes I would go," he insisted he had "no regrets," writing that "Rain must sometimes fall in everyone's life." His determination was, once again, on display: John set out to find a night business school that he could attend while stationed on the West Coast and began taking the "courses they had to offer in the way of secretarial and stenographic studies."

However, by the beginning of 1945 the tone of his correspondence grew increasingly somber. On February 9 he sent a note to Miss Baxter referencing a telegram: "Oh, by the way, did you receive the telegram I sent you? Undoubtedly you were aware of the hinting of coming events. From this date henceforth our destiny will be held in the hands of Fate. I am planning to write to you as frequently as possible, for I know you'll be very concerned."

LEAVING HOME AND HOMELAND

Although my dad was reluctant to tell us about his family's dramatic escape Christmas Eve when we were children, he grew more interested in sharing those stories as he neared his death. Luckily, my sister Jane took up the challenge. With dogged determination and infinite patience, she interviewed my father at least twenty-five times over the course of a year before his death. I listened to those extraordinary tapes only after he was gone, and after it was too late for me to ask my own questions. My reluctance to talk with him, and my ignorance about basic facts of his life, is humiliating and painful to admit. I permanently lost the opportunity to ask the hundreds of questions that I now wish I had asked. Nonetheless, I am enormously grateful to my sister Jane for capturing his life story and preserving it for me, and others, to hear. Not only does the sound of his voice, his idiosyncrasies and cadences, bring him back to life for me, it helps breathe life into the experiences he describes. I can feel the fear, grief, pain, and relief. I can be there with him.

My grandfather, Děda, had been an engineer employed at a major munitions factory, Zbrojovka Bruno, in Brno, Czechoslovakia, after World War I. It was only in writing this autoethnography that I discovered that his story, and his heroism, has been written about by others (Krčál 2012; Luza and Vella 2002; Wyllie 2006). Described as "a technical whiz," my grandfather had helped develop "a new type of machine gun—the BREN—which he sold to the British before the war" (Luza and Vella 2002:85). According to my father, Děda absolutely loved his job, and he made a speedy ascent from technical director to CEO, "supervising even its division of automobile productions" (Luza and Vella 2002:85). That changed, however, with the German Nazi invasion and occupation of Czechoslovakia in 1939. Děda was summarily demoted and replaced by a more trusted German official. Although he was accused of collaborating with the Germans during his lifetime, in fact Děda was an active and important member of the Czech resistance movement (Luza and Vella 2002; Wyllie 2006). There seems little doubt that the information supplied by my grandfather from the weapons factory, and transmitted to both London and Moscow, did damage to the German cause. According to Luza and Vella (2002), my grandfather "was excessive in his resistance efforts as he was in everything else, willing to do anything to damage the Nazis, even though he worked under their noses as one of their essential technical experts" (85). Among other things, Děda had considerable dealing with Albert Goering, the half brother of Hermann Goering, a ranking Nazi officer and Hitler's designated successor. My father recalled the many times Albert Goering was housed and hosted in the Staller family home (Luza and Vella 2002; Wyllie 2006). Information gained from these exchanges between Albert Goering and Děda was transmitted by my grandfather to allies in London and Moscow.

Děda's active participation in the underground meant he was gambling with his own life and put the safety and well-being of his wife and two sons in jeopardy as well. In a memoir of the Czech resistance, Radomir Luza recalls my grandfather's position this way:

It was a touchy question whether Staller should remain in such a dangerous position, working cheek by jowl with the Germans. He was providing
crucial intelligence about the levels of industrial production and the new
munitions they were developing. Father [Vojech Luza] thought the risk
was worth it; that is, he thought, I suppose, that the information was worth
Staller's life. (Luza and Vella 2002:86)

More than a few of Děda's friends and accomplices were executed.
According to a current historian of the Czech resistance movement, at the
height of the German occupation "there were 100 executions, at least, a
month. A gallows was set up in a schoolyard in Brno and every day when
you passed that school yard you heard someone being executed" (Vella
2004). Although not a detail my dad had described in his interviews with
my sister, he must certainly have been acutely aware of these gallows in his
hometown. He was also aware they were meant for the likes of Děda and
his family. In my father's opinion, the family survived only because the war
ended before Děda was caught.

However, things went from bad to worse in 1949 with the communist takeover of Czechoslovakia. Stalin's paranoia and desire to control
the Soviet bloc are legendary. According to Vella (2004), "Because the
communists very correctly recognize that if you would resist Hitler you
are obviously the kind of person who is capable of resisting Stalin or
resisting any communist takeover," they ruthlessly rounded up, tortured,
imprisoned, or killed those they could identify. It was in this context
that Děda was interrogated at a Bratislava police station. Although he
had been interrogated before and steadfastly asserted he had no "antistate
intentions" this time, according to Dad, his interrogators had first confirmed that they knew that Děda had smuggled out information against
the Nazis, then commented, ominously, "they were very smart and the
Nazis didn't catch you" and posed the clinching question: "Why should
we think you aren't working against us too?" It was not an idle question;
it was a direct threat.

That evening Děda's sons found him sitting alone in a darkened room.
He said simply and decisively to them, "We are going." On the tape, my
father's voice breaks, he pauses, and he finally gets out through audible
tears, "He bet everything." And then, after a moment's silence, his voice
stilled choking with emotion, "I would never have had the guts."

It was impossible for me not to be caught up by the story and catch the grief from the anguish in his voice. Listening to the mixture of pain and admiration moved me to tears. My tears were of compassion, of understanding, of sympathy, of pride, and of grief.

JOHN'S FILE: THE TELEGRAM

In addition to John's growing melancholy, he was anxious about the escalating and increasingly brutal war. When Miss Baxter asked about his Christmas holiday in 1944, John answered, "Well, to tell you truthfully I was very much concerned over the critical situation in the European theatre" and "set this day of the year aside for solemnization." Instead, in his letter he reflected on the joy of spending Christmas 1943 in New York City "visiting you and the other members of the staff. It was very kind of you folks to have made my visit during the Holiday season such a pleasurable one. I shan't ever forget. Believe me, I am very grateful" (February 9, 1945).

It was also in this letter that John referenced the telegram, noting, "From this date henceforth our destiny will be held in the hands of Fate." I thought I might have come across John's mysterious telegraph from January 1945 as I turned the page of his case file. There before me was a Western Union telegram on a fragile, yellowed sheet of paper addressed to Miss Helen Baxter of the Children's Aid Society. It was dated 5:37 PM May 28, 1945, and issued from Washington, D.C. Its seventy-seven words read:

> The Navy Department deeply regrets to inform you that your ward John Chester Munn Chief Yeoman USN was killed in action while in service of his country. The Department extends to you its sincerest sympathy in your great loss. His remains were buried at sea with full military honors. If further details are received you will be informed. To prevent possible aid to our enemies please do not divulge the name of his ship or station.
>
> Vice Admiral Randall Jacobs Chief of Naval Personell [sic]

John Chester Munn died as chief yeoman, United States Navy. He never got to go to stenographer school. He never got to finish his education, get married, or have children. He never got to say a proper good-bye to Miss Baxter or to Faith.

The words in the telegram had caused my hands to shake and my heart to beat faster. I could hardly read through my tears by the end of the paragraph. At my shaking fingertips was the actual telegram Miss Baxter had received on that fateful day over fifty years ago. If its content stunned me, a stranger, five decades later, what must it have been like for Miss Baxter receiving it on that day? What was it like for her to learn her ward had died this way? At what instant did she realize this is what happened? As she received the telegram? When she saw the heading? Did she feel it in her gut before she read the words? Was she sitting down? Did she collapse? Were her tears immediate? Did she cry out to her office mates? Did she leave work early that day? Was she still doing social work as she processed this news?

Years before, John himself had prepared her for this moment. He had written:

> I hardly approve of the method in which the Navy informs the next of kin of the deceased personnel. It's abrupt and too formal in form. I honestly think it is very inconsiderate as far as the comforting of one's bereavement. Yes, I know. The Navy Department can't afford to overtax its office personnel in Washington. I imagine they have enough to do taking care of the living as well as looking out for the welfare of the decedents' survivors. (October 8, 1942)

With historic hindsight, when I reach this early letter in John's case file, I seem to always shed anticipatory tears. There is something eerie about knowing how the story ends, knowing John's fate, but knowing that neither John nor Miss Baxter could have known it at the time the words were either written or read. But it also suggests to me that there is something very much alive about them even to this day. They are not lifeless, inert characters—not pickled fish or desiccated botanical specimens—in fact, far from it. They currently loom as active players in the theater of my life.

Miss Baxter remained busy in the aftermath of John's sudden death. She received correspondence and condolences from the navy. This included John's personal effects and Purple Heart. She dealt with lawyers, and, in an attempt to sort out John's family tree—from a legal perspective in order to administer John's estate—she contacted dozens of people, hospitals, social service agencies, and other institutions. She accounted for, and oversaw the distribution of, John's life insurance policies (some $10,000 in all), his bank accounts (over $1,000), and twenty-four war bonds.

FAMILY HISTORY: WHAT REMAINS?

All the allocation and shedding of possessions from the Homestead seemed hard enough. Then came a more stunning emotional revelation. I hadn't counted on the fact that the family that inhabited the Homestead loomed larger than I had originally thought. There were also friendly family ghosts. My father's brother had predeceased him. My mother was an only child. All four of my grandparents—on my maternal side, Mama and Fa, and on my paternal side, Babi and Děda—had died long ago. This meant that, unlike other families where artifacts might be dispersed through sprawling family trees, in my family it had all come to rest in a single, concentrated, spot: the Homestead.

Downsizing wasn't limited to disposing of, or allocating, material things from my immediate nuclear family. It was suddenly about sorting through our entire family history, in photographs, documents, and artifacts, from *both* sides and deciding what would survive and what would not.

What would happen to Fa's christening gown? Or Děda's engineering sketches? What was to come of three sets of family silverware (real silver, the kind you need to polish)? Or the impossibly fragile, but inexpensive, rose-colored glassware that appeared on Thanksgiving and Christmas? Worse yet, what was to happen to grade school products like Fa's composition book? Or Mama's nursing school textbooks, class photograph, and diploma? What about old passports, for heaven's sake?

As we cleared out these things, my mother rediscovered other remnants of our family history, including wartime correspondence between *her* parents: victory-mail, or V-mail as it was commonly know, from Fa, who was serving as a surgeon on a navy battleship in the European theater, to Mama and my mother, who were living back home in New York City.

Then there was the war on my father's side of the family. Virtually everything the family had owned but the clothes on their backs had been left behind when they fled Czechoslovakia. But after the cold war ended, Dad had carefully retrieved items from the Czech Republic with the help of family friends who had been left behind, and these things now resided in the Homestead. They included large oil paintings, a gaudy, oversized table clock, and a humongous ornamental vase.

I was acutely aware that as one of the two siblings in my family who remained childless, the family line (at least my branch of it) ends with me.

It seemed intuitively obvious that objects of significance or value should end up in the hands of my sister or brother with children—my nieces and nephews—who might eventually stake a claim. But would they even want these things? Would these items possess any meaning for them a generation from now? What should be kept as significant and what not?

All these things served to reveal the geological layers of my family's history through the experiences of its individual and collective members. As we sorted, we made decisions about which things were to be saved a bit longer and which were to be forever discarded. No matter how apparently innocuous the thing might appear on its face, each disposal carried its own unexpected emotional punch. One less artifact to aid in the story's future telling.

MISS BAXTER'S MISSION AND THE *BUNKER HILL*

In addition to all the legal and business affairs of administering John's estate that were thrust on Miss Baxter, there were much more personal—and undoubtedly emotional—tasks. For one, Miss Baxter was responsible for informing Faith of John's death. In addition, she exchanged a series of letters with women who had been a support network—some of them surrogate foster mothers—to John. This small community of mourners consoled each other but also wondered about what had happened to John and shared information when they could. Many also expressed concern for Miss Baxter. Wrote one, "I can well understand how deeply you are shaken as I know that he worshipped you, and I feel that was a strong tie between you. You acted as his guide and comforter always a reward which never can be taken from you, so feel comforted in the fact that you were an inspiration to him always." It is impossible for me to read these words, even today, without tearing up thinking of Miss Baxter's pain and her loss.

Among other things, these women attempted to piece together the story of what had happened to John. In keeping with wartime policy, there was little information initially. "I have no details from the Navy Department," Miss Baxter wrote to a friend.

> The telegram merely said that he was killed in action and was buried at sea. I wrote to the Admiral who signed the telegram asking for the date and also for details when they were available and could be given out. . . . I do not

know what ship John was on for I had the same address as you—Torpedo Squadron 84. In one of the letters I spoke of this and hoped that he might be able to tell us the name of his ship but apparently that was against regulations. . . . I have a feeling too that he was in the Okinawa campaign because we have been told in the papers a number of our ships were damaged by those beastly suicide planes there.

Indeed, Miss Baxter's suspicions were correct. John had been on the *Bunker Hill* when it was attacked off Okinawa on May 11, 1945. It took almost a month before the navy publicly released news of the *Bunker Hill*. The next day, June 28, the *New York Times* reported the story in horrifying detail (Loftus 1945). The captain of the *Bunker Hill*, George Seitz, had been sending fighter planes against the Japanese for fifty-eight consecutive days. Then, in a matter of thirty seconds on the morning of May 11, "two suicide planes crashed on her deck . . . and transformed her into an inferno of flames and exploding ammunition that riddled her decks and bulkheads and blasted holes in her sides." Each of the two Japanese pilots had released a 500-pound bomb before hitting the *Bunker Hill*. One crashed into thirty-four planes waiting on the flight deck; the other crashed through the flight deck and exploded in a gallery deck below.

Gasoline lines and fully fueled planes ignited, exploding ammunition from the parked planes and turning the flight deck into a pyre. Dense, black, billowing smoke rose hundreds of feet from ship. Below deck the vessel had turned into a furnace. It took a full four hours to bring the ship back under control. The battleship was melting below deck and being consumed by raging flames above. The *Bunker Hill* began sinking, in part, from being dowsed with tons of water in an attempt to combat the flaming gasoline and oil. Perhaps worst of all, she was straight on course for Kikai, "one of the strongest Japanese staging points for suicide planes." In a dangerous and dramatic move, the captain decided to abruptly turn the vessel around, as "tons of water, burning gasoline and oil on the hanger deck sloshed away from the fire fighters and poured over the edges of the deck into the sea." According to the *New York Times*, the *Bunker Hill* "literally dumped the heart of the inferno on her hangar deck into the sea." "On the following day, although the *Bunker Hill* was still in the battle zone, 352 men were buried at sea in ceremonies that began at noon and ended at dusk" (Loftus 1945:5). One of them was John Chester Munn, a CAS client and Miss Baxter's ward.

The *Bunker Hill* limped back home to the United States, a "blackened hulk" and the "most extensively damaged warship ever to enter the Puget Sound Navy Yard for repairs." Her "decks were warped and twisted and her gun side had been virtually destroyed. . . . One elevator, melted almost in two, hung in the smoking, blackened hanger deck . . . the hanger deck was demolished; the island structure, which had been engulfed in flame after the second plane struck, was in shambles of torn catwalks and twisted steel" (Loftus 1945:5).

The *Times* printed five photographs with its story. The reproductions are the kind of grainy microfilm war photos that under other circumstances I would have paid little heed. However, it was impossible not to linger over the fiery inferno images without wondering about John. When I first read the telegram, I had envisioned in my mind's eye a solitary death for John. Instead, I learned that 393 men had been killed in those moments on the *Bunker Hill*. Another 264 were wounded, and 19 were missing. In this mayhem, where had John been? What had he been doing? Did he know what happened to him? Did he have a fleeting thought before he was gone forever?

THE CHRISTMAS EVE CROSSING

As soon as possible following my grandfather Děda's frightful interrogation and decision to leave Czechoslovakia, arrangements were made using friends and networks in the Western world, the underground, and an active black market of human traffickers and couriers. On Christmas Eve, 1949, the family—including Babi and Děda, my uncle and his wife, and my dad—left fake Christmas presents (empty boxes that had been carefully wrapped and placed under the tree) and took the slow train from Brno to Bratcheslova. Prewarned about the number of Russian spies at major stations, the family exited the train at an "irrelevant station" before they reached their ticketed destination, my father remembering the irony of the station master's instruction to get credit for the unused leg of the journey as they detrained.

The family was met by a taxi, two black market guides, and a farmer. No names were exchanged. The taxi deposited the escape party, and their guides, in the middle of nowhere but closer to the Czech-Austrian border. The five Stallers—bracketed both front and back by human traffickers with guns—were hustled across an open field and into the woods. They spent the next three hours silently walking through the snowy forest, on a not quite pitch-black night filled with the eerie and discomforting sounds of wolves and owls and breaking twigs. Babi had weak ankles and difficulty walking, so her mouth had been taped shut out of concern that she might accidently cry out. I can summon up the surreal combination of fear, solemnity, the sense of interminable distance, and suspended time as Dad's voice spells out the story on tape. Even knowing the final outcome doesn't relieve the knot in my stomach as he recounts his journey, and I live it with him.

The party finally reached an icy cold river, still in Russian-occupied territory. The smugglers inflated a small boat capable of carrying only two people at a time. One by one, they ferried the family across: my uncle, an army deserter, first; next Děda, then Babi, and finally my aunt, until the only one left behind was my dad, for what "seemed like an eternity." I wept still more, listening to his voice recounting kneeling to the ground and kissing the frozen earth of a country he believed he would never see again.

The river crossing did not bring safety. They were still in Russian-occupied Austria, but the borders were heavily mined, although relatively less patrolled. The traffickers and their human cargo continued until they reached an old farmhouse where the five members of my family were secreted in a windowless, interior room. They spent a day and half in hiding—without food and with only a bucket for a toilet—leaving the farmhouse only with the evening darkness.

When the family finally reached Vienna, there was a meal and a bed for the first time in over two days. They spent another couple of days in hiding while falsified documents were obtained, each with a different name. My father was assigned the identity of an "Austrian student." The family bet on the fact that its fluency in German would be good enough to get it past Russian military, disguised as Austrian citizens rather than detectable as fleeing Czechs. They boarded yet another train in a Russian-occupied zone and separated from each other for safety—my grandparents in one car, my aunt and uncle in another, and my dad—once again—making passage all by himself. I can feel the sense of isolation he must have felt, falsified papers in hand and no familiar face in sight.

Fear grips my stomach even now, thinking back on my dad's account of the final moments of this harrowing journey. While he was still on the train, alone, and only 200 meters from the U.S.-occupied zone, the train slowed to a halt. Dad recalled the Russian lieutenant who entered his car along with two soldiers carrying automatic rifles. Out of the window, Dad could see that Russian soldiers were evicting passengers from the train, denying some people further passage, just yards from freedom. The Russian lieutenant took Dad's falsified passport, in which he claimed to be an Austrian student, and studied the picture. Then he looked at Dad. He slowly flipped through the pages of the passport. He turned back to the picture and again looked down at Dad. "It lasted forever," said my father, and "there was no place to run." I can still viscerally feel relief as my father recalled simply, "Then, the officers moved on."

Miraculously, the family emerged from the train one by one. They knelt together on the station ground in thanks, but not knowing what a future in exile would bring. Dad discovered only years later that my grandfather—who was not a religious man—had scrolled a single line in his diary, "God was merciful to us that night." My father's voice from the tape repeatedly calls the passage a miracle and tries to convince my sister, "You can not visualize it—it was a miracle, no doubt." My father also pondered the spiritual in his own life, claiming he "must" have had "a guardian angel. But not too many people have one. I could have gone wrong so many times," he said, only to ask out loud on the tape, "where were the guardian angels of all the Jews who died at the hands of the Nazis?"

Dad learned only later that he had been sentenced in absentia to two and a half years in prison for his "illegal border crossing." His family heard rumors that the smugglers who had helped them escape had subsequently been surrounded by Russian soldiers and had chosen suicide over capture. Even more significant, my dad heard from a close friend that a day or two after Christmas, authorities had advertised on Czech radio for "any information on the whereabouts of Karel Staller." It had taken the authorities several days to realize that Děda was missing. The family had benefited from the strategic timing of its departure on Christmas Eve. The holiday had provided protection and the advantage of time to cover distance.

On hearing this story, I finally understood why my father grew reflective and moody every Christmas Eve. At a time of year that brought only joy and celebration in my own life, I hadn't fully appreciated the complicated emotions that my dad must have felt each year on this anniversary. It was only hearing his story, in his own voice, after his death that brought the full meaning to the words I had heard since childhood: "Christmas Eve was the night Dad escaped." It also deepened my appreciation of a gesture, made by Mother, just minutes before his death. She pulled out a small, moth-eaten sweater from the back of a bedroom closet and rested it across his chest. It was the sweater he had worn during those harrowing days of escape. Now the same sweater would cloak him, for safe passage, one final time.

CONCLUSIONS: OUR FINAL REMAINS

I inherited plenty of stuff from the Homestead. Not much of it was of any monetary value, but much of it is emotionally laden. There are family photographs, my college letters, childhood books belonging to me and to my mother, Fa's letters from World War II, Mama's diary, scraps of lace that had adorned tabletops, and fabric curtains I remember from my grandparents' apartment. There is a framed etching of a coal stoker from the 1930s that had belonged to Fa and Mama but hung in the Homestead—on the wall of the second floor landing—for as long as I could remember. From my father's office, I couldn't bear to toss out his teaching notes, letters of recommendation for a handful of favorite students, day calendars, and travel logs. All these things are now nested in my own house, filled with other stuff that makes up the daily clutter of my life.

I also inherited the muff. Although my mother hadn't actually used the Christmas gift she received on the eve of my birth in decades, it had been carefully stowed and preserved. It is a motley, dusty old thing that I'll never use but nonetheless can't quite bring myself to throw out. So it will sit in my basement until I can face relinquishing this bit of my past. Or until I die and someone else, I'm not sure who, will have to do it for me, probably with no idea why the muff with its mothballs is in my basement in the first place.

I really haven't been able to bring myself to face reading through the piles of material I've received; procrastination and avoidance work better. Right now the scraps of my dad's professional and personal life, at least the ones entrusted to me, are gathered on shelves and in boxes in my basement. Fa's wartime correspondence and photographs of him in his navy uniform are housed in a clear plastic container in my library. Sitting at the top of this box is a small slate chalkboard—about the size of a paperback book—that had once belonged to my mother when she was young. Scrolled in chalk on the board is the word "doodlebug." My mother tells me it is Fa's handwriting. The doodlebug, of course, is my mother. How could I be entrusted with this ephemeral message from father to daughter, preserved in chalk on this slate, perilously on the cusp of erasure and complete extinction?

It turns out that a number of my friends—all of a certain age—are struggling with similar issues right now. I've had variations on a theme of this conversation over dinner tables and office desks. What should we do with our stuff? For example, what about the old love letters you don't really want your children to read? The theater ticket stubs that marked special events, the diaries in which we confided our deepest secrets, the yearbooks and teen magazines we pored over. Some have decided on public bonfires. Others have returned selected items to friends and rightful owners. Still others have just let things sit dormant.

How do you declutter your life in preparation for death? When and what do you cull? What story about yourself do you selectively preserve to be remembered? What will be the remaining image of your life and legacy? What incomplete story does that tell? In short, what should the pickled version of life look like? How does that align with the puzzle pieces held by others? What will get pieced together by children, family, friends, and maybe even strangers?

As I wrote this piece, I wondered about how John would answer these questions. What would he think of the record he left behind with Miss Baxter? Would he recognize himself in the stacks of documents and letters? What other things would he have wished to have had present in his case file?

What would he think of me reading his file and trying to bring meaning to it? Would he think justice had been done to him? What have I missed? What have I omitted that I should have said? What have I said that I should have omitted? What would John have wanted?

Somehow I feel quite confident that if John were here, he would have spoken his mind to me. Or maybe not—perhaps he would have simply put his thoughts into a letter to Miss Baxter. He worshipped her.

In 1942 John wrote Miss Baxter a letter of gratitude:

Miss Baxter, I don't know of any other person in the world who justly deserves more consideration than you. I sincerely mean it! Through your ceaseless efforts you have created a fraternal spirit that shall be carried on as long the Children's Aid Society exists. I know you have taken a keen interest in all of us. As for me, Miss Baxter, I am deeply grateful for your kindness. (June 15, 1942)

As a shred of evidence, in a single case file, it isn't a bad tribute from a fallen hero to his beloved social worker and guardian.

As social worker practitioners and educators, it may well be worth our time to pause and think about John and Miss Baxter the next time we record a note in a client's case record or in a student's file. What have we said? How will it be read and by whom? How will it define the person we inscribe? How long will it linger?

NOTE

1   John Chester Munn is an alias. His name has been changed according to the protocol of twentieth-century understandings. I'm not sure why. We should all be proud of this young man. We should honor his name, not hide it in a cloak of secrecy. I don't know if I could trace his family or they could find me even with his name intact. Nonetheless, I will play with it in my "renaming." If a genealogical detective from his family may some future day want to trace it, the clues are here, inserted with love and respect.

REFERENCES

Barbeau, E. J., and R. A. Lohmann. 1992. "The Agency Executive Director as Keeper of the Past." *Administration in Social Work* 6 (2): 15–26.

Bristol, M. C. 1936. *Handbook on Social Case Recording*. Chicago: University of Chicago Press.

Burgess, E. W. 1928. "What Social Case Records Should Contain to Be Useful for Sociological Interpretation." *Social Forces* 6 (4): 524–32.

Eliot, T. D. 1928. "Objectivity and Subjectivity in the Case Record." *Social Forces* 6 (4): 539–44.

Hamilton, G. 1946. *Principles of Social Case Recording*. New York: Columbia University Press.

Kagle, J. D. 1984. "Restoring the Clinical Record." *Social Work* 29:46–50.

——. 2002. "Record-Keeping." In *Social Workers' Desk Reference*, edited by A. R. Roberts and G. J. Greene, 28–33. New York: Oxford University Press.

Krčál, M. 2012. *Karel Staller: Život S Dvojí Tváří* (Karel Staller: Living with Two Faces). Czech Republic: Mlada fronta.

Loftus, J. A. 1945. "Big Flat-top Saved in Suicide Attacks. *New York Times*, June 28.

Luza, R., and C. Vella. 2002. *The Hitler's Kiss: A Memoir of the Czech Resistance.* Baton Rouge: Louisiana State University Press.

Vella, C. 2004. *The Hitler Kiss: The Czech Resistance.* C-Span Video Library, November 6. http://www.c-spanvideo.org/program/182014–4.

Witkin, S. L. 2001. "Reading Social Work." *Social Work* 46 (1): 5–8.

Wyllie, J. 2006. *Goering and Goering: Hitler's Henchman and His Anti-Nazi Brother.* Stroud, Gloucestershire: History Press.

CHAPTER 7

What Matters Most in Living and Dying

PRESSING THROUGH DETECTION, TRYING TO CONNECT

▸ *BRENDA SOLOMON*

I NEED TO WRITE THIS CHAPTER. I told Stan I would have it done by the end of the month. It is the twentieth.

In (Microsoft) Word, I scroll down under "file" and select "new blank document." So fitting. New blank document. Unlike tried or existing blank documents, this one has to be filled in and add up in some way to a chapter. The last blank document, though it had promise, saw extenuating circumstances and never became much more than, well, blank.

I give the document a title: BS trying to write a chapter. This is good. It does not put too much pressure on me or what, hopefully, will fill in what is not there. And it is likely a title I will remember if I lose it among the crowd on my desktop.

What I originally proposed for this chapter was something about my sister's death and the profession (social work, that is). I thought I had something to say about my need for some kind of help (while my sister was sick), and my expectation that hospital social workers would be able to, in some way, meet that need—by relating to me as a member of their profession and someone in need of assistance, that is, as a compatriot and another human being. In my mind, none of what I wanted or expected—in terms of getting help—ended up happening really, and I was going to write about why I thought that was so.

At this point, as I begin again many months later (with this new blank page), I feel the play of my sister's death and the unreachableness I felt surrounding her death more closely in the simple frustration of the moment, trying to write a chapter. As I see it, my sister's death marked the end of things as I knew them. When my sister left, in many ways, I went missing too. It wasn't that my sister's death began a new chapter in my life, it was more so like this: before my sister's death, there was one story about my life, and after my sister's death, there was another. Not only was I connected to her, but the tale I told myself about myself was connected to her as well. When she died, I felt profound loss—for her, and for the beliefs that helped propel me through and understand my life up to that point.

In life as it was I got things done. In life as it is I *try* to get things done. My experience of my sister's death made it difficult for me to simply go back to the work of "becoming someone"—not in the way I had before. Enduring my sister's death, I had become someone—else, or someone other than I had expected.

My desire to reach some socially mediated objective was muted. Even as the aims of my work before my sister's death were framed as social critique (and social critique was not exactly highly rewarded in the not-so-above-it-all university), for an aspiring scholar and professor it did count for something. But the single-mindedness with which I approached my academic career lost vitality, and my aims became focused in the physical and immediate—digging in the ground, making stuff with 2 × 4s, stacking wood, taking my cats for a walk; things like that. In this story of my life since my sister's death, things like writing this chapter just don't have the same charge. They don't matter as much. Yet here I am: trying. Something remains for me here—in this work.

While there are many things about life, as it is now, that are more *real* for me, I have not really arrived at a new story that I feel good about. I haven't quite found a new way of putting it together for myself that works for me. Even though this story is about living life more on my terms and outside of discursively arranged notions of success and a good life, I did not get here by my usual means, by my design. I did not steer off track; I was thrown here. And I usually get in trouble or where I shouldn't be and where I want to go by way of vigor—*my* vigor.[1] At least that is part of what I have always said to myself about myself. Yet here I am just the same. And this off-track place, where I find myself, has created a distance between me and trains and tracks and the choo-choo-chooing of life so that I may consider being on my way, arriving, and getting somewhere with some skepticism. As much fun as it is to believe in trains and tracks and the locomotion of life, I just can't go along with it enough to want to jump aboard and be on my way—at least not with the vigor with which I once did.

While I find the old story of my life, well, history, and, from where things are now, missing the point, I envy what it was like to believe in what I believed in then, with the vigor I believed it. Yes, that I miss a lot. And it was not a matter of having to acknowledge in the theoretical that vigor cannot overcome everything; it was a matter of having to acknowledge in the moment it happened that my vigor wavered and failed. It is one thing to refuse to acknowledge your limits; it is another to carry on past the point where the harsh enforcement of limits rocks your world. And from there I live in the murky mess of life where everything has its limits—where I can only try. And yet something in me still longs for a reinvestment, a re-formed vigor; a sustained belief in something in me that is unbelievable.

OK, maybe I should try to write this chapter.

Did I say it was Thanksgiving?

THAT THANKSGIVING

My sister died nine years ago. The first major holiday after her death was Thanksgiving. Every Thanksgiving since, I can feel the turkey and all the rest of it stuck in my throat as it stuck there that first Thanksgiving—and the surreal experience of trying to act like it was a holiday, like other holidays.

I think it is common for families to talk about the last Thanksgiving dinner during the current one—you know, the usual: who was there, what was said, how this pie was like or not like the one last year, and so forth. There are the various family stories that require retelling. There is the taking of one's seat—the place where you usually sit or used to sit when you were a kid.

Especially that first Thanksgiving without my sister, my family did very little of what families do. We talked, but only about what was immediately in front of us.

Pass the butter. The white meat is very moist. Would anyone like more wine?

The children offered some relief since they had their usual food needs to attend to. But my sister's absence hung in the air, between forkfuls, swallows, and meaningless remarks. Her place was filled up with children along a bench. She was there in someway it was felt. But mostly she was not there in all ways familiar and common—and that was what was mostly at the table—her absence.

And there was the turkey—dead and center on the white tablecloth. It could not help but feel more like a funeral than a holiday meal.

THIS THANKSGIVING: THE SIPPY CUP
AND THE SECURITY OFFICER

Since I chose to write this chapter, I needed time to write. And as it happened, it was Thanksgiving break; a week off from classes at the university. I thought it would be a good thing that my partner and our child go to my partner's parent's house for the holiday while I took the time to work on the chapter. So the Sunday before Thanksgiving I drove my family to the airport. And while I could feel right away that saying it was a good idea that they leave was, as it left my mouth, a bad idea, I had no idea what it would be like to actually say good-bye to my little girl, Clare, and my partner, Jennifer, at the airport. I recognized it right away, this feeling of dread and the problem of parting from them as if they might never return. I can't pretend that the ghost of Thanksgiving past and the fear of losing what I love most were not playing very loud in my heart. I accept that it just happens that way sometimes.

But I said good-bye and then good-bye again and eventually returned to the car. As I got in the car, I noticed Clare's sippy cup in the cup holder. I immediately thought back to a conversation I had had with Jennifer about the cup—how she was worried about leaving without it. With that in mind, I sprung into action and drove up to an airport entrance close to their departure gate. I got out of the car with the cup in hand and began walking quickly toward the entrance of the terminal when a neon-vested security person stopped me. He told me that my car would be towed if I left it at the curb. (It was early morning in Burlington, Vermont; my car was one of a handful parked curbside. The gate was a quick jaunt away. There would be no impact on traffic if I ran to deliver the cup.) I abruptly stopped in that stop-or-I'll-shoot kind of way and held that pose as I decided what to do. As I held the half-milk-filled pink sippy cup between the officer and me and considered making a break for it, I watched him examine the cup. I really thought he was considering its lethality.

I decided to reason with him.

I told myself to assume a very calm and friendly posture as I spoke to him. "I know you are just doing your job," I said, confirming his remarks, but then couldn't help myself and added, "but really, this is a matter of a sippy cup." I'm not sure exactly what I aimed to say when I said, "this is a matter of a sippy cup," but certainly I meant to suggest that in the history of the world sippy cups have not been used to hurt anyone, that the importance of getting a child's sippy cup to her was what was at issue here (and not homeland security), and that a child's need for her sippy outweighed any potential threat said cup could possibly present to people deplaning and boarding at our little Burlington Airport.

But clearly it was no use. There is no reasoning with a person who has been trained to do what the person is trained to do, especially if the person starts talking about how the person is just doing what the person has been trained to do; all the person is going to do is just that—and the cup doesn't have a chance.

Recognizing the futility of my attempt to make sense, in despair, and with some exasperation, I slammed the door as I got back in my vehicle.

What I failed to realize in my moment of need was that security guards are not there to make you feel secure nor to be helpful. Their job is to secure the area, as in keeping evil forces out of the way—to look for acts of potential terrorism, not for opportunities to assist travelers. That is all.

All contacts, including a call for help, elicit a detecting response, one that assesses whether or not the call for help indicates a threat to the homeland. Asking for help is asking for trouble. Literally. There is no wiggle room here.

As detectors, these guards are using categories of risk to the homeland to assess whatever they encounter, including a possible call for assistance. With this categorical sense-making at play, a request can only be worked up in terms of established categories of risk (to homeland). Thus it will not be met with say, a neighborly based, Burlington, Vermont, response, but rather an extralocally produced response, one that is textually mediated and studied and practiced to fit the work of detecting and the apparatus of homeland security (Smith 1990, 2005).

With this in mind, any human at an airport is a potential terrorist. Therefore travelers are instructed to aid in detecting work by not behaving as they otherwise might. Travelers following airport instructions or adhering to airport codes of conduct reduce their risk of being brought into a guard's scope of interest and allow guards to bring into focus those who may really be up to something.

If guards were to do something other than detecting, such as offering help, they would not be doing their jobs. Even as they were doing what might be called the human thing, or even the right thing, as they deferred to their own intellect and sensibility and considered such actions. It would still be outside of their work tasks to notice such things and offer assistance. And by doing something other than detecting, even if it was to help someone, would detract from the hypervigilance and suspicion that detecting work requires.

THE DARING TRAVELER

After my less than adequate show of disapproval by slamming the car door shut, I pulled my cell phone out of my pocket and put a call past security lines, into the airport, to Jennifer. But before my call went through, there was a knock at my window. I thought the security guard was going to arrest me or confiscate the sippy cup. Or worse yet, he might think that since I had to abort my mission to get the cup aboard a plane, my button-pressing phone call was an attempt to detonate the cup curbside! But when I looked up there was no security guard at my window; instead there was a woman, a woman who I imagined had raised all of her children some time ago, had a grandchild or two, and was on her way to meet them for the holiday. In any case, there she was, with her bag in tow, obviously on her way to board a plane. But instead of entering the airport, she was paused at my car and trying to get my attention. It was windy and cold and so it took some effort on her part to stand still and wait for me to lower the window and project her voice into the car. But she said very plainly and to the point, "Did you want the sippy cup to go to the woman and child that were with you? I saw them and will find them." She said this and then turned her head to avoid the direct gust of wind as it rattled the car. In my despair, I thought it was singularly the kindest and most human thing anyone had ever offered to do. Without thinking, I put my hand over my heart and said, "Thank you," and passed the cup to her through the lowered window.

With the security guard looking on, I passed my child's sippy cup and placed it into the hand of this traveler who, against the wind and force of the powers that be, had come to my aid, rescuing me from an obstruction of reasonableness. It was 5:30 in the morning and I was not fully awake, but I felt deep gratitude, comfort, and a renewed hope that not all independent thought had been wrung out of us.

It seems obvious enough that we are used to people behaving less like people in the infinite ways that people may behave, and more like automated people who behave in very predictable, limited ways. It is part of our daily life to expect no real person on the other end of the line or, when we do get a person, that he or she will profess to have no real means to help us—the scope of the person's authority is walled off and contained. In this context of scripted speech and preformed options, we accept an ongoing range of encounters with bodies and minds that convey emotions and understandings that are not their own.

Against this backdrop enters the woman at the airport who took the sippy cup. She saw the security guard's interference, must have understood the terms of security at the airport, and yet made a point of coming to my car and offering help. Because of the practices in place, she could not simply act out of human interest; she had to put human interest *over* airport protocols. To act in ways that honored a person-to-person connection, she had to dishonor the accepted terms of detection. One has to make some sort of conscious effort at critique and a calculation of risk to behave as one might if detecting practices were not in place—and taken for granted. In this way, to behave in a simple, kind, and compassionate manner was in itself complicated; it was, as a matter of *fact*, to misbehave.

At the airport, besides being on the lookout for perspective terrorists themselves, travelers are to keep their heads down and mind their own business and the business of those they are traveling with only. One thing is clear: you should *not* offer to take things into the airport for someone at curbside. Certainly, taking the cup from my car, the woman could be taken for someone who was at least willing to aid and abet a potential terrorist plot.

With all this in play, I pulled away from the curb and looked back at the woman over my shoulder, trying to assess the success of her attempt to carry out an ordinary act that by means of airport protocol (do not accept packages from strangers) had become nothing less than subversive—and potentially criminal. There were no indications of distress, and I felt relieved that the sippy cup will get to Clare. I imagined the expression on Jennifer's face as the woman hands the cup to her.

As I drove past the remaining entrances and exit to the airport and the several other neon-vested security personnel and finally away from the terminal, I thought first about what it would be like to be in Burlington alone without Jennifer and Clare for the holiday and then about the paper I had to write. As I drove, my thoughts drifted back to a time and events that will always be difficult to recall and hard to forget.

THE LAST TIME WE WERE ALL TOGETHER AND THE HOSPITAL

It was one week after my birthday, the last time my family gathered as family in the way that we were. I had a bonfire in the backyard and lit candles and grilled plenty of good food. I wanted my sister to be comfortable, and that was not altogether easy for her. I wanted it to be good for all of us, and that was not so easy either. Just a week before our family gathering, my sister was told that she would need to travel to a hospital with the latest fare in cancer treatment.

We went with the promise of a procedure that would buy her precious time. This procedure was known to have good outcomes. But my sister was not looking well, and I wondered why so much time had passed before this procedure was suggested.

In any case, during surgery it was assessed that her cancer had spread yet again and was set to kill her.

My brother-in-law and I were told this in one of those little empty rooms reserved for just that sort of thing located in and around the more occupied but no less stark large waiting areas of the hospital. As the doctors finished their remarks, I responded by saying that I did not want my sister to know she was dying. At the time even, I knew it was crazy to say this, and that it was crazy to have it be the first thing I said, but it was what mattered most in that moment—and besides, what was crazy and what was not crazy were not so clear to me any longer. All I knew was that I just couldn't bear to have her live with nothing other than certain doom. My brother-in-law just looked down at his folded hands and made no gesture at all. Although matters could not be made worse, it made it more real that he seemed devastated beyond words.

A few moments later I entered the recovery room. My sister was still deep in sleep under the effects of anesthesia. To look at her, you would not know she was dying. I remember trying to talk myself into killing her before she woke. It was the thing to do, I thought. If I had the guts to do it, then she would never have to deal with the devastating news, and with the final failure of her body. I so wanted to spare her the gruesome end. I thought it would be best.

At the same time I so wanted to believe everyone was wrong and that I was especially wrong; there really was a god that came with a stack full of miracles, and a miracle was well on its way. Or better yet, I wanted to believe all this cancer bullshit was a nightmare, and I would wake up and it would be gone. It all seemed so simple, really. One way or another, it all had to be a mistake.

As it turned out, the doctors had no intention of telling my sister she was going to die. When they met with her they said the procedure would not work in her case. Under their direction, my brother-in-law had already been in touch with another doctor in another section of the hospital who was working on another treatment that my sister might be a candidate for. This allowed my sister and brother-in-law to take up their let's-go-get-'em, best-seats-in-the-stadium way of approaching things that they both did so well together and enjoyed. Once again they had a focus for their energy and continued in the way they knew how to be together. I was relieved that they were still being themselves, although I felt very alone with the dread I felt.

As the two surgeons who delivered the good news of yet another possible cure left my sister's room, I followed them down the hall. I had to ask. Maybe I thought they would say there is no way to tell, or it is in God's hands or in her and her husband's hands or in the hands of the new treatment team down the hall, or something like that. But instead they said point blank, as they were walking slightly in front of me and I was struggling to catch up, "Five weeks, she has five weeks." I hesitated and then said very simply, "Thank you." But I resented them for telling me something no one should know—and that they said it with such certainty.

I kept walking, following the poorly lit hall all the way around to the other side of the unit to where there was some aspect of food service. There was a man sterilizing plates or something like that. And somewhere along there, I leaned against a wall and felt something, but certainly not the full impact of what I had just been told. I don't remember going back into my sister's room or most anything else that day. What I remember is experiencing those moments as if I were watching myself from somewhere above where I stood—as if it were on film. I think that the whole experience was too much to fully inhabit. There was something too powerful and repulsive about going into the hall and asking that question and getting that answer that made me step out and away from myself.

It was under these circumstances, whereby I was facing my sister's death and unwilling or, more likely, unable to talk directly with her about her death, that I sought the help of a social worker.

THE SOCIAL WORKER

As I look at it now, in the world of medicine and hospital life, I felt utterly lost. Everything I was experiencing was unfamiliar to me, unthinkable, not possible. It made me sick. I hated it. I was completely at sea. My sense of myself, my family, the world was adrift. I needed to talk to someone about myself to feel myself or like myself again. I needed to be in touch with some basic notions about who I was that were very much alive—and separate from my sister. I needed to be able to tell myself in the company of another person that I was someone who could handle difficult situations and would come through for my sister, my family, and her son. I needed someone to recognize me in some fashion—see an aspect of me that would help connect me to who I knew I was but just could not feel. I believed that if this could happen, then I would be better able to *be in* rather than just watch the last few weeks of my sister's life.

I assumed that if I said to the hospital social worker, "I am a professor of social work," she would show some recognition and have something to say to me about my work, and I would have something to say to her about her work—and she would say, as one professional to another, "Man, this all sucks. Sorry you are in this. How are you doing? Let me know if I can do anything to help." And I would begin to feel the weight of my feet in my shoes and be able to walk a little steadier.

In some circles this recognition of a colleague as a colleague is related to professional courtesy. According to a 1905 reference (see "The Duties of Professional Brotherhood" 1905), medical doctors had an understanding of what they should expect from one another that would suggest that what I was looking for from another social worker was not a new idea, nor too much to ask.

Considering the domain of the social worker's professional practice, I was a patient's sibling and a family member. And while the social worker acknowledged my professional status, what I remember most was that I felt I was being talked at. I couldn't believe it because I so didn't need to be talked at. Actually, I don't know when I would ever think I needed to be talked at. But without knowing what steps my sister had already taken, the social worker talked about the need for my nephew to be aided and by what means. I remember feeling overwhelmed as she discussed my nephew. It seemed clear that I was not someone to help. I was someone who was to help others. And while I recall little detail of the conversation, this is something I shall never forget: at some point in the meeting she said, "You are going to have to be the one to help your sister die." OK, so I was supposed to help my nephew live and help my sister die. I didn't think I could feel worse. I felt worse.

I realized right away that it was part of her practice to identify less vulnerable members of the family and recruit them into the work of helping with the dying patient and the other, more affected members of the family. Great! Not only was I in wicked need of help and unable to get it, but as an adult sibling, I was supposed to be positioned to offer critical help to my family. That I needed help myself clearly made matters worse.

As I sat there and listened to the social worker, I thought, "I know there is all this stuff that a hospital social worker dealing with death and dying issues is trained to do. But that does not mean that she should do it. And certainly not with me."

Instead of commonness between us, I felt the signs and symptoms of being social worked! I was handed some books on how to help my sister die. If you recall, I had less than a month to get really good at this helping someone die thing, and it infuriated me that someone might think I would spend the last month of my sister's life reading about it. As I saw it, I had a month to hang out with my sister and create alternatives to the experts' ideas of a well-planned death. And I had this crazy idea that this social worker might recognize my need for help and deal with it as a common response within the spectrum of responses family members have! I did not realize that I would be met with her preconceived notion related to what I should be able to handle and be interested in, especially in terms of meeting her theoretical suppositions about helping someone dying.

When talking to the social worker, what made me feel most in my skin was that I was outraged by her inability to relate to me in any sustained way outside of our hospital-mediated positions as professional social worker and patient. And I remained mad about the content of our conversation—how it was instructive and fit some therapeutic discourse that discouraged her from hearing what I had to say so as to listen for what I needed.

Rather, she had been trained and knew very well what to say and what I needed to hear. It was all very simple that way. I have to say, being as outraged as I was helped me feel myself again. As much *at sea* as I was, I knew a boat that could not float when I saw one. I knew reading books filled with expert accounts of how to help my sister die was not the raft I was seeking.

While I don't think that talking to people as if you are a social worker is the thing to do under any circumstance, certainly you should not talk to another social worker that way. That is, if a social worker takes an expert position in her or his work, it strikes me that it would be off-putting to most anyone seeking assistance; however, if a social worker takes this expert position with another social worker, it seems to accent, if not extend, the failure. Not only is the position off-putting, but it suggests that there is a gross lack of recognition of the other professional as one's peer—with even his or her own ideas about what he or she needs.

That said, social workers are not trained to respond to other social workers in need of help. The social worker whose help I sought was trained to look for signs and symptoms related to grief, loss, and end-of-life issues specific to some accepted practice in the field. She was trained to work with people in need of this kind of observation and remark and who would likely appreciate her intervention. In this context I was viewed in terms of her patient-care protocols. Other ways of engaging me were not likely to come into consideration. To the extent that she related to me as another professional, it may have propped up rather than relaxed her expert stance. As a social work educator, I may have put her in the position to offer with even more zeal that expert ability and knowledge that I did not seek, desire, or feel was in anyway helpful to me. All told, as much as I needed it and tried to illicit this kind of response, being a person with another person was not a *real* option for this social worker with me. As I looked into her eyes, it was as if no one was home. It was not that she wasn't a kind and compassionate person. She seemed lovely, really. As I see it, it was just that she was not thinking and feeling from her own experience; rather the thoughts and feelings she presented were transposed from the texts that mediated her professional life. And she thought she was doing right by me to treat me as she did. If she did think to act outside of these trained thoughts and responses, perhaps she believed it would be too personal to speak directly to how I was feeling. Perhaps she treated me as a professional who could actually handle something I really couldn't handle at all.

With this in mind, doing one's job is not only about looking at others in a way that reduces them to segmented aspects of experience; it is about doing the job of looking to edit out the full extent of one's own human capacity as one engages and looks at others. Doing one's job means editing out most of what is there. It is editing out what makes the observed a person and what makes the observer a person. It is dehumanizing work—and dangerous.

Although social work operates differently from airport security, I think that one of the problems with standards of care and evidence-based practice is that they reduce practitioners' interpretive authority and rather harness it with detecting protocols. These detecting protocols replace trust in practitioners and their person-to-person meaning-making practices with trust in extralocally studied and practiced methods of identification and accompanying scripted responses. These overarching methods and scripts fit the terms of institutional standards and overtake subjects and subjectivity in social working. They erase trust between people and replace it with trust in no one at all, in things like the state and corporations and in the interests of disembodied (homeland) security and disembodied (patient) care. Security and care without regard for bodies seems peculiar, and yet without much fanfare, this has become more so the terms of our work and the way we live our day-to-day lives.

Dorothy E. Smith (1990) refers to these professional processes as conceptual practices of power. Gerald de Montigny (1995), applying Smith's notion, discusses social work particularly in terms of an ideological practice. As he explains, "Our work converts the equivocal domains of daily life, with their chaos, uncertainty, confusion, and slippage into discursively fabricated and ordered accounts. Accordingly, even the ruptures, and the deep voids of madness, become manageable as social problems to be categorically defined and mastered" (25). Instead of bolstering social workers' compassion and interest in the complexity of human experience, and suspicion for accepted forms of sense-making that too quickly reduces human experience and too often pathologizes it, professional training and professional expert knowledge do more to advance detecting, in the way of security at the airport. Armed with specific problem-making criteria, social workers are set to identify theory-related aspects of a person's complex account of experience and place what might otherwise be random and inexplicable features of living a life into a coherent schemata to form a professional account of the person's feelings, behaviors, or mental state. By checking boxes on a form, or finding a list of symptoms to meet a category out of a manual, social workers have a means to reduce the totality of experience into narrow, problem-making terms. Along with this sort of detecting and categorizing come built-in methods of engagement and ways to solve the problem that fit the form that detecting has made of it. In this way the expert knowledge is reinforced by expert practice. By reifying the category, detecting brings into focus what is looked for. It leads to sightings. This, in turn, justifies the recruitment of more detectors to do the good work of helping people become identified. Detecting and categorization are believed to be the way to allow persons to solve problems, such as how to address my sister's death with planning for her son's care and the assumption that my sister needed my help or someone else's in order to die (I wish that were true because I would have made sure she never got that help!). The social worker at the hospital knew her death and dying theory and the current books to read and the right guide to follow in "helping someone die." She was an expert and did not need to question the tack to take in talking with me. She knew what to say and do in these circumstances. It was all figured out for her. It was all very clear and uncomplicated. She did not have to consider how to help or what I needed. She had knowledge without needing to think, or, more to the point, she could think without thinking. This is what has become (of) good practice (see also Jenks 1996; Moffatt 1999; Orr 2006; Smith 1999; Solomon 2005).

THE *OTHER* SECURITY GUARD

One day, in despair and unable to find anyone to talk to, I walked across the street to the research campus affiliated with the hospital. A campus. A place familiar and reassuring to me; a home away from home. I was drawn to it as one would be drawn to water in the middle of the desert. However, immediately I noticed the sign—just the kind of sign that is meant to stop people like me. It indicated that I must have a valid ID to access the grounds. About to turn away, I noticed, at the edge of the campus parking lot, the outline of a booth and then someone dressed in uniform who must be a security guard. I decided to talk to him. I remember the hot sun directly overhead. As I plodded along the scorched pavement toward him, it was as if what was left of me was being cooked out—that at any moment

I would begin to sizzle, then char, and finally crumble right there. I looked into the guard's eyes and attempted to make an appeal. It was a wonder that I tried, but I did. In any case, I said to him, "I am a professor at another university. My sister is in there (pointing to the hospital), and I just need to take a walk somewhere that might feel like home to me. I was just hoping I could take a walk." He took my university ID and looked at it and then again met my gaze and, with the utmost tenderness and warmth, said "Professor, take your walk." I felt tears in my eyes as I stepped past him. I looked back at one point. I wanted to say something. I wanted to remember him. But I could never forget him, and words were not necessary. I took my walk.

The strange part is, I remember analyzing all this as it was happening.

Just doing one's job or following the mandates of one's training in dealing with people in an airport, on a research campus, or in a hospital implies the subjugation of one's own sensibilities. It implies that some expert or expert discourse should preside over one's intellect and dominate any and all other discourses in dealings with other human beings.

In my terms, what makes a good professional social worker is being aware and critical of the formulas that comprise expert discourse and always choosing what I call connecting discourses over detecting or separating discourses. Social workers should always make sense of people's suffering in ways that extend their interest in the messiness of life and capacity to "be real" and potentially helpful.

It seems pretty obvious that we should not employ dehumanizing tactics at a point when people's humanness is in peril. Rather we should take actions that shore up people's sense of themselves and help them to be in close contact with what matters most to them.

Trying in this way is not at all easy. It is having the awareness of all that comes into play at any given moment and responding with the beauty and power and precision of a symphony. It is nearly impossible, but it is in the reaching—to take a sippy cup or to let someone take a walk—that someone is offered a chance to experience being seen and feel more like herself or himself. It is in a rich engagement and powerful exchange that something profound may take place and one's sense of one's self may be enlivened. It by pressing into and through expert knowledge and detection that we may take what otherwise would be a simple and common act of connection and experience something extraordinary.

THE END

In the end, in the final days with my sister, I remember thinking about all we knew between us, the years of education and experiences that were so important to us, and about the experts that surrounded us and all they knew, and about my brother-in-law, who was trained in medicine too. There we were, all of us with all this knowledge. Yet none of it helped us during those final days. It didn't matter if we knew all our colors, if we could sing to scale, if we knew all the parts of the body, if we understood the terms of cancer—even the one that was killing one of us. All that mattered was that we dared to continue to love when loving hurt so badly, and that we could look into one another's eyes and feel the depth of our connection. It was the hardest and most important thing to do. And considering our combined education, it is remarkable to consider that none of us had any real training that could help us with this critical task. Certainly it wasn't part of any of our jobs. And so we were all so utterly alone with ourselves, trying to find a way to be together that could at once sum up all that mattered and transcend all of what we had believed counted the most. In those final moments something was clear to me: we had been had. All the hospital protocols and medical jargon and expert discourses were a cloud that covered up the reality of our sheer and utter vulnerability. No one could help us, and so we were left with ourselves—at last—in some sort of free-fall, but still free. There was nothing to hold us to or make us follow or hope for or fear. We were on our own. Perhaps if there was a heaven, this is what it would feel like—something where dichotomies are resolved—where vast open spaces of intimacy surround you, and death looses its grip on life and life forgets its limits.

Social workers could be helpful in moments like this. But it would require more from them than the right terms and references and best practices. It would require that they dislodge themselves from these things and feel the full force of life as it is slipping away. It would require powerful actions that are done out of a deep connection with life, out of a knowledge of one's self as vulnerable and not knowing, out of a comfort to feel deeply enough so as to be moved by the sorrow that will invariably come your way, and with a bow to the complete lack of control over life that you have. In the contexts of institutions such as airports and hospitals, it would require a refusal to allow protocols and rules to override humanity. It would require listening deeply, sitting with a complex array of experiences and feelings that do not add up to any one thing, and wondering about the complexity with a philosophical interest and capacity to think outside the box and with attention to what is not there but might be possible. It would require an active mind and an open heart. It would require someone who does not thrive on being an expert but on living an exceptional life. It would require someone who is not bent on getting things done, who knows enough to set his or her sights on giving human connection a try. After all I've been through, I still don't have the capacity to act and feel in this way, but I know enough to ask this of myself—even as there are overwhelming indications in professional and personal daily living that do not support me in this endeavor. I just know it is what matters most—and worth trying.

LOST AND FOUND, FOUND AND LOST

When Jennifer called to say they arrived safely, I asked her about the sippy cup.

"I got it," she said.

"What did you say to the woman when she handed it to you?"

"What?"

"The woman, the woman who gave you the cup?"

"I packed the cup. I thought that was what you meant. The sippy cup was in my suitcase. What are you taking about? What woman?"

"No woman gave you a cup?"

"No, Bren."

I paused.

"Are you going to tell me what you are talking about?" she asked.

But I was deep in thought, imagining the woman in a little side room at the airport in shackles and missing Thanksgiving dinner with her family.

I felt sick.

I finally told Jennifer the story and she paused. I thought she was imagining the woman in shackles too. Then she said, "That was Clare's first sippy cup."

I said nothing. I didn't think I could feel worse about the whole situation.

Then she added, "Maybe she was able to leave the cup in lost and found."

The next day, I went to lost and found and looked. The cup was not there.

•   •   •

Every time we meet with someone, we have an opportunity to enliven or restore their sense of themselves and their belief in others. We should endeavor to never miss this opportunity. In the process of trying to get the cup to my daughter, I came in contact with the danger in security at the airport. It was the woman who took the cup who restored my faith in good will when she acted against or outside of standards and protocols that called for her to keep walking and ignore my distress. She did not get the cup to Clare, but her act to press into and through the meaninglessness was what mattered most. At the hospital I came in contact with a construction of help that could be no help at all. It was the security guard's action to grant me a walk, or his heartfelt response to my request, and not the walk itself that mattered most to me. And I'd like to think that it was the ability to feel the depth of our connection that mattered to my sister, even as that love could not keep her alive.

At the point that conceptual practices of power become well formed, they connote the boundaries of possible expression, put in motion what is prohibitive, and, as Butler (1993, 1999) suggests, set the terms of transgressions that would reveal their limits. But beyond transgression, calling for connecting practices (as I am doing here) puts in place an opposing referent from which social workers and other professionals may intend and articulate their practice, a practice "from somewhere" (Haraway 1997:292) that honors our relationships with one another, our trust in local concerns and practices, in what comes up between several people wondering aloud together, and insists on embodied subjectivity over disembodied objectivity (Haraway 1997; Harding 1993). Perhaps more than a flash in the night to illuminate the limits of powerful practices (Foucault 1977:35), a call for connecting practices seeks the formation of a transgressive space—an opposing opening within our social work imaginations toward an ethic of subjectivity and connection that may lead us to always listen and abide by what we might still be able to claim and account for as our *vigor*, a vigor that insists on these things and persists by way of simply trying to carry them out—that persists, quite simply, by trying to connect.

Disclaimer: As an institutional ethnographer, I consider this piece toward ethnography but not itself ethnography. In its current form it is more, and simply, a field note, if not a rambling account of various experiences. Even as I offer analysis, it is more a second field note rendered from a rereading of my first than it is analysis in the way of ethnographic work. Yet that is not to discredit this work. To the contrary, I wanted to write something that was not encumbered by academic protocols, in the way (I pronounce in this text) that frontline workers should attempt to shake off the effects of organizing discourses that arrange their everyday practices. That said, this attempt to shake off the accepted and bring it into relief is actually what a good institutional ethnographer would set out to do. So, even as I have placed academic protocols to the side and have not written an institutional ethnography per se, in writing this piece I have taken an institutional ethnographer' stance.

NOTE

1   As I struggled to make sense of my experience, I reread Kafka's (1989) "Letter to His Father" for a class I teach. In that piece, Kafka refers to "the consciousness of the Kafka vigor" (141). I found this way of talking about a belief in the force of family and their characteristic way of engagement helpful to me in thinking about my experience and articulating one aspect of it here in terms of my own vigor.

REFERENCES

Butler, J. 1993. *Bodies That Matter: On the Discursive Limits of "Sex."* New York: Routledge.

———. 1999. *Gender Trouble: Feminism and the Subversion of Identity.* New York: Routledge.

De Montigny, G.A.J. 1995. "Ideological Practice." *Social Working: An Ethnography of Front-Line Practice.* Toronto: University of Toronto Press.

"The Duties of Professional Brotherhood." 1905. *British Medical Journal.* BMJ Publishing Group. Digitization of the *British Medical Journal* (1857–1996) completed by U.S. National Library of Medicine (NLM) in partnership with Welcome Trust and Joint Information Systems Committee (JISC) in the UK.

Foucault, M. 1977. "A Preface to Transgression." In *Language, Counter-memory, Practice,* edited by D. F. Bouchard, translated by D. F. Bouchard and S. Simon. Ithaca: Cornell University Press.

Haraway, D. 1997. "The Presence of Vision." In *Writing on the Body: Female Embodiment and Feminist Theory*, edited by K. Conboy, N. Medina, and S. Stanbury. New York: Columbia University Press.

Harding, S. 1993. "Rethinking Standpoint Epistemology: What Is "Strong Objectivity"? In *Feminist Epistemologies*, edited by L. Alcoff and E. Potter. New York: Routledge.

Jenks, C. 1996. "The Abuse of Childhood." In *Childhood*, 84–115. New York: Routledge.

Moffatt, K. 1999. "Surveillance and Government of the Welfare Recipient." In *Reading Foucault for Social Work*, edited by A. S. Chambon, A. Irving, and L. Epstein. New York: Columbia University Press.

Orr, J. 2006. *Panic Diaries: A Genealogy of Panic Disorder*. Durham, N.C.: Duke University Press.

Smith, D. E. 1990. "K is Mentally Ill." In *Texts, Facts, and Femininity*. New York: Routledge.

———. 1999. "The Standard North American Family: SNAF as an Ideological Code." In *Writing the Social*. Toronto: University of Toronto Press.

———. 2005. *Institutional Ethnography: A Sociology for People*. Lanham, Md.: Alta Mira Press.

Solomon, B. 2005. "Traditional and Rights-Informed Talk About Violence: High School Educators' Discursive Production of Student Violence." *Youth & Society* 37 (3): 251–86.

CHAPTER 8

Will You Be with Me to the End?

PERSONAL EXPERIENCES OF CANCER AND DEATH

▸ JOHANNA HEFEL

"I'VE GOT CANCER AGAIN," I hear on my cell phone voicemail during the seminar break. Around me students are chatting and laughing as I take in this message, spoken by Hermann, my best friend and colleague, in a brittle, shaky, and at the same time agitated voice. I also hear "I'm in the hospital," and then the voice is replaced by a friendly, matter-of-fact voice that inquires whether I would like to hear the message again, save it, or delete it.

When Hermann fell ill with cancer, the physician advised him that he would have between a year and eighteen months to live. I promised him that I would be beside him in line with his needs and wishes until his life's end. A year later I too became ill with cancer and became not only a support person of a cancer patient, but a cancer patient myself.

We were both professors of social work at the University of Applied Sciences in Vorarlberg, Austria (and I still am). In an educational world permeated by economic principles and where everyone acts as an individual contractor, having cancer (along with all the challenges that the illness itself brings) is a liability that the system does not easily accommodate, if at all.

For me the cancer diagnosis was not something to keep secret but an opportunity to confront my private and professional circles with the transience of life, with illness and possible death. The promise to accompany my friend to the end had been given at a time when I was feeling healthy. Yet as he took his leave of life, I found myself in the midst of my own struggle with cancer and thus simultaneously attempting to cope with both our illnesses.

Furthermore, it is necessary in addressing a topic that currently affects many people and ultimately will affect everyone, namely, dying and death, to examine it from an individual and very personal viewpoint and to disclose it to an unknown audience. As a researcher I pass through different research phases, take up different perspectives, and try to courageously apply myself to this process.

Hermann died five years ago. It is now six years since the diagnosis of my cancer and the subsequent interventions and treatments. It is a good time to reflect on this life phase.

WRITINGS TO ENDURE LIFE

I would like to relax, express what I like, seek where my joie de vivre is, to sit down with my fear of surviving and write. (March 23, 2008)

The term biography is derived from the Greek *bios*, or life, and *grafe*, writing, and can in this sense be described as the writings of life (cf. Marotzki 2011). In this context, my diary entries express the struggle with and for my life and the struggle for the life of my friend and colleague who died. The noting down and description of the everyday, yet particularly my thoughts and feelings, the written reflection of personal and professional topics, have been a substantial part of my life for decades. Writing helps me to cope with living and shows—on rereading and with a certain distance—the paths of my development in relation to my younger self.

Writing also serves as an outlet for experiences; emotions become conscious and more understandable by putting them in words and writing them down. Changing perspectives acts as a release, fostering and helping me to gain distance (cf. Sperl 2010). During all these years, writing has become a necessity for me; more than a cherished habit, it is a part of my everyday life. Apart from personal diaries, I keep research and travel diaries. Writing in diary form is a dialogue with myself in a place of retreat reserved only for me, and a vital way for me to reflect on my life.

Autoethnographic research and writing is biographical research from the inside out and is concerned with an investigation into my own existence in a specific historical and cultural context. Opening myself up to this research method requires a readiness to admit who I am to myself as well as to grant to the public a window on my private life and my household of emotions: to turn my eyes once more to a phase of life that was extremely painful and marked by losses.

The explorative phase takes place in an involuntary sense through becoming ill with cancer and the confrontation with the finite nature of life, with dying and death. In this context, this leads to an orientation toward subjective experiences: those from early childhood and youth toward the issues of pain, death, and dying, and those in the present: sensing, experiencing, and learning illness, dying, and death. The investigative phase concludes with an inquiry into myself, rereading my diary entries as someone affected by cancer and a friend of someone dying. This contribution derives from memories written down in an interpretive and descriptive process, in which I reflect, describe, and reinterpret that which I have experienced, lived, and felt, comparing it with the corresponding literature. I consider this the integrative phase while I then document and discuss it critically in the respective context (cf. Fuchs-Heinritz 2005; Hitzler et al. 2011; Rosenthal 1995). The focus is on personal experiences as they are shaped and performed in social and cultural contexts.

FUNDAMENTAL EXPERIENCES: ENDURING PAIN, DEATH, AND DYING

Bearing pain without complaining was a matter of course for me throughout my childhood and youth. "What doesn't kill you makes you stronger!" was one of my father's key phrases and a guiding aphorism during my childhood and youth for dealing with life in general, and with pain in particular. My father, who was born in the early 1920s, was a physician who survived the Second World War seriously injured physically and emotionally. He was shaped by a strict Catholic upbringing and by the horrors of the war. He taught me and my siblings discipline, stamina, and a certain rigor and toughness toward oneself, among many other things.

Enduring Pain

I remember very clearly when, as an eight-year-old, I copied my older brother and jumped from the springboard to the pool wall. However, unlike him, I missed the target and hit my chin on the stone edge of the pool, causing a deep wound. My father drove me to the hospital, where he began

stitching the gaping wound without any anesthetic. When a nurse recommended an anesthetic, my father dismissed it as unnecessary, saying
"Johanna doesn't need that, she is brave." The green towel over my face,
the opening on my chin, the smell of disinfectant, and the fear of each new
stitch made me freeze and clench my teeth. The tears were flowing down
my cheeks, but I remained valiantly quiet, and sixteen stitches later I was
rewarded with praise and recognition from my beloved father.

Enduring Death

Both my parents experienced death at a young age. Johanna, my father's
younger sister, drowned in the garden pond when she was two years old.
When she drowned he was in the garden too, but as a three-year-old boy
he was not able to help her. His older brother, Konrad, committed suicide
at the age of eighteen. The trigger for the suicide was his failure on the
school-leaving examination in mathematics. Some weeks before the exam,
my father and Konrad had a conflict. My father was furious, and in this
emotional release he wished Konrad the failure. Konrad committed suicide
on his father's birthday with his father's gun, and my own father was the
bearer of that cruel message—he found him. For his entire life my father
felt guilty about both deaths.

My mother was orphaned at sixteen and was left to fend for herself. My
parents experienced the Second World War and the deprivations of these
years. My father was recruited in his early twenties as a beginning physician; my mother was a young girl at that time and, based on the experiences
with dying and death, became a nurse. Both of them lost many friends and
family members, but seldom had they spoken about their experiences.

I was an alert, curious child with a keen sense for the unspoken, and
when visiting the cemetery I always wanted to know the whys and where-
fores of Johanna's and Konrad's deaths. Therefore death was present in my
life from the beginning: as a burden and guilt for my father, and as loss and
absence for my mother. Added to this were the experiences and encounters
with death in my own circles.

When I was primary school age, I lost my beloved paternal grandparents
within a period of three years. I remember very clearly their laid out bodies: my grandmother in a black, austere dress—she always wore black—my
grandfather in a so-called Sunday suit with a white shirt. Both had rosary

beads looped in their folded hands. At the time it was still common to lay the departed out at home, so everyone who wished to could say their good-byes in peace. I also remember the cool air in the departed's bedroom, in which they were each laid out, the brass stand with holy water, and the rosary prayer of the attendees. We children had a black button sewn onto the collar of our coats before the funeral as a symbol of mourning. The wake and the farewell service took place in the church, and from there the funeral procession walked through the town toward the cemetery, where the family grave was located. Countless times I have read the quotation at the cemetery entrance that I find so comforting: "Here hatred and envy end, and all earthly suffering, here rich and poor, high and low are equal."

At that time I quite believed in a Kingdom of Heaven, and in a naïve way I imagined a big house with all the deceased up in heaven looking down on us. This picture gave me a feeling of security and shelter.

Later, during my teenage years, three boys from my friendship circle committed suicide within the space of a few weeks. They did not belong to my inner circle of friends, but I knew them from the Red Cross Youth Organization and was deeply affected. It was rumored that all three of them had problems in school, and I remember quite well that I did not want to believe this. We were not able to speak about our feelings, neither in our peer group nor in school. The bewilderment and particularly the speechlessness still hurt me today. Once again, a few years later, a childhood friend threw himself from a bridge into a deep gorge. Every time I drive over this bridge I think of him and how heartily and care-freely we had laughed together.

I experienced these suicides as confrontations with death as a state: the person is here and then, suddenly, she or he is gone. In contrast, dying is a process. My father expressed this precisely at the end of his life. A few days before his death, he said, "Do you know that dying itself is not so bad, if only it didn't last so dreadfully long."

Enduring Dying

When I was seventeen years old I witnessed a friend slitting his wrists, and the images of the blood-splattered walls and blood-soaked towels still haunt me and pursue me in my dreams. I was convinced that he would die. Fortunately that was not the case. I remember the smell in the apartment, the ambulance siren, the first-aider, the screaming friend and his yelling partner, and my struggle against vomiting. Even today I do not know how long I stayed there and when I left the apartment. I even do not remember how I came home. I never spoke to my parents about that evening. In my perception and memory this is a first, albeit brief, direct confrontation with a wish to die.

When I was pregnant with my daughter, my kindergarten friend Christian died of cancer. I visited him several times during his illness, and the last time, before he died, I saw him in the clinic. He fought with all his might against dying, and while in me a new life was growing, he had to let his young life go. It is difficult to express what I felt. I was shaken to the core seeing him dying, and at the same time I felt somehow guilty that I was alive and also pregnant.

My father faced dying fully aware and—as with many things in his life— he also wanted to plan and determine this last journey. When he sensed that his strength was leaving him, he visited his surviving friends and acquaintances. He said good-bye to long-standing colleagues and business partners and settled what he felt was important and necessary. When his strength left him, we put his bed in the living room so that he could take part in everyday life. His seven children took turns caring for him, so that usually two of us were present around the clock. My mother had already become ill with dementia at that time, and she surrendered hopelessly to her husband dying. The camp in the living room around my father's bed was somewhat biblical and corresponded to his tendency to be authoritarian: if we—in his eyes— sat idle next to his bed, he commanded us to read at least in order not to waste the time. During these weeks I corrected seminar papers, read articles, prepared courses, and had my last discussions with my father. These days reminded me of the Last Supper; as I wrote before, I was brought up in Catholic surroundings, and the scenery aroused pictures and tales of the Bible. He said farewell to all his children, sons- and daughters-in-law, and his sixteen grandchildren individually, giving everyone personal words on the way.

This conscious "making one's way along the final path" impressed me profoundly. I learned a lot for my life and death, not least of which being that we cannot determine the time of our death, and at the end everything and everyone must and can let go. But despite its inevitability, we can face death as we do life. For example, my father never lost his sense of humor and was able to continue to find himself and even his death amusing.

This process is also so painful. My father's older sister, whom we call Aunt Mia, died—at over ninety years old—a long and at times agonizing death three years ago. Over many weeks and months she was pursued by hallucinations, afraid of being put in a wooden box alive, of being poisoned and strangled. During her life I perceived her as a gentle yet tough lady who always took her daily walk; however, in the last few weeks of her life she suffered such that she was no longer able to leave the house. Her fervent wish was for us not to leave her alone to die, and so my siblings and I stayed with her. A few days before her death I cut her hair and we joked around and took photos. Her face was already showing signs of her forthcoming death, and her body was emaciated. She did not suffer from a specific illness; it was just the elemental end of a long, intensive life. She loved to be touched and stroked, and right up to the end she expressed contentment and discontent appropriately. She had an intense fear of hell, and despite our assurances that she had led a good life and would surely be going to heaven, she was particularly afraid of this at night. During one of my night watches, she cried terribly and asked me to help her to be able finally to die. I felt helpless but not overstrained because of my previous experiences with death. Above all, I felt terribly sorry for her and wished that she could pass away within the next hours. Her Catholic belief was deeply anchored, and the hope of reconciliation and reunion with those already departed was both supportive and frightening. Despite morphine she felt pain; her body was emaciated down to the bones, and every contact caused her agony. I found it hard to believe that her heart kept beating. Finally she died peacefully in her sleep, as my father had done. Her long-lasting and painful death struggle evoked fear about my own dying. It is not the fear of dying as a matter of fact, but especially the fear of unbearable pain and suffering a long time at the end of life.

ENDURING THE DIAGNOSIS OF CANCER

So, welcome to life, it has me again, even if it is a little painful right now. (June 29, 2007)

A year of mourning, good-byes, and letting go is behind me. In addition to losses through death, the ending of a fundamental love affair has rocked my life. After a bitter year of mourning, I decide to start a new diary: a book with many empty, unwritten, and untouched pages, unencumbered by words of mourning, loss, fears, and longings, which—by now in irregular intervals—recur in waves. This book shall accompany me in a new phase of life. On the first page I have stuck an excerpt from a poem by Hermann Hesse (1978) intended to give me courage and to look to the future confidently: "Courage, my heart, take leave and fare thee well" (187).

The pain I feel derives not only from the loss of loved ones and an ended relationship, but from a potential myoma in my belly. Over the past years numerous laparoscopic interventions have been necessary, but I'm not especially worried, although my feelings are ambivalent.

> Somewhere in a little corner it does indeed worry me, but first let's operate.
> (July 12, 2007)

However, I use the few days before the surgery to conclude the semester at the university and to spend as much time as possible with my friend and colleague, Hermann, who is ill with a recurrence of cancer. I don't want to acknowledge or permit rising feelings of fear and uncertainty about myself, and I manage to successfully block them out.

The surgery occurs without any complications; they remove one ovary, and everything seems to be fine apart from waiting for the histological result. I am told that this will take two weeks. Two days later we celebrate my son's twentieth birthday in the hospital; we drink sparkling wine and visit the delivery room where he and his sister came into the world. Despite the celebratory activities, everything feels different, and an odd, vague grief that I can't place comes over me. I had learned the lessons of my childhood well—that it's an advantage to suppress feelings of pain, weakness, and sadness, for to do so means being weak—so I manage. But deep inside I am depressed; I have vague feelings of having lost something essential to my life, but I cannot explain these feelings.

> Cancer, I have—had—cancer! (July 31, 2007)

An illness "that doesn't knock" (Sontag 1979:5) descends on me and overwhelms me. Yet, like others with cancer, my feelings and reactions are ambivalent and contradictory. Christoph Schlingensief (2009), a German film and theater director who died of lung cancer 2010, describes that he tried to "imagine" the distressing thoughts and finally felt relieved when the fear was clear and distinctly noticeable. David Rieff (2008) portrays the recurring confrontation of his famous mother, Susan Sontag, with cancer as a desperate effort to view the imminent diagnosis as any misdiagnosis. I myself reflect:

> I don't know how I should feel; I sense that I (still) don't want to wholly take this diagnosis in. My head and gut feelings gape apart from each other like a huge wound: My head reacts rationally and my gut is scared, it howls and is profoundly shocked. (July 31, 2007)

Cancer affects people physically, emotionally, and cognitively: it shakes one's fundamental identity and underscores the fragility and finite nature of life, awakening existential fears.

Externally, I carry on as normally as possible, whereas internally chaos, danger, and an overpowering fear of that which will come rule (cf. Baldauf and Waldenberger 2008).

> I am so strong, I comfort my children, who are so shaken, I calm those around me and hold myself steady. (July 31, 2007)

Existential fear and feelings of solitude intensify:

> To live with uncertainty and fear of new tumor forming, that I can manage. But this internal solitude, the longing for a companion, for closeness and contact on numerous levels—that makes is difficult for me to manage—now in particular. (July 31, 2007)

A recent consultation reassures me, apparently:

> The prognosis is good, I have time. (August 2, 2007)

A further required surgery is to be waited for patiently, and so I seek relief and create normality by resuming work.

> Today I turned on the PC for the first time in 2 weeks. 566 e-mails and a lot of work, the temptation is great to hop back into everyday life straightaway. (August 2, 2007)

Sharing the diagnosis of cancer can trigger a shock, which is often associated with partial amnesia affecting key events. Considered by itself, amnesia can be a healthy protective mechanism for the present and secures survival. The wearing off of a shock is slow and progressive; however, it is possible that the shock cannot fully be dissipated (cf. Andreatta 2006; Baldauf and

Waldenberger 2008). My key amnesia event is the consultation with the
surgeon two weeks after the first surgery. He informs me that the histological result requires a second surgery, and there is the possibility that
malignant cells have spread—but later I do not know anything about these
sentences; the only words I remember are that I have time to decide.

I am unaware of my shock. My external presentation is that I am stable
and strong. Internally I feel

> restless, the vulnerability and neediness is becoming apparent, it threatens
> and allows me no rest. Nevertheless, I can't bring myself to actually tackle
> anything. (August 6, 2007)

However, slowly the shock subsides and the reality sinks into awareness,
and I can admit the diagnosis of cancer in all its meanings.

> Selective perception—a prime example of how I have interpreted the talks
> with the doctors. Every plan that I have rightly made for myself consequent-
> ly now becomes nothing. The risk of a recurrence hangs in the air, perhaps
> there will also be an outbreak somewhere else. So the diagnosis is now clear
> and the second surgery is no prophylaxis. Chaos in my mind and gut, uncer-
> tainty, fear, and hope. (August 10, 2007)

While I describe my emotional instability in my diary entries, I function
externally in a familiar and long-trained manner; however, as the shock
abates, I sense myself and my instability and ambivalence even more clearly.

> I'm scared, very thin-skinned, but also full of hope and feeling gutsy. During
> the night I often sob, feel alone, I have such a great need to be held tight.
> During the day it starts again, a lot of things annoy me very quickly, and
> then I feel my imbalance. (August 14, 2007)

Baldauf and Waldenberger (2008) associate this great longing to be held
tight and carried with the primary fundamental experiences in the womb
and the experiences of having the presence of a reassuring and protective
partner. The feeling of solitude is closely linked to the longing to be picked
up, a familiar concept for myself. My surroundings and my place in life
are no longer tenable, and I have no control over what is happening in my
body. The unconscious and unresolved fear in my circles toward my cancer
and the advice and hopelessness consolidate my feelings of loneliness and

lead me to function outwardly more than ever according to my old patterns and the key phrase: "What doesn't kill you makes you stronger!"

This is the tremendous shock, to admit to myself now that I have calculated all the possibilities and impossibilities, but not that I could become ill with cancer and perhaps die—this insight pulls the carpet right out from underneath my feet.

> I had a very bad night, anxiety and uncertainty. I have created my own truth, now I want to put it behind me as quickly as possible. I want to live longer still and if possible, to be healthy. (August 11, 2007)

I realize that this second surgery is necessary now; they will remove my uterus, the other ovary, the fallopian tubes, the lining surrounding the abdomen, and a number of lymph nodes. The date is set for August 30, but the days up to it are governed by an extraordinary discrepancy between my behavior and my state of health.

ENDURING LANGUAGE

> My stomach is simply a battlefield, so maltreated and marked, everything severed, cut through, and churned up. Retrospectively, I think that my stomach before had something almost "virginal," in the sense that it was unspoiled by the fight of medicine with knives. (September 19, 2007)

Physicians avoid the term cancer—they speak about tumors, carcinoma, or a CA. The linguistic terms for cancer are each borrowed from warfare: tumors grow invasively; cancer cells take up residence in colonies; they attack the body, weaken, destroy, and finally annihilate the immune system. In rare cases, the body's defenses are strong enough to resist the attack and require radical interventions in the form of operations, chemotherapy, and radiation. These medical measures carefully and systematically eliminate, evacuate, kill, and annihilate not only the malignant cells but also— as collateral damage—the benign cells. The cancerous cells are bombarded with chemotherapy culls, and radiotherapy does not exclusively contaminate malignant cell tissue. In the battle against cancer, it is about winning or losing—living or dying. The enemy must be beaten via all possible means (cf. Noll 2009; Rieff 2008; Sontag 1979; Wilber 2000).

Sontag (1979) focuses on "illness as a metaphor" with the metaphorical images of cancer and tuberculosis. She describes the historical evolution of the interpretation of illness as punishment and the pitfalls of the theories of emotional causes of cancer. These one-dimensional theories neglect the complexity of potential causes of cancer and support the idea of bearing the blame for having cancer.

Both in my private and professional lives I am "supported by testimonies of compassion, but also I am horribly alone" (August 20, 2007). Moreover I am subjected to pseudo-psychological interpretations regarding the linear connection of workload, intensive living, and illness. In my close private circle I am exposed to comments such as "no wonder you became ill, you work so hard and take so much on," or "everything has a price, you have simply not looked after yourself enough, and now you must learn how to do that." These completely well-intentioned statements, albeit deeply hurtful, leave me feeling not only ill but guilty. I question my life up to that point; not because I lack the knowledge about the complex connections in terms of getting cancer, but because I am scared about the second surgery.

> A lot of exhaustion, headaches, and fighting tears—it's good that the surgery will be in four days, I've become increasingly unstable—fear is my constant companion. (August 26, 2007)

GOING PUBLIC

In my professional role as professor of social work, I decide to name my illness, to create a speaking area for the unspeakable and inform the staff, the students, and project partners about my medical condition. I do this after the first and before the second surgery, not knowing when and how I will come back again to the university.

Language as an essential instrument in social work is often afforded too little space in education. Linguistic difficulties in everyday life, in both professional and personal lives, come about particularly through insinuations, encryptions, silence, and encountering and confronting frightening and shameful subjects. Yet are not most tasks and problems that social workers deal with imbued with these phenomena? Is it not the case that vague statements and insinuations, cryptically formulated and unspoken, shape the everyday work of social workers, who are confronted by resistance and refusal? Ideally they are able to reflect on their own feelings of anxiety, shame, and overburdening in order to develop and mature their response to the daily demands of the work.

> Do relief and easing of a burden (for my part) and understanding (from those around me) occur when I share in an appropriate setting that I am trembling for my life? (August 24, 2007)

These thoughts motivate me to choose the path of opening myself up, to declare the diagnosis of cancer, to write it down, to refuse to spread a cloak of silence over my illness and the predictable absences (due to the second surgery and the convalescence, which required time away from the university), and in doing so, to minimize the room for ungrounded interpretation as much as possible. Cancer would no longer be a disease that affects people "outside" in potential occupational fields, such as in the hospital or in the palliative ward. Cancer now has a face and a name within the University of Applied Sciences, stated in all clarity and made personally visible.

At the time of my diagnosis, the summer term had just ended. Most of the students were already on holiday, while some were on field placements that I coordinate and supervise. I want to pass on this information personally, but I have no other option but to advise the students first by email about this change. I am unable to say how long I will be absent, as that will be clear only after the second surgery. I sit a long time in front of the computer and consider every word, formulating, deleting, trying to find the right expressions, deleting again, and in the end I clearly state, along with information about the course, that I have cancer and do not know when I will teach again.

Students are suddenly confronted with an unfamiliar closeness to existential issues such as a life-threatening illness, the transience of life, and possible death, not theoretically in a case example or a literature study but through a living encounter with me. This leads, three months after the second surgery, when I start teaching again, to activity and discussion of the topics mentioned, but it also triggers anxiety concerning their own health, dying, and death. In one of my notes I call this decision "the school of life for all participants."

There is no time before the second surgery for personal meetings and discussions, but many students answer my email, wishing me well for the

coming weeks, thanking me for the openness, and recognizing and prais-
ing my courage to be honest. As I return to work after the second surgery, I
notice insecurity, reserve, and also resistance from some of the students. My
colleague and friend Hermann is at this time visibly suffering from cancer
and wants to continue teaching, but in contrast to me he does not speak
with or in front of the students about his illness. He is—in comparison to
the time before his illness—less often at the university and therefore less
accessible to the students. His voice is not so strong, owing to chemotherapy and medication, and it is clearly visible that he is seriously ill.

Within the contemporary, neoliberal university, anything that impairs
productivity is a liability. This is demonstrated in the use of language,
which is oriented and established by the vocabulary of economics. In
the business university culture, students are recruited as customers, and
studies are referred to as products. Knowledge and competence are to be
shown and created—the diktat of effectiveness and efficiency determine
most of the contents. Nowadays universities must self-display on the market and withstand the competition with excellent products (cf. Mautner
2010). In this sense social work is one of the products, and with market-
corresponding skills, problems will be managed. The business vocabulary
and attitudes are adopted without being reflected on or questioned, which
has also left its mark on both the individual participants and the profession of social work.

In linguistically characteristic style, the market economy orientation
should not unsettle the customers; quite the opposite, once recruited and
gained, they should be linked to the corresponding products, which are formulated in such a way to ensure that the interest is not lost and the appeal
of something new remains present.

Lecturers as representatives and appointees of the system are required;
knowledge and experiences are to be taught bit by bit in bite-sized por-
tions, embedded in an enjoyable setting. The students' evaluations verify
their satisfaction and dissatisfaction and lead, not least of all, to professionally skilled lecturers being deprived of teaching contracts.

In this environment, acceptance and frustration-tolerance of a nonfunctioning element is low. This element must be removed as soon as possible
from the market and exchanged, thus corresponding to the mechanical
image of lecturers as service providers and reducing this to functionality.

LETTING GO

Oh, children. As I was hanging up the washing on the balcony, my two grown kids came walking home from the car park: my heart skipped, I felt so happy and heavy at the same time—letting go, continually letting go. (August 26, 2007)

Letting go of the image of a healthy body, carefully approaching the idea of a wounded and ill body, takes a lot of strength. By researching information on "my cancer," I try to counter the feeling of vulnerability. Knowledge fills me with confidence and for the time being gives me support.

Later, after the second surgery, I am required once again to let go, and at first I can hardly get hold of my situation:

Quicksand. Attached and hooked up everywhere. Over and over I am amazed that it is ME—detached from my body by the epidural anesthesia. (September 10, 2007)

Loss of integrity and control over my own body raises renewed anxieties and grief. I have vague memories of the hours and days after the second surgery. I float in and out of consciousness and cannot feel my belly and legs because of the epidural catheter that pumps analgesic into my spinal cord. There is another catheter in my urethra, and a central venous line under my wishbone. I never felt that helpless and sick before, and I am afraid of nevermore being able to get out of this bed. My head aches dreadfully, and the 130-mile distance to my family and friends feels like thousands of miles.

Holding on and letting go, or, in other words, not being able to hold on or control, is a metaphor for doing and being. Ken Wilber (2000), whose wife Treya died of cancer, describes the two polarities of resistance and opening. In her diary excerpts, Treya depicts the confrontation with life and death in a highly personal and moving way, reflecting life in the face of death. "Passionate serenity—to be passionate in all one's duties of life. To care about all things to the core with respect to oneself, but not in the slightest to cling to anything" (335f). For me she is a pioneering companion in the bitter moments of uncertainty and letting go. I read this book for the first time after the second surgery and then a year later when the oncological follow-up care diagnoses a liver tumor—luckily a benign one. I had to wait ten days for the result.

Many authors have described the process of mourning as occurring in phases or stages. I find myself in the phases of both fragile emotions and searching, finding, and separating. In the mourning process, a number of phases can be passed through at the same time—the sequence is not linear (cf. Bowlby 2008; Kast 1994, 2010; Kübler-Ross 1997, 2008).

Being reliant on the medical apparatus and on the help of hospital staff increases my fear of dependence on others. A wild determination to do everything by myself drives me on, and I act on this. The third day after the surgery I am able to walk some small steps, and from this day on I practice every day and expand my walk. A chaos of contradictory feelings seizes me. Uncertainty, fear, and grief but also a powerful intention to survive, faith in my strength and resilience, take up residence in my life.

> Life has become so uncertain, what must and would I like to let go, to let be, to deliberately say good-bye to? How will I continue my life and how do I avoid the fear that the cancer will come back? Question after question— I often have the feeling of walking over quicksand or on brittle ice and this is the way my steps are: small and unsure. (September 17, 2007)

The term "mourning work" (Kast 1994:40) is justified. I experience, suffer, and pass through deep emotional hard times and periods of meaninglessness and emptiness. A wide range of feelings of uncertainty, meaninglessness, overburdening, anger, fear, as well as unbridled joy in this now fragile life are daily companions. I am still far away from "deliberately say good-bye to" as I write down in my entry, but I am on my way.

With regard to my professional situation, I feel insignificant and question the meaningfulness of the high levels of personal effort and commitment I have deployed over the last few years. With the distance provided by my illness, I perceive a system that demands self-exploitation, up to and over my capacity limits, and I must realize that the daily business of the institution goes on without me. This insight hurts and at the same time is healing as I recognize the need to critically reconsider my work habits and workload and to create space for other activities.

> To figure out what does me good, supports me, strengthens me. This is what I would like to take time to do—sufficient time. (September 19, 2007)

This reevaluation process extends to the integral relationships in my life. Analogous to the concepts of language discussed previously, I find myself thinking through relationships, many of which have existed for many years, and this produces new, solid, and also volatile ones. Prior to the second surgery, a discussion developed between my grown-up children and me about the above-mentioned surgery. Intuitively, I spoke of our first shared room (the uterus), in which they were held and nurtured, and now neither they nor I required that anymore to live. A relationship had been started after only a few minutes based on the deepest bond, love, and happiness, and what is inexpressible can remain unspoken.

In this context, love for me means letting go of requirements and perceptions and remaining in contact. After the second surgery and rehabilitation period, a new phase of life begins.

> A memorable day: I live alone, without children or a partner. The three of us [my children and I] begin a new phase of life: Julia had the last day at work yesterday, Tobias starts studying, and I will live alone. (September 30, 2007)

With my son moving out (my daughter had already moved out), a stage of life comes to a distinct end, and my grieving process meets this new life stage.

> I hadn't thought that everything would be so tiresome. When will it finally stop? Only physicians, treatment and medication—my mood is groggy, I feel as if I'm wounded, the scars are like a memorial. (October 6, 2007)

This situation forces me to recognize demands on myself and images of fear, longing, and hope regarding health and illness. After I am discharged from the clinic, my oncological rehabilitation—above all with the need for health and regaining my strength, for physical and mental functioning—collides with everyday reality. It is not possible to work part-time without reducing my contractual commitments, which on financial grounds is not an option. There is no flexibility in terms of reduced workload due to ill health: either I work or I am ill. Therefore I continue to work and notice very clearly that the condition of my health is as unstable as previously. So although I am more aware of my need to moderate my work life, material circumstances rule this out. Thus I must find other ways to cope without further compromising my health.

A central concept that I teach students is the salutogenic concept according to Antonovsky (1979)[1], which rejects the dichotomous approach between being healthy and ill of classic conventional medicine and is oriented to a multidimensional continuum concerning health and sickness, in which stress-inducing and protective factors are key. People are regarded holistically, whereby the sense of coherence represents a central basis, which is supported by three components, namely, understandability, manageability, and meaningfulness. Up to the present I have understood it only theoretically, and now I experience it from a personal perspective. On this understanding I have adopted many resistance resources in my life so far, upon which I can now fall back and which support me to process constructively the shock from the cancer and to integrate it into my life.

Given that I consider my life fundamentally to be meaningful, harmonious, and precious, I have a lot of internal assets that allow me to cope with times of crisis. I find myself reflecting on how to cope and realize that it is important for me to experience myself as an active producer and shaper of my own life. This could perhaps partly explain my fear of losing control and being dependent on others. But I learned and am still learning to ask for help and receive assistance, and this enriches my life. My own transience does not scare me anymore; I am coming to terms with it and live my life more aware and intensively than before.

> Life is limited and precious and today at the cemetery the priest said: Don't give life more hours, rather the hours more life. In this sense I try to live and today at the cemetery with both my children I felt so rich, happy and reconciled. (All Saints' Day, November 1, 2007)

At All Saints' Day there is a prayer at the cemetery—a Catholic prayer, and therefore a family tradition that I continue. I take a lot more time to reflect on what still remains from life.

ENDURING GOOD-BYES / DYING / DEATH

> The dense silence and peace in death can be physically sensed, present and highly attentive. (January 12, 2008, the day Hermann died)

Six months before falling ill myself with cancer, my friend and colleague Hermann was also diagnosed. In the previous sections I have purposefully left this narrative strand out, and it can now be placed and read like a film over what I have written so far.

"Since there is death, we should care for the people around us and not think that life is able to eliminate this" (Noll 2009:150). The relationship between Hermann and me was open and warm from the start. We shared an office at the University of Applied Sciences. We conceived and tried out new teaching concepts and shared the opinion that teaching should be an appropriate mix of benevolent demands and support. We were both influenced by the political movements of the 1970s and 1980s, and both interested in sociopolitical themes and developments. From a collegial shared office, over time a deep and intimate friendship developed.

> Tears early in the morning at the office—yet not mine, Hermann's: the results of the checks are not ok. He is terribly afraid—it really hurts me to see him so desperate. Life and death, death and life—but not yet, please later. (October 19, 2006)

Hermann had already fallen ill with cancer two years previously and had survived the respective medical interventions and treatments. The oncological checkups had always been satisfactory up to this point, and the results were negative, which in medical terminology is considered to be positive, as no relapse or metastasis was detectable. However, metastasis was exactly what had now been confirmed.

I found myself at this time, as mentioned previously, enduring the diagnosis of cancer in a sensitive phase of my life. My partner had not long ago separated from me, and my emotional state was unstable. Hermann becoming sick again reactivated my feelings of grief and fear of being abandoned.

> Hermann has cancer again. His voice sounds sad, thin, on the verge of tears. I have an awful night behind me—lots of tears and grief—does this also mean letting go again? (October 23, 2006)

For Hermann, the reappearance of cancer evoked an ardent will to live expressed in implementing long-cherished plans, such as a house move and remaining professionally active.

> He still manages a lot at the University of Applied Sciences, tries to finalize as much as possible—it reminds me of the situations before the birth of my children or before I set out on a big journey. (October 29, 2006)

The metaphor of a journey is also explored by Tiziano Terzani (2007), who, when he becomes ill with cancer, talks about life and death, of journeys in foreign lands and inward journeys to oneself. His key insight is that death and life are two aspects of the same thing, and that the direction of the journey goes from outside to inside.

My upcoming journey is not to a foreign country; I'm not traveling geographically, but rather in the sense of Terzani's metaphor: I am standing at the start of a journey inward, which ends with the death of a beloved friend and colleague. I do not speak to him about this metaphor. From today's view, his journey leads finally to his death while I am still alive. When I wrote down these words about the big journey, I did not know that I too would be diagnosed with cancer. From the beginning, Hermann's aim is to survive; he wants his wife and me to give him a boost, to confirm his belief that he will overcome his illness. And I comply only too gladly, as hope is the last thing to die, although in my diary I write down my fears and concerns.

> Hermann will nevertheless now undergo chemotherapy; I'm worried for
> him and about him. I don't want to lose yet another person that I care about,
> whom I've let get close to me, whose presence is so joyful and does so much
> good. (November 11, 2006)

The communication between physicians and oncology patients is of great importance in this emotional, highly sensitive situation. Ultimately it is about life and death, short-term prospects of the meaning of life, and the physical and psychological quality of life. The asymmetry between physician and patient reinforces feelings of helplessness and of being at someone's mercy. Thus communication can affect compliance and coping strategies. Hermann's hope that he will once again beat the cancer is undermined by the communication between his physician and himself. This physician had bluntly informed him that according to relevant empirical studies he would live for about another eighteen months. I am not present when Hermann receives this information; I suspect him of keeping this situation private.

I am convinced that good communication requires adequate time and space and an atmosphere in which asking questions is encouraged and physical and mental pressures can be discussed. As I describe in the section "Enduring the Diagnosis of Cancer," I had partial amnesia when the physician in the hospital informed me about the necessity of a second surgery. Some days later I visited my gynecologist, who has known me for the last twenty years. He took the time to show me the process, prognosis, and possibilities of treatment and asked me how I felt and whether I had questions. I remember his words quite well: "If you were my wife, I would suggest surgery as soon as possible." These words were very helpful because they showed me his personal and emotional concern.

The emotional sensitivities, psychological issues, and problems in confronting being ill with cancer should be addressed equally along with the social environment of the person with cancer. Important significant persons and relatives are similarly included in the communication process, as long as this is desired. My second surgery is in a different hospital from the first, and fortunately my brother-in-law is the head anesthesiologist of the gynecology division. We have known each other more than thirty years, and he is the only one who dares to name the word cancer face to face with me. For me it is a helpful dialogue because I get information and my emotional needs are addressed. He answers comprehensibly and clearly and takes my concerns seriously. Lang et al. (2009) refer to the importance of a dialogue between doctors and patients. Along with the appropriate cognitive and treatment-oriented skills, communication skills such as active listening should without doubt be an integral part of medical studies. As mentioned above, Hermann is deeply disappointed and frustrated about the nature of the discussions with his physician. I have the impression that the helplessness of the physician is reflected in these consultations. In Hermann's case it appears to me that his physicians hide themselves partly behind technical language and avoid engaging with him on a personal level. I am lucky that my gynecologist and my brother-in-law are caring for me. David Rieff (2008) focuses on the handling of the truth between physicians and someone ill with cancer, his own uncertainty in discussions with his mother, Susan Sontag, concerning cancer and her prognosis, and his efforts to learn communicative skills from a physician who supported Sontag until the end of her life with expertise, attention, and human dignity. Nevertheless, there is no patent remedy; it is always an interplay of individual personalities and situations. However, respect for the patient and his or her views of a good and harmonious life should always be in the foreground.

Hermann has highs and lows, he has become extraordinarily thin, it hurts so terribly. I hope so much that he survives it! It is an arduous path, fatigue spreads, everything takes a lot of energy, I'd prefer to just stay in bed. (December 19, 2006)

At this point I believe that Hermann is at death's door; his physical constitution is appalling. I feel tired and drained, the daily work is exhausting,
and I work hard on caring for Hermann and all his needs and wishes. My
feelings are ambivalent: I no longer believe that he will survive; the evidence is that he will die. But in spite of everything I want him to live. The
chemotherapy is working well, the physician says, but it is also destructive.
Hermann fights, and I recognize several phases of coping with grief, according to Kast (1994) and Kübler-Ross (1997, 2008), in Hermann as well
as in myself. The spectrum of contradictory emotions is expressed in Hermann's spirit of optimism and desire for something fresh, such as the move,
but also the deep feelings of grief and loss.

We end the year with a walk.

> A wonderful walk with Hermann, nature has gone crazy: spring warmth,
> the shrubs are sprouting, the first flowers are sprouting and it's the 31st of
> December. Hermann will no longer come to the University of Applied
> Sciences. I've expected this already, I'm very sad, and it is absolutely the
> right decision. Oh, how much I wish that he will still survive everything.
> (January 1, 2007)

As if all this isn't enough to deal with, Winfried, the father of my children, has a heart operation, and so I commute between both ill men, my
work at the university, and my mother with dementia. I feel increasingly
overburdened, and yet I always find the energy to get up every morning
and to continue. I consider myself fortunate that I have been successful at
building resilient, protective factors into my life. The positive life model of
my parents, my childhood and youth in a large family, the relationships in
my family and friendship circles which are supported by trust and appreciation, belief in my strength and courage to take on and cope with difficulties
and challenges, and, in particular, my extraordinary lust for and humorous approach to life have shaped my identity and proven to be sustainable,
stable, and robust (cf. Welter-Enderlin 2010).

> Hermann thinks that 2007 is the year of conclusions. Will he die? Will
> Winfried's heart operation go well? This waiting is bad. In 2007 I would like
> to simply live life, aware of every day. It sounds so easy, but it's so unbeliev-
> ably difficult. (January 6, 2007)

And so weeks pass. Winfried's heart operation goes very well and is satisfactory. Hermann seems to rally and a planned operation is canceled; instead the physician prescribes another round of chemotherapy.

> There is a quiet doubt inside me, whether this physician is really telling him the truth, whether Hermann is telling me the truth. (February 21, 2007)

A few days later, I note:

> Medicine has abandoned Hermann. There is no operation, but a so-called preserving chemotherapy.

At this time, we speak about good-byes and dying, Hermann knows about my experiences with dying and death and asks me repeatedly for details about my feelings of being a companion to those dying and about their last hours. Finally he asks me to be there with him to the end, and cautiously, almost fearfully, he inquires whether I'm prepared to fulfill his wish, not only for him but also to assist his wife. I promise him that I will be with them to his end.

Although I feel drained, psychologically stretched, and shaken, physically I feel healthy and up to the task. Hermann is a modest man and has few demands. Besides the wish that I be with him to the end, he expresses some wishes that seem to me quite strange and too late to fulfill. One of his wishes is to keep teaching. At times he is so weak that I have to collect him from the seminar room and accompany him to our office, where within seconds he falls asleep on the sofa. At such moments I feel my heartstrings pull. He has become small; his skin is ashen with a gray shimmer. He rests, and I'm afraid to ask myself the question of whether perhaps one day he'll fall asleep here and not wake up again. Yet he doesn't give up; his will to live is strong, and he devises plans. Together with his wife, my children, and me, he would like to travel to Rome. As promised I go along with him, and we plan the trip. I do not believe it will be realized, but I am not able to say this. I am afraid to disappoint him and let him down. Looking back on these days and reflecting, I remember one of my thoughts was that I would never work if I were in this situation. But at that time I was not yet affected by cancer. Fortunately I recovered quickly from the surgeries and I am still fine, and meanwhile I do not dare to say what would be when— I have learned that life is too complex and we are shifting.

Hermann's physical constitution no longer permits him to pursue his hobbies: hiking and working with stone. In the search for new possibilities, he discovers painting. Thus, from the last months of his life, large and small formatted pictures emerge along with a fragmented book with the title *A Network of Love: Thoughts on Society and Spirituality*. In the foreword Hermann writes:

> It is not my first book, but it is completely different from those so far. I'm a scientist, this side is very important to me, and it should have some influence on this book. However, it shall be a socio-spiritual book of reflection. Here comes a new chapter that I didn't know until now. This scientist in me calls it the path to a transpersonal sociology and with it philosophy, from which sociology once evolved.

Apart from spending as much time as possible with Hermann, listening attentively and asking him what would be helpful, I find that writing and reading are indispensable to me. My private entries are especially helpful in getting through these weeks and months. The professional knowledge of the complexity of this life situation, on both a physical and a psychological level, encourages and enables me to cope better with this situation. Hermann writes: "Cancer creates fear, but it also shakes you into motion, it creates possibilities, it is creative, it is alive—only without limits." To me the painting and writing in his book, the shared reflections of his physical and emotional health, are clear evidence of the process of letting go. In my perception he integrates cancer into his life, and I ask myself if he reconciles himself with it. In comparison to my situation, there is the crucial factor that I have cancer for the first time, and Hermann has metastasis and a shattering prognosis.

Yet it is infinitely difficult to be Hermann's companion and to witness his life come to an end. Inevitably I am confronted with the finiteness of my own life, with memories of experiences of partings from the past, and with fears about dying and death.

Spring is approaching, and eating is becoming increasingly difficult for Hermann, yet one day he really surprises me:

> I cooked for him and he ate much more than the days before—he almost fell asleep at the table. I try to be there for him, there's nothing else I can do. (May 9, 2007)

At the university Hermann's presence and teaching trigger some unease. Hermann does not speak openly at the university about his illness, as I will later do. I hear comments like "The students cannot be burdened with that," or "In this condition he can't teach in a qualified way," and as he has to be in the hospital for two weeks, a course is taken away from him without his agreement. The reasons given for this are that it will ease his burden and that students need continuity. I charge those responsible with burying him while he is still alive, a cruel and unfortunately consistent image for those who are socially excluded. The reaction is criticism about my emotional behavior and the reassurance that this is for Hermann's own good. But who knows better what someone's good is than the one who affected by such decisions? The system has no room for nonfunctioning personnel.

Despite his illness and vulnerability, right up to the end of his life Hermann does not hide or retreat, although this is what many people expect and even want him to do. Ariès (2002:747) portrays the history of death in his comprehensive work and describes the triumph of medicalization, the tendency to keep severely ill people out of sight of the general public. In Western society, primarily those people who are dynamic, sporty and physically tuned, healthy, and shapely gain recognition. Physical attractiveness and bodily integrity as normal standards are not questioned. Thus when the reality of illness and death invades the protected world of teaching and students, it evokes displeasure, uncertainty, and stress.

I made the promise to be with Hermann to the end at a time when I considered myself to be healthy. However, now it is summer, and while I become ill with cancer myself, Hermann is increasingly saying farewell to life. We mutually support one another to bear the burden of the finiteness of life together, and my diagnosis of cancer intensifies and deepens our friendship and bond. He shows me that a strong soul and a great spirit can inhabit a body marked by illness: the body is only the outer shell, yet without this shell we cannot live.

Not many words are needed between us; we are able to understand each other and mostly understand what is going on inside each other.

> Hermann has declined again, he looks gray and can only eat purees, he often chokes. He's scared. Even if he doesn't say so, I can sense it. (October 6, 2007)

Baldauf and Waldenberger (2008) describe the oppressive and constrict-
ing atmosphere in the space around those who are frightened. Fear can
be transferred and often leads to defensive reactions; unconsciously your
breathing adjusts and becomes shallower. In the last weeks before Hermann
dies, I experience this extremely clearly. When I am with him, I consciously
breathe deeply.

Being touched does him good, and he feels protected. His wife, Elisabeth, and I care for him at home. He lies on the sofa in the living room
and falls asleep exhausted after saying a few sentences to us. When we want
to leave the room to leave him in peace, he asks us to stay. If he hears our
voices, when we caress him or hold him, he feels well and safe in our presence. He describes how it awakens memories of his childhood and makes
him feel happy, safe, and calm. I rub his back with caution; the skin feels
dry and thin. I know the risk of bedsores, and I remember my father who
died nine years ago—his comforting groaning when I rubbed his back. The
words "loving means to let go" occur to my mind, yet I am not depressed.
I feel very close to Hermann and Elisabeth in this intimate atmosphere.
Hermann is emaciated to the bones; lying on the sofa, he relishes this
health care bound in love. It is a situation of peace and friendship.

Those dying must be taken seriously, and they have wishes up to the
end, even if these possibly seem to be incomprehensible and illusory.
Hoffmann (2011) vividly describes the fear of social death and the requirements for hospice care. One of the principles in the hospice movement is
to speak *to* those dying and *not about* them. Another one is truthfulness:
"To conceal nothing from the party, to gloss over nothing about their
situation and to take their fate, fears and anger concerning their impend-
ing death seriously and to bear it, instead to allow them to fight it and not
avoid it" (79).

Will it always continue like this up to the end of my life? One good-bye
after another? I fear Hermann is the next, I try to brace myself internally,
and I am scared, not about his death, not about being with him. I'm scared
about the emptiness after death, of further holes in my life. A web of holes
and cracks that spread over the web and can barely be patched. And even if
they are interwoven once more, these places remain vulnerable, they threat-
en to tear again. (November 21, 2007)

Toward the end of the year, the exhaustion and pressure take their toll on my already weakened and affected health:

> I have the feeling of losing face if I show myself to be weak, fearful, and not in control, if I show vulnerability. However, it is contradictory, as I would like to be uncontrolled. Nobody should control me, even the feeling of having to be in control. (November 24, 2007)

I recognize that I need therapeutic and supervisory aid, and that they are sources of strength. These "islands of time" of dialogue and reflection allow me to observe and broach the pressures; to express negative feelings, fear, and distress in a secure environment; and to practice mindfulness with regard to my limited resources. For some time I have been learning to listen to my body's messages, and the experience of illness has made me more aware of and sensitive to myself. I start the day with a morning walk and a good breakfast. I learn to accept necessary medical appliances for the rest of my life and reframe them as a most welcome break in my day-to-day business. I meet friends and go to the cinema, and step by step I dare to make plans again for my future life.

Student (1999) stated that the inhumane approach to those dying frequently derives from stress and fear: the fear of the dying, the fear of a painful loss, the fear of feelings of powerlessness and helplessness and, particularly, of one's own death. Becoming aware of and acknowledging my own fears helps me to support Hermann.

Hermann works up to the end.

> Hermann is weak, his breath rattles. This week I picked him up from home to teach and drove him back home again. My heart hurts, I like him so much and the time is now so limited. (December 15, 2007)

Hermann's wish and decision to work until the end is a great challenge for me, but I have promised to be with him on this path right up to the end.

Hermann and Elisabeth have been a couple for many years. On December 29 they get married, and the celebration takes place with their closest family circle. As they make their vows, the room is filled with their love and also with the rattling and whistling of Hermann's breath. His voice is fragile, and his words are interrupted time and again by awful coughing fits and the struggle for air. The atmosphere is terribly beautiful, and I find myself holding my breath.

The choking fits increase and become unbearable for him. His fear grows. Hermann decides to enter hospice care, yet not without making sure that he can go home anytime. Two days before his death, we work on curriculum ideas, knowing and sensing that the time for the final good-bye is near. Elisabeth and I alternate and are also both together with him; we give each other mutual support. To see someone die is infinitely hard; toward the end it is just about being there—there is nothing else you can do—and letting the person go. Simply sitting there, holding his hand, breathing together, and waiting.

One last time in his life, Hermann drinks a sip of beer and eats a small bit of veal sausage. He fights with a shortness of breath, and coughing fits shake him. Nothing happens against his will, and when I go home late that night I say good-bye to him, sensing that he is already going. A few hours later, Elisabeth rings me. Hermann has died peacefully in his sleep.

ATTEMPT AT A FRESH START

Not a single word written for three months, I am utterly exhausted. I was with Hermann until the end of his life on this earth; he died peacefully on the 12th of January, 2008. As always I've performed wonderfully: it was a matter close to my heart to give him a warm and worthy send-off, to support Elisabeth, as I promised Hermann I would. I gave my best, supported by our deep friendship, by the many people whom I knew from Hermann's stories and who have now become faces and voices. And letting go hurts so dreadfully! I miss Hermann so painfully! (March 23, 2008)

The emptiness after the funeral and the settling of the pending organizational tasks hurt psychologically and physically. A stay in an oncological clinic for treatment and convalescence for a number of weeks permits me to rest and to discover my life energies again. Outside my usual surroundings, along with the applications and treatments that do me good, I'm given time and space to look back and recognize that for months I have lived at the limits of being overburdened physically and psychologically, and that fear has been my constant companion. Fear is frequently taken as negative, but it has a double function as a threat and a chance for further development. The present involuntary confrontation with illness and the subsequent voluntarily intensive confrontation with dying and death enable me to ac-knowledge fears, and to endure and integrate them. As I exceed the bound-aries set by fear, I realize what a rich life I lead. I am aware of my survival from cancer, and at least the matter of fact is that we all have to die—but I did not yet. The finality of life has become less important.

Retrospectively I can comprehend the five phases described by Kübler-Ross (1997, 2008) of denial, anger, bargaining, grief, and acceptance in both Hermann and myself, although not consecutively. I have an image of myself "like I've fallen out of the world," as I am confronted with cancer, imminent dying, and death. My diary describes the denial and suppression of the diagnosis, the fear of losing independence, and the gradual adoption, acceptance, and integration—the initial uncertain steps after the opera-tions, the impatience with the (subjectively perceived) long recovery, the anxiety about Hermann, and for many months my feelings of loss and grief. I often mention that my heart hurts, and at the end I no longer crave for Hermann to survive, but, having consented to say good-bye to each other, that he may die peacefully.

Saying good-bye means mutually letting go, and often it is more diffi-cult for the survivor than for the person dying. During the months with Hermann and falling ill with cancer, I became closer to myself: the con-frontation with the finite nature of life led me to rethink and reestablish priorities and to give more importance to the everyday. Time has different dimensions, and my way of looking at my life has changed. A considerable challenge lies in pulling back from the obsession, the benefits, and also the shortcomings, instead of consciously enjoying the small moments of hap-piness and the richness of my life. This leads the way from loss and death to joie de vivre and a more conscious lifestyle.

On an individual level, I view the confrontation with the diagnosis of cancer as a personal development, learning, and maturing process, a confrontation with my life and my current life situation, embedded in a social context. As a social work academic, I am interested in the social level, attitudes, and handling of illness, dying, and death. How are dying and death changing in the twenty-first century? What effects does the market economy diktat, prevalent over all areas of life in the Western world, have on the handling of dying and death? I share the critical view of Gronemeyer (2011) that dying and death are apparently not taboo subjects; they are, so to speak, on everyone's lips, yet in a distanced and technocratic manner. In accordance with all other areas of life, dying is also unquestionably permeated by concepts of economic principles and action strategies. The "flexible dying" of the twenty-first century allows one to choose between clinics, care homes, dying at home, palliative wards, or alternative clinics. In neighboring Switzerland there is also the option of supported, self-determined dying. The same also applies to the funeral style and the reception. Customers decide on the coffin, flowers, candles, music, through to the gravestone; everything is possible and feasible. Dying and death have become modernized, and in this sense the institutional and economic control of medicine is a logical conclusion. At the same time, however, dying has become individualized and therefore a fact pushed to the edge of society.

Since life seems to consist of a series of more or less planned projects, the last project is planning for dying and death. In addition, the never-ending possible exchangeability through the market and the derived insignificance of the individual's experiences show what massive effects they have in all areas, on both the individual and society, and not least of all on the handling of dying and death. "A consumer merely disappears, who can be replaced by another" (Gronemeyer 2011:278)

Elias (2002) describes the problematic of modern societies in handling dying and death as a loss of tradition and the search for other options. Since the old-fashioned conventions no longer seem to be suitable and adequate, it is necessary to develop new rituals. The threat to one's own life and the finiteness become real in the encounter with those dying, and thereby the dying triggers fears and uncertainties in the living. The consequence is to institutionalize and force out dying and death from social life.

The hospice movement takes another path and enables people to end their lives with dignity. The fact is that we all die and one day will be dead. Taking on these facts and not avoiding them, by integrating those dying into everyday life, enriches our own life and death. For the handling of dying, death, fears, and grief opens up doors to oneself and enables a conscious and differentiated view of the value of life. On a social level, death has primarily become an object for medicine and biology, whereas the integration of dying and death into society would mean that we let go of a market economy image of functionalism, and instead of talking about human capital, we talk about people and develop adequate attitudes.

I end with a poem by Hermann Hesse (2003:13):

The pruned oak tree
How they have pruned you, Tree,
How you stand so strange and peculiar!
How you have suffered a hundred times,
Until nothing in you was but defiance and will!
I am like you, with the cutting,
Long suffering life, I did not break
And I dip my forehead daily in the light
Out of the suffered brutality.
What in me was soft and tender
Was scoffed by the world to death,
Yet my essence is indestructible,
I am happy, I am at one.
Patiently I shoot new leaves
From the branches fractured a hundred times,
And in defiance of all woes I remain
In love with this crazy world.

NOTE

1   Aaron Antonovsky (1923–1994), an American Israeli medical sociologist, developed the theory of salutogenesis, which describes the relationship between health and illness, and focused on the study of health in opposition to the traditional pathological model. Antonovsky explained how specific personal dispositions serve to make individuals more resilient to daily life stressors. A key aspect of his theory, "sense of coherence," consists of three factors: understandability, manageability, and meaningfulness. Understandability means that whatever happens to a person, he or she is able to understand it. Manageability describes the handling of situations as well as applied coping strategies. Meaningfulness is the sense of meaning in one's life. Meaningfulness serves as the motivational factor of the three, and they all reinforce each other.

REFERENCES

Andreatta, P. M. 2006. *Erschütterung des Selbst- und Weltverständnisses durch Trauma* (Trauma of Self-Conception and Conception of World). Kröning: Asanger Verlag.

Antonovsky, A. 1979. *Health, Stress and Coping.* San Francisco: Jossey-Bass.

Ariès, P. 2002. *Geschichte des Todes* (The Hour of Our Death). 10th ed. Munich: Deutscher Taschenbuch Verlag.

Baldauf, D., and B. Waldenberger. 2008. *Das Getragenwerden und Gehaltensein als tröstender Beziehungsraum. Eine psychoonkologische Begleitung für Krebspatienten, Angehörige und Betreuer* (Holding and Guarding to Solace: Psycho-oncological Support for Cancer Patients, Relatives and Caretakers). Würzburg: Diametric Verlag.

Bohnsack, R., W. Marotzki, and M. Meuser, eds. 2011. *Hauptbegriffe Qualitativer Sozialforschung* (Central Terms in Qualitative Research). 3rd ed. Opladen: UTB.

Bowlby, J. 2008. *Loss: Sadness and Depression.* New York: Basic Books.

Canacakis, J. 1987. *Ich sehe deine Tränen. Trauern, Klagen, Leben können* (I Can See Your Tears. Living with Mourning and Grieving). Stuttgart: Kreuz Verlag.

De Beauvoir, S. 1985. *A Very Easy Death.* New York: Pantheon.

Denz, H. 2007. Ein Netz von Liebe. Gedanken zu Gesellschaft und Spiritualität (A Network of Love: Thoughts on Society and Spirituality). Memorandum.

Elias, N. 2002. *Über die Einsamkeit der Sterbenden in unseren Tagen. Humana Conditio* (Loneliness of the Dying). Frankfurt am Main: Suhrkamp.

Fuchs, T., A. Kruse, and G. Schwarzkopf, eds. 2011. *Menschenbild und Menschenwürde am Ende des Lebens* (Humanity and Human Dignity at the End of Life). Heidelberg: Universitätsverlag Winter.

Fuchs-Heinritz, W. 2005. *Biographische Forschung* (Biographical Research). 3rd rev. ed. Wiesbaden: VS Verlag.

Girtler, R. 2010. "Feldforschung als Ethnographie" (Field Research and Ethnographie). In *Handbuch Qualitative Methoden in der Sozialen Arbeit* (Compendium of Methods in Qualitative Research in Social Work), edited by K. Bock and I. Miethe, 289–94. Opladen: Verlag Barbara Budrich.

Gronemeyer, R. 2011. "Auf dem Weg zur Selbstverwaltung des Sterbens" (On the Way to Self-Administrated Death and Dying). In *Menschenbild und Menschenwürde am Ende des Lebens* (Humanity and Human Dignity at the End of Life), edited by T. Fuchs, A. Kruse, and G. Schwarzkopf, 267–79. Heidelberg: Universitätsverlag Winter.

Hesse, H. 1978. *Stufen. Ausgewählte Gedichte.* (Steps—Selection of Poems). Baden-Baden: Suhrkamp Verlag.

———. 2003. *Verliebt in die verrückte Welt. Betrachtungen, Gedichte, Erzählungen.* (Loving This Crazy World: Reflections, Poems and Narratives. Frankfurt am Main: Suhrkamp Insel Verlag.

Hitzler, R., R. Bohnsack, W. Marotzki, and M. Meuser, eds. 2011. *Hauptbegriffe Qualitativer Sozialforschung* (Central Terms in Qualitative Research). 3rd ed. Opladen: UTB.

Hoffmann, M. 2011. *Sterben? Am liebsten plötzlich und unerwartet. Die Angst vor dem Sozialen Sterben* (Dying? Preferably Suddenly and Unexpected. The Fear of the Social Death). Wiesbaden: VS Verlag.

Kast, V. 1994. *Sich einlassen und loslassen. Neue Lebensmöglichkeit bei Trauer und Trennung.* (Getting Involved and Letting Go: New Livability During the Process of Grief and Separation). Freiburg: Herder Spektrum.

———. 2010. *Was wirklich zählt, ist das gelebte Leben. Die Kraft des Lebensrückblicks* (What Genuinely Matters Is Experienced Life. The Power of the Life Review). Freiburg im Breisgau: Kreuz Verlag.

Koch, U., and J. Weis, eds. 2009. *Psychoonkologie. Eine Disziplin in der Entwicklung* (Psycho-Oncology—a Developing Discipline). Göttingen: Hogrefe.

Kübler-Ross, E. 1997. *On Death and Dying.* New York: Scribner.

———. 2008. *Verstehen, was Sterbende sagen wollen. Einführung in ihre symbolische Sprache.* (To Understand What Dying Persons Want to Say. Introduction to Symbolic Speech). Munich: Knaur Taschenbuch.

Lang, K., C. Schmeling-Kludas, C. Schölermann, F. Kunkel, and U. Koch. 2009. "Kommunikation mit onkologischen Patienten. Ein evaluiertes Trainingsprogramm für Ärzte und Pflegende" (Communication with Cancer Patients: An Evidence-Based Training Program for Physicians and Caretakers). In *Psychoonkologie. Eine Disziplin in der Entwicklung* (Psycho-Oncology—a Developing Discipline), edited by U. Koch and J. Weis, 239–50. Göttingen: Hogrefe.

Marotzki, W. 2011. "Biographieforschung" (Biographical Research). In *Hauptbegriffe Qualitativer Sozialforschung* (Central Terms in Qualitative Research), edited by R. Bohnsack, W. Marotzki, and M. Meuser, 22–24. Opladen: UTB.

Mautner, G. 2010. " Language and the Market Society." In *Critical Reflections on Discourse and Dominance.* London: Routledge.

Noll, P. 2009. *Diktate über Sterben und Tod* (Dictates on Death and Dying). Munich: Piper Verlag.

Pockrandt, B. 2006. *Grenzgänge im Angesicht des Todes. Biographische Narrations-analyse zur Kontingenzverarbeitung im onkologischen Feld* (Limits at Death's Door. Analyzing Biographical Narrations to Handle Contingency in Oncology). Kassel: University Press.

Rieff, D. 2008. *Swimming in a Sea of Death: A Son's Memoir*. New York: Simon & Schuster.

Riemann, F. 2009. *Grundformen der Angst* (Fundamental Forms of Anxiety). 36th ed. Munich: Reinhardt Verlag.

Rosenthal, G. 1995. *Erlebte und erzählte Lebensgeschichte. Gestalt und Struktur biographischer Selbstbeschreibungen* (Narrative Studies of Life. Gestalt and Structure of Biographical Self-Description). Frankfurt am Main: Campus Verlag.

Schlingensief, C. 2009. *So schön wie hier kanns im Himmel gar nicht sein. Tagebuch einer Krebserkrankung* (In Heaven It May Never Be as Beautiful as It Is Here. Journal on Being Affected with Cancer). 5th ed. Cologne: Verlag Kiepenheuer & Witsch.

Sontag, S. 1979. *Illness as Metaphor and AIDS and Its Metaphors*. New York: Anchor Books.

Sperl, I. 2010. *Geschriebene Identität—Lebenslinien in Tagebüchern* (Written Identity—Experiences of Life in Private Journals). Munich: Herbert Utz Verlag.

Student, J.-C., ed. 1999. *Das Hospiz-Buch* (The Hospice-Book). 4th ed. Freiburg im Breisgau: Lambertus.

Terzani, T. 2007. *Noch eine Runde auf dem Karussel. Vom Leben und Sterben* (Once Again a Turn on the Merry-Go-Round: Living and Dying). Munich: Knaur Taschenbuch Verlag.

Van Stap, S. 2006. *Meisje met negen preugen* (Girl with Nine Perukes). Amsterdam: Prometeus.

Welter-Enderlin, R. 2010. *Resilienz und Krisenkompetenz. Kommentierte Fallge-schichten* (Resilience and Competence in Crisis: Annotated Case Histories). Heidelberg: Carl-Auer-Systeme Verlag.

Wilber, K. 2000. *Grace and Grit: Spirituality and Healing in the Life and Death of Treya Killem Wilber*. Boston: Shambhala.

Yalom, I. D. 2008. *Staring at the Sun: Overcoming the Terror of Death*. San Francisco: Jossey-Bass.

CHAPTER 9

Holding On While Letting Go

AN AUTOETHNOGRAPHIC STUDY OF DIVORCE IN IRELAND

▸ *ORLAGH FARRELL DELANEY AND PATRICIA KENNEDY*

THIS AUTOETHNOGRAPHY is a joint endeavor about our experience of the divorce process in Ireland. In this study we engage in dialogue to reflect on how we got through the process and what we learned from the experience. We hope that sharing our insights will help others who are facing divorce. We focus very much on our resilience, on what helped us bounce back and get on with our lives. Our friendship is central to our experience and demonstrates the importance of support and sharing in trying times.

Our friendship began over ten years earlier when Orlagh approached Patricia to supervise a proposed Ph.D. dissertation on infertility. Shortly afterward Orlagh developed chronic fatigue syndrome (CFS)[1] and had to withdraw from the university where she also worked. Our friendship endured despite our very different lives.

Orlagh lives alone in a cottage in a remote corner of rural Ireland. She tries to live "the good life": living simply, lightly, harmlessly, and mindfully; growing vegetables; rearing sheep, donkeys, goats, hens, and dogs; trying to make a difference; challenging contemporary notions of what it means to be a success as a woman; and calling on complementary therapies and philosophies for inspiration. Her small rural community consists of scattered individuals and families that form a diffuse support network of which she is very much a part.

Patricia outwardly lives a more conventional life: in a big city; a senior academic; a mother of four children; traveling; writing; trying to make a difference by living differently within the mainstream. While living in the city can give the impression of community, it can be an isolating and fragmented place in contrast to Orlagh's more supportive community. Patricia's busy household filled with children and animals is a safe haven where all five of them in their own individual ways are growing toward the light.

As we were both traveling toward ending our marriages, we decided we wanted to document and make sense of what we were going through and to share this with other people. Making a documentary was empowering for us at a time in our lives when we often felt we had little power or control. There is a profound silence on the subject in Ireland where the family law court takes place in camera. We decided that, given Orlagh's health, an oral record would serve us best. We also felt that our dialogue as two close, trusting friends would bring us to greater depths of understanding. As we wanted to reach a wide audience, we decided to make a radio documentary. *There Was Love* was recorded over a fifteen-month period between 2008 and 2009 and was broadcast on RTE, the Irish national radio station, in 2010. A year later when we set out to write this autoethnography, we realized that time had given us even greater insights. We decided that we would excavate our personal journals to see what we had written to our private selves and how this added depth to the public stories we had shared with the radio audience. We draw here on private journals we had both kept for decades. We also draw on the transcripts of recording of our dialogue for radio. In this autoethnography we reflect on our resilience and describe our insights.

DIVORCE IN IRELAND

Following a constitutional referendum in 1996, legislation was enacted that facilitated the introduction in 1997 of no-fault divorce. A couple must have lived apart for at least four of the five years before proceedings are issued. The parties do not have to have been living in separate houses. At least one of the parties has to be domiciled in the Republic of Ireland or have lived in the country for a year before bringing proceedings. The court must be satisfied that there is no reasonable prospect of reconciliation, and that both parties and any children are properly provided for. The family law court is held in camera, which guarantees that only the parties, their legal representatives, the judge, and court officials are entitled to be present. Ostensibly to protect the privacy of the parties concerned, in camera ensures that the general public and those who access the family courts are often provided with no information concerning the procedure involved in such cases, the orders that can be made, and the circumstances surrounding those orders. This ensures that what happens within goes unreported and unresearched.

The number of divorces granted in 2009 was 3,341, a 14 percent increase since 2002 (Courts Service Annual Report 2009). In 2009 we were two of those statistics. While numbers have been rising, there remains a deep silence on the experience of divorce. We wanted to break the silence. At the same time, we wanted to reflect on what we were experiencing, to acknowledge and make sense of the pain we were feeling, and to explore where we were sourcing strength to persevere. By regularly sharing our experiences with each other, we were able to gain more perspective; at the same time our friendship strengthened, and with it, mutual support. Hence this autoethnography began when we were both engaged in the divorce process.

RADIO DOCUMENTARY

As two friends with shared values but very different lives, we recognized that working together from different positions would add value to our analysis. The *Doc on One*, a weekly documentary feature on RTE, invites submissions from those interested in making documentaries. Radio is mass media. It is everywhere. McLeish (1994) states that radio "acts as a multiplier of change, speeding up the process of informing a population; it provides information; it acts as a watch-dog on power holders; it enables social and political debate; it contributes to artistic and intellectual culture; it disseminates ideas; it enables groups and individuals to speak to each other; it mobilises public and private resources" (9).

We met with the producer and set off on our journey to break the silence. As our working title, *Holding on While Letting Go*, would suggest, we aimed to explore the issues that can arise from the experience of marital separation: managing loss (emotional, financial, and material) while at the same time trying to hold onto one's dignity, self-respect, integrity, and values. The producer, agreed to take a backseat other than to teach us how to use the equipment. We set about recording the background sounds of both our lives: animals, rural Ireland, and silence in Orlagh's case, and the sounds of the city and a busy family life in Patricia's case. We aimed to capture the seasonal changes and their impact on daily living in the urban/rural divide; surviving major events and holidays; the presence and absence of children; caring for animals; preparing for court appearances; our experiences with the legal and judicial systems; the importance of support; and living with CFS. We planned the documentary to capture the passage of time, to mark the seasons and festivals, and to present cameos of each of our lives, our friendship, and the outcomes of our divorce applications.

Over a period of fifteen months, we learned to use recording equipment and, with and without the producer present, recorded eight hours of material, which was condensed into a thirty-two-minute documentary. Completed in March 2010, *Holding on While Letting Go* became *There Was Love* and was broadcast for the first time in June of that year with a listenership of approximately 200,000 and a further 100,000 podcasts. At the end of the broadcast listeners were invited to respond via a designated page on the RTE Web site (http://www.rte/doconone/there was love). What was included in the final documentary was constrained by the in camera requirements and privacy laws. Another obstacle to full disclosure was our shared awareness that the men we were divorcing and Patricia's children were among the potential audience. Yet we wanted to be honest. We realized that what we could actually say was determined by how we said it. Here we share what we have learned from discussing our experiences with each other as we were going through the divorce process and making the documentary, its aftermath, and our reflections a year later. We present two parallel narratives, intertwined as one: the public one, censored for radio, and the private additional insights and explanations, including excerpts from recorded dialogue and our very private, personal journals kept before, during, and after two decades of marriage. We learned about ourselves and our friendship. This is our story of resilience.

Resilience is generally associated with bouncing back, having the ability to cope, recover, and move on. It is a skill, talent, or attribute that people carry in varying quantities. It is associated with overcoming adversity, bouncing back, surviving, and, for some people, coming out of a crisis situation stronger and more resourceful. Walsh (2003) defines resilience as "the ability to withstand and rebound from disruptive life challenges" (1). She refers to Luthar, Cicchetti, and Becker's observation that "it involves dynamic processes, fostering positive adaptation within the context of specific adversity." Walsh contrasts those who get stuck in a victim position with those who bounce back, as resilient. She suggests that "resilience involves key processes over time that foster the ability to 'struggle well' surmount obstacles and go on to live and love fully." Referring to the work of Luthar and Ziegler (1991), who emphasized personal traits possessed by the "rugged individual," Walsh suggests that this view has changed over time to incorporate family and wider socioeconomic influences.

FROM *HOLDING ON WHILE LETTING GO* TO *THERE WAS LOVE*

During the fifteen months we were recording, both our statuses changed from married to divorced. When we began our project, we felt we were desperately trying to hold on, to survive. By the time we had finished, we had traveled from the proposed title of *Holding on While Letting Go*, reflecting how we were feeling at the time, to *There Was Love*, something the process showed us. Holding on while at the same time letting go permeated the initial ten to twelve months of our documentary making. At times we were barely holding on through difficult times of worry, stress, and uncertain finances. The letting go was threefold: letting go of love, or our ideas and concepts of love; letting go of the deep disappointment it involved; and trying to be let go of, or set free. On one level we had to be prepared to let go of our homes and security, and on another level, our hopes and expectations. We also had to let go of anger at things that were said and done, broken promises, and frustration with resistance and intransigence. While experiencing this we were trying to hold on to our sanity and dignity and, through our research, our power and our voices. We were aware of this, but through making the documentary we became aware that there was love in our lives, even though we may not have been aware of it or felt very loving. We found this very healing. Writing this autoethnography a year later has helped us reflect further.

Dyer and McGuinness (1996) suggest that historically resilience was used to describe a pliant or elastic quality of a substance or organ. Reviewing several sources, they highlight the importance of bouncing back, rebounding, adaptability, and buoyancy. They define resilience as "a global term describing a process whereby people bounce back from adversity and go on with their lives" (227). It is a dynamic process highly influenced by protective factors, which they describe as specific competencies that are necessary for the process of resilience to occur. They propose that competencies are simply the healthy skills and abilities that the individual can access. Competencies exist in three domains: individual, interpersonal, and familial. They note that there "is a shifting balance between vulnerability and resilience."

Listening to the recording, we were both struck by the change of tone as time went on. At the beginning, when we were both anticipating divorce but it was still something stretching before us in the distance, our voices were tired, strained, anxious, tense, and stressed. While we cannot capture this tone here in the written word, we can reflect on the words used. The following excerpts from the documentary reflect our "holding on."

PATRICIA: I still don't know when I'm going to get a divorce, but it looks like I'll have a court date sometime in winter. Hopefully by the end of the year things will be resolved.

ORLAGH: Your first court date is coming up soon, how are you feeling about that?

PATRICIA: I think about the kids and the significance of the day their parents get divorced . . . it is before and after from then on. . . . I just think I need closure and I need to move on and I feel strong enough to deal with whatever will come out of it.

This is the determination identified by Dyer and McGuinness (1996) as a feature of resilience. Orlagh's excerpt below shows the importance of social support and the strong sense of self, to which we both held firm. On a private level we were recording much stronger sentiments. We talked about sleepless nights, nausea, panic attacks, exhaustion and physical weakness, and distress. Patricia had dramatic weight loss and an abscess on her breast, which the doctor said was stress induced. For Orlagh, the symptoms of her condition worsened. Orlagh's words also reflect determination.

Over a four year period I was scheduled for court many times. Because my jurisdiction was rural, the family law courts sat for two days three times a year maximum. The case lists were huge, and even if you were listed you could sit around all day and never be called. Often I found out just before

5 PM the previous evening that the "other side" had got an adjournment—another three-month wait. Because of the CFS in particular, each court visit took days to prepare for and weeks to recover from. My sister always took me, and Patricia would often be there as at times were other very supportive friends. I would have all my documents, which I had gathered and frequently updated, mostly of my own volition, in a wicker basket, which was really heavy. By the end of the four years, its handles had completely worn. I wore a long black coat with a silver angel broach and my hair pinned up. Always on my wrist I wore either blue or orange prayer beads, which gave me comfort and strength. At times of necessity I withdrew completely from the group conversation as we waited. I prayed that I would have the strength to just not pass out from weakness, and that if I was called to be heard my stressed-out brain would not completely turn to fog. For my loyal supporters I always brought a car picnic lunch of egg salad sandwiches and homemade rocky road. All I could ever swallow was the green tea as I tried to smile and hold on to what bit of dignity I could. In my wicker basket was every receipt, statement, letter, and piece of history that I thought could help my case. My legal team were often quite dismissive of my "overpreparedness." Yet eight or nine appearances later, when my case was finally heard, it was every one of those pieces of paper that ultimately kept the roof over my head.

My family are incredibly good to me; my older sister Fiona in particular is a constant through all the struggles. In the uncertain years pending the long-awaited court decision, I had to remain open to the reality that I may have had to sell and move. On the rare times I could go driving, I would find myself staring into people's homes and imagining what it must be like to know each day you could actually live there. Of course that was naïve because nobody knows what anybody's story really is. I often fantasized about how I would make the house truly my own if I were allowed remain living there. I tried to insulate myself from any risk of future adversity.

When the house did become mine, I had the geometric stresses checked or "divined," as it is called in Ireland, by a wonderful little man in his eighties. He identified all the "bad lines" and single-handedly hammered in rods all around the outside of the house to improve the energy. It felt like out with the old and in with the new. He was concerned about me living alone and unwell in such an isolated area, and he said he would add me to his nightly list of prayers. To this day he remains on mine.

Our days and nights were dark. There were times we were desperate, at the edge of our limits in all sorts of ways. The radio documentary facilitated us in recording our dialogue. Our discourse occurs at several levels as we explore the physical, environmental, and psychic implications of our experience.

PATRICIA: Orlagh, you know that dark night you mention? When I think of my dark night I can look up at the lights of Dublin. Your dark night frightens the life out of me because of where you live. There are no streetlights; not even in the distance. At this time of the year your dark nights can go on for a long time. Could you explain to me what that is like or how you survive that? I don't think I could.

ORLAGH: Yes, Trish. There's that kind of dark night and then there's the internal dark night. I'm fine. . . . I'm fine with nature's dark night. There's a blanket of stars, and very often there's a huge moon that comes up at the back of my hill. I go out in my pajamas because the dogs go out for their last pee. You can hear the goats give the odd "maa" in their shed. Nan the sheep comes around for one more biscuit—and that's fine. You can hear that awful banshee-like wail of the fox on the back hill—nothing of that frightens me. I love that. . . . I love all that. But the dark nights that I've been through since the separation and becoming ill can last for weeks. And I have cried, I have cried loud scary noises. You try and avoid going there. You want your mind and your reasoning to take you to the next level without having to go down into that deep dark difficult emotional place. But you can't. You have to go through it to get past it. I remember one night, just before the separation, lying on the couch in the kitchen. And it was quiet and it was dark except for . . . some very loud snoring from the bottom of the house . . . and my heart was just broken.

You know Trish, I would never have considered myself to have been of low self-esteem, and I can say that now with certainty nor would have anyone else. Yet I obviously did not either know enough or think enough about self-love. Why else would I have "put up" with so much for so long? Certainly I paid into all the drama and dysfunction, and I overinvested in Dan at a huge cost to myself. When I made what I call the "heart lock" into Dan (he was my first real love), I was so invested so fast I really only ever considered him. I only rated what he thought of me, and that was so up and down. I now realize I never stood a chance with the "other presence," the alcohol. The huge collateral damage from the drinking—when the person you love, and who you want to love you, constantly turns to everything else except you for pleasure and fun, who basically uses you and always boomerangs back to you eventually to be put back together. It is no wonder you think less and less of yourself and, despite previous good judgment, find yourself clinging on even tighter to the ever-decreasing bits of love and promises you receive.

I woke up thinking about how I used to get up early, travel for hours and teach, and travel home and do more work. What would Dan do? There all day with his music. He was often out running when I got home. Then when I discussed my work and the "politics" of it, terrible tension would ensue. It was my own repeated mistake to mention it. I only had to walk in the door from my "big" job and an argument would ensue. Once I taught a series of classes at a women's shelter and I know I helped them, but at times when I got in my own door I felt like a fraud. I have worn out shoes over the years running and walking, stressed and heartbroken. Yet I would walk back in my gate open and hopeful. What if I had came home from teaching to find him with a shovel, tending the crops or feeding the animals? Something cooked, delighted to see me? I took loving very seriously. Dan always suited and cared for himself. When he didn't, we both thought it was major. I had nothing to compare with. I thought love was forgiving and making the best out of everything.

We had to be careful with what we said in the radio documentary for legal reasons. We were interested to see the differences between what we were saying to each other in the public world of radio and the private thoughts we had recorded, never expecting to make them public. Thus when writing this autoethnography we decided to look at our personal journals, which were written in private for our personal reflection. Orlagh found that writing poetry helped her make sense of what she was experiencing:

NO
I can't pretend anymore
The things I took for love,
The energy I put into being light
The everymoment of pleasing
And still I'm at it.
Can anyone love anyone that long
When teeth clog and breath smells and piles droop?
My mind is gone in a circle with you.
What if this or what if that?

I have wiped too many shitty arses
to give up this house
and go into the world of renting spinsters.
Whatever way I say it or whatever
way you hear it,
It is still NO.

Patricia wrote:

This time nineteen years ago I was getting ready to be married and now I am preparing for divorce. Both are big events, one the beginning, the other the end. At least with a wedding you can plan and you know the date. But with a divorce it seems to be someone else, the state or the system dictates. In 1985 when we were a young couple, Irish emigrants in London, I had written in my journal:

We were happy in our attic flat. I would blink awake at dawn and watch silently and lovingly as he would pull on his warm long-sleeved vest. I would envy the cloth as it hugged his vibrant skin. "Gotta go," he would sing, "gotta go." Bending to kiss me, he would slip out the door and I would slip out of bed, oblivious to the cold morning air, and race to dress before he could leave without me. I would place my hand in his as we glided slowly through the silver dawn. Six minutes later we would pass the Earls Court Exhibition Centre which stood proud but shabby in its usual place. Turning into the station, we would smile at the grumpy vendor as he counted the coppers falling through his tanned fingers. Racing down the steps we would notice the transport workers going off duty and ambling home to their grey council flats. The camaraderie of these workers always brought a smile to our faces. A chubby man would sing "Hello Young Lovers" when he saw us coming. I loved when the train would slow down and sometimes even stop. I could steal a few extra seconds with him but the journey always had to end. As the early train would whisk him away from the station I would take a deep breath and plod through the early morning commuters towards our lonely flat, a nothingness now that he was gone. I would trudge up the stairs exhausted at 8 AM and think: it's not the big things that I love about you, it's the small things; like the way our toes rub together in the morning when we awake; and the way you always drown your cereal in milk and afterwards, you'll leave without washing your crumby plate; when you steal a glance at a newspaper in fear that I'll reprimand you, accuse you of ignoring me, not loving me. You're always right, I do, and that is why I love you.

Patricia's sense of self as a younger woman was very much linked to her then-lover. Looking back as a divorced older woman and mother, she could reflect on those early days and the intervening years.

What strikes me now is the phrase he used "gotta go" which as a young woman was not threatening. To me it was a description of his job demands. It seemed exciting. As the decades wore on and I became a wife and a mother four times, these all too familiar words when I asked for help, love, company, often with a child in my arms, one balanced on my hip and two other playing by my feet, were signalled by a raised right hand and the words "Back off."

It took him, after 21 years, between 8 and 10 days to erase any proof of my existence in our home. I had left taking with me as little as possible, only the children, some clothes, some books and my etchings. I wanted to leave as unobtrusively as possible. Ten days later I went to get a book from my former bedroom, to find it had grown. It was wider, longer, and deeper. He had cleared away my marks. When I later asked him why he had never cleaned our bedroom during the decades we slept together, he answered: "It was always your stuff, your mess." How stupid of me. True to myself I reacted by making pints of pure organic juice and drinking it. I ground organic free trade coffee beans and I lit candles and oil burners, geranium oil of course. I sat at the kitchen table with fresh air blowing through the kitchen, all doors and windows open to clear my mind, and I started reading a novel. It was a Jane Urquhart novel, chosen for its cover, fresh green and blue foliage.

Orlagh also reflects on her early relationship. An excerpt from her journal of several years earlier:

Now after 7 it is a glorious evening. I was working in the university all day and got home to the birds singing. Two days ago I heard the first cuckoo of the year. I love the sound of that little bird! I have just watered the tomato plants and early leeks in the polytunnel and the trees in the garden which are trying hard to flower. All around the yellow gorse is in full coconut bloom. Everything is so incredibly beautiful when it first appears after the long winter. I have made a pot of basmati rice and spiced lentils for dinner and warm apple sponge for dessert. The smells fill the house as does the ylang ylang oil burning in the bathroom as a surprise for Dan who must be out on a long run with the dog?

The love and care is palpable. In dialogue as the divorce process continued, obstacles were overcome, not easily but with determination and care. We showed determination to live well, care for each other, children, and animals and to value our friendship. The documentary making made us find words to describe what we were experiencing, and this helped us to clarify not only for a radio audience but for ourselves. Making the documentary enabled us focus on what we were going through in a different way. We were able to step back a little and reflect on our reactions, and furthermore to share these and discuss them with each other. Knowing we had a potential audience encouraged us to choose our words carefully, and this too helped reflection. In trying to explain our situation to others, we were clarifying for ourselves.

Walsh and McGoldrick (1991) suggest that "family resilience thus involves varied adaptational pathways over time, from a threatening event on the horizon, through disruptive transitions, and subsequent shockwaves in the immediate aftermath and beyond." For example, "how a family approaches an anticipated loss, buffers stress and manages upheaval, and effectively reorganises and reinvests in life pursuits, will influence the immediate and long term adaptation for all members and their relationships" (227).

ORLAGH: Trish, you recently moved house—how is that for you?

PATRICIA: Because my husband was refusing to cooperate and had stalled proceedings for several years, I felt I had to move, with the children, out of the family home. I rented a house near the children's schools and moved in, dogs, fish, turtles, and all of the equipment four children bring: bicycles, trampolines, musical instruments, etc. It was difficult trying to raise a deposit, find a suitable home, negotiate a lease, and all in the week schools and the university reopened after the summer holidays. We are settling down—life goes on and it feels like normality. The way I feel about it is when a marriage is dead you have to leave it and move on or it rots around you. It was time to have separate houses and to try to come to some kind of agreement and get on with our lives—all of us. I'm happy anyway, and you know—we are fine.

I got up early on Saturday morning and came downstairs. There was a small creature lying at the bottom of the stairs. It took a while for me to realize it was Tommy, my daughter's pet hamster. It had been killed in the night by one of our dogs. They had raided his cage and, judging from the large mounds of excrement on the beige carpet of the rented house, had eaten vast quantities of hamster food. Later on that night I was searching for the dog and discovered he had jumped over the garden wall with a giant leap on the trampoline. Orlagh, while I am laughing now my journal entry captures the true heartache I was feeling:

Mauve, violet, purple, all shades of the same essence, the essence of sadness and grief, loss and pain. I used to have green and blue dreams, dreams of turquoise, indigo, violet, emerald sea snakes swimming in electric blue seas, pink sea mountains of salt floating wordlessly on azure seas, white crystal mirroring blue calving glaciers, silver dolphins and breaching whales like I saw in Alaska. These dreams are gone now. I dream in muted tones of mauve and purple, too much brown added, and beige. My four children; golden; each and every one of them golden; and the brightest summer yellows, their hair, their souls, their minds, bright and shining like a summer's day, a path of silvery moon across the sea, washing peacefully ashore, swoosh, swoosh, swoosh, bringing comfort to all who sit on golden sands listening, breathing in and out with the sea's patterns. Because of those sunshine kids with the green blue eyes I stayed, I stayed longer than I should have and wilted like the flowers on the table near me as I write; the flowers, a duty gift given to me by a husband who no longer cares, who let me down, two roses, a sunflower, a few sprigs of leaves.

I rented a house nearby, two up, two down. I sought refuge there. It had a bright blue mosaic in the hallway, pouring out under the front door to draw me in. It welcomed me. The light was bright in that small house. I surrounded and filled it with flowers, geraniums mostly, reds and pinks, around the doors and windows, floor to ceiling in the porch, for protection I had read, protection from evil. A yew tree I placed at the back door, in the sunshine, for rebirth, for moving on, for new beginnings. I made and drank as much juice as I could swallow and fed it to my sunshine children, cranberry, pomegranate, beetroot, and pear, all to protect and keep them strong. I burned oils, geranium to keep them safe, lavender relaxed, and tea rose for love. Each time my children left to stay with their father, I felt the pain and sorrow pour from my skin, my tissues, my sinews and bones, years and years of pain and sorrow and sadness, my dead sister, mother, father, my bitter marriage, my sick child, my childhood poverty and pain, all liquidized and flooding from my shoulders, back, glands, all pouring from me, down my back and from my back onto the floor, and lay there at my feet.

Here I was facing the rest of my life, an ex-wife, against my will spending nights, enforced exile away from my children. "But you choose it, you left him," the voices hum. It is true, I did, but it was to survive, to learn to love myself, to breathe so that I could mother my children and my own inner child. I found myself a new roommate: my almost nine-year-old son, blonde, strong, green blue eyes, full of fight and angst and passion but safe in my bed and sleeping more soundly than he had in years, stirring only slightly at night to reach for me, to whisper he loves me, to throw a muscular male but still baby arm around me. I am truly blessed. I asked him last night if he liked my room and he answered: "I like any room when you are in it." He then went on to ask me, "What happened in your day?" Another little body appears sometimes, an even smaller person, a little blonde girl, blue eyes, and red lipstick and matching nails, dressed always immaculately in matching pajamas and slippers, she too slips between the sheets and throws a slim but very possessive and protective arm over my broad shoulders. This little woman is far more secure, confident, and assured of her place in the world. I can hear, further along the hall, the breathing of the two older boys. One of them today looked at me most sincerely and said: "You are a fabulous mother," much as I had reassured my own mother on her deathbed. The third boy, the middle one, has been in love with me since well before his birth, kicking wildly against the caverns of my rib cage, and on birth asserting with his cries: "I am here, now look after me." Yes. I am truly blessed.

ORLAGH: Trish, when you tell me how much solace and fun you get from being a mother, I am aware that my situation is so different. Between the ages of thirty and forty were the "infertility years." It became a black chasm that I really had not expected to fall into. Initially I was ambivalent about having children, but that was considerable progress from my preceding stance of "dead set against." As it turned out, it was an incredibly short trip to "obsessed with becoming pregnant." I remember it as the saddest, loneliest, most painful time of my life. With hindsight it is hard now to separate it from all the sadness and struggle that ran parallel to it at the time. I researched it inside out, initially to help myself to counter the medical management at the time who, because it was unexplained, kept sending me home between three-month appointments to relax. But then the research turned to the issue of infertility or involuntary childlessness itself, and I devoted my master's thesis to breaking the silence that surrounded infertility in Ireland in the late nineties. It was when I was continuing that research at the Ph.D. level that I met you, who was to become my supervisor and ten years on one of my dearest friends. To this day I am the only person I know or am related to that does not have children. Oftentimes through the whole lengthy divorce proceedings I was told by lawyers how lucky I was not to have children in my circumstances. A few years previously I would have given them my political lecture on involuntary childlessness. Today, thankfully, that deep pain has morphed down into experience, maybe even wisdom, and takes its place alongside all the others. Anyway, these legs are too sore for soapboxes.

When you are quilting your life, all the patches don't have to be your own. My dear friends Marcella and John, who live close by, had a much-longed-for baby over two years ago. Marcella kindly says she is birth mother and I am earth mother. Little Abbey hugs my sheep, rides my donkey, collects eggs, and sits on my German shepherds. Her first shoes were pink wellie boots—my gift to both her and myself. She drinks green tea from her own little cup, which she gets from the dresser. She has her own tin of treats from which she chooses one thing for now and one for her pocket. My name was her first word. We all have designs for our lives, but often it is beyond us what stitches us together.

PATRICIA: Orlagh, you are divorced now. The last time I was here you were getting ready for court and getting all your documents ready. Here you are now getting ready to reap more than one type of harvest.

ORLAGH: Yeah, Patricia, I'm here and I know I can stay here. That's a huge relief after huge stress. My solicitor used to say, "You know it could be four years before you could be getting your divorce and anything is sorted," and I thought she was crazy! . . . It is such an arduous system . . . and if there was any other way? There is collaborative law where both sides work together and promise to never go to court, that definitely needs to be promoted. It is so costly unless you are legally aided, and stressful, and a few years out of your life where the love you started out with is forgotten about and totally abandoned, and that is sad.

PATRICIA: Yes, Orlagh, when my divorce happened it was quick—almost sudden. It was a very wet day when I got divorced. I'd been up at five o'clock that morning. It was lashing rain, and I was very tired. I was conscious that while we were in love once and did all sorts of things together, we had arrived at a situation where we are staring ahead and sitting behind our legal teams. Our case was straightforward, so the judge granted the decree of divorce, and he wished us both the best of luck for the future. We went our separate ways. I walked out of the court and along by the river. There I was after more than twenty years of marriage, exhausted mentally and emotionally. I was tired and hungry, so I went and had my breakfast, and then I went to the cinema and slept, because I was too tired to go home. I was too tired to talk to anyone, and people want details. I felt grief and loss, and it was difficult to know who to turn to, who to talk to, and there is grief. Recently, one of the children said to me that they saw my wedding photos. But you don't cancel out your wedding; it is just you have reached a different stage of your life. And I suppose I felt there is no more need to argue, and we were moving on, and that maybe we could be good parents from now on. It is just a different chapter.

ORLAGH: I know how you feel. The other day in my handbag I found these little orange beads and I had a flashback to the day in the high court. I had my stress beads, my prayer beads, and I was flying around them when I was on the stand (box), and they burst and they went everywhere! And after I got down, the court clerk said [primly], "And what are these?" And everyone was picking up my stress beads! And I found a few of them the other day and I thought— nobody is cut out for that kind of stress! It is more with hindsight that I feel the relief. I think this time last year such and such was happening. It was dramatic and there were so many courts. Sometimes when I walk up the road, I think, "It is all over. I'm here. This is my home." My heart just lifts. Or when I see the animals pottering around, or I'm pottering around and I think, "It is all over. It is sorted. I can stay here." For years I lived with "Will I be able to stay here? Where will I go? How will I start all over again?" I see it clearly in my journal:

> There is no more material struggle. God willing you will get to keep the house. When you disconnect from everyone else's aspirations and all the conditioned messages there is nothing you need or want that you don't already have. Stop bobbing for apples—you are in Eden. Driving home from Lila's over the hill I saw a newly cut field, the silage dotted in black bales. From the distance it looked like a golden bread pudding with dark currants. The flowering whitethorn trees were like brides on a day that was soft tar hot. The distant drone of a lawnmower on a Sunday afternoon. Beetroot stained hardboiled eggs on salad leaves from the polytunnel.

PATRICIA: It was the first day of November, the first day of winter and we watched the sun going down together. We were saying that it was really nice and that we had come a long way. And we just sort of said—"thanks be to Jesus that it is all over"! We had gone full circle from the beginning of the New Year, through spring, summer, and autumn. Our lives had changed as gradually as the tress and fields. And looking back to the previous winter as the New Year stretched before us, Orlagh had written:

It is the sky that prompted me to write. Done with the "happy new year" calls, the skyline caught my attention and startled me into thinking about the end of another year. Full darkness at 5 PM. Blue black spills over Eagle Hill and back to the east there are luminous shades of yellows—it struck me as a sign of hope. Today walking down the road I was filled for a moment with forgiveness, probably aspiration more than authentic. Still it is a relief from all the thoughts and reflections that have plagued me since the split. Something very huge in me is being healed. Love from so many people and in so many guises is coming towards me now having looked to one source for love for the past 20 years. I breathe and try to release my ex-husband into the New Year and claim it for myself. New Year's Day, up at 5 AM which is becoming usual. It is black dark outside. I have had rye toast and green tea. Will I promise myself only the best for myself for this year? Will I ask the greater powers for what is best for me? I will. Last year was a momentous year for me. Probably one of the most difficult in many ways. I feel like I had been tunnelling a way out for a long time. Spoonful by spoonful I was clearing my way out alone. Now it is like I can see the daylight. I have spent the last while considering how it all went wrong or moreover how right was it ever actually? That seems cruel and disloyal but in order to break free, necessary? As soon as it is right I will feel the forgiveness.

It is interesting to see how Orlagh was moving on. It is clear that the New Year represented a very important milestone for both of us. It seemed to symbolize the passage of time, letting go of the old and moving on into an unknown future. Patricia's situation was still unresolved, so her journal told a very different story.

It is New Year's Day and I face it with trepidation, not knowing what lies ahead. I will undoubtedly end up in the divorce court and have to do battle for custody of my babies. Last night I tried to let go of my fears and anxieties as we waved goodbye to 2008. In the afternoon I surfed in the wild Atlantic Ocean, aware at how privileged I was to have my thirteen year old son at my side, encouraging and teaching me, my other three children playing in the sand dunes. And later on as the New Year rang out we walked with the other inhabitants of the small western village where we were staying. Safe in the shadow of the mountains, led by six men in kilts, playing the pipes, and another six holding blazing torches, the bells rang out. There was hope.

Making the documentary gave us the opportunity to stand back and look at ourselves and what we were experiencing and expressing. The stress is palpable. The holding on is as tangible as the letting go. This didn't surprise us. We had anticipated it in our working title. What did surprise us, though, was that there was always love. This came out so strongly in our words: familial love, love for friends, self-love and preservation, love of nature and the countryside, but most of all the love we had shared with the men we were divorcing. When we realized this, we both found it very comforting as it helped us appreciate that our marriages and our emotional investments had not been in vain. We had believed in our relationships for a very long time and had tried to keep our marriage vows until it hurt too much to continue and we needed to call a halt.

There was love.

PATRICIA: We met when we were both around nineteen. We knew each other for about a year before we started going out together. We met in the university rowing club. I would have said it was love at first sight, I don't know how he'd feel. We were young, although we didn't think so at the time. . . . I'd like to believe love is eternal, love doesn't die. Different challenges come your way. I think things change over time. When you are young you have plenty of time to put into a relationship. If you are tired or sad or bored, you can go to the cinema or for a meal or something. Once you have got a career or you have children, you sort of peel away all of that distraction and you have to deal with the reality. I don't think love dies, but I think you can kill it—by neglect. We graduated in the 1980s in the midst of an economic recession and emigrated to London, both aged twenty-one. It can be difficult for a young migrant couple, forced to depend on one another in a foreign land, without the support and companionship of family and friends. Orlagh, I know you very well now, but my early perception of you was that you were this fairy-tale couple, living up in the wilderness, madly in love. And you'd arrive into my office usually with some organic food, or a homemade gift, and the way you spoke about your husband, he was like some hero. When I met you both, I can remember you walking along hand in hand, with your long, flowing hair. It is interesting now looking back—what a few years can do, or maybe how our perceptions can change?

ORLAGH: Yes, Trish, it is interesting to me who we become to make things work. There is no doubt I was 100 percent invested in love and the concept of love, and I think possibly who I signed up with would have got that part of me, that whole part of me. But yes, I was in love. I wouldn't have stayed for twenty years otherwise! But at a huge, huge cost . . . a cost I didn't recognize til toward the end. When ME came, the cracks became craters. I thought it was all the stuff of soulmates, all the uphill struggle, Dan and me against a loveless world. I thought I could make up for all previous hurts against him and vice versa. Another night on the couch, now early in the kitchen in my flannel nightshirt, the clock ticking. Dan snoring down the hall in "our" bedroom. How many years have I been doing this? Every morning searching, trying, stuck, lonely, waiting for the click of Dan's shower. Filling myself with optimism and hope that he will bring some light into today. Waiting, waiting, suppressing, suppressing, squeezing myself into his perspective like an ugly sister into a glass slipper.

PATRICIA: Orlagh, what kept you hanging in there that you didn't give up?

ORLAGH: I think, Trish, it is what you see in the beginning, whether it's a spark or a glimmer or a big bright light of love. What causes you to fall in love; you are slow to give that up. And it is not like it goes out completely. There are flashes of it, there are glimmers of it. God knows there were enough reconciliations in our situation, and you believe and you are highly invested. It is interesting to examine. It was easy to blame it on things like the infertility, differences, poverty. I think really you can talk yourself around a lot. And I had become very isolated, I had isolated myself. And the image you put out there as you say is: everything is fine here.

My legal team used to say to me that nobody starts off in love or marriage and thinks it is going to go this way. And even though we have to dig in and fight our corners and argue for what is ours, it is hard not to be saddened. Nobody wants it to go sour or to go bad. My solicitor said the most dignity that can be afforded one party by the other . . . she promotes that and I respect that. And it is one thing I took away, that in my case, not too much was said that was not honest and true and respectful, and that is a small thing to hold on to. Because there was love, there was always love, or else we would not have been there or been married.

We both realized that there were different loving relationships in our lives. Our families of origin were important as role models and as a source of support.

PATRICIA: It struck me having met your family, how much a part of your life they are and the love that is there. . . . I think it might be nice for other people to hear that things can change and how the love can flow back in from another source.

ORLAGH: Oh yes, it is very interesting to me that when I withdrew the love, when the love died . . . all the love was going in one place, and when it shrank away from my marriage, it opened up toward everyone who had, bless them, essentially been waiting in the wings. And I think essentially I am a strong woman. I am not physically strong at the moment, but I am a strong woman. I have good supportive relationships. Bernie and I have been close since we were nurses together in the States for a while over twenty-five years ago. Since her husband's untimely death twelve years ago, she has raised four children and is putting them through college. We are like "significant others" in that we run all the big stuff past each other and often the not so big stuff. With her calm presence and psychotherapy background, she gets to the core of things directly. Despite finishing up her BA in fine arts, running parish committees, and working in bereavement, she frequently travels from the other side of the country to see me, often laden with all the things that keep me healthy and that I can barely afford alone. Dotted through the year are Zen cards that come in the mail with money for me to "treat myself." We both know that money pays bills and helps keep me solvent.

Through all my struggles, my older German shepherd, Credence, never left my side. He was always protective, but since I became ill, wherever I lay he lay, for hours and hours when necessary. When the sadness overwhelmed me and I'd slide down the wall into the "sitting cry" (yes, it could be a yoga pose), he was there in front of me staring his wordless love. When Wei, my second shepherd, came to us from dreadful circumstances, skeletal and a nervous wreck, my older dog was tolerant and, when he finally realized he was here to stay, began to teach him and essentially raised him into the peaceful, loyal creature he is today. When I would come home from the many nonevent or adjourned court hearings, those dogs were there for me; through every bout of illness they were there. When the symptoms were so bad that all I could do was sit quietly in the rocker, often it was enough of a healing to just watch them.

My older dog's hips had been deteriorating fast, and that one night, as he ambled down to my bedroom where he always slept, his back legs went completely and he never stood again. How he looked at me said everything, and the next morning, with the help of wonderful friends and neighbors and four-wheel drives, we got to the vet. My neighbors, both big strong men, carried him to the first jeep, tears running unashamedly down their faces. Another jeep with my dear friend in it awaited us down in the valley. I feigned strength and calmness for him. When we finally returned with his body wrapped in his favorite quilt, another dear friend hacked through frozen ground to lay him to rest above my bedroom window. How I wished the ground had not been so cold for him. That night I had to push on my heart with my hand to hold in the pain and just let the overflow come out my eyes. Surely this was the last thing to lose. Through the darkness of that snowy winter night I lay there, and through my sobs I tried to let him go on his final journey, unable to thank him enough for his unwavering loyalty and real actual love. At 5.30 AM a ball of yellow light flew in and past my bedroom window. It was over in an instant. I let myself believe it was him on his way. After I grieved for a couple of weeks, real physical grieving, my younger shepherd stepped into the breach and continues to do so today. I thought my twenty-year relationship with Dan and all that it entailed was the stuff of soulmates, but I wonder if we humans don't overcredit ourselves.

New animals have come over the last year, mostly rescued, but who is rescuing who? Little Gracie, a long haired collie-cross, was dumped in a forest at nine weeks old, weighing just four pounds. A year on she is happy, healthy, and looks like a dog from a Disney movie. Zebulon, a German shepherd pup, was the only surviving pup in a litter that came unexpectedly during last winter's fierce snow. Another unfulfilled dream, two donkeys, a mother and son who would have been bred, year-in, year-out, came to me last autumn, Ike and Corabeth, a nod to *The Waltons*. You could say they are rescued, but that suggests that I rescued them while really we rescued each other. Besides a nonbullying policy, it is a ruleless environment, nonhierarchical and peaceful. My dogs, though loving and peaceful, would defend, and at night they become my ears. When you have no particular partner or child or career, it is wonderful to have such a purpose and a cause that is valid and worthwhile. A dear friend calls it my "little ministry in the mountains." I believe very few spiritual teachers compare with animals. They have an amazing ability to forgive, to love, to be ecstatic with joy and trust, even after hardship, to be truly content with very little.

PATRICIA: I know what you mean, Orlagh. I grew up in a very loving environment. I grew up in a very humble home. My parents died in their seventies, and my father was still buying my mother flowers, and giving her valentine cards. She'd sit on his lap and say, "Every day is like a honeymoon." It may sound a bit gushy, but you know they were people who met when they were sixteen. They went through very hard times and didn't have any financial resources, but there was loads of love. And I could see that in my brothers in particular; that they had that kind of romance and I suppose maybe that was what I was looking for.

For most of 2009, even though we were working toward a divorce, my husband and I shared the same house. It is not the environment I grew up in.

I'm sitting in my living room and it's quiet now, but usually from 3 PM on it is hectic in this house! The two younger ones are in from primary school, and they might have four or five friends with them. The two dogs are barking. There are different types of music. There is rap competing with rock and roll. There is drum practice and base guitars with the amps on full. There is a football being kicked around the place, and me screaming in the middle of it! Then there is dinner and homework and scouts or swimming or whatever is on. Then there are other evenings when their father is here and I'll carry on as normal, but we'll kind of move around one another. I never really watch TV, so he may be in the room with the TV with some of the children, and I may be downstairs playing draughts with somebody. We just move around one another. It's like a dance I suppose—a domestic dance. There's no arguing or anything, and people come in and think we are a very loving family and say, "What's wrong with you, why are you breaking up? You look very happy together." I have a friend in Cork who calls it the "Hillary and Bill" approach. I suppose you learn to live separate lives within the same house, you learn avoidance techniques. There are no arguments, there's no ill will or shouting . . . you just learn to work around each other like two adults sharing a house. My fear is my children are learning this is normal behavior for a couple.

ORLAGH: My life is so different. Where I live I am the only woman on a quiet road of three miles. Scattered around are hill farmers who watch out for me and my animals. They fetched and carried for me in the snow, constantly checking in to see if I needed anything in the village. My closest neighbor shops for me regularly. My family, sidelined for years through circumstances, are center stage. They are all embracing and affirming and tell me now that they are proud of me. When I was "successful," had important jobs, academic achievement, awards, etc., they never said that. When I asked them why, they said, "Nothing you ever did was as hard or took as much courage as this." For all this kindness, I worry that I can do so little in return. I bake for them all, I pray, I send out love. I light the candle and listen openheartedly to their worries and concerns. Over the last few years Seamus, my wonderful counselor and spiritual guide, has listened to me mentally trudging around the cycle of "I'm not doing anything worthwhile, I'm not accomplishing anything, what can I do that is worthy?" He sits back in his old chair in his peaceful, faded office, lights his pipe, and reminds me again of my little "ministry in the mountains" where I have it all and where "being" is enough. He says. "Orlagh, if through just being who you are your life really touches a handful of people—you are doing well."

And through the fifteen months of recording, the friendship continued and deepened. We were like two infants learning to walk on our own after decades of having husbands we thought we could lean on. Making the documentary meant that we had to have regular conversations, which began to give shape to our lives, and in a way they gave us a structure in which we were forced to really notice what we were experiencing and to reflect on this and on our reactions. We could safely confide in one another, rant, and vent our frustrations, but once the recorder light was on we presented in a much more controlled manner. We were able to support one another because all the reflection and trying to figure things out assured us that we really heard and understood each other and could provide support based on that mutual understanding.

Dyer and McGuinness (1996) identify adversity as an antecedent to resilience. They write of the importance of the presence of at least one other caring person in the person's life at some point, even briefly: "The example of this caring individual and the mirroring of the person's inherent worth are crucial to the development of resilience" (227). Effective coping, they argue, is the primary consequence of resilience and the sense that having overcome one adversity, the person has mastered the skill to overcome more. Hetherington and Kelly (2002) write on the divorce process as involving an escalation of predivorce tensions, separation, and reorganization of households and relationships. Thus new challenges unfold over time.

ORLAGH: Thanks so much for visiting, Trish. I can't believe it's nearly a year since we started this! This time last year you drove on your "skinny"' wheel without a spare! Today you have no petrol!!

PATRICIA: I know, Orlagh, and today the gear stick came off in my hands!! It's nice to see your place and you looking so well—with your lovely orange jumper. It matches the orange pumpkins on top of your dresser. What are they?

ORLAGH: They are little organic Japanese orange pumpkins I grew. Yes, thanks. I am good. And all the animals are good. I have eight chickens now, and the dogs are great. Nan the sheep has been shorn and the goats are "themselves," and the cat is ignoring us. All is well, there is life after divorce!

PATRICIA: I talked to Orlagh on the phone when I got my divorce, but I hadn't seen her, and she felt she only had half a divorce until I got mine, and she was very stressed out. Then I went to see her, but I didn't tell her I was coming because she wears herself out cooking when she is having visitors, so I just arrived, and it was lovely to see her, and we were both exhausted. What was really nice was that she gave me a present of a rocking chair . . . and I asked myself, "Why didn't I ever get myself a rocking chair?" And I think maybe that was part of being married, you know, when someone says: "I will get you a rocking chair" and it never happens. God—why didn't I buy myself a rocking chair, they aren't that expensive . . . the rocking chair is kind of a new me . . . I can grow old in that rocking chair. But I could have had a rocking chair for the last forty years. It is kind of interesting the things that affect you. She sent me off with a rocking chair and ten eggs from the hens.

REFLECTIONS A YEAR LATER

The documentary is part of the process—a story of how, as two women in Ireland, we experienced the disintegration of our marriages and eventual divorce. The autoethnography is a reflection of the documentary process and the divorces, illustrating how no story is final or comprehensive. The recording of the documentary was very much a collaborative effort between us and the producer. However, we both felt that we had a very different vision of the shape the documentary would take. One issue we both felt very strongly about was the inclusion of music, and it proved to be a contentious issue, as the producer disagreed with the approach we wanted and she pulled rank. As a result, we had to drastically cut the sound tracks we had both wanted, and which we felt could convey better than words the mixed emotions we were experiencing. At the beginning Patricia wanted Tom Waites singing "Hold On" as a backdrop to her voice. Over the years that she shared a house with her husband but lived separately, she would take comfort from that song, night after night, as court dates were adjourned and she felt like a puppet, dancing to someone else's tune, reminding herself to "hold on, hold on." Orlagh was very keen to include Kate Bush's *Ariel* recordings as a backdrop to her voice as she had always been an inspiration to her, a beautiful woman's voice, living her life fearlessly, poetically.

By the end of the documentary and the final recording session, Patricia was in a different place. The days of holding on were over. It was time to move forward, let live, and start celebrating life. She wanted to include an original song, written and sung by her brother Billy. His song "Let's Party" evoked for her where she was going in life. The pain, uncertainty, and suffering were over. It was time to move on. He had been her main supporter through the whole process, and his voice singing "I'm going out tonight. Party!" said it all. She wanted to move on and celebrate the rest of her life. The critical attributes of resilience identified by Dyer and McGuinness (1996) are malleability and pliancy, rebounding toward a direction in life; and a sense of self: not just high self-esteem but a sense of one's unique path in life. This involves acceptance and appreciation of what has happened in one's own life: "the thread of enduring values weaves the foundational fabric for the sense of self" (277). Third, they refer to determination, "stick-to-it-iveness"; a quality of persevering until the task is completed or the goal is achieved. Hurdles exist but can be jumped: "It is a value of fortitude with conviction, tenacity with resolve. They suggest that "there is little black or white thinking, that the resilient person addresses the shades of gray and resourcefully problem solves." Finally, they stress the importance of a prosocial attitude: the ability to draw people into one's life during times of adversity supports the process of resilience. Prosocial behaviors can also be learned through the support of others.

We learned so much from making the documentary as we were progressing toward divorce. Having to discuss, share, and record our feelings, thoughts, and experiences during a very challenging period in both our lives forced us to focus, reflect, and evaluate. Knowing it was to be broadcast worldwide made us hyperaware of how we wanted to put an end to pain and hurt and not utter angry, bitter words but celebrate our friendship—our mutual support, the love and beauty in our lives, and our own determination to move on, to not only survive but grow. We were aware that the resilience we displayed was very much due to this determination, the social support and networks we embraced. When the documentary was broadcast, we realized we had achieved our goal. We had reached people with our self-disclosure. Feedback through various networks showed us this. A year later we began to see more clearly what for various reasons we hadn't said—the gaps, omissions, silences. This chapter is an attempt to reclaim our full stories and our shared story. Now we feel that it is safe to say: yes, there was love, but there was compromise, disappointment, pain, sadness, anxiety, and grief. And as life went on, we brought with us threads and shadows of other grief and losses in our lives—in Orlagh's case, infertility and CFS, and for Patricia, the premature deaths of both her parents and her sister, and the ongoing health problems of one of her children. But we bounced back, are still bouncing back, and intend to bounce even stronger in the future. We engaged iteratively with our research and our personal experiences. In this autoethnographic piece, our personal experiences were central. Through the use of documentary, we could employ narrative as a constructive way of representing and understanding our experience (Clandinin and Connolly 2000:18). The narrative revealed the intimate details of our stories and our lives. Listening to our own narrative over and over again was an iterative experience. We were struck not only by our own words, the words we chose, but also by the tone of voice we used. The strain and stress and alternatively the relief and relaxation were palpable to us. We were surprised by our emphasis on love. Like autoethnography, radio documentary is a very creative and appealing means to break the silence. Our piece was heartfelt, and by allowing the documentary content to reveal cameo-like pictures of our lives, we used evocation rather than cognitive contemplation as means (Ellis 2000).

Because of our friendship, our conversations were real, warm, and intimate. We feel the medium of radio gave them added value as the emotions in our voices reached places the written word could not touch. Muncey (2010:148) prepares the autoethnographer for the expectation of criticism and the ammunition needed to counter it, and "the vulnerability of revealing yourself, not being able to take back what you have written or having any control over how readers interpret it. It is hard not to feel your life is being critiqued as well as your work" (Ellis 1999:671–72). This was amplified in our case by the choice of radio as medium. Muncey seeks immense satisfaction from the personal growth that ensues from autoethnography. We have both experienced tremendous satisfaction from doing this work on many levels. The very fact that while doing the work we were pursuing our divorces suggests that there was intense personal growth and at times great difficulty and struggle. However, as researchers, there has been immense satisfaction in doing this autoethnographic piece. It is exciting to be doing what is essentially a groundbreaking piece in the Irish context and hopefully paving the way for more such work, both on divorce and in autoethnography in general. We have learned so much and are beginning on a path we believe will provide further satisfaction and personal growth.

To conclude and depart for now, we heartily concur with Ellis (1999:671–72), who advises that autoethnography provides an avenue for doing something meaningful for yourself and the world. We will finish with our own words, first from Patricia:

> I was so happy to walk through a safe, warm, bright house, the mosaic, fifteen shades of blue, my children safe and sleeping. I walked from room to room and child to sleeping child and kissed each one and stroked their hair and thanked God for their presence, for the very fact that they were alive. I saw through the house elements of myself I had forgotten, and I saw new aspects of myself emerging. I glimpsed my running shoes and shorts, my kayaking gear, my lovely new feminine Doc Marten sandals, and my new flowery top, drawing attention to my new sense of discovery that color, fabrics, style, a long time missing, were returning. There were less blacks in my wardrobe. There hung cerulean, azure, turquoise, indigo, emerald, moss, and the deepest greens and purples, colors of healing and nature and letting go. I saw my laptop, near the shelf which held all the books I had written and edited. I saw the light shining on my red guitar, my CDs. Mixed with all of these items, in center stage, the children's school bags, material for lunches. I knew that no matter what parts of me were emerging, I was only complete when surrounded by my children. I knew that they would grow up and find their own ways in life and that was fine, but now at their age these small children needed to be with their mother and I with them. I knew the physical pain of being away from them, the physical pain in my stomach, the emptiness. All I could do was hold on and believe that they would get through all of this and things would work out . . . and they will.

And the final words from Orlagh:

> Tonight in the wild garden I sit in the old armchair I rescued from the forest. Mu my cat is with me. The harvest moon is starting to rise from behind the trees. Divine. The scented night stock I planted from seed, weeks and weeks ago, is finally blooming and smells between sweet and aniseed. I contemplated spending a full night outside some night, just to really feel part of it all. I wonder if I could? I am too sore tonight. It is exactly a year since I heard Mu crying in a hedge, a gash in her leg. I called her Moonlight because it was a full moon night. For weeks she ignored the food I left out for her, preferring to chase and eat bugs. She lived in fear of my dogs. Now she has her own

cushion on the red chair by the range, the dogs asleep below her. I'm sitting on the front step with the very last bit of daylight writing this. The skyline is the burning reds and oranges of Africa. My chimes are ringing to the long awaited breeze. Across the fields are the lights of a tractor—the gentle sounds and smells of late summer crop saving. The dogs are still mooching around outside, the house still too warm for "good sleepin." One huge lone star is in the sky—what is that? Perhaps it is Venus, where all us women hail from?! I am in shorts and a teeshirt and bare feet. It feels so unencumbered. I baked all day and had to cover up with a long skirt and shirt to take the dogs to the bog hole so they could dip. I couldn't even eat till 9 pm. I'm so sore and tired, yet it is hard to tear myself away from this beauty. It is a joy to be alive this night, here on this step with my pots of herbs and geraniums. It is the kind of beauty you want to grasp and retain, but you cannot. You can just be blessed by it and move on to the next now.

We hope our story will show others that it is possible to move beyond crisis and to bounce back, and that for many people adversity can lead to personal growth, to coming out of a difficult challenging situation not only intact but in many cases stronger.

NOTE

1   Chronic fatigue syndrome (CFS)—also known as chronic fatigue and immune dysfunction syndrome (CFIDS), myalgic encephalomyelitis (ME) and by other names—is a complex and debilitating chronic illness that affects the immune and central nervous systems.

REFERENCES

Bochner, A. P. 2000. "Criteria Against Ourselves." *Qualitative Inquiry* 6 (2): 266–72.
Clandinin, D. J., and F. M. Connelly. 2000. "Narrative Enquiry: Experience and Story." In *Qualitative Research*. San Francisco: Jossey-Bass.
Courts Service Annual Report. 2009. http://www.courts.ie.
Delaney, F. (Orlagh Farrell). 1999. "The Silent Period: Women's Experiences of Infertility in Ireland." Master's thesis, UCD, Dublin.
———. 2002. "Infertility: The Silent Period." In *Motherhood in Ireland: Creation and Context*, edited by P. Kennedy, 64–76. Cork: Mercier.

Denzen, N. K. 1997. *Interpretive Ethnography*. Thousand Oaks, Calif.: Sage.

Dyer, J. D., and T. M. McGuinness. 1996. "Resilience: Analysis of the Concept." *Archives of Psychiatric Nursing* 10 (5) (October 1996): 276–82.

Ellis, C. 1999. "Heartful Autoethnography." *Qualitative Health Research* 9 (5): 669–83.

———. 2000. "Creating Criteria: An Ethnographic Short Story." *Qualitative Inquiry* 6 (2): 273–77.

Ellis, C., and A. Bochner. 2006. "Analyzing Analytic Autoethnography: An Autopsy." *Journal of Contemporary Ethnography* 35 (4): 429–49.

Field-Belenky, M., B. McVicker-Clinchy, N. Rule-Goldberger, and J. Mattuck-Tarule. 1986. *Women's Ways of Knowing. The Development of Self, Voice and Mind*. New York: Basic Books.

Hetherington, E. M., and J. Kelly. 2002. *Divorce Reconsidered: For Better or Worse*. New York: Norton.

Luthar, S. S., and E. Zigler. 1991. "Vulnerability and Competence: A Review of Research on Resilience in Childhood. *American Journal of Orthopsychiatry* 61:6–22.

McLeish, R. (1994). *Radio Production*. 3rd ed. Oxford: Focal Press.

Moss, P., and I. Dyck. 2002. *Women, Body, Illness*. Lanham, Md.: Rowmann and Littlefield.

Muncey, T. (2010). *Creating Autoethnographies*. London: Sage.

Reed-Danahay, D. E., ed. 1997. "Introduction." In *Auto/ethnography: Rewriting the Self and the Social*. New York: Berg.

Rinpoche, S. 2008. *The Tibetan Book of Living and Dying*. London: Rider.

Rosenthal, A., and J. Corner, eds. (1995). *New Challenges for Documentary*. 2d ed. Manchester: Manchester University Press.

Ruby, J. 1995. "The Image Mirrored: Reflexivity and the Documentary Film." In *New Challenges for Documentary*, edited by A. Rosenthal and J. Corner, 34–47. 2d ed. Manchester: Manchester University Press.

Spry, T. (2006). "Performing Autoethnography: An Embodied Methodological Praxis." In *Emergent Methods in Social Research*, edited by S. N. Hesse-Biber and P. Leavy, 182–211. London: Sage.

Walsh, F. 2003. "Family Resilience: A Framework for Clinical Practice." *Family Process* 42 (1).

Walsh, F., and M. McGoldrick, eds. 1991. *Living Beyond Loss*. New York: Norton.

CHAPTER 10

The Pretty Girl in the Mirror

A GENDER TRANSIENT'S TALE

▸ *ALLAN IRVING*

We experience the world once, in childhood, the rest is memory.
—Louise Gluck

Art struggles with chaos but it does so in order to render it sensory.
—Gilles Deleuze and Felix Guattari

ONE IS NOT SIMPLY / one is not / one is ever after / one is as much as this. As I write I am wearing a pretty light pink silk dress with frilly short sleeves and lacey white panties, and I have sprayed on some perfume. I am feeling excited and very feminine. Among a number of frocks and dresses, this one is my favorite. If I were to go to the local café wearing this dress and making no attempt to "pass" as a woman (I have a beard)—a genderfuck—it is very likely I would feel the violence of compulsory gender. I wish I had the courage. In 1988 at the Philadelphia Institute of Contemporary Art exhibition of Robert Mapplethorpe's work, a striking self-portrait of the photographer as a transvestite greeted visitors as they entered the gallery. Writing in the exhibition catalog, David Joselit (1988) comments that "Mapplethorpe's hair is teased into a woman's hairdo; his eyes are open and his lips parted in an unspeakable expression of softness, imploring, and—perhaps—fear. His upper torso is bare and strikingly resembles a woman's breasts" (19). S/he is very pretty, as I have wanted to be.

Joselit suggests that

> the message Mapplethorpe delivers is that the experience of any masculine or
> feminine identity is the sensation of an unstable, constantly readjusted succes-
> sion of poses. In his work, the crossing of boundaries between aggression—or
> phallic drive—and submission is not simplistically developed as an opposition
> between masculinity and femininity, it is experienced as a drama that takes
> place within the entire range of sexual identities. (21)

Convergent with this assessment, my cross-dressing story unfolds within a
transgender discourse drawing on philosophical, literary, and cultural references in my life.

The term transgender came into widespread use in the 1990s for an
expansive range of ways of living a life, including cross-dressing, and that
calls "attention to the fact that 'gender' as it is lived, embodied experienced, performed and encountered, is more complex and varied than can
be accounted for by the dominant binary sex/gender ideology of modernity" (Stryker and Whittle 2006:3). Transgender subverts and disrupts
and denaturalizes the notion that biology/anatomy and gender line up in
a natural arrangement and opens up vast possibilities for the interweaving
of bodies, identities, and desires. Gender is not an essential truth out there,
a mimetic material entity that is foundational, but rather a linguistic and
performative construction. Cross-dressing is not some aberration where
anatomy and gender fail to line up as has been mandated but simply a wish
to live a life in a certain way, with certain sartorial practices.

The next five paragraphs were written last, after the rest of the chapter was finished. I received with appreciation and enthusiasm the invitation from Stanley Witkin to write an autoethnography; it is all too rare in
social work to have an opportunity to write outside its crushing, arid, and
sterile empiricism, an artless positivism sanding away all traces of intensity and feeling. For me the world is a place consisting of the sand-grain
manyness of things and feelings that cannot be measured or counted. The
decision to write an autoethnography about my cross-dressing was made
after a number of days of intense anxiety, doubt, and shifting microcli-
mates, textures, and tonalities of mood—the simple pleasure and openness
and airiness of wearing a skirt or dress. This aspect of my life had been a
clouded secret for a long time, and now all the flying instants of memory,
many painful, would need to be called up from the midnight blue world

I inhabited growing up. But the opportunity to try to piece something of my life together within a more expansive cultural framework, however fragmented, was very appealing. The writing, I imagined, might be an unmaking and a making as I sifted through the rubble of a life. From about age twelve, I now realize, I began to live in a threshold liminal world, and I less and less wanted to be contained within any single group or location—what I now call a beige modernism. Instead, I remember always desiring to escape the Enlightenment network of classifications that "normally" locate people in fixed cultural spaces.

My embrace of postmodernism from the early 1990s on brought me to rethink our dominant culture's inscriptions of gender dualisms and wish for unitary identities. All through high school, long before I ever heard of postmodernism, I felt intensely that an imperious rationality and reason, the high values of the eighteenth-century Enlightenment, were monsters of entrapment that kept us from a magical, poetic, and diaphanous existence. Rationality, I sensed, bridled creative forces, subordinating them to objectified representations. Recently I was asked if I considered myself a rational person and I responded, "Not very much," receiving a look of disapproval and concern that I might very well be suffering from some DSM aberration. French philosopher Arnaud Villani (2006) writes, "what threatens this powerful life, is not the *singular* subject, always anomalous and in fragments, but rather *the myth of the rational subject*, with its abstract ideas, its immense pretension, its sanctification of a limitless progress" (246).

I have tried to write this chapter from desire and how I feel, knowing that memory is endlessly decaying; how could I feel these decayed memories, how could they return for me, always altered, perhaps mostly dimly in their resounding absence? I am always excited by the textures of the "female" clothes I wear, and I hoped my writing could feel and express the textures of a life. Once I began writing, I found that the thread, once pulled, kept unraveling into complexities that had been hidden, a territory of the unknown, a territory of indiscernibility. On several occasions long periods of time went by when I couldn't write, blocked by the absolute unsayableness of what most would probably see as the simplest of things. I would wait, a patient outlasting, until the whisperings of the past would again speak, until I imagined stones on fire, tulips in winter gardens, a song of loss that could break the hearts of beasts, a dark moon edged with fire and blood, until I was caught off-guard as in a sun shower.

I have been influenced by the thought of Gilles Deleuze, a philosopher, and his often coauthor Felix Guattari, and their book *Anti-Oedipus* (1983), concerned with the liberation of desire. They completely reject the Kantian ideal of a unified and rational subject and focus instead on multiple desiring "intensities," which under modernity have been restricted, forbidden, and repressed. Deleuze and Guattari create an ontology of desire that establishes flows of desire that can be compared to Foucault's flows of power. Desire is everywhere and everything (Hickey-Moody and Rasmussen 2009:46). They envision desire as productive and unfixed, where sexuality and gender are flows of desire that are open to transformation, where desire is a fluid indeterminacy, beyond categorical distinctions and hierarchical organization (Shildrick 2009:121, 124–25).

Angus Fletcher's *A New Theory for American Poetry* (2004) frames a way I have thought about what I have written here. Fletcher makes a distinction between poems that seek a consistent, logical truth and those that desire to represent a coherent, nearly chaotic vision that admits a complexity that it cannot fully comprehend. Consistency, in Fletcher's analysis, occludes large swaths of "reality," the story, to create an artificially demarcated truth. Coherence, on the other hand, lets uncertainty, doubt, and provisionality in, to intrude, leaving a sense of magical wonder and surprise for the writer and perhaps the reader.

Cross-dressers spend a great deal of time, as I do, in self-display before a mirror. Consequently the trope of the mirror is ever present. It is a heterotopian mirror where "I" both design myself "male" within a modernist, humanist logic of self-reflection and at the same time fashion myself, as a queer self, within a postmodern aesthetic that is an other, a pretty girl, and often as neither male nor female, something very different from both (Huffer 2010:199). (Huffer describes Michel Foucault's heterotopias as "little laboratories of pleasure where becoming-other can be tried out for a while, in ways that are more intense, more sustained" [125]). Judith Butler offers a thought on how the mirror female for the cross-dresser "confers an ideality and integrity on the body and that the very sense of the body is generated through this projection of ideality and integrity." This mirroring, so much a central feature of transgender life, can even, Butler (1993) suggests, "transform a lived sense of disunity and loss of control into an ideal of integrity and control" (75). Foucault (1998), with his usual discernment, describes the mirror as offering the "kind of mixed, intermediate experience that forms between utopias and the utterly different emplacements that are heterotopias":

> The mirror is a utopia . . . since it is a placeless place. In the mirror I see myself where I am not, in an unreal space that opens up virtually behind the surface; I am over there where I am not, a kind of shadow that gives me my own visibility, that enables me to look at myself there where I am absent—a mirror utopia. . . . But it is also a heterotopia in that the mirror really exists, in that it has a sort of return effect on the place that I occupy. Due to the mirror, I discover myself absent at the place where I am, since I see myself over there. From that gaze which settles on me . . . I come back to myself and I begin once more to direct my eyes toward myself and to reconstitute myself where I am. The mirror functions as a heterotopia in the sense that it makes this place I occupy at the moment I look at myself in the glass *both utterly real*, connected with the entire space surrounding it, *and utterly unreal*, since, to be perceived, it is obliged to go by way of that virtual point which is over there. (179)

This encounter of myself as both myself and other disrupts the binary of Enlightenment reasoning and allows for possibilities, alternatives, to open, however fleeting. For special moments I really am the pretty girl of my desire, the artist Cindy Sherman lying in a reverie wearing panties and bra and holding a mirror.

However, these mirror moments of ecstasy are always on the edge of disintegration. The philosopher G. W. F. Hegel thought about the subject and the world, or thought and being, as two mirrors facing each other, holding out the promise of identity by self-recognition but at the same time "the threat of dispersal and abyssal decay through the effect of an infinite regress of mirror reflections" (Szafraniec 2007:41). Asja Szafraniec writes that "when we take into account that the figure of a mirror reflection stands as much for a unifying movement as for an infinite structure of deferral, it becomes possible to interpret the entire splitting movement of difference as mirror-based" (41). The notion that the mirror can be unreliable is illustrated in the paintings of Francis Bacon, where there are unsettling recurrent motifs of mirrors that do not reflect or reproduce exactly (Van Alphen 1992:57).

It began, the cross-dressing, at age ten, in 1955, in the basement of our house in Toronto. Although I do not remember the first time, the

excitement of putting on a red skirt of my mother's was intense and exquisite. My body was flooded with new, pleasurable sensations and wild sexual
feelings that were blistering, a fiasco in my mind and body. I was male, so
I thought, and yet here I was in this dark cellar, a basement archive of *ars
erotica* (clothes stored) feverish with the rush of desire, beyond control,
wearing an item of clothing very clearly identified as female. As I erotically fantasized and daydreamed that I was a pretty girl, my orgasms would
explode almost immediately when I put on this skirt and other markers of
femininity. Usually in the early years of gender femaling I would feel disgust and shame after masturbating and vow that I would not do this again,
always fearful that I would be found out. By the next day the arousing imaginings of being a girl would return as strong as ever, and the cycle would
repeat itself. Almost without exception, this is the pattern described by
all cross-dressers.

Several years earlier, before it all began, a practice that has only deepened
to the present, I became aware of how attracted I was to pretty girls, and
especially their clothing, in our neighborhood. Already I was feeling the
emotional ebb and flow and ambivalence of the sometimes desire to be a
girl. I have a vivid memory almost sixty years later of playing with Maeve,
who was my age, sweet, with golden red hair, who lived two houses away,
wearing a fetching ruffled dress with frilly petticoats peeking out, a lovely
delicate flower. Over the next days I was consumed with cravings to look as
she did, to wear similar lacey feminine garments, dreamy dresses and panties, to be as adorable and pretty as Maeve. How wonderful it must feel.
It was the captivating atmosphere that swirled around her, her style, her
mannerisms, the mist that she brought to the room. Even today there are
evocative remnants of what was present as we were together many years ago
one bright morning, now a tactile absence endlessly coming into being,
still erotically alluring, although decaying each day in a lavender twilight of
memory. To be her. To be Maeve.

In grade eight I was infatuated with Ann, a captivatingly pretty girl in
my class. By then, as a male, I found her sexually desirable, but even more
compelling, I wanted to be her, to look like her, to have her hair and breasts
and delicate, soft skin, and I spent much of my time that year dreaming
and imagining what it would be like to be living her life and putting on her
cute girlie skirts and dresses each morning. In line with teenage girl fashion
of the 1950s, she often wore a pink poodle skirt (now seen as one of the

defining icons of the 1950s—they were considered flirty, and the epitome of girl femininity) that I ached to be dressed in, and I would fall into reveries about this skirt, marked by sexual and gender craving. I spent the days in class stealing glances at her, lost in many conflicting desires and longings. Being male was painful and troubling that year. I felt so trapped wandering between two worlds. It would be years before I knew of the idea of liminality or the words transvestite or cross-dresser, transgender or queer.

Fantasy, as can be seen in my descriptions of Maeve and Ann, has shaped, and continues to shape, my cross-dressing imaginings and is a gentle way of constructing possibilities. To close down transgender fantasy in its many intensities and variations as abnormal is to define the limits of reality in a restrictive and destructive way. Fantasy is a "method" (not one usually taught in research classes, alas) that allows me to imagine myself otherwise. My body and its several gender expressions and desires does, through fantasy, enter a reality of becoming a pretty girl. This is a reality I need to inhabit some of the time, a reality that I do not consider in any way pathological but as one of many ways to live a life. It resonates for me with Nietzsche's (1974:240) proposal that we become poets of our lives and Foucault's (1997:262) plea that we can be artists of our lives.

"For we live with those retrievals from childhood that coalesce and echo throughout our lives," Anna says in Canadian writer Michael Ondaatje's novel *Divisadero* (2007:136), "the way shattered pieces of glass in a kaleidoscope reappear in new forms and are songlike in their refrains and rhymes, making up a single monologue." In *Human, All Too Human*, Nietzsche (1986) writes that the "undissolved dissonances in the relation of the character and sentiments of the parents survive in the nature of the child and make up the history of its inner sufferings" (295). I know that in our disconsolate and opaque house in Toronto, the dark flow tides of despair I have so often felt over my life began before I was a year old. Moods are compelling, contagious, and intensely interpersonal, and they alter the perceptions of not only those who have them but also those close to them. In my first few years in Toronto, misery hunted my parents down and rode their minds and spirits. The atmosphere was one of clouds, mist, fog, and vapor, my existence. Cross-dressing, at least in part, has been a way for me to inhabit and live another existence, one where I now find a sense of fulfillment and even happiness.

My mother was a social worker and my father a professor of philosophy. They met in 1938 when she was a student in one of his classes at the University of British Columbia. I was born the night of March 13, 1945, in Vancouver, an excruciatingly painful birth described in searing detail in one of my mother's journals (her journals have been in my possession since her death in January 1981). Not at all a happy event. The day had been, by my father's account (he sometimes wrote passages in my mother's journals), "dreary, drizzly, rainy and without sunshine," and when the hospital phoned at 11 PM to tell him of my birth, he went upstairs in our house at 1650 Wesbrook Crescent, on the university's campus, and stared out over the Gulf of Georgia. He wrote, "The wind was blowing a terrific gale; there was a snowstorm; and one could hear the wild waves roaring in the blue Gulf, beating at the cliffs of the Point Grey Promontory. Such was the night Allan was born—wild and stormy like the world at war—and like the ordeal of human birth." And like my life was to become. A number of studies have documented that, from a seasonal perspective, March is the peak month for the onset of episodes of depression, and given how much depression I have struggled with, perhaps it was an unfortunate month to be born (Jamison 1993:132). That same month my father accepted a position as a professor of ethics at Victoria College at the University of Toronto, where he remained until his death in February 1965, and moved his family to that city, resigning from the University of British Columbia.

When I entered high school in the fall of 1958, my craving for crossdressing accelerated. Early in September I saw Oakwood Collegiate's sexy, eye-catching cheerleaders in the school colors of blue and gold practicing their routines, handstands, and cartwheels in their very short pleated miniskirts and yellow panties. Getting through the school day was torture, and right after school I rushed home to put on a little flouncy skirt of my younger sister's and pretend I was a pretty and desirable cheerleader, taking pleasure in showing my panties in a mirror and attracting the male gaze. The pretty girl in the mirror. If only I could remake myself, recast myself, have acceptable and legitimate access to the world of feminine clothes, and be cute, pretty, and desirable. Being forced always to be visible as a male, where the brutal binary of male/female ruled in the drabness of late 1950s Toronto, came close to tearing me apart. Driven by intensities and multiplicities, I unraveled each day, feeling ill at ease at always having to appear as "male." Why couldn't I be female some of the time, and just have this

accepted? Go to school in a dress if I wanted? High school slipped through
my fingers into nothingness. The experience for me is best captured in the
work of Samuel Beckett, where everything is philosophically twilit and
there is only in memory a profound series of dwindlings.

It always had to be a secret, a dark, preoccupying secret. From the beginning I was troubled that the clothing I wanted to wear and that erotically
excited me did not correspond to the male I was supposed to be. What was
going on? It was the 1950s. The word transgender was not in use. Following each episode and the intense sexual release, I would be sure that this
dressing would never happen again; usually within a day the almost uncon-
trollable desire would return and the pattern would repeat itself, as it has
now for fifty-five years. As I entered my teenage years and high school it
was painfully apparent to me that there was clearly something very wrong,
but what? I was abnormal, deviant, and I increasingly lived with the terror
of being discovered. Each day I lived in a swamp of killing shame. Once
the feelings of shame settled in, I could not look at anyone, especially girls,
without blushing (this in itself was a tell-tale sign of my guilt), certain
that they could see what I was up to and would reveal that I was a pervert. Perhaps surprisingly, I never felt or thought I was gay; I was always
very attracted to girls/women and so much wanted to be with them, to be
in their company. However, I found it almost impossible to ask girls out
on dates (in my final year of high school I did have a "steady" girlfriend,
which lasted for two very troubled years) since I was not a "normal" male.
I withdrew. I began to feel very alone; even though I had friends, there was
a crushing sense of isolation since I felt and perceived myself as so different
from others and had to hide who I was. Deleuze and Guattari (1987) capture exactly what it was like, "the upheavals caused by a monster force, the
Secret, threatening to bring everything tumbling down" (205).

There was no one I could talk to for, as Derrida (2001) realized, "if there
is something absolute it is the secret. We are never finished with the secret,
there is no end, and it clearly has to do with not-belonging" (57–59). Foucault vividly recalled why he felt he had to keep his gay way of being in the
world a secret for as long as he did: "In my personal life, from the moment
of my sexual awakening, I felt excluded, not so much rejected, but belonging to society's shadow. It's all the more a problem when you discover it for
yourself. All of this was very quickly transformed into a kind of psychiatric
threat: if you're not like everyone else, it's because you're abnormal, if you're

abnormal, it's because you're sick" (quoted in Huffer 2010:23). I did not feel safe revealing my secret, and it is only in recent years that I have started to tell a very few others.

As far as I know, I was never observed cross-dressing, and I was always careful to keep my cross-dressing separate from the rest of my life. In his book *Male/Femaling* (1997), Richard Ekins uses the word "aparting" (134) to describe the cross-dresser who wants to maintain a definite boundary between his male and male/femaling world. Until about twenty years ago, this was what I desired. After each episode of cross-dressing, I would often feel shame and disgust, put my sister's or mother's clothes (later my first wife's clothes) back as quickly as possible, and for a brief period return to a male world. Once I started buying my own clothes in the late 1980s, I went through many purgings common to cross-dressers who feel there is something very wrong with their desires. This involved getting rid of all the female clothes I had accumulated, certain that this would be the end of my cross-dressing. This never happened, of course. By the 1990s there began, within a postmodern construction, to be much more discourse about transgender and queer practices, and I gradually abandoned viewing my desire to be a pretty girl as pathological; rather, it was just one way of life that is as normal as any other, and one that brought me considerable pleasure and sexual excitement. For some years now, I have not engaged in purging, and I have an extensive collection of women's clothes. I enjoy shopping for pretty dresses and cute little skirts and have a number of favorite female clothing stores on the Internet.

The strategy I adopted to maintain the "aparting" and to ensure that the outside world would never doubt that I was a complete male was to participate in sports—football and hockey in high school and rugby in university; to work one summer in the rugged wilds of northern British Columbia; to go drinking with the guys; and to wear clothes that would never be seen as feminine.

Desolate body, unwanted being, desperate cross-dresser, wanting to wake up as a pretty girl, like Virginia Woolf's Orlando. Marjorie Garber writes in her splendid *Vested Interests: Cross-Dressing and Cultural Anxiety* (1992) "that transvestism is a space of possibility structuring and confounding culture: the disruptive element that intervenes, not just a category crisis of male and female, but the crisis of category itself" (17). Cross-dressing is a cultural signifier bringing into play gender, sex, sexuality, and gender material culture in the artifact of clothing. Female clothing has, in the lived reality of my life, allowed me to play repetitively with identity and self-image and being other. Gender for me has been until recently a troubling presence; in the past few years I have come to feel as though I am neither male nor female but exist outside this binary between these two constructed polarities, in a liminal place of difference—a gender queer. I like being both. As a male I seldom feel vulnerable but often aggressive, although not desirable; as an imagined attractive female wearing a cute little skirt, lace top, and panties, I feel vulnerable, fragile, desirable, flirty, pretty, gentle, dreamy, and magical. I much prefer these feelings, and it is how I would like the world to be. I have always found it remarkable that the material culture of clothes—gentle, soft, tactile, lacey, delicate, flirty, pretty—can so affect how I feel about my body. I find pleasure in both the sexuality of being dressed as a girl/woman and the feeling of being a girl/woman. My desire to be a girl or woman is appeased by dressing, and I have never had the transsexual wish for surgical change (sex reassignment surgery) to a woman. I do like having two identities as well as the excitement of being able, by the passport of clothes, to transgressively enter the world of the opposite. A recent study of cross-dressing in Britain confirms that most cross-dressers feel the same desirability of femaleness (Suthrell 2004:197–98). Almost every day I feel the desire for part of the time to be a girl, to go about my everyday activities wearing pretty clothes. In the mirror I am this girl, although I am almost always aware that I am only an image of this girl, a specular example of created and desired femininity.

My cross-dressing predilections have from the beginning to the present largely reconstituted traditional and mainstream cultural imagery—television, film, music, magazines—of the 1950s, when I was growing up, of the aggressive male and the pretty gentle woman. My imagined fantasy picture of myself was to be girly, wearing ultrafeminine clothes that were delicate, frilly, diaphanous, and fetching. To the outside world and my peers, on the other hand, I strove to present a hypermale image. The 1950s are hailed by fashion historians as the golden era of feminine expression: swing and flared skirts and dainty flared dresses, the popularity of petticoats, pleated skirts, and pink pumps, all of which I found beguiling and trance inducing as I was growing up. I intently observed female film stars of the era—Marilyn Monroe, Natalie Wood, Brigitte Bardot, Carroll Baker, Connie Stevens, Elizabeth Taylor—and found their ultrafemininity irresistible. Unlike many males, I didn't picture myself as a male lover to these lovely women but romanticized about being them. Natalie Wood especially drove me mad with desire to be her. By the late 1950s most of my male friends were constantly trying to get me to look at the women in *Playboy* magazine. Of course I did not reveal that I didn't find the models particularly appealing, much preferring a less obvious expression of femaleness in pretty and tactile clothes.

I was very influenced by the popular music of the 1950s on as it began the historical process of destabilizing gender as something fixed, essential, and attached to anatomical characteristics. The performer Little Richard was one performer who early on contributed to deconstructing fixed gender identities. The album cover for Alice Cooper's *Love It to Death* (1971) showed the male members of the group dressed in lacy, see-through lingerie, wearing considerable amounts of mascara. The famous cover of David Bowie's album *The Man Who Sold the World* (1971) shows him draped across a covered daybed with long hair and wearing a blue and white patterned dress, revealing his interest in cross-dressing and questions of gender identity. The frock he wore in the cover photograph had been one of six purchased for Bowie by his wife from the offbeat fashion designer Michael Fish, who designed dresses for males. Mick Jagger also wore one in a 1969 Rolling Stones concert. The Bowie album cover was banned in the United States when it was released since cross-dressing was seen as not only too controversial but also disturbingly aberrant. With this album Bowie ushered in the era of glam and glitter rock, which was a major influence in subverting the idea of gender as fixed and suggesting that gender identity was constructed, fluid, playful, and performative (Auslander 2006:21, 44, 121; Perone 2007:16; Stevenson 2006:44). For me these popular culture expressions of ambiguous gender identity began the long, arduous process of normalizing cross-dressing and the idea of a transgender existence.

In the 1970s I also became intrigued by the paintings of Paul Gauguin done in Tahiti and Marquesas Islands from the 1890s until his death in 1903. He was fascinated by the *mahu*, men who dressed as women and performed feminine social roles, as depicted in his *Marquesan Man in a Red Cape* (1902), with the *mahu* looking very feminine and delicate with a flower in "his" long hair. The *mahu* are seen as a third gender, neither male nor female. In some of his writings from this period, Gauguin used Polynesian androgyny to castigate rigidly defined European gender roles (Reed 2011:21–22).

In her lectures, *A Room of One's Own* (1957), Virginia Woolf comments that if there were "other sexes" beyond male/female, "nothing would be of greater service to humanity" (29). Her transgender novel *Orlando* had the year before positioned her as a writer and thinker who unsettled the idea of gender as inevitably lining up with particular anatomical features. Virginia Prince, who founded *Transvestia* magazine in 1960, the only publication of its time for male cross-dressers (it ran for 100 issues into the 1980s), did suggest another gender, which she called "femmiphilia" (lover of the feminine), a "male" who manages to transcend the borders between genders. American writer Djuna Barnes's lesbian and transgender novel *Nightwood* (1936) is one of wild intensity in the Deleuzian sense. The central character is a cross-dressing doctor—Matthew O'Connor—and through his many monologues the novel envisions gender as moving far outside the Enlightenment binary of male/female, suggesting much more fluid ways of thinking about gender identity, such as "a third sex" (157). One night when Nora, a character in the novel, visits O'Connor, she discovers his predilections. On his dresser she observes "some twenty perfume bottles ... creams, rouges, powder boxes and puffs. From the half-open drawers of this chiffonier hung laces, ribands, stockings, and ladies' underclothing. In the bed lay the doctor in a woman's flannel nightgown" (85). Very much as I do, O'Connor in the novel studies and looks at women in his endless desire to be a woman. "Am I not the girl to know of what I speak," he says (97), often referring to himself as a girl or a woman. O'Connor is perpetually distressed that although he is anatomically male, in his dreams and emotions he is very much an attractive woman.

In *Nightwood* gender is depicted as a variable array of constructions and not essentialized as masculine or feminine, but both in different combinations. In fact, sex (anatomy), sexuality, desire, and gender are not seen as lining up as male or female in a fixed, certain determination but as unstable and shifting. The novel sensitively portrays the pain and conflict engendered by a self that is anything but fixed, embodied in the difficulties experienced by those whose gender identities are complex and blended and that do not correspond to culturally prescribed heteronormative conceptions. Gender and anatomical sex are decoupled, and anatomy is not seen as a constraint on the expression of gender. My own life experience as a cross-dresser is very much that of O'Connor in the way that sex, gender, and sexuality for me have been culturally incongruent with what is expected and seen as acceptable, so that my desire to go out wearing a dress or a skirt, even in our back garden, has been blocked by my fear of the unwarranted attention and ridicule this would inevitably create. It would also, as O'Connor, observes be to dress "the unknowable in the garments of the known" (145). Outcast, outsider, abject, marginal, because not able to fully live within the binary of Western reason. Why would pieces of cloth create such dissonance?

Djuna Barnes's *Nightwood* foreshadows Judith Butler's understanding of gender not as essence but as performance. For Butler (1990, 2004), there are no fixed gender differences, and gender has no ontological status outside the repetitive performative acts that constitute it. "If gender is the cultural meanings that the sexed body assumes, then a gender cannot be said to follow from anatomical characteristics in a causal manner. Taken to its logical limit, the sex/gender distinction suggests a radical discontinuity between sexed bodies and culturally constructed genders" (1990:9–10). We can construct and re-create our gender for moments, for longer periods, or permanently. In order for my cross-dressing desires to be fully in play, I have had to recognize that I am not a stable subject and acknowledge that I have never been completely within a heteronormative "male" matrix. For Georges Bataille, it is only that which is shaped by the immediacy of erotic desire and experience that is meaningful (Hussey 2006:83). Butler makes the persuasive case that biomedical and heteronormative conceptions of gender produce a subject position and hence a subjectivity:

Gender is thus not the product of choice, but the forcible citation of a norm, one whose complex historicity is indissociable from relations of discipline, regulation, punishment. Indeed, there is no "one" who takes on a gender norm. On the contrary, this citation of the gender norm is necessary to qualify as a "one," to become viable as a "one," where subject-formation is dependent on the prior operation of legitimating gender norms (Butler 1993:32).

Out of the murmur of memory and dream, remembered, imagined. Only speaking of instants where atoms briefly assemble. An autoethnography depends on memory and in my writing becomes a literary philosophical narrative where imagination shapes memory to its own creative ends. Weaving has often been invoked as a metaphor for the process of memory. Memory is not so much archaeological recovery as it is processual, the result of the weaver's shuttle and loom ever creating new and different patterns, designs, and forms, an assortment of configurations from memory and with each sentence an innovative delineated self (Olney 1998:20).

Today I am wearing a lovely white lace eyelet short skirt, a pink T-shirt, lace nylon panties, and a lacey pink bra. It makes me feel alluring, much more aware of my body and its movements, and flirtatious. It is practical on hot summer days as well to wear short skirts—so much cooler. A playful summer pleasure: to feel both pretty and cool. What is the matter with men?

Ghostly presence. A few years ago when I was living in Toronto in a dismal and sorrowful state, I was returning to my apartment one evening about eleven after meeting a friend for drinks. The route to the apartment took me past Victoria College at the University of Toronto where my father had taught philosophy for twenty years. As I passed the college where I spent many days with my father as I was growing up, I was suddenly taken over by the first part of the sentence where God asks Job, "Where were you . . . ?" (38:4). (The full quote reads: "Where were you when I laid the foundation of the earth?") All the anger, hurt, and suffering I had endured as a teenager and beyond poured out as I walked into the college's grounds screaming at my long dead father: Where were you? Where were you when I needed you? Where were you when all I wanted was for you to draw me close with gestures of affectionate and protective love? Where were you when I was uncertain, lost, and astray and in desperate need of consolation? I knew that night I had a hunger for delicate touches when I was little, a hunger never fulfilled. I sat on a bench shouting and sobbing, mercifully ignored by the few late-night campus strollers. In a journal entry for March 13, 1961 (my sixteenth birthday), my mother had written, following a visit to her psychiatrist, that when I was younger she did not really like me, right from the moment of the difficult birth in Vancouver. She is unambiguous that she much preferred my sister and had wanted her first child to be a girl. All the pain, sadness, and anguish of my life spilled out on the college lawn that winter night—everything I had repressed for many years.

Explanations abound for why one cross-dresses: medical/psychiatric, psychological, emotional, sexual, cultural, sociological . . . artistic, philosophical, fantastical, imaginative. Not surprisingly the predominant feeling I had for many years after I began to cross-dress was that there was something very wrong with me; I was a pervert, deviant, sick, abnormal, disturbed, confused, and, like most who grew up in the 1950s and 1960s, my desire had be kept a dark secret. It is only in the past few years, and many therapists later, that I have set out to explore my desires to dress as a girl or woman and to talk about it with a few close friends who I knew would not judge me. Even this has been painful. Wearing dresses and skirts was, and still is, seen as a disruption, a violation of the construction of masculinity. In the Book of Deuteronomy, where Moses lays out various moral laws and codes, including the Ten Commandments, he issues a law against cross-dressing (22:5): "A woman shall not wear a man's apparel, nor shall a man put on a woman's garment; for whoever does such things is abhorrent to the Lord your God." Annie Woodhouse writes in *Fantastic Women: Sex, Gender, and Transvestism* (1989) that

> Masculinity is treated as a thing in itself, something to be achieved by all men. Those who do not evince a convincing image of masculinity have failed and, in the common parlance of insult, they become effeminate. It is no accident that transvestites are commonly thought to be homosexual; after all, any man who is effeminate cannot be heterosexual, there must be something "wrong" with him. (136)

Although I dislike, despise in fact, all these categorical terms, it is worth mentioning that almost all cross-dressers are heterosexual (what a ridiculous term) as I am, although it is an ambivalent, and divided heterosexuality: on the one hand wanting a "male" intimate relationship with a woman, and on the other wanting to be the pretty woman who attracts the man. Such confusion.

Today I am in a Beckettian mode, wanting to offer commiseration to myself for the impossibility of not ceasing before having been and to reach a state of achieving "the extinction of this black nothing and its impossible shades" (Beckett 1995:154). Simply spending the day looking through a "glass black with the dust of ruin" (129). When I read my mother's account of my difficult birth, I think of Beckett's lines in *Waiting for Godot* (1954): "astride of a grave and a difficult birth. Down in the hole, lingeringly, the grave-digger puts on the forceps. We have time to grow old. The air is full of our cries" (104). As well, when I think of her journal expressing a wish for a girl, I find some almost enigmatic solace in Beckett. In his novel *Company* (1979) are lines that hang around me: "a mother stooping over cradle from behind. She moves aside to let the father look. In his turn he murmurs to the newborn. Flat tone unchanged. No trace of love" (66).

Eventually I created company for myself as a girl, holding myself in my arms. However, in no interpretive way do I consider my cross-dressing as an aberration. It is a way of being that would be as "normal" as any other construction of oneself and fully satisfactory if it weren't for a repressive society that pathologizes and reproves a "male" in a pretty dress.

The wish of my mother for a girl rather than a male child provides one explanation from a psychoanalytic perspective of my desire to cross-dress. In Otto Fenichel's *The Psychoanalytic Theory of Neurosis* (1945), one of the classics of psychoanalytic literature, transvestitism, a perversion, is the result of the male identifying with his mother and fantasizing that the woman possesses a penis, hence overcoming the fear of castration. The female identification might also represent, Fenichel notes, an identification with a little girl, such as a little sister. In Fenichel's interpretation, "the transvestite act has two unconscious meanings: (a) an object-erotic and fetishistic one: the person cohabits not with a woman but with her clothes, the clothes representing, symbolically, her penis; (b) a narcissistic one: the transvestite himself represents the phallic woman under whose clothes a penis is hidden" (344–45). Most of the therapists, psychiatrists, and psychoanalysts I have seen over the years have subscribed to some version of Fenichel's account. Toward the end of the summer in 1964 I was in a very painful emotional state over a breakup with my girlfriend of two years and my obsessive cross-dressing. My father arranged for me to see a psychiatrist he knew through university connections. I smoked cigarettes at the time, and in the first visit, after I told him about my cross-dressing, he excoriated me for the cigarettes and practically ordered me to give them up and smoke a pipe as he did, something that represented maleness. I did, but it did not "cure" the cross-dressing. It is, I realized years later, not something to be cured but to be embraced and enjoyed. Ever since I started buying my own clothes over twenty years ago, I have gradually accepted and get great intellectual, emotional, and sexual pleasure from not living my life entirely within the gender binaries and boundaries prescribed by my upbringing and by society.

When Fenichel published his book in 1945, transvestism was considered a perversion; however, now it is judged to be a mental disorder (I see it as neither) by the lofty standards of the American Psychiatric Association in the revised fourth edition of its DSM IV—*Diagnostic and Statistical Manual of Mental Disorders* (2000). The manual uses the term "transvestic fetishism" (574–75). This "mental disorder" is characterized by the "cross-dressing of a male in women's attire . . . and in most cases, sexual arousal is produced by the accompanying thought or image of the person as a female (referred to as 'autogynephilia')." The clothing is arousing since it is a symbol for a desired femininity. The description notes that "the cross-dressing becomes an antidote to anxiety or depression or contributes to a sense of peace or calm."

From the late 1960s through the 1980s, one of the best-known interpreters of gender identity and gender dysphoria was a psychoanalyst and professor of psychiatry at UCLA, Robert Stoller. In *Sex and Gender* (1968, 1975), he described, in widely quoted passages, the mechanisms of transvestite behavior:

> The whole complex psychological system that we call transvestism is a rather efficient method of handling very strong feminine identifications without the patient having to succumb to the feeling that his sense of masculinity is being submerged by feminine wishes. The transvestite fights this battle against being destroyed by his feminine desires, first by alternating his masculinity with the feminine behavior, and thus reassuring himself that it isn't permanent; and second, by being always aware that even at the height of the feminine behavior—when he is fully dressed in women's clothes—that he has the *absolute insignia of maleness, a penis. And there is no more acute awareness of its presence than when he is reassuringly experiencing it with an erection.* (1968:186)

In 1985 Stoller said much the same thing in *Observing the Erotic Imagination*:

> When I am like a female, dressed in her clothes and appearing to be like her . . . am I still male, or did the women succeed in ruining me? . . . No. You are a male. No matter how many feminine clothes you put on, you did not lose that ultimate insignia of your maleness, your penis. And the transvestite gets excited. What can be more reassuringly penile than a full and hearty erection? (30)

Charlotte Suthrell, in her cross-cultural study of transvestites in Britain and the Hijras of India, *Unzipping Gender* (2004), sees cross-dressing as complex cultural practice. Many "male" cross-dressers find (and this has been the case with me) that they take pleasure in the imagined, often fantasized, experience of the other. The way into a feminine aesthetic through clothing allows for an expanded experience of being in a world that is felt to be more appealing and hence escaping being a prisoner of gender. "Female" clothing, just from an artistic perspective, is for me so much more beguiling and enchanting (color, texture, adornments), and often when I am shopping for clothes, either in a store or on the Internet (for cross-dressers Internet shopping has been a wonderful development), I find myself under a kind of elusive, dreamy spell. In those moments I am the pretty girl in the mirror. Suthrell found from her interviews that cross-dressing can be a reaction to social pressures and allows for a feeling of relaxation and comfort when dressed. For many cross-dressers, especially in the early years of the practice, there is a strong autoerotic dimension. This aspect emerges when looking at oneself in a mirror when dressed, becoming the desired and dreamed for girl—and finding the image pleasingly erotic. Suthrell quotes one cross-dresser's account of the auto-erotic phase: "The sexuality of dressing as a woman is essentially a male sexuality. . . . I find I want to make love to my own feminine image; this is why so many transvestite sessions end by the transvestite making love to himself" (60),

The term auto-gynephilia was invented in the late 1980s to describe "males" who are sexually aroused by the thought and image of themselves as women surrounded by fantasies of the "woman within." My own long experience as a cross-dresser encompasses all these facets, and more and more I feel almost all the time that I am both male and female at once, and that, although a long time in coming, I now live in a more magical world.

Cross-dressing has given me more intense feelings, ones that feel like sharp stings of electricity running through my body. There are many ways in which I identify with the Romantic movement of the early nineteenth century, a reaction against the cold rationalism of the eighteenth-century Enlightenment. In their critiques of the Enlightenment, Romantic writers and artists placed a great emphasis on beauty, the irrational, the imagination, feeling, the poetic, intuition, longing, desire, the sublime, the mysterious, dreamy thoughts, reveries, and aesthetic appreciation generally. All these words and the train of feelings they invigorate are crucial to my fluid, fleeting identities, my desire to continually confuse boundaries and to narratively, through memory, reach into the past. All these characteristics of Romanticism are far outside the hardness and violence of rationalism and empiricism and their denial of tender touching. One of the early Romantics was the English poet and essayist Samuel Taylor Coleridge, who was particularly intent on restoring feeling and the imagination to our mental lives. His poetry is full of daydreaming imagery, as in his well-known "Kubla Khan." Coleridge made a detailed study of Kant's philosophy and concluded that Kant's view of the mind was far too restricted to encompass the full range of human experience (Botting 1999:108). Franz Schubert's Romantic compositions, such as the song-cycle *The Pretty Milkmaid* and his *Quartet No.14 in D Minor, Death and the Maiden*, especially the exquisite second movement, *andante con moto*, both favorites of mine for many years, are associated for me with cross-dressing—what would it be like to be a pretty milkmaid or a beautiful dying maiden? Another Romantic writer, Emily Brontë, in her lovely piece *The Butterfly* (1842, 1996) with its imagery of birds, flowers, and butterflies, brings to my feelings and understandings sentiments of gentleness, compassion, kindness, flowingness, delicateness—all sensations that are much more a part of my life when I am cross-dressed. Recently I bought a delicate and sweet butterfly bracelet, the butterfly being a symbol of renewal and transformation. It may seem unusual to link the Romantic movement with cross-dressing, but both bring to me some wonderfully heightened and sensuous/sensual feelings and erotic, arousing thoughts. Pleasure. Intensity. Ecstasy.

There is another link to be made as well. I have a particular interest, going back to 1991, in postmodern philosophy, culture, and the arts, and there are many connections—even convergences—to be made between Romanticism and postmodernism (Larrissy 1999), and hence cross-dressing. One convergence can be created from the late, unfinished work of the British Romantic painter J. M. W. Turner and his allusiveness and the randomness and the chance wanderings of smoke, clouds, mist, and steam in his paintings. Romanticism and postmodernism are about the fragile process of becoming, an indeterminacy of process, and never being complete, never finished (Massey 2005:115; Vaughan 1999:44). Here we can call on a vocabulary of postmodernism of contingency, nonlinearity, unpredictability, chance effects that converge with how I experience cross-dressing and an always present ontological uncertainty, where all closed and fixed coordinates of modernity now are let go and I float and drift as mist, as vapor. It's ethereal, ghostly, and precarious. Invoking another metaphor, my cross-dressing bears some resemblance to a palimpsest where various levels of becoming and being female keep being erased by the everyday, although imperfectly, and hence continue showing up beneath the standard surface rendering of maleness I present to the world. The imperfect erasures are an ever present source of hope for me where my own mirror counterdiscourses might one day become something more than that.

However, there is an ethical point to be made here. I feel often when I cross-dress that I am a mist that cannot, and should not, be interpreted, cannot be captured or contained, cannot be induced to explain, cannot be subjected to an assertion of power, a will-to-meaning. Lynne Huffer (2010) asks, "What would it mean to think of the queer subject as an atmosphere?" (117). An acceptance of nonmeaning is required. In Samuel Beckett's novel *Murphy* (1957), Murphy is exhausted by the struggle to endlessly explain and simply wants to achieve a state of being where he is "improved out of all knowledge" (62). The philosopher Stanley Cavell (1976) thinks we might be best served in life by undoing "the curse of meaning" and knowing that haunts and grieves us. It is Cavell's insight that it is not the failure or abandonment of meaning we should be concerned about, but rather its "total even totalitarian success—our inability not to mean what we are given to mean" (117). For Gilles Deleuze (1998) it is not only that words mislead and lie: "they are so burdened with calculations and significations, with intentions and personal memories, with old habits that cement them together, that one can scarcely bore into the surface before it closes up again. It sticks together. It imprisons and suffocates us" (103).

Through cross-dressing I am able on occasion to jettison the silt of all this mental detritus and reach a state of pure intensity.

Today I am wearing a short, cute halter dress with a little flare and pink nylon panties, perfume, and a necklace. I love how it feels on my body, silky, soft, delicate, and how the dress moves, flutters, when I walk. It is a hot day, and this little outfit feels cool and nonrestrictive and fills me with erotic and almost breathtaking emotional exhilaration. My whole body is tingling, flooded with sensations. Wearing feminine apparel for me heals the Cartesian mind/body split, the Cartesian error, restoring the body to its own potentially wild, transgressive existence as the mind recedes.

Time's pretense of ordering. The triviality of endings. No one can ever hope to understand why losses come, heart's grief, what was taken away. Cross-dressing has located me in different worlds. The female image of myself in the mirror reflects back my other self, a lovely attractive and desired woman. Endings we all know are not easy. I have no transformative, redemptive ending to offer. Like the voice in Beckett's (1995) story "The Calmative," I have often wished for only "the mirrors to shatter . . . and to vanish in the havoc of its images" (63). Be again, be again. And as always, I am with Beckett: "There's my life, why not, it is one, if you like, if you must. No need of a story, a story is not compulsory, just a life, life alone is enough. What counts is to be in the world, the posture is immaterial, so long as one is on earth" (116). Time has done its work. The memory now comes faint and cloudy of the story I might have told, one that is nothing but pure mist and gold.

REFERENCES

American Psychiatric Association. 2000. *Diagnostic and Statistical Manual of Mental Disorders*. Washington, D.C.: American Psychiatric Association.

Auslander, P. 2006. *Performing Glam Rock: Gender and Theatricality in Popular Music*. Ann Arbor: University of Michigan Press.

Barnes, D. 1937, 2006. *Nightwood*. New York: New Directions.

Beckett, S. 1954. *Waiting for Godot*. New York: Grove Press.

———. 1957. *Murphy*. New York: Grove Press.

———. 1979. *Company*. London: John Calder.

———. 1995. *The Complete Short Prose, 1929–1989*. New York: Grove Press.

Botting, F. 1999. "Virtual Romanticism." In *Romanticicm and Postmodernism*, edited by E. Larrissy. Cambridge: Cambridge University Press.

Bronte, E. 1842, 1996. *The Butterfly*. Translated by S. Lonoff. In *Charlotte and Emily Bronte: The Belgian Essays, a Critical Edition*, 176–79. New Haven: Yale University Press.

Butler, J. 1990. *Gender Trouble*. New York: Routledge.

———. 1993. *Bodies That Matter*. New York: Routledge.

———. 2004. *Undoing Gender*. New York: Routledge.

Cavell, S. 1976. *Must We Mean What We Say?* Cambridge: Cambridge University Press.

Deleuze, G. 1997. *Essays: Critical and Clinical*. Minneapolis: University of Minnesota Press.

Deleuze, G., and F. Guattari. 1983. *Anti-Oedipus*. Minneapolis: University of Minnesota Press.

———. 1987. *A Thousand Plateaus*. Minneapolis: University of Minnesota Press.

Derrida, J. 2001. *A Taste for the Secret*. Malden, Mass.: Blackwell.

Ekins, R. 1997. *Male Femaling: A Grounded Theory Approach to Cross-Dressing and Sex-Changing.* London: Routledge.

Fenichel, O. 1945. *The Psychoanalytic Theory of Neurosis.* New York: Norton.

Fletcher, A. 2004. *A New Theory for American Poetry: Democracy, the Environment, and the Future of Imagination.* Cambridge: Harvard University Press.

Foucault, M. 1997. *Ethics, Subjectivity and Truth: The Essential Works of Foucault,* edited by P. Rabinow. Vol. 1. New York: New Press.

——. 1998. *Aesthetics, Method and Epistemology: The Essential Works of Foucault,* edited by D. Faubion. Vol. 2. New York: New Press.

Francis, E. 1999. "'Conquered Good and Conquering Ill': Femininity, Power and Romanticism in Emily Bronte's Poetry." in *Romanticism and Postmodernism,* edited by E. Larrisy. Cambridge: Cambridge University Press.

Garber, M. 1992. *Vested Interests: Cross-Dressing and Cultural Anxiety.* New York: Routledge.

Hickey-Moody, A., and M. L. Rasmussen. 2009. "The Sexed Subject in-Between Deleuze and Butler." In *Deleuze and Queer Theory,* edited by C. Nigianni and M. Storr. Edinburgh: Edinburgh University Press.

Holy Bible. 1989. New Revised Standard Version. Grand Rapids, Mich.: Zondervan.

Huffer, L. 2010. *Mad for Foucault: Rethinking the Foundations of Queer Theory.* New York: Columbia University Press.

Hussey, A. 2006. *The Beast at Heaven's Gate: George Bataille and the Art of Transgression.* New York: Rodopi.

Jamison, K. R. 1993. *Touched with Fire: Manic-Depressive Illness and the Artistic Temperament.* New York: Simon and Schuster.

Joselit, D. 1988. "Robert Mapplethorpe's Poses." In *Robert Mapplethorpe: The Perfect Moment,* edited by J. Kardon. Philadelphia: Institute of Contemporary Art.

Larrissy, E., ed. 1999. *Romanticism and Postmodernism.* Cambridge: Cambridge University Press.

Massey, D. 2005. *For Space.* London: Sage.

Nietzsche, F. 1974. *The Gay Science,* translated by W. Kaufman. New York: Vintage.

——. 1986. *Human, All Too Human,* translated by R. J. Hollingdale. Cambridge: Cambridge University Press.

Olney, J. 1998. *Memory and Narrative: The Weave of Life Writing.* Chicago: University of Chicago Press.

Ondaatje, M. 2007. *Divisadero.* New York: Knopf.

Perone, J. 2007. *The Words and Music of David Bowie.* Westport, Conn.: Praeger.

Reed, C. 2011. *Art and Homosexuality: A History of Ideas*. New York: Oxford University Press.

Shildrick, M. 2009. "Prosthetic Performativity: Deleuzian Connections and Queer Corporealities." In *Deleuze and Queer Theory*, edited by C. Nigianni and M. Storr. Edinburgh: Edinburgh University Press.

Stevenson, N. 2006. *David Bowie: Fame, Sound, and Vision*. Cambridge: Polity Press.

Stoller, R. 1968, 1975. *Sex and Gender*. Vols. 1 and 2: *The Development of Masculinity and Femininity*. New York: Science House.

———. 1985. *Observing the Erotic Imagination*. New Haven: Yale University Press.

Stryker, S., and S. Whittle, eds. 2006. *The Transgender Studies Reader*. New York: Routledge.

Suthrell, C. 2004. *Unzipping Gender: Sex, Cross-Dressing, and Culture*. New York: Berg.

Szafraniec, A. 2007. *Beckett, Derrida, and the Event of Literature*. Stanford: Stanford University Press.

Van Alphen, F. 1992. *Francis Bacon and the Loss of Self*. London: Reaktion Books.

Vaughan, W. 1999. "Turnabouts in Taste: the Case of the Late Turner." In *Romanticism and Postmodernism*, edited by E. Larrissy. Cambridge: Cambridge University Press.

Villani, A. 2006. "Why Am I Deleuzian?" In *Deleuze and Philosophy*, edited by C. V. Boundas. Edinburgh: Edinburgh University Press.

Woodhouse, A. 1989. *Fantastic Women: Sex, Gender, and Transvestism*. New Brunswick, N.J.: Rutgers University Press.

Woolf, V. 1928, 1973. *Orlando: A Biography*. New York: Harcourt Brace Jovanovich.

———. 1929, 1957. *A Room of One's Own*. New York: Harcourt Brace Jovanovich.

CHAPTER 11

Reality Isn't What It Used to Be

AN INQUIRY OF TRANSFORMATIVE CHANGE

▸ STANLEY L WITKIN

SCENE 1: NAVIGATING LIMINAL SPACE

I AM IN A HOTEL ROOM IN MIAMI, Florida. The hotel is the site of the 1986 annual conference of the Council on Social Work Education. Besides its educational function, the conference also serves as a site for potential employers and job seekers to meet face-to-face. I sit in a hard-backed chair facing four members of the faculty search committee of a midwestern university. I am interviewing for a faculty position.

"How would you describe your approach?" one of them asks. Four faces wait expectantly for my answer.

I hesitate while my mind races through possible responses—frantically evaluating and discarding them. Not wanting to delay any longer lest I appear unsure, I say "eclectic" in what I hope is a confident-sounding voice. However, even as the word becomes audible, I know that it is the wrong answer. Indeed, the expressionless faces of the search committee seem to confirm my fears. They wanted something more substantive, I tell myself, a specific theoretical position that I would explain and, if necessary, defend. Too late, I am not getting this job.

Some years earlier it would have been easy to answer their question— "behavioral," I would have averred confidently. But that position no longer held sway with me. In fact, it seemed antithetical to much of what I now believed. So much had changed, but I had no conceptual box in which I could locate or package my thoughts.

Although I still held a position as an associate professor in the School of Social Work at Florida State University, I had been on leave for the past three years, living in Oregon and working in the field of computer software. I had not anticipated returning to academic life; however, the company I worked for folded, and the volatile nature of the software industry in the mid-1980s convinced me that giving up my tenured position was too risky, especially given my family responsibilities. I was not convinced, however, that I wanted to return to Florida State and therefore was exploring other academic positions.

Reentering academic life was not easy. I had not read a social work book or journal article for three years. I left the university at a time when I was increasingly questioning the beliefs that formed my professional identity. Changing fields allowed me to put these questions on hold. However, as the interviewer's question made clear, returning to the academy required that I figure out what I believed and how I wanted to represent my professional self. At the time of the interview, I didn't have an "approach," at least not one that I could articulate extemporaneously. For the search committee, this was unacceptable; for me, it was an indication of the need to continue to explore the nascent and somewhat inchoate ideas that had been percolating for some time. Eventually this led to a sea change in my assumptions and beliefs about social work and life itself. What follows is an inquiry into and narrative about that change.

INTERLUDE: BELIEF CHANGE

How does belief change happen? Not superficial or surface change but transformative change where foundational presuppositions, assumptions, and understandings are replaced by new ones—a "paradigm shift" in which what was invisible becomes visible, and foreground and background reverse positions. If you listened only to scientists and researchers, you might think that such change occurs (or should occur) in response to research-generated data, that is, rationally. Yet I have never met a single person where "data" of this sort were the primary catalyst for such change. Transformation, if it happens at all, seems more than the outcome of a deliberative, intellectual process. Strongly held beliefs are anchored to our lives in complex ways, and their dislodgement and replacement involve equally strong influences.

And because we rarely seek to change these beliefs, particularly if the direction of change is from a more conventional way of understanding to a more marginal one, these influences are usually neither planned nor anticipated.

This autoethnography is an exploration of such a change in my professional life and also in my personal life as the two are inextricably intertwined. Unlike dramatic portrayals of awakenings or life-altering epiphanies, the change was not cataclysmic but a long process in which unexpected encounters and events loosened and sometimes shook the foundations of my beliefs and, over time, led to new interpretive lenses for understanding the world. It also involved trying to navigate new terrain without the use of familiar orienting devices and dealing with colleagues who responded to my changed beliefs with incredulity and criticism.

Social workers commonly engage with others who express the desire to change or whom social workers want to change. Of course, social workers too may seek self-change in professional and personal domains. Sometimes these changes are simple, "first-order" changes in which assumptions and foundational beliefs remain intact. At other times the changes sought entail a dramatic shift in one's assumptive world and the beliefs those assumptions support. Although there may be a "final straw" that invites causal ascriptions, deeper analysis may reveal a more complex process involving a mélange of relationships, circumstances, and events, contributing in unpredictable or unimagined ways.

My inquiry explores circumstances and events in my life that in hindsight were instrumental in laying the groundwork or providing the impetus for transformative change. By exploring the particularities (and peculiarities) of how such change occurred in my life, I hope to shed some light on why such change is so difficult and therefore infrequent. I also hope to provide a deeper understanding of the social and cultural contexts that enable or hinder transformative change, increase empathy for those struggling with or against such change, and stimulate new ideas for its facilitation.

SCENE 2: THE CHILDREN'S HOME

It is mid-1969 and I have recently graduated from the University of Minnesota with a bachelor's degree in social welfare. This was a new major and consisted of a small number of social work courses heavily supplemented by courses in psychology, sociology, and the liberal arts. Like many of my generation (and still today), I was drawn to social work because of its congruence with my political values and my desire to do something meaningful. Although I originally considered psychology, obtaining a Ph.D. degree seemed daunting—particularly the statistics requirements. Mostly I wanted to understand social life and relationships (including my own). I loved social psychology and was fascinated by the works of the symbolic interactionists like Herbert Blumer, George Herbert Mead, and Irving Goffman. My teachers included the social theorist Don Martindale and the historian David Noble, both of whom dazzled me with their (quite different) ideas about why people in the United States act as they do. Given my interests and self-assessment, social work seemed liked the best (i.e., most pragmatic) option.

Wanting to remain in the Midwest following graduation, I applied for and was offered a job at the Taylor Children's Home in Racine, Wisconsin. Founded in the 1860s as the Taylor Orphan Asylum by funds bequeathed by Isaac Taylor, himself a former orphan, the Children's Home was now a "residential treatment center" for male youth. At the time of my employment, the original nineteenth-century, Gothic-style building that housed the orphans, although in disrepair, was still being used for some administrative offices and the on-campus school. The residents—boys between the ages of ten and seventeen—lived in new, brick housing units. I worked as a teacher—one of two—for a subgroup of children who were deemed unable to attend public school, usually due to behavior issues. The other teacher, a veteran educator whose teaching experience exceeded my age, was a middle-aged woman of matronly appearance, conservative dress, and strong countenance. In contrast, I was young, male, and scruffy, with no experience as a classroom teacher. Aside from intermittent, informal advice from my more experienced colleague, I was pretty much on my own, expected to manage up to eight children of varying ages, abilities, and propensities for violence while keeping them from hurting themselves, each other, or me. Learning was a bonus.

My classroom was a small, unadorned former bedroom located in the basement of the original, and now crumbling, orphanage building. As a learning environment it was far from adequate for *any* students, let alone those labeled as incorrigibles and failures by the educational system. I recall one day when, in the middle of a lesson, a flushed toilet on the floor above us resulted in water dripping from our ceiling, creating havoc in the room and ending any chance of learning for that day. Such events communicated

to the students a powerful message about their lack of worth, further confirming their alterity and hopelessness.

I drew on my limited knowledge of behavior modification from my
undergraduate psychology classes, particularly abnormal psychology, to
develop a structure that I hoped would produce some level of order and
safety. I tried tangible and symbolic rewards and occasionally punishments
incorporated into point systems and token economies. However, despite
my attempts at manipulating antecedents and dispensing consequences
in a contingent manner, my classroom remained a volatile and challenging learning environment. I felt isolated and found the stress of the job to
be unrelenting. Finally, some physical encounters—being hit with a chair
while breaking up a fight and having a nail thrown at me that landed just
under my eye—convinced me (after two years) that it was time to move on.
Since my degree was in social welfare, I sought work in that field, eventually
finding employment as a caseworker at the Clark County Department of
Social Services in Neillsville, Wisconsin.

SCENE 3: CLARK COUNTY MIGRATION

Clark County was a rural, dairy-farming area, home to about 31,000 resi-
dents, including a small indigenous population who were members of the
Winnebago tribe (Ho Chunk Nation). Neillsville, the county seat, had a
population of about 3,500. County politics were very conservative. George
Wallace, the segregationist governor from Alabama, won the 1972 presidential primary in the county. In contrast to the surrounding environs, the
Department of Social Services was relatively liberal. There was a new, young,
MSW-educated director who hired people in his own age cohort (twenties
and thirties). Many of them, like myself, were relatively new graduates from
outside the area. Neillsville also was home to a residential treatment center.
Many of its staff—teachers, cottage parents, and social workers—were of
this same age cohort. Together these two organizations produced a subpop-
ulation of relatively well-educated young adults who had decidedly different
ideas, politics, and ideals from those of most of the locals. While this group
provided important social support, it also kept me an outsider to the community in which I was living and to the people with whom I was working.

Once again I struggled to find my way, albeit in a more supportive and
open environment. This time I was working primarily with children in foster

care and their biological and foster parents. I also worked with families where abuse or neglect was suspected or adjudicated. As with most government social service positions, I had to navigate a web of regulations, manage mountains of paperwork, and somehow find the time to provide services to the children and families on my caseload. As in the Children's Home, many of the situations confronting me were complex, and I felt ill prepared to handle them. Complicating matters were the conservative, sometimes bigoted views of some people with whom I needed to work, and in some cases depend on. For example, shortly after beginning my new position, I met with the juvenile court judge, an elderly man (who fortunately retired soon after) who lectured me about working with "Indian children." He wanted me to understand that they were like animals, and that despite what we might do to "civilize" them, they eventually would "revert" back to their savage nature. I sat there shocked at what I was hearing and dumbfounded about what to do. I was a twenty-something social worker beginning a new job, and he was a senior, respected judge who would be making decisions about my clients. Could I afford to alienate him? Could he threaten my job security? Deciding that discretion was the better part of valor, I bit my lip and sat silently through his monologue, realizing that explicit opposition at this point would serve neither my interests nor those of my prospective clients.

Like most of my colleagues, I found a way to cope with the day-to-day demands of my position, bending rules when needed (and when I could get away with it), prioritizing demands, and responding to periodic crises. Regulatory mandates, particularly foster care home visits, also structured my day. Often this meant visiting dairy farms and talking with farmers as they went about their chores. Feeling ever the city slicker, I tried to get a picture of how things were going while nimbly walking through the barn and staying clear of the backend of the cows lined up in their stanchions. I would also talk with the foster children and gather information from other sources, such as school officials. I used a "good enough" approach; that is, gathering enough information from different sources to make what seemed to be a reasonable assessment and, if needed, recommendations and suggestions. I tried to be pragmatic—what did the child and the foster parents need in terms of support?—rather than theoretical (or, at least, explicitly theoretical). What I could do, materially and socially, was limited, but I attempted to work the system to obtain and provide what seemed to be most needed. Where possible I also worked with the biological parents toward the goal of returning their child(ren) to their care, or in some cases relinquishing their parental rights. Here too I tried to be pragmatic, although moral and psychological judgments related to their fitness to be parents were inevitably made.

If I had been asked about "my approach," I probably would have said it was behavioral. There were two reasons for this. First, I did not have another descriptive term (although "social work" might have fit). Second, I encouraged foster parents to use simple behavioral techniques such as contingent rewards and time out with their charges, and my work with foster children was somewhat based on providing differential consequences for their actions. Occasionally I would have the opportunity to assume a more therapeutic role, talking with clients about their "inner" as well as external problems.

SCENE 4: BECOMING PROVOCATIVE

I am in my office at the Department of Social Services. The office is small, accommodating my desk and a couple of chairs in front of it, but not much else. The décor is characterless, in keeping with general ambiance of the building occupied primarily by government offices that serve people who are poor, downtrodden, and marginalized. Across from me sits Nancy, a woman in her mid-forties wearing a shapeless dress and a sad expression. She appears passive and forlorn. In a subdued voice she tells me about how her husband and four children walk all over her and how she feels worthless as a human being.

This is not the first time I have heard Nancy's tale of woe. As I listen, I wonder what I can do that supportive services, therapy, and medications could not. Certainly nothing I have tried has seemed to make any difference. In desperation, I turn to something called "provocative therapy," a controversial approach developed by a social worker named Frank Farrelly when he worked at the Wisconsin State Psychiatric Hospital. I knew a little about provocative therapy from a presentation by Farrelly that I attended. As I understood it, provocative therapists confronted people in ways bordering on caricature and parody with their self-presentations and characterizations beyond what they can accept. For instance, rather than counter clients' declarations of incompetence or sadness, the provocative therapist not only agrees but goes even further in his or her characterization of the person's self-identified deficits, telling them, for example, that they might as well give up or consider a life more appropriate for such a worthless human being. No matter how low a person might go in their self-effacement or debasement, Frank would go lower. Comments such as "I'm just no good" might be met with "You're right. You're worthless." Frank was relentless. As he put it, "I drive people sane." Watching Frank practice provocative therapy was shocking, an unrelenting stream of put-downs seemingly without boundaries. But, and this is critical, there also was humor. Frank was funny, a master of the one-liner or quip, like a therapeutic version of the classic comedian Henny Youngman.[1] Frank's ability to express the humor in what seemed like a hopeless situation communicated a powerful metamessage of caring. This message enabled his clients to endure his "insults" and return for additional sessions.

Still, his comments were shocking and disrupted the expected relational positioning of the client and social worker.[2] For example, on meeting a client who was obese, Frank quipped, "Oh my God, the Goodyear Blimp has been loosed from its moorings!" The resultant sense of uncertainty (e.g., Is he kidding? Nuts? Should I leave? Stay?) generated space for new possibilities. Also, somewhat paradoxically, some people seemed to feel that finally, here was someone who understood them! I could imagine the client thinking something like, "I hate that I'm obese, and this guy gets it." Eventually Frank's quips and antics evoked protests from clients, thereby redirecting and mobilizing their energy toward change. In fact, at least in Frank's case, there seemed to be no point at which his provocation became overt support. Clients simply stopped reacting with shock or anger and responded more like you would to a friendly, somewhat bizarre, jokester.[3]

Nancy's passive demeanor and self-effacing behavior reminded me of some of Frank's clients. Intrigued by his success and desperate to do something that might have an impact, I started agreeing with Nancy's characterizations of herself:

SHE: I'm useless.

ME: I agree, you can't seem to do anything right.

This response got a noticeable shift in Nancy's posture but not much else. I tried my best to imitate Frank's delivery and communicate caring despite the apparent insensitivity of my words. When Nancy complained about how badly her children were treating her, I sided with them, telling her that her she might as well be wearing a "kick me" sign. Nancy responded with a sigh and what I took as a look of incredulity. Hey, *something* was happening! This new approach not only seemed to get Nancy's attention but, after a period of uncertainty in which she appropriately tried to make sense out of my sudden change toward her, actually saw her arguing against my assessments: "I'm not so bad." Eventually she even reported a few small successes with her family—attempting to assert herself and not accept being treated poorly.

Despite this positive movement, I was too uncertain and anxious about causing possible harm to go to the lengths that Frank did, which left me as a somewhat unprovocative provocative therapist. For example, in Frank's version of provocative therapy, even successes are met with suspicion; however, I found this difficult to do. My previous training in behavior modification informed me that I should reinforce Nancy's gains and not risk undermining them. So I let go of my provocateur role and we both returned to our more typical positions.

On reflection, my ineffectiveness with Nancy and my desire to help her led me to consider an approach that on its face seemed to violate many of the tenets of social work practice. Choosing this particular approach was circumstantial. I had actually seen it demonstrated, and there seemed to be a similarity between Nancy's situation and some of Frank Farrelly's successful cases. Despite my shock at provocative therapy's methods (a reaction I shared with clients), my inability to help Nancy change made me more open to exploring plausible reasons for its effectiveness.

Although my experience with provocative therapy may have had transformative potential, and certainly contributed to my developing understanding of change, it did not lead to significant changes in my beliefs or my approach to working with clients. Professional and organizational factors were aligned against such change. Beliefs about the appropriate social worker–client relationship and the meaning of ethical practice highlighted the potential for harm in using this approach. Job expectations, supervisor reactions, and legal considerations provided additional cautions. Also, I did not see the relevance of provocative therapy to my own life. Thus I viewed it as an exception to the rule—something that might be useful in certain unusual situations, a last resort when nothing else seemed to work. Nevertheless, the highly unconventional nature of the practitioner-client relationship in provocative therapy rekindled (albeit on a low flame) my interest in relationships and their importance in helping others change.

Whether I helped Nancy in the long run is uncertain, as other changes independent of my work with her occurred in her life. Still, my brief foray into provocative therapy demonstrated to me that there were many ways of instigating change. It also somewhat lessened the authority of mainstream explanations of the causes and amelioration of human suffering—that there was a single, "right" approach—and increased my curiosity about other perspectives.

SCENE 5: BECOMING A "REAL" BEHAVIORIST

Despite this foray into provocative therapy, my assessments and judgments continued to be guided more by the regulatory and organizational demands of the job than by explicit theoretical perspectives. If anything, my familiarity with behavior modification from my undergraduate days and its growing popularity in social work drew me in that direction. I was attracted to behaviorism's scientific aura, its relatively straightforward application, and its easy-to-discern effectiveness. In an environment in which I often felt that there was little I could do to make much of a difference, this approach was appealing. Therefore, when offered an opportunity to attend a professional conference, I chose one with a behavioral theme—the Rocky Mountain Conference on Behavior Modification in Denver, Colorado. I cannot recall how I found out about this conference or why I chose this particular one (although I am sure that going to Denver was part of the appeal), but I do remember being excited about the prospect of learning more about "behavior mod." The featured speaker at this small conference was Michael Mahoney, who had recently received his Ph.D. degree in psychology from Stanford, where he worked under Albert Bandura, the originator of social learning and self-efficacy theories. Mahoney was interested in self-control, which at the time was a radical concept for many behaviorists since it involved the notion of "cognitive mediation," something that operant behaviorists like B. F. Skinner did not acknowledge. Short of stature and boyish in appearance (Wow, he looks younger than me!), Mahoney was an engaging and entertaining speaker, and I found myself taken in by his presentations—even the one on self-control in pigeons. I returned from the conference energized and committed to learning more about behavioral approaches and particularly Mahoney's work. What I did not know was that Mahoney would take me on an intellectual journey that would have a substantial impact on the evolution of my thinking.

SCENE 6: BACK TO SCHOOL

In 1973 I decided to return to graduate school and obtain a master's degree in social work. Since I enjoyed living in Wisconsin, I applied to the social work program at the University of Wisconsin-Madison and fortunately was accepted. Once there I began working with Sheldon Rose, a professor in the School of Social Work well-known for his expertise in behavioral approaches, particularly as applied to groups. I found Sheldon to be warm, bright, and charismatic. I voraciously consumed his courses on behavior modification and group work. What made Sheldon's work somewhat different from that of others in the field was his background in social psychology. This led him to integrate ideas from group dynamics with a behavioral approach. For example, we were taught to be concerned with group-level factors such as group cohesion that were not easily reducible to individual explanations. Understanding group interaction as generating realities different from the actions of individuals provided an important connection for me to the social interactionist ideas that I found so compelling as an undergraduate student.

Working with Sheldon felt cutting edge and important. There was a scholarly and scientific aspect to the work that was appealing. It was empirical and pragmatic. We identified and counted behavior and demonstrated our efficacy by showing change in the desired direction following the application of our interventions. At the time, being a behaviorist was to be part of an alternative, minority community. We were the radicals and outsiders, daring to think outside of the "touchy-feely" box of our colleagues. Sheldon attracted an inner circle of students who were generally considered among the most promising future academics. I liked being part of such a group. So when my academic adviser, a newly minted Ph.D., brought up the idea of applying to the doctoral program, I was intrigued. Sheldon was supportive of the idea, and the opportunity to continue my studies and work with him was attractive. I applied and was accepted into the Ph.D. program.

The doctoral program was heavily oriented toward research, and I quickly was immersed in courses on research methods and statistics. I encountered young, bright, energetic instructors like Joel Levin and Larry Hubert who introduced me to the world of quantitative research design and analysis.[4] This was esoteric knowledge that seemed capable of providing definitive information on causal questions of importance. I was excited to acquire the tools that would enable me to determine whether our attempts to help others were actually effective. There was an enticing, puzzle-solving aspect to methodology and statistics that I found intellectually challenging and satisfying. As I progressed in this area, the questions and puzzles grew more sophisticated; for example, statistically significant results were no longer enough—we needed to conduct "post-hoc comparisons." Analysis progressed from univariate (one independent variable) to multivariate. This was heady stuff, and I began to see myself as a social scientist who possessed specialized knowledge and skills that could unlock some of the mysteries of human behavior and guide social work in a useful way.

I decided to focus my doctoral research on marital relationships. This topic enabled me to keep a hand in the social psychological, interactionist literature that had long interested me. Additionally, I was hopeful that such study might help illuminate the mysteries and challenges of my own marriage. Some of the leading scholars in the field of behavioral marital therapy, such as Robert Weiss and John Gottman, were exceptional writers whose theoretical and empirical work was stretching the boundaries of applied behaviorism. I recall Weiss posing the question, "Can a relationship be crazy?" In other words, could we posit an entity called a relationship that transcended the individuals who constituted it, and could that entity be characterized as dysfunctional? For a behaviorist this was a radical line of thinking. Gottman too seemed to recognize the limitations of a strict behavioral (i.e., operant) approach to relationships (Gottman 1982).

Despite the relatively radical slant of such thinking, all were committed to the methodological orthodoxy of behaviorism—that empirical research, expressed quantitatively, was the best way of discovering what marital relationships were *really* like. I was fascinated by both aspects of their work: their conceptual creativity and their attempts to empirically explain relationships. I used Weiss's marital interaction coding system in my dissertation and related research (Witkin et al. 1983) and later published an article on sequential analysis (based on Gottman's work) and its potential applications in social work (Witkin 1988). On the other hand, concepts like temporal form seemed to express something important about relationships that was not captured by behavioral methods. Viewing couples' attempts to coordinate their actions as analogous to how jazz musicians coordinated their playing seemed more illuminating of how interaction patterns developed over time than did attempts to reduce such processes to discrete, measurable units. Although ideas like this kept my social interactionist flame from extinguishing, as a married student with two children, living in a tiny apartment, I was highly motivated to complete my degree and start earning a livable wage. Thus practicality won out and I decided to put these other ideas on hold.

During this same period, single-case designs found their way into social work. Used extensively in operant behavioral research, these designs involved the collection of data on single organisms over time, for example, the number of pecks a pigeon made on a disc that was connected to the release of food using a particular reinforcement schedule. Single-case designs were seen as providing a way to integrate research methodology with practice. The logic of these designs followed that of the classic experiment: the manipulation of an independent variable (i.e., the treatment or intervention) and the comparison of response rates in the presence and absence of treatment. Since there was no control group, individuals were compared with their own behavior before and after treatment. The aim, as in experimentation, was to be able to make a causal claim of the form: treatment X causes outcome Y; for example, contingent reinforcement for toothbrushing increases its frequency.[5]

Single-case designs seemed like an exciting development to me and my colleagues. This was a time (early 1970s) of shrinking resources for social programs[6] and increased competition for those resources that were available. Legislation mandating the evaluation of social programs required proof of their worthiness to receive, or continuing receiving, funding. Also, new specialties such as family therapy were drawing their own professional boundaries, calling into question social work's historic and somewhat exclusive claim to expertise with this population. These developments in themselves would have been challenging, but the situation became even more urgent with the publication of articles, by social workers no less, that raised serious questions about the effectiveness and even the beneficence of social work practice.[7]

Single-case designs seemed to offer a way of responding to these resource challenges and evaluation concerns. Here was a way to bring science into the practice arena, to provide empirical data on the efficacy of practice, and to separate truly effective practice from the misguided efforts of social workers. Doing so, I believed, would help shed social work's "do-gooder" image in favor of the scientific practitioner and bolster social work's claim to resources.

I was excited by these developments and devoted myself to the study and application of single-case designs. In fact, my first attempt at publication was a manuscript on single-case designs that I submitted to the journal *Social Work*. Although it was rejected for being "too technical" for the journal's readership, I consoled myself with the belief that this decision confirmed the woeful state of social work scholarship and practice knowledge and was but another indication of the importance of our work. Ironically, it also affirmed my nascent identity as social scientist, and so I displayed my rejection letter as a badge of honor, proudly showing it to my fellow students who readily accepted this interpretation.

There was something seductive about hitching one's star to the science bandwagon. It felt potentially revolutionary for the profession. Clients' problems would be operationalized—converted into measurable concepts— enabling them to be monitored and examined over time. Interventions— also operationalized—would be applied in ways that would potentially reveal their efficacy. We (practitioners) would be guided by data rather than by intuition, clinical hunches, altruism, or the latest practice fad. Human suffering would be subject to experimental logic—controlled and manipulated. And amazingly, I was one of the chosen few who would help engineer this new era of scientific social work. Nancy was a distant memory. It was a heady time.

SCENE 7: MAHONEY RETURNS

Yet while all this was going on, other seeds were slowly germinating. As I noted previously, my encounter with Michael Mahoney at my first professional conference years earlier led me to follow his career. Not only was Mahoney a prolific author, but his interests veered toward a critical understanding of science. As a dutiful fan, I followed along. In 1976 Mahoney published the book *Scientist as Subject: The Psychological Imperative*, in which he described the "storybook image of scientists"—a man in a white coat who rigorously employs the scientific method in the impassioned and rational pursuit of truth. He then took apart this image, revealing the gap between this idealized picture and the actualities of scientific practice. Borrowing from Kuhn's seminal work *The Structure of Scientific Revolutions* (1962)—another enlightening book through which I persevered— Mahoney portrayed scientists as "people," members of a community whose behavior was guided by its rules, rewards, and sanctions, and who, like the rest of us, aspired to be recognized and successful. He also showed that science as practiced was a lot messier than the sanitized version we read about in textbooks.

Mahoney's work steered me toward philosophical critiques of many taken-for-granted or, in my case, unexamined ideas underlying not only the conduct of research but my understanding of "reality." For example, I had not considered the idea that facts relied on theoretical beliefs and assumptions. Rather than reflections of the real, facts were seen as claims requiring communal recognition. As Mahoney (1976) wrote, "A 'fact' is not a fact until it has received peer approval, and herein lies at least one reason for scientists' quest for recognition. If they want their work to be contributory, they must strive to get it publicly recognized—i.e., acknowledged, replicated, expanded, and so on" (119).

This notion of the "theory-ladenness" of facts, among other such ideas, ignited new lines of thought that had heretofore been unknown to me. I had never thought of facts as anything but constituent parts of reality. To view them instead as authoritative claims that depended on various assumptions was a dramatic shift in my understanding, one of many that were to come.

Another important and unexpected event took place at a conference of the Association for the Advancement of Behavior Therapy (AABT). As a card-carrying behaviorist, I eagerly attended these conferences to learn about the latest research and practice techniques. Perusing the program, I noticed that Mahoney was chairing a symposium on science, so I went. Two of the speakers, unknown to me, were Ian Mitroff and Walter Weimer. Mitroff (1974) had recently completed a study about theory change among geophysicists in response to the Apollo moon mission in which soil samples from the moon were collected. Based on interviews with several eminent scientists, he found that not only were most resistant to changing their theories even when confronted with seemingly disconfirming samples, but some went further by deriding their competitor colleagues in quite colorful language. Weimer (1979), a philosopher, critiqued what he called justificatory theories of science; in plain language, theories that justified their positions through unacknowledged leaps of faith. He argued (as did Mahoney) that empiricism was self-contradictory in that its own premises were beyond empirical verification, and that scientific logic was a rhetorical rather than a truth-based system.

I sat transfixed through these presentations, captivated by their arguments and the questions they generated. Although I did not think about it at the time, it now seems quite ironic that at a conference on behavior therapy I was hearing ideas that undermined the basis for behaviorism! How was I to reconcile the questions raised with the work that I was promoting and undertaking? I did not know. Besides, completing my dissertation was my highest priority. This was not the time to go meandering off into new areas of inquiry or to challenge my work.

Like many people, I was good at partitioning my life based on the demands of the situation. So I tucked these questions away and completed my dissertation on a comparative study of two communication programs for couples. My methodology was conventional, my measures standardized, and my analyses quantitative and complex enough to demonstrate my worthiness to enter the fraternity of doctorates. It also landed me an assistant professor position at Cornell University in the Department of Human Service Studies located in the College of Human Ecology.

SCENE 8: HIGH ABOVE CAYUGA'S WATERS

Despite my less conventional interests, I began my academic career still committed to the empiricist methodology of behaviorism. This was the creed of my community, and it informed my teaching and my research. It did not, however, define the intellectual community that was Cornell. And I soon found myself, once again, confronting ideas that challenged the canon. Two people, Karl Weick and Ray Rist, neither of whom I had known or even heard of before coming to Cornell, were important in unsettling my beliefs and in helping me to begin formulating an alternative. Weick's influence was indirect, coming to me through my graduate assistant, Laurie, who was taking his courses on the social psychology of organizing. Laurie was excited about these courses and shared with me her course syllabi, which were unlike anything I had seen before. The readings were multidisciplinary and unusual, the assignments creative, and the ideas fascinating. I was intrigued by Weick's ability to generate new terms for relational realities. Enactment, loosely coupled systems, and galumphing provided novel interpretive lenses for generating new understandings (see, for example, Weick 1976, 1979). Once again I encountered the metaphor of a jazz group, in this case illustrating how organizations "enact" their own environments that they then "discover." My juggling act was growing more complex.

Ray Rist was a colleague in my department. Although relatively young, he was considered a rising star in the academy. He had already published books and numerous articles on topics such as school desegregation and integration efforts in the United States, and social science methodology. A sociologist by training, Ray was an ethnographer and a proponent of qualitative research. Despite his success, I thought his approach lacked rigor, and we engaged in some spirited discussions about this. Never defensive, Ray invited me to participate in his qualitative research seminar. Seeing it as much as a challenge as a learning opportunity, I agreed. Although I stubbornly held my ground during the semester, the group discussions about topics like meaning and understanding, and Ray's interesting research projects, resonated with my "latent" philosopher. The experience further loosened my previously unshakable confidence in the discovery of truth through empirical research.

SCENE 9: EVALUATION IN THE REAL WORLD

One of my responsibilities at Cornell was to direct the evaluation of a social services training project in upstate New York. The project, which spanned several counties, involved different training programs for state social services staff and managers. Naturally I was determined to do all I could to develop and implement a rigorous evaluation. This meant developing a strict research protocol, using a pretest-posttest design to assess changes in knowledge and performance over time based on standardized self-report measures and performance indicators. Duly prepared, I confidently embarked on the evaluation—and was stunned by how quickly my plans unraveled. What I did not anticipate was the impact of administrative and political factors. Neither the training nor the evaluation held the same meaning for many of the participants as they did for me. For example, being allowed, or in some cases compelled, to attend the training could function as a reward or a punishment, which had a substantial impact on participants' assessment of its value. For many workers, the evaluation was another form of potential sanctioning, and many were reluctant to participate. Also, there were numerous disruptions, absences, and restrictions, which left my "rigorous design" barely recognizable. In one agency, for example, no space was allocated for my primary performance measure—role-plays with the workers. The only space available was the bathroom, not quite the setting I had in mind, but we used it. I *had* to have performance measures.

Although I continued my evaluation efforts while attempting to make adjustments and accommodations, the experience was frustrating. It also helped me to see (although I could not articulate it at the time) how methodological prescriptions and descriptions of evaluations differed from what they looked like in "real time." There was so much going on that was not captured by my measures. How could the realities of the text and experience be so different? Another question mark appeared.

SCENE 10: LIFE HAPPENS

In the summer after completing my first academic year at Cornell, my wife (now my ex) was expecting our third child. The pregnancy had gone well, and, given the excellent health of our other two children, we had every expectation of another healthy child. It was not to be. The birth of our son Joshua raised little initial concern, although we were puzzled about why he would not nurse. Still, he looked fine, and the doctor gave him an Apgar score of 9.[8] Some hours later, after I jubilantly returned home, I received a call from my wife. "He has a cleft palate," she blurted out crying. Oh God, I thought. This is terrible. Tears started rolling down my cheeks. The cleft was of the soft palate, which is why it was not visible to us. This also seemed to explain his inability to nurse.

I hung up the phone trying to process this unimaginable development. Little did I know, however, that the magnitude of Josh's problems was only beginning to be revealed. Shortly thereafter, we learned that Josh had a ventricular septal defect (VSD)—a hole in the wall between the right and left ventricles, a hypospadias,[9] rocker bottom feet, a vertical talus, and most ominous, the possibility of a genetic disorder—trisomy 18—that, according to the literature I read at the time, was usually accompanied by "severe mental retardation" and death by age seven. Suddenly the cleft palate seemed almost inconsequential. At one day old, Josh's color was bluish and he was hypotonic. We did not think he would survive. Since the hospital did not allow children on the ward, I brought our other two children, aged two and seven, to the window of my wife's first floor room so they could see their brother for what we thought would be the first and last time.

On the second day of Josh's life, a decision was made to transfer him to Upstate Medical Center in Syracuse, where they had a neonatal intensive care unit (NICU). Walking into the NICU was entering a world I did not know existed, an alien world of babies in incubators, many of whom were so small and wrinkled that they resembled hatchling birds. They were attended by people in gowns and masks who checked the multiple tubes attached to their tiny bodies. It was also a world of strange sounds: beeps from various monitors and alarms when someone's little heart or lungs stopped working. In the midst of this cacophony of sight and sound lay Josh. It felt surreal and too much to process.

One of the hardest things to deal with was the uncertainty. At first the concern was simply Josh's survival; however, about a week after he arrived at the NICU, his condition stabilized enough that he was sent home. We were given a stethoscope and told to monitor his heart rate because an increased rate would be the first sign of (his expected) heart failure. Josh's chromosome studies came back normal so, to our great relief, we were able to eliminate trisomy 18. Still, the future remained uncertain. At this point, the only diagnosis we had was from one doctor in the NICU who told us Josh had "cerebral palsy."

Daily care was quite taxing. Feeding was a huge chore since Josh did not suck and the cleft made him prone to aspirate the drops of milk that were sprinkled into his mouth using a lamb's nipple. Aspiration also caused Josh to make scary choking sounds until the milk ran out of his nose.

Life took on a fractured quality. I felt terrified and numb at the same time. Still, even with Josh's overwhelming needs, our other children needed us too. I wondered how they understood what was happening and the changes it had brought about in their lives. It could not have been easy. I tried to maintain a sense of normalcy and shield them from the nightmare we were living. So when a fair came to town, I took them, smiling and laughing on the outside while struggling to keep my panic from becoming visible.

Josh survived. Surgery repaired his cleft palate and his vertical talus. Casting corrected his rocker bottom feet. His VSD miraculously closed spontaneously. What could not be fixed were Josh's significant developmental challenges—at around six months we were told that his lagging head circumference was due to "lack of brain growth." When I asked what we should do, the physician replied, "take him home and love him." I was stunned, unable to fully comprehend what was said. It felt like we and Josh were being sentenced to some unspecified type of incarceration of indeterminate length with no possibility of appeal. Still, all was not negative. Despite these issues and his high degree of dependence on others, Josh was unceasingly happy, highly social, and attractive—features that endeared him to the many people involved in his education and care.

About a year after Josh was born (1978), I left Cornell and took a position in the School of Social Work at Florida State University in Tallahassee. Although I had never envisioned living in Florida, the sunny climate was a draw as Josh's fragile condition kept us homebound—and his uncertain prognosis threatened to keep us so—during Ithaca's long, cold winters. As Josh's survival was no longer a pressing concern, my attention turned to how to help him develop his potential, whatever that might be.[10] Like most people, my firsthand knowledge of people with disabilities was limited, and their invisibility was not something I thought about. Therefore I turned to what I knew—the academic literature—for guidance. I was particularly interested in the behavioral literature since, despite my growing doubts, that was still my primary orientation. Given Josh's age, I focused on early intervention and education programs. Whatever I had imagined I might learn, this was not it. Not only did the language seemed insensitive, but the very humanity of people with disabilities—their uniqueness, talents, strengths, relationships—seemed missing. In short, this was an impoverished view of people that I could not accept.

Josh was my son and I loved him. Despite how others might see him, I saw a little boy reaching for life, an emerging personality who brightened my days with his smile. He was decidedly different from the "mentally retarded" or multiply handicapped person depicted in the literature. He was a whole person defined not by his disabilities, but by all his qualities and relationships. My feelings were captured in a song by the folksinger, now Unitarian Universalist minister, Fred Small. Based on a true story about a man named Leslie who was born with significant disabilities and adopted as a baby by a loving couple, the chorus goes,

> Leslie is different
> Like everyone in the world
> He's kind of awkward, kind of fragile
> Kind of graceful, kind of tough
> He's kind of slow, he's kind of clever
> He's just Leslie, and that's enough

Having Josh in my life led me to reflect on what it meant to be a person and whether Josh had the same rights of citizenship as other people. I remember listening to an audiotape by the spiritual teacher and author Ram Das in which he told the story of a couple whose young child had fallen into a swimming pool and suffered serious brain damage. According to Ram Das, one of their greatest challenges was to come to terms with a new model of what it was to be human. As I listened, I realized this was also my struggle. Did Josh have to demonstrate or earn his humanity through displays of certain qualities or competencies? On its face such a notion seemed absurd if not immoral; however, that was how much of society seemed to treat him.

Unfortunately, although Florida had a more hospitable climate, it also embraced a separatist view of people with disabilities that kept them out of the mainstream of education and society. In Tallahassee children with disabilities were required to go to a "special school" out of sight of "typical" children. I contacted the education administration and school principal, arguing that Josh had a right to attend his neighborhood school and that the school system had a responsibility to provide him with an appropriate education. When they were unresponsive, I sought out other academics and parents of children with disabilities who felt similarly. Eventually we formed an advocacy group called the Family Advocacy Coalition for Excellence (FACE). For the next several years we struggled with school administrators, school boards, and sometimes parents to reform the education system. As with many advocacy efforts, it often felt like two steps forward, one step back, but progress was made. Increasingly I felt that I was living a disconnected life: my professional life in which I espoused empirical research and behavioral interventions, and my personal one in which I railed against segregated education, dehumanizing categorizations (e.g., developmental age), and "factual" assessments that justified the very conditions I found objectionable. Although I tried pushing the behavioral envelope by exploring cognitive processes (for example, how people misconstrue events or probabilities), I did not have an alternative approach that would unify these disparate dimensions of my life.

SCENE 11: DROPPING OUT, TUNING IN, AND STARTING ANEW

Then, in 1983, an unexpected opportunity arose once again. A friend, also a social work academic, asked me to join him in his personal computer software business in Eugene, Oregon. What? Leave academia? Move three thousand miles away to work in a field I knew almost nothing about? Ordinarily I would have rejected such a change, but the timing and circumstances made the offer enticing. I was not particularly happy living in Florida, the salary offered was considerably more than I was making, and it sounded like a potentially interesting venture. Not insignificant were my memories of my father telling me about the regrets he had about roads not taken. I did not want to look back some day and wonder "what if." Finally, after visiting Eugene and learning that Josh could attend a "typical" school, I requested and was granted an unpaid leave of absence from FSU and headed west. While space limitations do not allow me to detail my experience in the software industry, most relevant to this context was that my "dropping out" and eventual return to the academy three years later had the effect of enabling me to start over. Although, as scene 1 illustrated, reentry was not easy and returning to FSU not my first choice, the time interval generated a sense of a "new beginning," an opportunity to explore the effects of a confluence of events on my thinking. As a tenured associate professor, I had the freedom to determine the direction my "new" career would take. I no longer was interested in being a quantitative, behavioral researcher nor limiting my exploration of the many questions and issues that had surfaced over the years. Instead, I decided my "second career" would focus on the study of alternative models of understanding that seemed more congruent with my values and those of the social work profession.

I started reading further in the areas of the philosophy of science, particularly the social sciences, and alternative methodologies of inquiry. During these explorations I came across Ken Gergen's article on the social constructionist movement in modern psychology (1985). Reading his paper felt like an epiphany as many of my inchoate ideas were articulated. Meanings could always be otherwise, and relationships moved to the foreground. Even truth and reality were no longer inviolable, but claims associated with particular historical, cultural, and social contexts. Now I had a new concept and term, social construction, that seemed to hold promise. While this was going on, I was collaborating with my colleague, Shimon Gottschalk, whose knowledge of continental philosophy dwarfed my own. Shimon was a supportive colleague who patiently accompanied me on my intellectual meanderings. Together we published several articles that helped me begin to carve out a new scholarly path. The articles also served as a kind of public announcement (to those who knew me) that my beliefs had changed. Additionally, I began to write about social construction and its potential for social work.

SCENE 12: NEGOTIATING A NEW ME

Not all my colleagues shared my enthusiasm for this new scholarly turn. In fact, some seemed to consider me more like a traitor to the scientific, empirically based social work movement. This became clear after I published an article in *Social Work* critical of the empirical clinical practice (ECP) movement in social work (Witkin 1991).[11] In my article I attempted to unearth some of the unexamined assumptions of ECP and to show that it was inconsistent with its own criteria. Shortly after the paper's publication, I was notified by the editor that a rejoinder was to be published. While that in itself did not surprise me—I knew the paper would be controversial to some—what was surprising was that it was authored by one former and two current colleagues at FSU, and that the focus of their rejoinder was on my "revised views" (see Harrison, Hudson, and Thyer 1992)! Apparently my colleagues considered *changing* my views over seventeen years a valid point of critique. More troubling was the somewhat personal nature of the criticism. University colleagues, two of whom had been friends, writing a critique without warning that was based on my supposed inconsistency—I was not sure what to make of it.

This wouldn't be the only time I experienced criticism or bewilderment regarding the changes in my beliefs. Its most extreme expressions occurred followed my appointment as editor-in-chief of *Social Work*. Here the focus of criticism was not my belief change per se, but what they had changed to. The combination of being in such a visible and influential position while espousing social constructionist (or, as some called it, postmodern) beliefs unleashed a range of responses.

Some were blunt. "Have you lost your fucking mind?" a senior colleague well-known in the field for his research expertise asked me at a conference. Taken aback, I responded with a simple "no" and went on to say something about how I was interested in exploring alternatives to mainstream research. Another senior colleague was more circumlocutory in his criticism, telling me of his concern about the "antiscience" movement in the profession. Since he was unwilling to name me directly, I played dumb and told him that I was unaware of such a movement. Some people refused to speak with me at all. At another conference, a collaborative-minded colleague urged me to talk with the social work representative from the National Institute of Mental Health (whom she knew) about funding possibilities for multiple methodological approaches to research. Coincidentally, as we were talking he walked by, but when she called out to him to talk with me, he quickened his pace and walked hurriedly by, shaking his head and waving his hand in a gesture that we both interpreted as "not interested." Finally, some attacked me in print. "The postmodernist high-jacking of American social work reached its apogee with Stanley Witkin's editorship of the profession's lead journal, *Social Work*" (Stoesz 2002). Not much subtlety there.

I write about these incidents, not because they offended me, but because they illustrate how the social environment can present challenges to developing and maintaining transformative belief change. We all live within knowledge communities that generate, maintain, and reflect the beliefs and commonsense assumptions of their participants. These communities provide order, sensibility, and cohesion to their members. Beliefs (and the people who hold them) based on different assumptions or on devalued or nonrecognized criteria are potentially disruptive or threatening and therefore often marginalized.

This seemed particularly true in my case given the high visibility of my position as editor of *Social Work*. As a former mainstream researcher and supporter of empirical practice, I found it hard to explain such change according to the beliefs of that community.[12] At the interpersonal level, these changes evoked feelings of perplexity, discomfiture, or betrayal among those who saw me as a supportive colleague. Therefore, short of disavowing their own beliefs, my positivist-oriented colleagues countered my new beliefs, ignored them (and me), or engaged in ad hominen critiques. I interpreted the more personal attacks as about differences in our visions about the profession and my detractors' belief that I was undermining their hard-earned progress toward a more scientific and respected social work. Taken together, the effect was to challenge my change and to exert pressure to "return to the fold."

My metamorphosis from realist-empiricist to social constructionist relocated me outside my former community and into a new one. It meant, for example, that I no longer saw empirical data derived from research as unproblematic, nor as the ultimate arbiter of knowledge claims. Instead I now saw beliefs as expressing values, and both as expressions of historical, cultural, and social dynamics. Moreover, I viewed claims to objectivity and truth more in terms of power (e.g., their rhetorical authority) than as a reflection of the real. These changes had profound effects on how I understood myself and others as well as social work practice, research, and education.

SCENE 13: JOINING A NEW CLUB

I felt excited and anxious about the path I was on. My career felt reinvigorated, yet I lacked a supportive community in which I could safely explore these developing ideas. That changed when I learned about the Study Group for Philosophical Issues in Social Work, a loose collective of academics disenchanted with the growing influence of mainstream scientific thought in social work. I first learned about this group through Howard Goldstein, a creative scholar, author, and prolific letter writer. It was through letters some years earlier that I first connected with Howard. He had read an article I had written on cognition and wrote me a long letter that both commended my efforts and raised penetrating questions. This was the beginning of a letter-writing exchange that eventually led to in-person meetings and an important friendship.

I found the camaraderie and support of the study group to be invaluable. Many of the core members, like Ann Hartman, Joan Laird, Dennis Saleebey, Ann Weick, and Howard Goldstein, had forged highly successful careers based on their creative scholarship. Their interest in alternative ideas provided a haven in which I could think out loud without looking over my shoulder, and their own writings were catalytic. Howard was a role model for going against the grain of conventional thought. His brilliant insights and impeccable prose were inspirational, and his "curmudgeony" "bah-humbug" countenance only accentuated his caring and warm heart. My editorship of *Social Work* overlapped with his editorship of the journal *Families in Society*, and we would exchange ideas and drafts of editorials. His critiques were straightforward—no sugar coating or gratuitous back slaps here—yet constructive, helping new ideas emerge. It is hard to overestimate what his support and friendship meant to my explorations of social construction.

The study group eventually evolved into an organization called the Global Partnership for Transformative Social Work, which continues to provide support for "thinking differently" and exploring new or unconventional pathways. I continue my participation in this community without, I hope, closing the door on new possibilities.

REFLECTIONS: SOME LESSONS LEARNED

What ideas or insights, if any, might social workers and other readers glean from this narrative? My own reflections lead me to identify four interrelated, nonexhaustive conditions facilitative of transformative change.[13] When reading, keep in mind that retrospectively extracted from the narrative, these conditions appear more lucid and linear than how I experienced them.

First, there needs to be some inducement to change that is stronger than the inclination to maintain the status quo. If things are going well, why change? In fact, the opposite is often the case—we resist change. Change generates uncertainty, which may seem less desirable or more risky than the current situation.

Our assumptions and beliefs generate orientations (tendencies to view events or people in certain ways, to adopt certain perspectives or positions) and sense-making templates that provide a sense of stability, predictability, and understanding to our lives. These are not easy to give up, as evidenced by my continued adherence to a behaviorist orientation despite growing questions and doubts. As a behaviorist I saw things in terms of contingencies and consequences. I focused on overt behavior with little regard for its potential meanings, contextual nuances, or social dynamics. I made sense of things using this framework and countered and reinterpreted others' interpretations or experiences to fit this framework.

On the other hand, my fascination with relationships and the frustrations I experienced in my work with youth and later on with adult clients evoked a vague but troubling sense that my positivistic behavioral approach (although I did not articulate it in this way at the time) omitted important aspects of human experience. However, although I flirted with change—my brief foray into provocative therapy—I retained my behavioral orientation. It was not until after the birth of my son Josh and the profound and personal disconnect between my own experience and how people "like him" were depicted in the literature and its implications that the scale tipped toward change.

Second, there is an awareness that certain assumptions, beliefs, perceptions, or understandings are connected to the troubling state of affairs. I began to see, for example, how narrowly focusing on Josh's overt behavior reduced his personhood in a way that I found unacceptable.

This awareness does not come easily. Foundational beliefs are often implicit or taken for granted. They form the presupposed backdrop for other beliefs. Additionally, as noted previously, we enact the environments that we discover, or, in constructionist terms, we "actively construct the world of everyday life and its constituent elements" (Gubrium and Holstein 2008). This makes it difficult to let go of assumptions and beliefs that serve us in various ways. Becoming aware of them *and* connecting them to our undesirable state of affairs requires language to name these beliefs and a way of explaining the connection. This does not occur in isolation. Beliefs become manifest in action. My beliefs and their implications became apparent in my attempts to make sense of what was happening in my life and with Josh. I needed others—books, talks, relationships—to see how these beliefs rested on several assumptions about reality.

Third is the recognition and availability of a constructive alternative. We do not simply discard our beliefs without having replacements. To do so would leave us adrift. Alternative positions provide a standpoint that illuminate beliefs and assumptions and provide a new vocabulary for describing our experiences. They help us make sense out of situations in ways that the previous ones did not, and they enable us to move forward from the position in which we previously were stuck.

Not all alternatives, however, lead to transformative change. My dissatisfaction with operant behaviorism led me to explore cognitive models. Although they provided some new concepts, they were not transformative in the sense of replacing foundational assumptions and beliefs. It was not until I encountered social construction and the radical shifts in understanding it proposed that transformative change begin to take form.

Fourth is the need for social support. It helps to have encouragement in times of uncertainty. The trajectory of change is rarely linear, and it is crucial to have support for staying the course. Role models or experienced others can facilitate the articulation of ideas, boost self-efficacy, allay fears of isolation or "craziness," and provide living proof that "it" can be done. Change always occurs in a social, relational context. Both the genesis of change and its maintenance are subject to the vicissitudes of social processes. My changes altered the relationships I had with colleagues. It positioned them to be supportive, neutral, or oppositional. They did not request such change, and to the extent that it invited them to change similarly, it may have been viewed as unwelcome or even threatening, as possibly illustrated by their reactions of incredulity and hostility.[14] The pressure to return to the fold can be difficult to resist without other sources of support. For me, it was essential to find a new community (the Study Group for Philosophical Issues) that encouraged and affirmed my changes.

FINAL THOUGHTS

I have attempted to provide a narrative of transformative change that captures some of its complexities. My narrative contrasts with those that focus on a single, proximal event—usually a religious conversion or traumatic experience—that is considered to be the cause of the change. In my experience, such change is not reducible to one event but the confluence of many events and contingencies. Although some events, such as the birth of my son, are more salient than others, it is hard to know what its impact would have been without all that preceded and followed it, for instance, my hiatus from the academy. Rather than focusing on a single event, it may be more useful to think of transformative change as involving a constellation of events and responses to them. From the single-event perspective, the proximal context associated with change influences its interpretation. A life-changing experience at a revival meeting will be given a religious interpretation; an "a-ha" experience in therapy will be given a psychological interpretation. Looking at transformative change in a more complex way allows for greater diversity in interpretation and perhaps less adherence to a single story to explain how such change occurs. This is not to deny that cataclysmic events that drastically alter people's circumstances or undermine their understandings can lead to transformative change; however, it is not inevitable. Also, I would argue that while such events are potentially catalytic in generating change, they are not necessary for transformation to occur. This is fortunate since we cannot nor should we engineer cataclysmic events in people's lives. As a counterexample, it is not uncommon for students who go through our social constructionist–oriented MSW program to graduate quite changed, although not traumatized, by the experience. During the two-year program they are exposed to and actively engage in numerous experiences—reading, dialogue, lectures, film, field work, supervision—in which their ideas are critically examined, sometimes challenged, and new ideas are proposed. For some this process gradually shifts their understandings in profound ways, for example, from an individualist to a social-relational orientation, from understanding truth as a discoverable, transcultural, atemporal, noninterpretive statement of reality to one that is contingent, plural, local, and historically, culturally, and socially embedded.

It is hard to live in a random universe. We need to make sense of our lives, to discover (or generate) a thread that seems to hold together the variegated tapestry of our experiences. When we have such a thread, we protect it. When it is frayed or cut, we attempt to repair it or find a new one. Social workers and other helping professionals often work with people whose life tapestries are barely holding together. By understanding the complexities of change, I believe we might better assist them in repairing or, if necessary, creating a new tapestry of their lives.

NOTES

1   Youngman developed a style of comedy based on brief comments or retorts to various situations. For example, "I went to the doctor the other day. I said Doc, my leg hurts, what should I do? He said limp!"

2   Looking at this today, I can explain the relational dynamics in ways that seem, to me, reasonably convincing. For instance, from a positioning theory perspective (e.g., Harré and Van Langenhove 1998), the situation could be described as one in which the therapist assumed a position that seemed to disavow the responsibilities associated with those of "therapist." At the same time it positioned

the client as not-a-client in the expected sense, creating for them a sense of uncertainty about the rights and responsibilities of each. However, at the time I contemplated employing this approach, I had no such understanding. In fact, I was motivated more by my feeling of helplessness and the need to do something that might change things for the better.

3   In 1974 Frank and Jeff Brandsma published a book entitled *Provocative Therapy*.

4   Both Levin and Hubert, faculty in the Department of Educational Psychology, have had distinguished careers. Levin in particular has achieved international acclaim, having published more than 375 scholarly papers and been the recipient of several honors and awards from professional organizations.

5   I am struck by how my memory of events does not seem to quite jell with less impressionistic information. For example, I had originally written about the impact of a book, *Single Case Experimental Designs*, by two psychologists, Michel Hersen and Donald Barlow, on single-case designs in social work. Although this book did have a substantial impact, it was not published until 1976, after the publication of some articles on the subject in social work journals and during my final year of doctoral study. Some research helped me to recall that a publication in 1974 by Michael Howe in *Social Service Review* was an important introduction of these designs to the field and to me.

6   A result of the ending of Lyndon Johnson's Great Society.

7   Joel Fischer's "Is Casework Effective: A Review," published in the profession's flagship journal, *Social Work*, in 1973, was the most controversial of these publications. Based on a review of eight studies of social work practice, Fischer concluded not only that there was no evidence to support a claim of social work's effectiveness, but that almost half the studies reviewed showed that clients' conditions actually deteriorated. Not surprisingly, his study evoked strong responses both pro and con, but it was hard to dismiss its potential implications for the profession. At the time I was firmly in the "pro" camp, lauding the exposure of the well-intentioned, but unscientifically based, social work practitioners.

8   An Apgar score is a commonly used measure of a newborn's overall level of health. The highest score is 10.

9   A condition in which the opening of the urethra is on the underside, rather than at the end, of the penis.

10 I am finding it difficult to express the challenges involved in Joshua's care
    during these early years without them overwhelming the rest of this au-
    toethnography. There were so many scary, emotionally wrenching events.
    For instance, Josh developed a high fever the second day after arriving
    in Tallahassee and had his first of several seizures. We rushed him to the
    emergency room, where he underwent a spinal tap. This was how we met
    the person who was to become our pediatrician.

11 The empirical practice movement was the forerunner of what is now evi-
    dence-based practice. Basically, proponents of ECP advocated for the use
    of single-case designs and empirical measures based on a positivist-ori-
    ented philosophy.

12 Interestingly, according to the empiricist doctrine, such change would be
    rational only if it were based on empirical data; however, this would re-
    quire generating data that negated the unquestioned superiority of empir-
    ical data, a highly unlikely occurrence. Also, since empiricist metatheory
    denies or does not acknowledge its own presuppositions or values, basing
    change on such criteria will not have much credibility.

13 I am not willing to call these necessary conditions, although they likely
    are sufficient.

14 This is why some programs designed to help people cope with stress emphasize
    the importance of developing, guiding, and nurturing social support.

REFERENCES

Farrelly, F., and J. Brandsma. 1974. *Provocative Therapy*. Millbrae, Calif.: Celestial
    Arts.

Fischer, J. 1973. "Is Casework Effective? A Review." *Social Work* 18 (1): 5–20.

Gergen, K. E. 1985. "The Social Constructionist Movement in Modern Psychology."
    American Psychologist 40:266–75.

Gottman, J. M. 1982. "Temporal Form: Toward a New Language for Describing
    Relationships." *Journal of Marriage and the Family* 44:943–62.

Gubrium, J. F., and J. A. Holstein. 2008. "The Constructionist Mosaic." In
    Handbook of Social Constructionist Research. Edited by J. A. Holstein and J. F.
    Gubrium. New York: Guilford.

Harré, R., and L. Van Langenhove. 1998. *Positioning Theory: Moral Contexts of
    Intentional Action*. Oxford: Blackwell.

Harrison, D. F., W. W. Hudson, and B. A. Thyer. 1992. "On a Critical Analysis of Empirical Clinical Practice: A Response to Witkin's Revised Views." *Social Work* 37:461–64.

Howe, M. W. 1974. "Casework Self-Evaluation: A Single-Subject Approach." *Social Service Review* 48 (1).

Kuhn, T. S. 1962. *The Structure of Scientific Revolutions*. Chicago: University of Chicago Press.

Mahoney, M. J. 1976. *Scientist as Subject: The Psychological Imperative*. Cambridge: Ballinger.

Mitroff, I. I. 1974. *The Subjective Side of Science: A Philosophical Inquiry into the Psychology of the Apollo Moon Scientists*. New York: American Elsevier.

Stoesz, D. 2002. "From Social Work to Human Services." *Journal of Sociology & Social Welfare* 29 (4): 19–37.

Weick, K. E. 1976. "Educational Organizations as Loosely-Coupled Systems." *Administrative Science Quarterly* 21:1–21.

———. 1979. *The Social Psychology of Organizing*. Reading, Mass.: Addison-Wesley.

Weimer, W. 1979. *Notes on the Methodology of Scientific Research*. Hillsdale, N.J.: Erlbaum.

Witkin, S. L. 1988. "Lag Sequential Analysis in Social Work Research and Practice." *Social Work Research & Abstracts* 24 (3): 17–20.

———. 1991. "Empirical Clinical Practice: A Critical Analysis." *Social Work* 36 (2): 158–63.

Witkin, S. L., J. Edleson, S. Rose, and J. Hall (1983). "Group Training in Marital Communication: A Comparative Study." *Journal of Marriage and the Family* 45 (3): 661–69.

CHAPTER 12

From Advising to Mentoring to Becoming Colleagues

AN AUTOETHNOGRAPHY OF A GROWING PROFESSIONAL RELATIONSHIP IN SOCIAL WORK EDUCATION

▸ *ZVI EISIKOVITS AND CHAYA KOREN*

I gave your proposal a lot of thought and considered it very carefully. I am anxious about leaving my secure job as a social worker with older persons but see a great opportunity here to learn what academia is all about. So I'm taking this chance and here I am.
—Protégé

Welcome to being my assistant. You will not have to make photocopies or make me coffee. I can do that for myself, and besides I have a secretary. You and I will work together, write together, teach and do research together. We don't count hours here, and you don't have to sign in, but you can never sign out. We agree on something that needs to be done and we do it. It can be here, at home, wherever, as long as it gets done. Your academic apprenticeship starts today and will be fun. When you end it you will know how to write articles and proposals and teach like it is the best show in town.
—Mentor

THIS CHAPTER DESCRIBES AND ANALYZES the experience of academic apprenticeship and mentoring from the perspective of mentor and protégé. Several themes are addressed, including the dynamics of the personal and the professional over time; the development of interpersonal relationships; emotions; power, control, and related gender issues; strategies of negotiation; the position of the protégé among peers in light of the relationship with the mentor; writing together; coteaching; doing clinical work and arguing about topics related to clinical work; separation and individuation; and maintaining collegiality and friendship. Several of these topics are examined from a process-oriented, developmental perspective, which focuses on the transition from the role of assistant to that of colleague. Finally, we address what we learned from each other over the years of our collaboration and specifically in the process of writing this autoethnography.

MENTORSHIP, AUTOETHNOGRAPHY, AND SOCIAL WORK: MORE THAN MEETS THE EYE

PROFESSOR: Are you okay talking about your own experience?

PH.D. CANDIDATE: Of course, but nobody at the university has ever asked me about that before.

—C. Ellis

Mentorship, autoethnography, and social work share more than meets the eye. While searching and reading about these topics for the purpose of writing a literature review, we could not help but realize how much they have in common, especially when written from the dual perspective of mentor and protégé.

Autoethnography requires being able to deal with emotion as well as a capacity to be reflexive (Ellis 1999), and the same holds true for a functional mentoring relationship (Johnson and Huwe 2002) and, in many ways, for a meaningful client-social worker relationship (Miehls and Moffatt 2000). One of the aims of mentorship is to enhance professional and personal growth and development (Sambunjak, Straus, and Marusic 2009), and similar claims have been made regarding the outcomes of a good autoethnography (Ellis 1999); hence the necessity for both members of the mentoring dyad to be reflexive and able to deal with emotions (Eby, Rhodes, and Allen 2008). Another similarity between the three undertakings is evident from the suggestion that the social worker's identity is enriched when he or she develops a reflexive self that enhances growth and openness toward the other (Miehls and Moffatt 2000). Autoethnography requires the ability to confront less than flattering discoveries about oneself. Honest autoethnographic exploration and a meaningful mentoring relationship will both generate many fears, self-doubts, and emotional pain (Ellis 1999). To develop as a professional academic in general and as a social work academic in particular, the protégé must be able to deal with constructive criticism. A mentor might, at times, have therapeutic impact on the protégé (Sambunjak, Straus, and Marusic 2009), and autoethnography can have meaningful therapeutic value for its authors and its readers (Ellis 1999). The relevance of the therapeutic dimension in social work training seems obvious. Autoethnography is a process, as is mentorship in social work. No two mentoring relationships are alike, and each autoethnography is unique. Finally, autoethnography aims to turn a personal experience into a cultural interpretation (Ellis 1999), while a mentor should enable his or her protégé's personal insights to enhance overall professional development (Sambunjak, Straus, and Marusic 2009). Continuing this line of thought about the similarities between the three endeavors, there is a growing literature on integrating the personal and the professional self through reflective experiential learning in social work (Taylor and Cheung 2010).

The similarities mentioned between client–social worker and mentoring relationships do not preclude differences between the two. One such difference, which is directly relevant to our own autoethnography, is the role of friendship. While client-therapist relationships share many characteristics with friendship, the general tendency in both scholarly literature and practice is a strong preference that they be kept distinct (Callaghan, Naugle, and Follette 1996). In a productive mentoring relationship, by contrast, friendship plays a major role (Martins 2005; Wishart 2006).

To examine the possibilities offered by autoethnography in improving the quality of mentoring relationships, we briefly reviewed definitions of mentoring, theoretical frameworks, and empirical findings related to mentoring relationships in academia in general and social work in particular and asked what is known about functional and dysfunctional mentoring. Finally, we examined methodologies used by empirical studies and suggested that some critical questions can be explained only by doing qualitative research and more specifically by autoethnography (Ellis 1999), such as the one we conducted.

WHAT IS MENTORSHIP ALL ABOUT? DEFINITIONAL ISSUES

The mentorship is especially productive when the mentor believes he or she can learn from you, and the relationship is a two-way street.
—Katherine Hansen

Mentoring in academic education can be traced back all the way to Socrates's protégé, Plato (Campbell 2008). Within academic disciplines of human behavior, it can be illustrated by relationships between such important personalities as Sigmund Freud, who mentored Carl Jung, and Harry Harlow, who mentored Abraham Maslow (Eby, Rhodes, and Allen 2008). All these dyads are characterized not only by the stature of the figures involved but also the different professional path ultimately developed by the protégé, a path that often led to new schools of thought and considerable conflict with the mentor. In other words, being mentored does not by any means imply staying on the beaten path. Quite often new paths are opened up, and much time and reflection are needed by others in the same professional field in order to recognize the similarities and the differences between mentor and protégé.

Mentoring within the profession of social work has received little attention (Collins 1994; Wilson, Valentine, and Pereira 2002). The literature that exists refers to two main domains: one relates to the mentoring of students and social workers within agencies (Collins 1994), while the other relates to mentoring students and young faculty within schools of social work (Wilson, Valentine, and Pereira 2002; Simon et al. 2004). The latter is the focus of this autoethnography. While the specific literature on mentoring in social work is scarce, most general literature on mentoring is also pertinent to the particular circumstances of social work.

Mentoring is an old phenomenon, yet there is no consensus on its definition. The disagreements revolve around several issues, such as the appropriate level of emotional intimacy, age differences between mentor and protégé, duration, formality, and the functions of the relationship (Eby, Rhodes, and Allen 2008; Sambunjak, Straus, and Marusic 2009). For example, Johnson (2008) and Mullen (2008) refer to situations in which the student is assigned to the mentor as formal academic mentoring, while informal mentoring would mean that two parties chose each other of their own volition. Campbell (2008), by contrast, argues that as long as mentorship takes place within an academic setting, it is considered formal even when the participants choose the relationship.

This lack of consensus makes comparisons across studies difficult, particularly when no operational definition is provided (Johnson, Rose, and Schlosser 2008). On the other hand, it can be said that operational definitions may become impediments in the conceptual development of the term, restricting it to its measurement. However, several issues related to mentoring are generally agreed on (Eby, Rhodes, and Allen 2008): (1) each mentorship relationship is unique; (2) mentoring is a partnership of knowledge acquisition and learning; (3) mentoring is a process; (4) a mentoring relationship is reciprocal yet asymmetrical because, although mutual benefits exist, the stated goal is protégé growth and development (Zerzan et al. 2009); and (5) the relationship is a dynamic one, and its impact increases over time. Mentor-protégé relationships can be mistaken for other types of relationships, such as adviser-advisee, teacher-student, supervisor-supervisee, coach-client, or role model-observer, which are akin but not synonymous. These relationships, including mentor-protégé, can be evaluated across several relational dimensions, such as context, influence, mutuality, relationship initiation (formal or informal), intimate closeness, interaction, and power differences (Eby, Rhodes, and Allen 2008). The uniqueness of the mentor-protégé relationship is that it can be simultaneously high in mutuality, informal or formal, high in intimate closeness and change from a high to low power differential (Eby, Rhodes, and Allen 2008).

Eby, Rhodes, and Allen conclude that faculty-student mentorship should be viewed as an essential part of a student's educational experience, providing an opportunity to learn beyond the classroom and to identify with the specific academic institution. It includes providing knowledge, support, and guidance on academic issues such as classroom teaching performance and research skill building, as well as nonacademic issues connected with identity and personal problems. It builds both student-faculty relationships and student-to-student relationships.

The lack of consensus relating to definitional issues has an impact on the theoretical framework and on operational definitions of the concept of mentoring, as will become evident in the following section.

MENTORING RELATIONSHIPS: THEORETICAL FRAMEWORK

If you treat an individual as he is, he will remain as he is. But if you treat him as if he were what he ought to be and could be, he will become what he ought to be and could be.

—Johann Wolfgang von Goethe, *Wilhelm Meister's Apprenticeship*

Initially mentoring was treated as a developmental issue (Hunt and Michael 1983; Levinson 1978). Levinson (1978) suggested that mentorship is an essential stage in young adult development, with emphasis on male development, while Hunt and Michael (1983), emphasized how the different developmental stages of the protégé and the mentor (age and age differences, gender, duration of mentorship relationship, and personality) play a part in the relationship. Other developmental models relate to attachment styles based on attachment theory (Wang et al. 2009). Yet others refer to Bandura's (1977) social learning theory, which relates to modeling (Johnson, Rose, and Schlosser 2008). Hunt and Michael (1983) addressed additional contextual issues, such as academic environment, events or changes that may lead to new stages of the relationship, and the outcome of the relationship for both participants and academia.

Functional models such as Kram's (1985) add mentor functions, including behavior and roles. These functional models relate to the difference between career and personal mentoring. Variance theory (O'Neil and Wrightsman 2001) integrates developmental and other models relating to (1) primary factors including roles, personality context, and diversity; (2) relationship parameters including degree of mutuality and reciprocity, breadth and depth of the relationship, degree of congruence between protégé's and mentor's needs, values and goals, and sensitivities; and (3) interpersonal terms, including what actually happens within the relationship.

More recently perceived similarities between mentor and protégé (Owen and Zende-Solomon 2006) and commitment fit (Poteat, Shockley, and Allen 2009) have also been addressed. Although attempts are being made to establish theoretical models of mentoring relationships, there is still a need for a more solid theoretical grounding in this domain (Johnson, Rose, and Schlosser 2008).

BETWEEN FUNCTIONAL AND DYSFUNCTIONAL MENTORING RELATIONSHIPS

When students come to me for advice concerning their mentor relationship, I always say that as long as the advantages outweigh the disadvantages, you're fine.
—Chaya, former protégé

Most of the literature presents the functional part of mentorship by indicating positive aims, motives, and outcomes for protégé as well as for mentor (e.g., Zerzan et al. 2009). Protégés were found to benefit by professional and personal growth and development (Sambunjak, Straus, and Marusic 2009), career advancement, productivity, initial employment, psychological health benefits, and professional confidence and identity development. The benefits to the mentor have received less empirical treatment (Johnson 2008) and include personal satisfaction in seeing the student's growth, personal fulfillment through working with talented students and passing along skills to the next generation of scholars, staying current in one's field of research, gaining a reputation as a talent builder for academic apprenticeship, and establishing relationships that become more collegial and reciprocal (Johnson 2008; Zerzan et al. 2009).

In spite of the mutual benefits, since we are dealing with relationships, some fluctuation can be expected, and some unpleasant elements arising from conflict, value differences, and divergent interests may lead us to the dark side of mentorship. Thus focusing solely on the bright side would necessarily lead to an incomplete picture (Johnson and Huwe 2002).

Dysfunctional mentorship means that the relationship is no longer functional for at least one member of the dyad. This could result from an interaction between the following parameters: (1) a poor match between mentor and protégé with regard to personality, communication style, relationship style, career stage, or career interests (Sambunjak, Straus, and Marusic 2009); (2) the mentor's technical incompetence (i.e., he or she is not familiar with essential methodology needed for the specific dissertation); (3) relationship incompetence (i.e., the mentor has poor interpersonal skills); (4) mentor's neglect of the protégé; (5) relationship conflict (i.e., clashing expectations regarding what the mentorship should entail) (Sambunjak, Straus, and Marusic 2009); (6) violation of boundaries; (7) exploitation; (8) attraction; (9) unethical or illegal behavior; (10) abandonment; (11) problems connected with cross-gender and cross-race mentoring (i.e., a poor fit between the two parties due to gender or racial differences); or (12) protégé traits behavior (Johnson and Huwe 2002).

A dichotomy between functional and dysfunctional mentoring might seem too simplistic. We therefore suggest that mentors and protégés examine their relationship based on these parameters and locate the relationship on a continuum, with one end presenting the functional and the other the dysfunctional possibilities mentioned above. Such conceptualization may enable us to examine the balance between advantages and disadvantages; the extent to which basic needs are being met; and emotions and emotional states in the mentoring relationships (Johnson and Huwe 2002).

METHODOLOGY

> By exploring a particular life, I hope to understand a way of life, as Reed-Danahay (1997) says.
> —C. Ellis

Most studies on mentorship in academia examine the protégé's perspective (Johnson, Rose, and Schlosser 2008). The same holds true for the literature on social work mentoring (Wilson, Valentine, and Pereira 2002). Studies from the perspective of mentors are scarce in the academia in general (Sambunjak, Straus, and Marusic 2009) and in social work in particular (Collins 1994). Examining an inherently dyadic structure from the perspective of only one individual provides a limited picture of the phenomenon (Eisikovits and Koren 2010; Thompson and Walker 1982). However, recent quantitative (e.g., Allen and Eby 2008; Poteat, Shockley, and Allen 2009; Wang et al. 2009) and qualitative studies (e.g., Gardner and Lane 2010) have examined the relationship from a dyadic perspective, thus providing a more comprehensive view (Eisikovits and Koren 2010; Thompson and Walker 1982).

Within the profession of social work, research has shown that mentorship is an important factor in facilitating career development, career success, and career satisfaction of both protégés and mentors in social service agencies (Collins 1994). Within academia, new faculty in departments of social work believe that mentoring provides them with multiple benefits, including improved teaching and research performance (Wilson, Valentine, and Pereira 2002). Quantitative studies on mentorship in academia relate to relationships between a series of variables (e.g., Poteat, Shockley, and Allen 2009) and to outcomes of mentorship (e.g., Sambunjak, Straus, and Marusic 2006). They do not, however, address the meaning of the mentoring relationship, a meaning that can be captured only through qualitative analysis (Sambunjak, Straus, and Marusic 2009). We identified one such study recently conducted on the personal mentor-protégé relationship using an autoethnographic approach (Gardner and Lane 2010). Not only did it give the authors the opportunity to relate their unique experience as mentor and protégé, but it also served as a means for learning about such a relationship specifically within the context of a nursing education program. In a broader sense, then, this study facilitates the identification of the general from within the particular.

Procedure and Analysis: How We Do It and What It Means

Using an autoethnographic approach that relates to the perspective of the mentor and the protégé elicits in-depth, insider perspectives on an academic mentorship relationship from the viewpoint of both participants in the process. Our autoethnography is mainly retrospective and relates to the mentorship by recalling the process (Ellis 1999; Gardner and Lane 2010). We generated joint and separate accounts of the various stages in the relationship, both in writing and orally.

Ethical Considerations

As Ellis (1999) points out, our stories and experiences are told within the context of our lives and those who share our lives. Telling our stories necessarily reveals aspects that relate to the lives of significant others, who are not always interested in such exposure. We addressed this issue by shielding identities and altering information without changing the essence of our stories and experiences.

Our autoethnography is more evocative (along the lines suggested by Ellis and Bochner 2007) than analytic (as suggested by Anderson 2007). We present our narrative as a whole while discussing its meaning and integrating relevant literature.

●   ●   ●

Here is our narrative of mentoring, as we understand it at this time.

ZVI: My colleague and friend Stan always finds these creative ways to think about social work. His conferences are not conferences in the classical sense but rather opportunities to raise ideas, free oneself from the chains of academic convention, and talk about the professional and the personal all at once. He is teaching us all to think outside the box (e.g., Witkin 1999), which is just fine with me and goes along well with autoethnography as described by Ellis and Bochner (2007). So when he asked me to participate in his new idea, this book, I paid attention. Then I spoke to Chaya, and what we present here is the outcome of our joint endeavors. I thought that this "rite of passage" would be a good opportunity to further our relationship. It would give us the chance to reflect on our work and relationship retrospectively and see what we and others can learn from it (Ellis 1999). I said to Chaya, "Now that I've lost you as my assistant, let's see what went on and what we can make of it."

CHAYA: I thought of it as gaining a colleague, but I guess we cannot avoid the fact that I am no longer his assistant, and I think it is a great opportunity for us to reflect on what these years were all about. A few months ago Zvi told me that he had been invited to write a chapter on using autoethnography in social work and suggested that we write something together, asking if I would be interested. "Of course I'm interested," I said, "I enjoy working with you and I am honored that you chose me." We had to think of a topic that concerns us both in order to write an autoethnography together. I do not remember all the ideas that surfaced, but it didn't take long to settle on writing about the mentoring relationship and using ourselves as a case in point while aiming to turn a personal experience into a cultural interpretation (Ellis 1999).

ZVI AND CHAYA: We both feel that this is a great opportunity to reflect on our five-year mentoring relationship as it shifts toward a more collegial one, while also sharing our experiences with others to enhance the understanding of mentoring relationships (Ellis 1999). However, along with this excitement and due to the evocative, emotional aspect of our experience (Ellis and Bochner 2007), uncertainties and anxieties arose.

ZVI: I read our draft over; it seems to me we are missing out on something. It reads too rosy. It is too nice to be authentic. I think we are missing some of the heavier emotional stuff; we are glossing over the times we really did not like what went on: that we hurt each other, that we wished this thing would be different.

CHAYA: (*Sighing*) You are bringing up something that if I think out loud I agree with. I guess there is no way around it; we need to get into the real stuff.

ZVI: I guess we will need to elaborate more on the personal aspects of the relationships we have. How we deal with boundaries? How we hurt each other? What we expect from each other? What is our mutual place among other close people? Family? Other friends? Colleagues at work?

CHAYA: Perhaps we should look at some questions that express some of our concerns. As we move on, we should double check if we address them. For instance: What will working on this project do to our relationship? How will it affect it?

ZVI: What consequences can we expect from openly dealing with the hardships and heartbreaks that were part and parcel of the overall experience? Will we be able to be honest and authentic about our experience?

CHAYA: What will we discover about our relationship and ourselves? What will we share with our readers without harming others or ourselves?

•   •   •

And so our story begins.

CHAYA: Do you remember, Zvi? It all started with the initiative of my primary Ph.D. adviser at the time, who was previously my M.A. thesis adviser. We both realized that neither of us had sufficient knowledge of how to conduct an extensive qualitative study, which has been described as potential reason for a dysfunctional mentoring relationship (Johnson and Huwe 2002). She asked me if I would want you to join as Ph.D. adviser, and I was very excited about the idea because I knew that you were considered *the* expert on qualitative research in our faculty, and I was hoping that you would agree.

ZVI: I was interested and could help with qualitative methodology but had little interest or knowledge in gerontology at that time. But why were you interested in doing a qualitative study? I told you all the disadvantages of being a qualitative researcher in an essentially positivist academic environment. I continued using this dissuading strategy as you told me you remained interested.

CHAYA: I had some interest in qualitative research as graduate student. I was quickly persuaded that I need to first learn quantitative research skills and that I can consider qualitative research at a later stage. Thus my M.A. thesis was quantitative. Data were collected using a structured questionnaire that included several quantitative tools. To collect data from older persons, it was recommended to read the questions and the optional answers to them and fill in their choices. The topic was on the meaning of life after losing a spouse. The issue of meaning in life triggered very interesting in-depth discussions with the research participants, which fascinated me much more than the statistics I performed on the questionnaires. Thus I decided that my Ph.D. thesis would be qualitative.

ZVI: OK. This took care of it. I decided that if you wanted it badly enough, we should try it. I did have a vague interest in old people's emotional world. I grew up with aging parents and was getting to the age myself in which I needed to deal with some issues of aging. So I figured perhaps you could teach me something. With our mutual interest in place, we started to search for what else brings us together. Although, in a way, we were the product of "matchmaking," I think it is safe to say that we chose each other, as we both had the option to refuse but did not. From the onset our mentoring was informal (Johnson 2008; Mullen 2008), although some would refer to it as formal owing to the academic context in which it occurred (Campbell 2008).

CHAYA: As a Ph.D. student I began to attend your seminar on theory building. At the first meeting of this seminar, each student introduced himself or herself and the research topic. I was one of the last students to present and was grateful that I just finished reading "Narrative Research: Reading, Analysis and Interpretation (Lieblich, Tuval-Mashiach, and Zilber 1998), which I thought would come in handy. At the time I was working as a social work practitioner at an old-age home and hoping that with a Ph.D. I would be able to get more exposure to academic life, have an opportunity to research a topic that I was curious to learn more about, both theoretically and empirically, and improve my employment options. The topic of my dissertation, "The Meaning of Second Couplehood in Old Age," reflected the meaning old age has for me, as a period that is not necessarily only about decline, loss, and deterioration but also an opportunity for growing and development (Koren 2011). This coincided well with the stage of life in which I found myself at the time: forty-three years old, married with three young children, believing that it is never too late to try and fulfill goals and dreams like mine, which were to develop an academic career I never had the opportunity to fulfill earlier because I was busy raising our children and supporting my husband's career by working only part time.

Zvi, when you asked me in class about my proposed research topic, I said that I wanted to learn more about older people who had created a second couplehood relationship in old age through their life stories. You listened and asked me, "Do you know what an 'epiphany' is?" I remember thinking that fortunately, at some point in my past I took an English literature course in which I learned short stories by James Joyce, who refers to the concept of epiphany. I said yes, and I could see that you were surprised. Then you proceeded to ask me, "So what is it?" I explained that epiphanies are turning points in the protagonist's narrative. I think you were impressed. I realized that prior knowledge and a broader education, which went beyond the specific discipline of social work, would be far more useful than I'd imagined.

ZVI: It certainly helped me realize that you had a well-rounded general education-al background. After class I approached you and said you should make an ap-pointment with me through my secretary. As dean of the College of Health and Human Services at the time, I was extremely busy, and it was quite an elaborate process to schedule a meeting with me. I personally made sure that the meeting would happen (and you told me that you were flattered by this). This was the rite of passage by which mentorship began (Hunt and Michael 1983), and we know now, in retrospect, that it was a statement of intentions by both of us.

CHAYA: I prepared for our meeting intending to present what I had worked on up to that point on my dissertation. However, when our meeting started you suggested that we leave the research aside because you wanted to discuss "some-thing more important." You were looking for a research and teaching assistant and said that you wanted to interview me for the job. I was very curious to hear what you had in mind; the way you said it convinced me that it would be worthwhile.

ZVI: I was dean of the College of Welfare and Health Sciences. That alone was a full-time job and kept me busy from morning to night. It was a growing col-lege. I wanted it to grow faster, and the university placed a high priority on it. We were trying to develop many graduate programs and new administrative units. I tried not to neglect my academic career, as I knew that I would want to return to my role as a researcher and a professor before too long. My writing and research were at the heart of my professional preoccupations, but my time was consumed by administration and organizational development. I was think-ing at the time that a good research assistant would serve as a viable link with my academic work, and so I was searching for a serious and reliable person who could do the job. In addition, I was very ill. I had been suffering from a chronic intestinal disease, which required surgery. I had indeed been operated on twice, but both surgeries failed. So when you came into my professional life I did not have a large margin for error. I also had little time for experimentation. I got the word out that I needed someone reliable who could collaborate with me on research and that—given that I required a full-time commitment to a position with little compensation—it would be unfair for me to employ someone who was not interested in an academic apprenticeship and a Ph.D. The position was such that it would be worthwhile only for someone who had a broader motiva-tion than merely making a salary (Eby, Rhodes, and Allen 2008). I also told you that for the last ten years I have employed research and teaching assistants who went on to develop academic careers, an expected outcome of faculty-student mentorship (Eby, Rhodes, and Allen 2008). I really had these high, perhaps un-realistic expectations from the job. I wanted someone who would be willing to begin an academic apprenticeship yet be capable enough to behave like a col-league; to be free yet committed to the job and never try to count hours and look at the clock; to be interested in the kind of research I do, yet to be coura-geous to argue with me rather than just submit to my ways; to be committed to me personally and tolerate my health status. I really did not think such person existed, but still I wanted someone like that. I had this intuitive feeling that Chaya comes as close as one can to this ideal. It was an intuitive feeling that had no rational grounds. It worked. I remember telling you at the beginning that I do not expect you telling me things about yourself that I would refuse to share with you. I told you that I was married with a son living abroad and told you about my health situation briefly.

CHAYA: I went along with your modeling and told you that I too am married for twenty years, with three children, and that I was working part time as a social worker in an old-age home alongside my studies. I also signaled that I was ready for a change and had every intention to get into academia. I told you that I was willing to take certain risks to grow within my limits. I was struggling between my security needs and my urge to develop.

ZVI: I was happy to hear this because I wanted someone in a stable personal situ-ation, someone upon whom I could rely in terms of personal and professional availability. You left me with a feeling of being there in every way.

CHAYA: You told me about a previous assistant who would disappear every time he had a fight with his girlfriend, and another assistant who had to take mater-nity leave, which you fully supported. Nevertheless, despite the empathy you have for their human situations, and because of your own personal circumstanc-es at the time, you were seeking a different experience. I thought to myself that there are advantages to being older than the average Ph.D. candidate. I felt I could really and fully dedicate myself to academic work with you, and that this was a great opportunity for me. I felt you were warm, willing to give, and not condescending; you conveyed at the same time that you needed me, and as such you were conveying strength in your vulnerability. My practical side was also satisfied with the feasibility of the arrangement. I thought to myself, although all three of my children were of school age, I could still manage three full work-ing days at the university. My children were young but not too young to be able to take care of themselves a few hours after school until I returned home. I felt that my personal situation fit in well with what you were looking for.

ZVI: All of the above was a solid indication that there would be a good match between us as mentor and protégé (O'Neil and Wrightsman 2001).

CHAYA: Regarding the so-called more professional skills and qualifications for the job, you emphasized that academic life in Israel requires English proficiency. Today this reminds me of the joke you often tell about the value of Hebrew manuscripts for academic accreditation: "If God were to apply for a tenure-track position at the University of Haifa, he wouldn't be accepted because he only wrote one book and it's in Hebrew." I laughed, and today I tell this to my students. At the time I responded that, to some extent, I'm bilingual as I was born in the United States and immigrated to Israel as a young child with my family. In the years since then, I had kept up my English through reading, and when I write in English, I think in English.

ZVI: I remember you told me that at the time, you had already submitted two articles, which were cowritten with a colleague in English.

CHAYA: And on that basis I told you that you could definitely rely on my English proficiency. I further had the impression that my competencies were adequate enough to constitute a solid base for building a confident relationship. I felt safe about my English and felt this is important to you so we could go with that.

ZVI: I offered you to be my research and teaching assistant along with being your dissertation adviser, provided that you quit your job as social worker in the old-age home and dedicate your efforts to academia. I told you that I do not believe in part-time commitments, and that academic life is in many ways like priesthood and involves total dedication and commitment.

CHAYA: I responded that as long as the work interests me I don't mind working 24/7. You told me that you would try to get me full employment as research and teaching assistant and that it would not make sense for me to work with you on a part-time basis. It took me some time to fully realize how right you were. I was overwhelmed by your offer, since I realized that this was the opportunity I had been waiting for: someone to mentor me in developing an academic career. I felt you had given me a vote of confidence and that you believed in my ability to fulfill your expectations as your research and teaching assistant, and I very much wanted to accept your offer on the spot. However, I felt that I had to consult with my husband before doing something drastic like quitting my job, which came with a certain degree of security, as well as a monthly salary, a pension program, social security benefits, etc. Later on, when often overwhelmed by work, I reminded myself that this is far more enjoyable than my previous work at the nursing home. Once the scholarship was approved, I gave notice of resignation to my previous employer and began to work with my mentor-to-be, who turned out to be one of the most significant figures in my life on the professional as well as on the personal level. This does not mean it was all a rose garden; there were definitely cloudy periods with rain and storms along with the sunshine, and this should be mentioned in order to avoid a biased picture.

I felt compassion for your medical situation. I watched you suffer, and there were days when I wondered how you could come to work. I felt the desire to help you with your academic work and relieve you of some of the teaching obligations and research assignments. I was eager to start with the literature review on existential phenomenology in social work, the first assignment you asked me to work on. Remember that? I started reading up on phenomenology and gradually realized how phenomenological my thinking was and how much I was attuned to this perspective, and later I employed it as a theoretical framework for my dissertation. I remember how I identified with the existential-phenomenological ideas of subjectivity, stating that reality is constituted by multiple subjectivities, and that each person interprets situations in his or her unique way, thus learning the distinction between real and true. I felt in a way that I had "come home" in both the professional and personal sense. Sharing a worldview is a key aspect of a functional mentoring relationship (Kram 1985). On the professional level we share an existential-phenomenological worldview, which is neither the mainstream perspective taught at the schools of social work in Israel nor an approach that has been adopted by most social workers in the field. Moreover, we shared a disagreement with, and even hostility toward, the reigning psychodynamic perspective, which maintains that most of our personality lies in the unconscious and can be retrieved only by the therapist, who therefore knows more about the person in therapy than that person knows about himself or herself (Van Deurzen 2010).

ZVI: Our joint hostility to the psychodynamic perspective grew out of the belief that such perspectives facilitate an abdication of responsibility by people for their own behavior (Spinelli 1989). Our conversations at the time focused on concepts and experiences of power, symmetry/asymmetry in therapy and life, responsibility and the inevitability of decision making, as well as freedom and the limitations imposed on it. I remember talking to you about the rigidity of using the DSM and the diagnostic categories. I told you about the case of a person in a mental hospital who was catatonic. He told me that he was made out of glass and broke every time they gave him an injection in his back. I persuaded him to get the shot on an imaginary line between his leg and his back.

I drew the line, and the nurse gave the shot without the guy breaking. You told me that this was a great example of focusing on the experience rather than the diagnosis, and we used this example to teach experiencing rather than knowing. In another instance we discussed our personal experience of being named as diagnostic categories ("the diverticulitis by the window") rather than by our names, and how deindividuating that was. The professional and the personal were mixed together, and we often did not know whether we were talking about "them" or "us."

Several things contributed to making our relationship closer. I felt that despite of my suspicious nature, I could trust you. You were reliable and loyal. In my Hungarian culture, these were and remain essential. You were sensitive to my health situation and were able to take it into account in a manner that bordered on sacrificing your own comfort and time. You would do a whole series of tasks, which you alone assigned to yourself, and would complete them even before the deadlines we had agreed on. I often thought it was too good to be true. Once I develop this level of trust, I am more effective and pleasant in my working environment. Your quiet way of being was in sharp contrast to my hyperactive and direct style, and when these blended together they "produced" a Zvi that seemed more tolerable for students and colleagues. That along with the high quality of your work could be considered an additional benefit of mentorship for the mentor (Johnson 2008).

CHAYA: On the personal level, it turned out that you and your family are from the same origin as my husband's family. This contributed to a sense of cultural affinity, which enhanced the functional mentoring relationship (Johnson and Huwe 2002; Sambunjak, Straus, and Marusic 2009). I was familiar with the culture, which is characterized by a certain sense of humor and some level of cynicism, both of which I lacked but understood well and have since improved to the point where I find myself at times telling your jokes in my classes. For instance, you used to tell and retell the joke about your mother-in-law: "In the beginning I did not like her, and now I like her as much as I did in the beginning." Our good fit is due to the combination of similarities and differences, and the way in which we complement one another in the personal, psychological, and sociocultural realms (Johnson and Huwe 2002; Sambunjak, Straus, and Marusic 2009). For example, you have the tendency to be associative when teaching your classes (e.g., when a student asks a question, you answer in-depth even when the material is not part of the lesson plan), which makes them very interesting yet at times hard to follow. For instance, you can take off on the topic of conflict and move it between the personal inner levels of conflict to the social structural one when the class is dealing with just understanding the Conflict Tactics Scale (Straus 1979), which aims to measure intimate partner violence. At times, however, by the end of the session you hadn't covered everything you wanted. Here is where I came in, with my tendency to be very structured or, as you say, "obsessive," in the positive sense. The truth is that at the beginning I was offended that you referred to me as "obsessive," and I even thought about how I might change this trait. Following the "honeymoon phase," this was the first time I felt offended and recognized some level of misfit between us, until things were cleared up by your explanation regarding the functionality of my "obsessive nature" (in the sense of style, not disorder).

ZVI: I kept trying to persuade you that your "obsessive style" helped me organize my "scattered brain" and get where I wanted and needed to be.

CHAYA: And when I realized this we agreed to preserve it.

ZVI: With time, your obsessiveness softened, and my scattered brain got more structured. My students told me that my associative teaching style works well as long as you told them where it was headed. So our cotaught classes were organized and scattered, systematic and associative at the same time, and my associations and your presentations made it "the best show in town." This does not mean that all the students were satisfied with the two of us teaching together. However, this way of complementing each other worked throughout the relationship we developed and seemed to be functional for both of us.

CHAYA: I agree. Student opinions varied to some extent, and some perceived our teaching as overwhelming, but overall our role division turned out to be functional. For instance, you were conscious of the fact that you tend to live in space, phenomenologically speaking, while I live in time. That often meant that you could stay overtime at a meeting when you enjoy it, without paying attention to the clock; I, on the other hand, tend to value "clock time" and try to remind you that while we both enjoy the space in which we find ourselves, time is almost up, and we have to switch spaces. You came to expect me to move you in and out of spaces and keep your time, which was often an unrewarding task.

ZVI: Indeed, you kept moving me in space. I used to say that you are my GPS. I do know this is not always pleasant, and the audience tends to be hostile toward you rather than me. I was recently more aware of this and tried to spare you from it.

CHAYA: This in itself is wonderful for me to hear because I have difficulties using GPS when I try to get from one place to another. However, you are right. It hasn't always been great fun to stop your narrative and remind you that we need to go. But you got better at this, and I feel more comfortable doing it. We had, as I am sure you remember, our ups and downs.

ZVI: Yes there is no doubt about it that our relationship has had several turning points, some filled with satisfaction and happiness and others with anxiety and suffering, but also the latter helped to deepen and broaden the relationship. We learned that we could deal with most difficult issues openly as long as they were based on mutuality and honesty.

CHAYA: I agree. For instance, after about three months of being your assistant, you told me that you felt I was very distant, and that this would not have happened were you in your usual state of health. You said that if it weren't for your medical situation, you would have invested more energy in getting to know me better by now. This remark made me anxious because I felt you had touched a sore spot. I know that I am usually a reserved person and that it takes me time to open up gradually.

ZVI: I felt I was to blame

CHAYA: And I felt I was. We had many discussions about the issue of distance. They involved personal needs, gender, working style, and cultural values.

ZVI: I remember once telling you about how bad I am with reacting to rejection. I told you my story of immigrating and feeling rejected by my foster parents as a new immigrant in the kibbutz, and how I never forgave them for it. I told you how, as a second generation of Holocaust survivors, I was compared to my deceased brother.

CHAYA: I once shared with you how, during late adolescence, I interpreted being rejected in my family of origin, and how sensitive I was to this. So, on the personal level, we shared this extreme sensitivity to rejection. But, as you recall, it took quite a while to talk these things over.

ZVI: I was aware that you made great sacrifices raising a wonderful family, and I needed to create the opportunity to make up for your "lost time," so to speak. I also recognized the youth and vigor in your willingness to learn and catch up. Yet I was afraid to point to these issues openly because I feared you would misinterpret them.

CHAYA: Your primary concern, as you told me, was to produce opportunities for your mentored students and let them use these. You explained to me that you believed we needed to be particularly aware of this among women.

Your personal investment in this was quite impressive, and it was known that you invested a lot in academic apprenticeships of students, most of whom happened to be women. Here again, our beliefs and interests met. Yet we did take some time before we addressed these openly.

ZVI: We both grew up in guilt-ridden cultures and blamed ourselves for whatever was wrong between us. The case of closeness/distance in our relationship was no exception. While the distribution of self-blame became part of our routine in the relationship, it always helped to discuss things openly, and we never blamed each other.

CHAYA: Yet I felt at that juncture that I needed to learn to open myself up to you and yield to the pressure arising from your expectations of me. I could not ruin it all by appearing closed and distant. This could be interpreted as an illustration of wanting to please due to asymmetry in mentor-protégé relationships, but in this particular issue it went well with my need to take chances at opening up emotionally, even at the price of possibly getting hurt. After all, the relationship was asymmetric by definition, yet this was functional for me at that point in my development.

ZVI: This was also part of the recurring theme we grappled with throughout our relationship: boundaries and their problematic nature in cases when professional and personal intertwine, as happens in case of mentoring (Johnson and Huwe 2002).

CHAYA: Thinking of this retrospectively, I guess it was an invitation to friendship, which is an important aspect of functional mentorship (Kram 1985; Martins 2005; Wishart 2006). Although I felt frightened to open up, I wanted to expand our interpersonal ties and friendship beyond the formal, professionally based one. On the professional level, I knew you were satisfied with my work. As far as that was concerned, I was under the impression that I passed that test. I felt that I wanted to do all I could professionally. There were things I did that I felt were naturally part of the job requirements, but apparently you did not take things for granted, and you let me know that you were grateful for my help (for example, preparing your electronic presentations, and, occasionally, teaching a class for you owing to your very complicated health situation). But then again, I saw this as part and parcel of your mentoring role, because you often listened to how I taught and commented and gave me guidance on improving my pedagogical methods. Your comments referred to details both of content and of style, usually trying to teach me how to be less uptight and more sensitive to my audience.

ZVI: My message was that it is not enough to know; you should be able to share it. "What" and "how" need to go hand in hand.

CHAYA: After several years of watching you and teaching while you were watching me, I overcame my own need for extensive preparation, and I can now finish a whole class without being enslaved by my electronic presentation.

ZVI: As I always told you, "It is there but you should not let it control you."

CHAYA: My weak spot was the ability to combine the professional with the personal without going overboard, on the one hand, and without hiding, on the other. I was afraid that I would overstep my own boundaries, but I was determined to make the relationship work. So I said to myself that I must be more open with you, tell you about my family and my children, and share things with you besides professional ideas, open up, and become a friend. I remember deciding this, but I don't remember what actually happened that started changing things. I was actually glad in a way that I had the opportunity to work on being able to combine the professional and the personal. Later it helped me to realize how our personal relationship enriches our professional one, and the other way around. I started to feel this being transferred to my other relationships. It taught me that it takes quite a bit of professionalism to relate on both the personal and the professional level simultaneously, rather than fighting it because I was afraid of crossing boundaries or mixing them (Johnson and Huwe 2002).

ZVI: My professional education had clear-cut and rigid instructions concerning the distinction between the personal and the professional, yet it provided fewer and less concrete instructions concerning the ability to blend and combine those (Johnson and Huwe 2002). I always had trouble with it for both personal and professional reasons. On the personal level, I had difficulties with developing hierarchical relations and was quite informal and often straightforward, which could also be seen as abrasive. My clinical training was permeated by warnings against countertransference, and my ethical education was geared to avoid the consequences of such mixing at all cost. In light of this, experimenting with the issue in my relations with you was quite complex, and I often felt that I was not able to regulate the interpersonal distance without feeling too close or too far from you. Such challenges occurred often. Chaya, a good example was our meetings to help prepare for your first qualitative interview with a spouse in second couplehood.

CHAYA: We discussed the experience of exposure of the interviewees throughout the interview process and how it affects what we ourselves reflect about in our own personal relationships. For example, I interviewed a couple (each member individually) regarding their previous marriage. Each struggled with trying to share the most intimate parts of their lives with me while trying to avoid a complete exposure of themselves and their relationship. I felt this struggle was highly relevant to my own experience of sharing certain parts of my private life with others. Much of what was said was easily transferable to me. The very opportunity to compare and reflect on their lives along with my own was enriching, and discussing these parallels with you helped me understand better how to deal with them.

ZVI: You learned that similar situations are part and parcel of doing qualitative research, and that we all need to address them at some point in our working life.

CHAYA: It was not always easy; at times I felt exposed to you. What helped was that you made me feel that I am not alone in feeling exposed and dealing with the specific content issues that came up.

ZVI: We all grapple with private issues as we attempt to understand the intricacies of other people's lives (Arnd-Caddigan and Pozzuto 2008).

CHAYA: As I was experiencing this process of trial and error, I gained much understanding of my private life and became strengthened by your support and personal input. I simultaneously felt relieved and much closer to you, through the intimate elements of the experience. I further realized that my choice of research topic was not just the result of my belief in the ability of old people to continue to grow in old age. It had to do with hope. While conducting the interviews, I realized that in the case of each interviewee who told me something about his or her lifelong marriages, there was something I could identify with relating to my own marriage, and that their descriptions of their second couplehood relationship helped me see my own relationships in a new light.

ZVI: Our learning continued to combine the professional with the personal, and often concepts, emotions, norms, and reflective understandings came together in a continuous process of growth for us (Arnd-Caddigan and Pozzuto 2008).

ZVI AND CHAYA: Another turning point in our relationship relates to understanding friendship, including companionship, sharing, and self-disclosure. When these are chosen and voluntary, they are likely to lead to a sense of "we," a mutuality of affection and interests (Wilson 2000).

ZVI: During the second Lebanese war in July 2006, Haifa, where the university is located, was bombed for days. Chaya lives near Tel Aviv, which was not bombed, and when the war broke out she went home to her family and avoided Haifa for several days although she did return to the university long before the war was over. I felt deeply offended that she did not share with me and our other colleagues the first days of crisis. I gave her the message that her blood is not worth more than ours and that I saw her action as a sign of disloyalty to me and to our colleagues as a group. I guess this had to do with some local cultural difference based on the idea that people need to stick together when harm and danger come. Such beliefs were part of the collectivist ethos that was prevalent in the formative period of the state but could have faded during the time of the last war. One could grow up on this as I did, or one could not (as Chaya did not). But I sure took it personally, as I was not aware of her value system at the time. It brought about a lengthy and somewhat tense conversation about what we expect from friends at times of crisis or danger, like war.

CHAYA: My first reaction was that, as a mother to three children, how could I endanger myself by coming to Haifa? On the other hand, do I enjoy the company of my friends at the workplace only in peaceful times or take part in times of crisis as well? How can I balance family and friendship? And I couldn't avoid the question: how significant am I to you, in fact? I didn't want to hide behind my insecurities, however, and after realizing how much you were hurt, I once more faced the fact that I was probably more significant to you and to some of my other colleagues than I'd let myself believe. Once I understood that we are mutually important for each other, the question of danger ceased to be an issue. I returned to the university on a daily basis. I discussed these issues with my family, and they eventually understood the inevitability of traveling to Haifa to join my friends and colleagues during the workday and returning to my family at the end of it as we are used to in our country; life must go on.

ZVI: Our different perceptions and behaviors in such situations caused conflict and disappointment. It was difficult to resolve the differences between us, yet an understanding was reached about the fact that we all despise war and should stick together during such times, along with the understanding that your family also needed you in order to feel safe. However, the most critical point in this event was the realization that even when it is hurtful, we can reach an understanding, which takes into account the perspective of the other. This strengthened our relationship and enabled us to overcome many work-related tensions to come.

CHAYA: Closeness and mutuality have their costs. An important phase in our relationship was realizing that we all live with others and have additional working relationships we need to respect. For example, I had to realize that I was not the only student you enjoyed working with, and that sometimes there were perhaps other students that you preferred to work with rather than me. The realization dawned on me after an article you and I submitted twice had been rejected. I suddenly realized that my friend, who was also your Ph.D. student (though not your assistant), was scheduled to work with you many more hours than she had previously been. Previously I felt uncomfortable when she told me that she needed more time to work with you. After that, I felt that the situation was reversed; that she had much more working time with you than I had. This was happening at a time when I felt that you were disappointed in me because of the rejected article, and I constructed a scenario whereby you were moving on to another, more promising student after I had failed you. I felt betrayed and abandoned; licking my wounds while you both went on to work on something else. Because of insecurities about my professional and personal abilities, I was sure, at the time, that you thought you would get better results by working with her. Only recently have I been able to discuss this incident with you, but it felt good that we could eventually talk about it.

ZVI: Your insecurities and my lack of attention to them because of my overloaded professional life were a constant source of tension in our relationship. On the one hand, we had a close mentoring relationship and an emerging friendship; on the other hand, I was involved in a series of mentoring relationships, which were taking up more of my time than you or I expected, and this often created letdowns.

CHAYA: I obviously did not always like it and would have preferred it to be different. Yet I finally realized that each student has one mentor, but each mentor has several students. One indication of growth and development for me in our joint work consisted of realizing that each mentoring relationship is unique, and that several such relationships can coexist simultaneously rather than at the expense of one another (Eby, Rhodes, and Allen 2008). It took me a long time to realize that you can enjoy working with various students and colleagues, and that you don't think one is better or worse than the other, but merely different. I realize now that our mentoring relationship is unique, without value attribution of better or worse. It is simply different and unique, in the same way that most of the older persons in my study speak about old age: "It's not better or worse than other periods in life, it's simply different."

ZVI: Nowadays when we write together I say, "You've come a long way, I'm proud of you. I am glad you got ahead just in time, as I start going downhill."

CHAYA: I tell you, "You're not going anywhere . . . you are just the way I knew you years ago."

ZVI: The literature mentions the personal satisfaction that mentors have seeing the fruits of their investment (Johnson 2008; Zerzan et al. 2009). However, you often make me think about the Sisyphean task of a mentor, which has received little if any attention in the literature. The more you invest, the better they turn out, but the bigger the loss when they leave. I keep investing in these people, and they grow up and depart, and I am left there to start all over again. Yet I also think about the fact that each and every mentored student gave me another fresh perspective on a series of professional issues and on myself. Each helped me stay open to the future and understand the unique combination of loss and change. It became an antiaging device, providing me with renewed energy and willingness to learn.

CHAYA: Throughout our mentoring relationship, I was confronted by colleagues' remarks that I was exaggerated in my devotion to the role of assistant and that being involved in so many projects and responsibilities would eventually be harmful to my dissertation; that I should start cutting down on my involvement in so many projects with you. Some even went overboard and remarked that I was being exploited and that they had to tell me because they had my best interests at heart. Fortunately I never felt that way and never took them seriously. I replied that I understood from the start what I was getting into, and that I wasn't afraid of hard work, and that what I learned through working on other things applied to my dissertation, for example, qualitative analysis. What could seem to others as dysfunctional in the mentoring relationship (Johnson and Huwe 2002) was actually experienced as very useful.

At present, a little more than two years after the conclusion of my Ph.D. degree, I have an even greater appreciation for the projects I was involved in. They exposed me to researchers abroad and to conferences in which I presented the results of my work with you. As part of my apprenticeship in academia, you taught me how to write research proposals. After I finished my Ph.D., I submitted one on my own. It was recently funded, and I also have lots of data to write from.

ZVI: And since the rejection of that first article, you have published more articles than your peers, some of which we have written together and share authorship for.

CHAYA: I do not take this for granted. I know that a big part of it was due to the mentoring I received and the process I went through.

ZVI: I feel that you keep me on my toes, you don't leave any stone unturned, and I learned from you to be more precise, more thorough, and more grounded in what I write. I also learned from you to be aware of issues concerning what we don't understand and the parameters of what we do. This fostered my authenticity and intellectual honesty.

EPILOGUE

The least happy element in all this is the approaching end. We both know we must let go and nevertheless have difficulty doing so. We very much enjoy working together and have a keen understanding that we have to part, in the sense of transforming our relationship from a mentoring to a collegial one. Indeed, we are in the midst of this transformation even as we write this chapter. In writing about ending the mission of mentorship, Martins (2005) states that not all successful relationships must end with the grave, meaning that if the relationship comes to an end after the mentoring is over, it does not necessarily indicate that the mentorship was unsuccessful. However, we value our relationship too much to settle for anything less than its continuation, which we are now working to ensure. We hope, furthermore, that our experience can serve as a source of innovation to others. One way of doing this is finding a framework, which can accommodate the transformation from mentor-mentee to colleagues. At present, for example, we are coauthoring research proposals in which we are coprincipal investigators. We are also coadvising graduate students. These situations place us in a position in which we are learning to be colleagues. It is not easy, as Zvi is still senior and often tends to behave in an overprotective manner, while Chaya often continues to feel mentored.

Initially our mentoring relationship focused on creating "we-ness," on emphasizing the similarities which led to closeness. As the relationship evolved, we learned that the most difficult part of we-ness in our mentoring relationship is recognizing that the world is not the result of one's own individual making but rather a cocreation with a person defined as a fellow who becomes a constant presence in one's existential situation and acts on the other while the other acts on him or her. We are hoping to further evolve in our "we relationship" (Schutz 1970), which implies continued respect for each other's own subjectivity, while trying to cocreate together an intersubjective world reflecting our knowledge as it develops and our differences as they are changing content and shape.

The idea of copresence involves great sensitivity to the other's subjective meaning system while being constantly aware of one's own, as well as the fine line between the two. This simultaneity cannot be sustained completely over time, and therefore we experience in mentoring a continuum of degrees of we-ness, rather than a binary, either/or format. However, the simultaneity of consciousness is the basis for a spatio-temporal community created in mentoring, in which a true exchange of views can take place, associated with a willingness to grasp and internalize what has been exchanged. In mentoring, each party needs to be oriented to the other and his or her needs along with his or her everyday presence in our life. Mentoring that works is a true "thou relationship" (Buber 1958, 2000) in which the other is perceived holistically in his or her entirety. This is likely to lead to a high-quality collegial relationship. We discovered that the only way to overcome conflicts that naturally arise in such emotionally charged situations is to leave space for the other's individuality. This should be allowed even when such individuality looks objectively different from or unacceptable to one's own. This is likely to allow for parallel streams of consciousness that ultimately may enable taking the perspective and role of the other.

．　　　．　　　．

Mentoring was an opportunity for us to learn how to step out of our own consciousness, move toward the other, and therefore develop flexibility and experiential openness. However, these understandings came with much investment, learning, and willingness to change. Often they involved a painful withdrawal from the we-ness in order to fully realize its potential. This kind of involvement leads to a great deal of reciprocal, intergenerational learning, and an openness to accumulating substantive knowledge alongside experience. It allows the mentor to revise his or her settled mindset vis-à-vis new knowledge brought to the table by the protégé while also highlighting the advantages of insecurity as a catalyst for learning new content and acquiring new attitudes and values. In parallel, this relationship equips mentor and protégé with a sense of continuity and historical perspective.

In concluding, we would like to share with the reader the following notes we exchanged after Chaya's graduation ceremony.

My Dear Friend Chaya,

Now that you are one of the boys . . . I would like to:

—Tell you that I both love and value you for your tremendous willingness to learn and grow along with your unmet honesty and reliability.
—That I am losing the greatest assistant and winning the greatest
colleague.
—That I will compare for years ahead all my assistants to you and
that this is a terrible injustice toward them.
—That I hope our collaboration in all domains will continue inde-
pendently of where your professional life will take you.
—That I will always remain your friend and make sure I give you the
sense of support and security you need in order to flourish.

Hugs and congratulations,
ZVI

To Zvi,
My Dear Friend and Mentor,

Some reflections on what was, is and hopefully will be . . .

I started my Ph.D. with great uncertainty of how things will be . . .
but then I got the opportunity to meet you . . . and by the process of
working together I went through one of the most meaningful journeys
I made in life . . . learning way beyond the curriculum.

You offered me an opportunity that no one else has, to experience
academic life from within, and gave me of yourself beyond anything
I every expected or imagined possible.

I am glad that I dared to take chances on the challenges you offered
me, which were not all easy but certainly rewarding. Some more pleasurable than others.

It was and still is a great privilege for me to work side by side: with
you as your assistant and colleague. As you can see it is difficult for me
to relate to it in the past tense. . . . I truly hope we will continue our
collaboration in all domains regardless where I will end up being, as
I believe it can be.

From your friend and colleague who will be there for you always.

Love, Chaya

REFERENCES

Allen, T. D., and L. T. Eby. 2008. "Mentor Commitment in Formal Mentoring Relationships." *Journal of Vocational Behavior* 72:309–16.

Anderson, L. 2007. "Analytic Auto-ethnography." *Journal of Contemporary Ethnography* 35 (4): 373–95.

Arnd-Caddigan, M., and R. Pozzuto. 2008. "Use of Self in Relational Clinical Social Work." *Clinical Social Work Journal* 36:235–43. DOI 10.1007/s10615-007-0103-7.

Bandura, A. 1977. *Social Learning Theory.* Englewood Cliffs, N.J.: Prentice-Hall.

Buber, M. 1958, 2000. *I and Thou.* New York: Scribner Classics.

Callaghan, G. M., A. E. Naugle, and W. C. Follette. 1996. "Useful Constructions of the Client-Therapist Relationship." *Psychotherapy* 33 (3): 381–90.

Campbell, C. D. 2008. "Best Practices for Student-Faculty Mentoring Programs." In *Blackwell Handbook of Mentoring: A Multiple Perspectives Approach*, edited by T. D. Allen and L. T. Aby, 325–43. Chichester: Wiley.

Collins, P. M. 1994. "Does Mentorship Among Social Workers Make a Difference? An Empirical Investigation of Career Outcomes." *Social Work* 39 (4): 413–19.

Dewane, C. 2006. "Use of Self: A Primer Revisited." *Clinical Social Work Journal* 34:543–58.

Eby, L.T., J. E. Rhodes, and T. D. Allen. 2008. "Definitions and Evolution of Mentoring." In *Blackwell Handbook of Mentoring: A Multiple Perspectives Approach*, edited by T. D. Allen and L. T. Aby, 7–20. Chichester: Wiley.

Eisikovits, Z., and C. Koren. 2010. "Approaches and Outcomes of Dyadic Qualitative Analysis." *Qualitative Health Research* 20 (12): 1642–55. DOI: 10.1177/1049732310376520.

Ellis, C. 1999. "Heartful Auto-ethnography." *Qualitative Health Research* 9 (5): 683–99.

Ellis, C. S., and A. P. Bochner. 2007. "Analyzing Analytic Auto-ethnography: An Autopsy." *Journal of Contemporary Ethnography* 35 (4): 429–49.

Gardner, L. D., and H. Lane. 2010. "Exploring the Personal Tutor-Student Relationship: An Authoethnographic Approach." *Journal of Psychiatric and Mental Health Nursing* 17:342–47.

Gensler, H. J. 1998. *Ethics: A Contemporary Introduction.* London: Routledge.

Hunt, D. M., and C. Michael. 1983. "Mentorship: A Career Training and Development Tool." *Academy of Management Review* 8:475–85.

Johnson, W. B. 2008. "Student-Faculty Mentorship Outcomes." In *Blackwell Handbook of Mentoring: A Multiple Perspectives Approach*, edited by T. D. Allen and L. T. Aby, 189–210. Chichester: Wiley.

Johnson, W. B., and J. M. Huwe. 2002. "Toward a Typology of Mentorship Dysfunction in Graduate School." *Psychotherapy: Theory, Research, Practice, Training* 39 (1): 44–55. DOI: 10.1037///0033.3204.39.1.44.

Johnson, W. B., G. Rose, and Z. S. Schlosser. 2008. "Student-Faculty Mentoring: Theoretical and Methodological Issues." In *Blackwell Handbook of Mentoring: A Multiple Perspectives Approach*, edited by T. D. Allen and L. T. Aby, 49–69. Chichester: Wiley.

Koren, C. 2011. "Continuity and Discontinuity: The Case of Second Couplehood in Old Age." *The Gerontologist.* DOI: 10.1093/geront/gnr018.

Kram, K. E. 1985. *Mentoring at Work: Developmental Relationships in Organizational Life.* Glenview, Ill.: Forsman.

Levinson, D. J. 1978. *The Seasons of a Man's Life.* New York: Knopf.

Lieblich, A., R. Tuval-Mashiach, and T. Zilber. 1998. *Narrative Research: Reading, Analysis, and Interpretation.* Thousand Oaks, Calif.: Sage.

Marris, P. 1980. "The Uprooting of Meaning." In *Uprooting and Development: Dilemmas of Coring with Modernization*, edited by G. V. Coelho and P. I. Ahmed, 101–16. New York: Plenum Press.

Martins, A. 2005. "Ignition Sequence: On Mentorship." *American Academy of Child and Adolescent Psychiatry* 44 (12): 1225–29. DOI: 10.1097/01. chi.0000183462.57025.bd.

Mcauley, M. J. 2003. "Transference, Counter-transference and Mentoring: The Ghost in the Process." *British Journal of Guidance & Counselling* 31 (1): 11–23. DOI: 1080/0306988031000086134.

McGranahan, E. 2008. "Shaking the 'Magic 8 Ball': Reflections of a First-Time Teacher." *Journal of Teaching in Social Work* 28 (1/2): 19–34. DOI: 10.1080/08841230802178839.

Miehls, D., and K. Moffatt. 2000. "Constructing Social Work Identity Based on the Reflexive Self." *British Journal of Social Work* 30:339–48.

Mullen, C. A. 2008. "Naturally Occurring Student-Faculty Mentoring Relationships: A Literature Review." In *Blackwell Handbook of Mentoring: A Multiple Perspectives Approach.* Edited by T. D. Allen and L. T. Aby, 119–38. Chichester: Wiley.

O'Neil, J. M., and I. S. Wrightsman. 2001. "The Mentoring Relationship in Psychology Training Programs." In *Succeeding in Graduate School: The Career Guide for*

Psychology Students, edited by S. Walfish and A. K. Hess, 113–29. Mahwah, N.J.: Erlbaum.

Owen, C. J., and L. Zende-Solomon. 2006. "The Importance of Interpersonal Similarities in the Teacher Mentor/Protégé Relationship." *Social Psychology of Education* 9:83–89. DOI: 10.1007/s11218-005-2671-0.

Poteat, L. F., K. M. Shockley, and T. D. Allen. 2009. "Mentor-Protégé Commitment Fit and Relationship Satisfaction in Academic Mentoring." *Journal of Vocational Behavior* 74:332–37.

Sambunjak, D., S. E. Straus, and A. Marusic. 2009. "A Systemic Review of Qualitative Research on the Meaning and Characteristics of Mentoring in Academic Medicine." *Journal Gen International Medicine* 25 (1): 72–78. DOI: 10.1007/s11606-009-1165-8.

Schutz, A. 1970. *On Phenomenology and Social Relations*. Chicago: University of Chicago Press.

Simon, C. E., D. D. Bowles, S. W. King, and L. L. Roff. 2004. "Mentoring in the Careers of African American Women in Social Work Education." *Affilia* 19:134. DOI: 10.1177/0886109903262765

Spinelli, E. 1989. *The Interpreted World: An Introduction to Phenomenological Psychology*. London: Sage.

Straus, M. A. 1979. "Measuring Intra Family Conflict and Violence: The Conflict Tactics Scale." *Journal of Marriage and the Family* 41:75–88.

Taylor, P. G., and M. Cheung. 2010. "Integration of Personal/Professional Self (IPPS) Through Reflective/Experiential Learning." *Journal of Teaching in Social Work* 30:159–74. DOI: 10.1080/08841231003705248.

Thompson, L., and A. J. Walker. 1982. "The Dyad as the Unit of Analysis: Conceptual and Methodological Issues." *Journal of Marriage and the Family* 44 (4): 889–900.

Van Deurzen, E. 2010. *Everyday Mysteries: A Handbook of Existential Psychotherapy*. 2nd ed. London: Routledge.

Wang, S., R. A. Noe, Z. M. Wang, and D. B. Greenberger (2009). "What Affects Willingness to Mentor in the Future? An Investigation of Attachment Styles and Mentoring Experiences." *Journal of Vocational Behavior* 74:245–56.

Wilson, M. W. 2000. "Connection and Transition: Influences of Career Mobility on the Close Friendships of Women Student Affairs Professionals." *Journal of College Student Development* 41 (5): 529–43.

Wilson, P. P., D. Valentine, and A. Pereira. 2002. "Perceptions of New Social Work Faculty About Mentoring Experiences." *Journal of Social Work Education* 38 (2): 317–33.

Wishart, P. 2006. "Phyllis Stern: Mentor, Friend, and Collaborator." *Health Care for Women International* 27:563–65. DOI: 10.1080/07399330600770304.

Witkin, S. L. 1999. "Taking Humor Seriously." *Social Work* 44 (2): 101–4. DOI: 10.1093/sw/44.2/101.

Zerzan, J. D., R. Hess, E. Schur, R. S. Phillips, and N. Rigotti. 2009. "Making the Most of Mentors: A Guide for Mentees." *Academic Medicine* 84 (1): 140–44.

ORLAGH FARRELL DELANEY is a writer and researcher. In 2013 she cofounded *Lilith and Sige ememoirs* with Patricia Kennedy.

ZVI EISIKOVITS is a professor of social welfare at the School of Social Work, head of the School of Criminology, and director of the Center for the Study of Society at the University of Haifa, Israel. His current research interests are in multiple perspectives on child abuse and neglect, intimate partner violence, and intergenerational forgiveness between older parents and their adult children. He is also interested in methodological issues in qualitative research such as units of study that are more than one, the construction of typologies, and triangulation between various kinds of qualitative data coming from literary texts with art.

JAN FOOK is a professor in education (critical reflection) in the Faculty of Health, Social Care and Education at Kingston University and St. Georges, University of London, UK. She is former director of the School of Social Work, Dalhousie University, Canada. Her interests include practice research methodologies and the research and development of critical reflection.

JOHANNA HEFEL is a professor in the Department of Social Sciences and Organization Studies at the University of Applied Sciences Vorarlberg, Austria. She is coordinator of the Master of Clinical Social Work and cofounder of the Austrian Society of Social Work (http://www.ogsa.at). Her teaching and research interests include theory and practice in social work, clinical practice, reflexive learning, and critical discourses.

ALLAN IRVING lives in Swarthmore, Pennsylvania, and teaches part-time in the School of Social Policy and Practice at the University of Pennsylvania. He is currently working on an intellectual history of social work from the Enlightenment to postmodernity.

PATRICIA KENNEDY is a senior lecturer in social policy at the School of Applied Social Science, University College Dublin, Ireland. She has authored or coauthored eight books, the latest titled *Key Themes in Social Policy* (2013).

CHAYA KOREN is a lecturer at the School of Social Work and research fellow at the Center for the Study of Society at the University of Haifa, Israel. Her current research focuses on intergenerational relationships in the family, second couplehood in old age from an intergenerational and multicultural perspective, intergenerational forgiveness between older parents and their adult children, and ageism. She is also interested in methodological issues in qualitative research such as dyadic and family units and the construction of typologies.

NORIKO MARTINEZ has a private practice in Chicago, Illinois, working with children and adults, integrating mindfulness with both cognitive and psychodynamic methods. She is also lecturer at Loyola University Chicago School of Social Work, where she teaches in the areas of cross-cultural clinical work and cognitive integrative theory and practice.

KATHERINE TYSON McCREA, professor at Loyola University Chicago School of Social Work, is the founding editor-in-chief of *Illinois Child Welfare*. Her publications address child treatment, residential care for severely mentally ill, homeless adults, and practitioner-relevant research. Current research focuses are global social work, participatory action research, and practice and research for severely traumatized youth.

SATU RANTA-TYRKKÖ is a postdoctoral fellow affiliated with the social work program of the School of Social Sciences and Humanities, University of Tampere, Finland. Her present research interests focus on three distinct but often intersecting fields: ecological/eco-social social work, postcolonial issues in social work, and interfaces of social work and art.

BRENDA SOLOMON is an associate professor of social work at the University of Vermont in Burlington. Her scholarly interests include social constructionism and institutional ethnography for social work.

KAREN STALLER is an associate professor at the University of Michigan School of Social Work in Ann Arbor. She is also coeditor of the journal *Qualitative Social Work: Research and Practice*. Her current research focuses on historical developments in the services, programs, and policies dealing with runaway and homeless street youth in the United States during the nineteenth century.

STANLEY L WITKIN is a professor in the Department of Social Work at the University of Vermont in Burlington and the president and cofounder of the Global Partnership for Transformative Social Work. His recent writings concern applications of social construction to social work practice and inquiry.